CASINO GAMBLING
FOR THE
CLUELESS

Also by Darwin Ortiz

Gambling Scams

CASINO GAMBLING
FOR THE
CLUELESS
A
BEGINNER'S
GUIDE
to Playing
and Winning

Illustrations by Leslie Dunlap

Darwin Ortiz

A Lyle Stuart Book
Published by Carol Publishing Group

Carol Publishing Group edition, 1998

Previously published as *Darwin Ortiz on Casino Gambling*

A Lyle Stuart Book
Published by Carol Publishing Group
Lyle Stuart is a registered trademark of Carol Communications, Inc.

Editorial, sales and distribution, rights and permissions inquiries
should be addressed to Carol Publishing Group, 120 Enterprise Avenue,
Secaucus, N.J. 07094
In Canada: Canadian Manda Group, One Atlantic Avenue, Suite 105,
Toronto, Ontario M6K 3E7

Carol Publishing Group books may be purchased in bulk at special
discounts for sales promotions, fund-raising, or educational purposes.
Special editions can be created to specifications. For details, contact
Special Sales Department, Carol Publishing Group, 120 Enterprise Avenue,
Secaucus, N.J. 07094

Published by arrangement with Dodd, Mead & Company, Inc.

Manufactured in the United States of America
ISBN 0-8184-0609-7

10 9 8 7 6 5 4 3 2 1

for my parents,
who were willing to let me do
what I wanted with my life

Contents

A Note to the Reader

All gambling terms in italics in this book appear in the Glossary.
The Glossary also contains gambling terms that do not appear in the
text of the book.

Preface

Can you win at casino gambling? Absolutely; people do it all the time. Can you win consistently enough to become rich? Well, no—at least, not if you stay strictly within the bounds of honesty. If becoming rich is your goal, you should look elsewhere than Las Vegas or Atlantic City. I think that most people today are sophisticated enough to realize that anyone who promises to make you rich from gambling is either misguided or at least trying to mislead you. Casino gambling is first and foremost a form of recreation; at least, that's the healthy way to look at it. Many people find it exciting and the perfect way to escape for a while the pressures of their daily lives. They look at any losses they incur as the price they pay for their fun. After all, virtually every form of recreation costs money.

However, that doesn't mean that you have to approach the gambling tables resigned that you are going to walk away a loser or fatalistically believing that what happens is entirely out of your control. Anyone who tells you that gambling is all luck and that skill and strategy don't matter is misleading you just as much as the guy who tells you he can make you rich from gambling. If you listen to either of them you will end up poorer.

Gambling being what it is, there will always be times when ignorant, incompetent players will win and times when skilled, knowledgeable players will lose. However, in the long run you can be sure that your winnings and losses will be determined by the unbending mathematical laws affecting each bet you made. The essence of skilled gambling is to learn techniques that will help tilt the mathematical odds more in your direction. If you think that luck is more important than odds in gambling, consider this: The gambling casinos don't place their faith in luck. They have built their business on mathematics and that reliance has made the casino industry one of the most lucrative businesses in the world. If you follow their example, you will win more often.

The question arises, where can one go for reliable information on how to gamble? Many people turn to casino personnel as a source of information. It is common to see players in a casino asking a dealer or *pit boss* for playing advice. The notion that casino employees must be expert gamblers is one of the most widespread, and one of the most erroneous, gambling myths among the general public. Casino personnel have to know how to operate and supervise the games; they don't have to know how to gamble. You might think that just by watching the games day after day for years the casino employees would somehow absorb knowledge about how to gamble intelligently, but it doesn't work that way. The ignorance and misinformation about how to gamble to be found among casino pit personnel is staggering. It is indicated by the fact that most casino employees are lifelong losers whenever they get on the players' side of the table. This is a fact that will be verified by anyone who knows the industry. A few years ago, a well-known *pit boss* at a major Las Vegas Strip casino wrote a book about how to play baccarat. Among the choice bits of information he offered was the suggestion that whenever a winning player left the table the reader should try to get his seat because some of the good luck would adhere to the chair and the new player would also win. If this sort of thinking makes sense to you, by all means turn to casino personnel for your information on how to gamble.

Still other players try to emulate the playing style of *high rollers* they see at the tables. Because these gamblers are playing for high stakes and are being treated like VIPs by the casino, other players assume that they must know what they are doing. Actually, a high roller is only a person whose nongambling career earns him so much money that he can afford to gamble ignorantly without worrying about the consequences. What defines a high roller is the fact that he loses much more money than the average player. That hardly makes him an ideal role model.

Certainly, there are a few casino employees and high rollers who are knowledgeable players, but they are definitely in the minority. You can't assume that because someone works in a casino or gambles for high stakes, he must know what he is talking about. As the lucky-chair baccarat example I cited shows, you can't even assume that because someone wrote a book on gambling he must know what he is talking about. I won't ask you to make that assumption about this book. As much as possible, I have avoided asking you to accept anything I say on faith.

The advice contained in this book is based on the insights I have gained from a lifetime of experience gambling combined with a lifetime of studying, analyzing, and experimenting at the various casino games. I have tried to pass on to you, not only my conclusions, but the insights on which they are based. Rather than just giving you a list of dos and don'ts, I have tried to give you an understanding of why these techniques will help you be a winner. Don't do something because I say so; do it because it makes sense. I think that in reading this book you will come to see why my advice makes sense. You will obtain a deeper understanding of what the various casino games and gambling in general are all about—what is really going on below the surface level that is all the average player sees. That understanding can't help but make your recreational gambling a more enjoyable experience for you. It will also help you win more often, and that is the most enjoyable part of gambling.

I. The Game Plan

♣ Let's talk about basics. Before you even start to study the games, there are some essential points you have to consider. For example, just where do you plan to do all this gambling?

Where to Play

NEVADA VS. NEW JERSEY

In this country, anyone who wants to gamble legally has two choices, Nevada and Atlantic City. Most often the selection is based solely on geographical proximity. However, if you can afford to base your decision on other factors, here are a few to consider. Although Atlantic City likes to portray itself as Las Vegas East, the two areas are actually very different in many ways. Atlantic City cannot even begin to match the glamour of Las Vegas, nor, with only eleven gambling casinos, can it match the variety of top-flight entertainment and gourmet fare to be found in Vegas.

If your main concern is the gaming tables, there are three other differences you should keep in mind. Unlike Las Vegas, Atlantic City is not a twenty-four-hour-a-day town. The A.C. casinos are legally required to close from 4 A.M. to 10 A.M. on weekdays and from 6 A.M. to 10 A.M. on weekends. The casinos have been lobbying strongly against this restriction, so the situation may soon change.

A much more important consideration for the gambler with a limited bankroll is the fact that the East Coast clubs do not cater to the small bettor the way many Nevada casinos do. In Nevada, one-dollar and two-dollar games are plentiful, even on the Las Vegas Strip. You won't find a one-dollar game anywhere in Atlantic City.

Except for the Claridge, which recently opened five two-dollar tables, a three-dollar minimum is the lowest you will find at the blackjack tables. In about half the casinos, the lowest minimum is five dollars. To make matters worse, it is almost impossible to find a seat at these tables during the busy spring and summer months. During a recent visit to A.C., I couldn't find a single crap table with a minimum lower than ten dollars. This is a pretty hefty price for most players, particularly those who want to take full odds and would therefore have to go for twenty dollars a shot. When casino gambling was first legalized in Atlantic City, the Casino Control Commission mandated that each casino provide a specific number of tables at certain low minimums in order to ensure that players were not forced to bet over their heads. This laudable goal was soon abandoned, and now the casinos set their own table limits. It would be nice if the casinos were to show some regard for their less-affluent customers. However, as this is being written, the eleven casinos have just scored the most profitable month in the history of Atlantic City gambling. As long as a handful of casinos have a stranglehold on all the gambling money on the East Coast, they are not likely to change their policies. Those with limited funds may find they have a choice between risking it all in a few minutes at a high-limit game or contenting themselves with playing the endless rows of slot machines.

The most fundamental difference between the casinos of Atlantic City and Nevada is the almost total uniformity in the games, rules, and dealing procedures found in all the A.C. clubs as opposed to the wide variation to be found in Nevada. In Las Vegas, one can often find casinos offering *single odds* at craps next door to clubs offering *double odds* and single-deck blackjack tables right next to four-deck *shoe* games in the same casino. Some casinos offer exotic games like *Sic Bo* and *Pai Gow* or even novelty games like *Crapless Craps* and *Double Exposure 21*. Others stick to the traditional games. Nevada casinos also vary in the freedom they offer the blackjack player in regard to *splitting* and *doubling down*.

By contrast, once you've played in one A.C. casino, you've played in them all as far as dealing procedures, rule variations, and games offered are concerned. This is because of the difference in the regulatory structures of the two states. In Nevada, the state gives the casinos great latitude in how they conduct their operations. The policies of the individual clubs reflect the pressures of competition, judgments as to what kind of clientele each casino wishes to attract, and the preferences and innovativeness of management. In Atlantic

City, no such freedom exists. The Casino Control Act that brought legalized gambling to New Jersey stipulated that the Casino Control Commission should formulate uniform rules governing virtually every aspect of casino operations.

Last year, people throughout the country read about a controversial game of blackjack played by Frank Sinatra at the Golden Nugget in Atlantic City. I suspect that few people really understood what the controversy was all about. Sinatra demanded that the game be dealt face down from a hand-held deck rather than face up from a shoe, and he also insisted that his pal Dean Martin be allowed to cut the cards. If the same event had occurred at the Golden Nugget's other property in downtown Las Vegas, there would have been no headlines. It is not uncommon for Vegas casinos to alter their procedures to accommodate willful *high rollers* and celebrities. In Atlantic City, the action resulted in a $25,000 fine for the Golden Nugget. The Casino Control Commission had decreed that all blackjack games must be dealt from a shoe, with the cards face up, and that no nonplayer may be allowed to cut the cards; that is just what you can expect to find at any blackjack table in any one of the eleven A.C. casinos, as well as any new ones that may open up—unless you are Frank Sinatra.

Don't feel too sorry for the poor casinos that have to labor under this bureaucratic yoke. The casinos of Atlantic City have had considerable success in lobbying for the rules that they wanted from the Casino Control Commission. The result is that while competition determines many of the procedures followed in Las Vegas, A.C. is more like a monopoly. The casinos can do what they want because the players can't go elsewhere to get a better deal. The rules at craps are pretty much the same as those in Nevada. They even offer slightly better odds at some of the *proposition bets*. This is a moot point, however; if you are still interested in craps proposition bets after reading this book, I will have failed in my job. The A.C. casinos also give the roulette player a strong break with the *en prison* rule.

The situation is not as good for the blackjack player. The New Jersey Supreme Court ruled in 1982 that, under the Casino Control Act, the casinos did not have the right to *bar counters*. As a result, New Jersey offers the only blackjack games in this country where you can count cards without any fear of being thrown out. Unfortunately, immediately after this ruling, the casinos convinced the Commission to permit them to use up to eight decks of cards in the game. At present, all the A.C. casinos deal either six- or eight-deck games. This is very unfavorable for counters and also hurts other players.

Even prior to the Supreme Court ruling, the casinos had convinced the Commission to eliminate the *early surrender* rule at blackjack. This rule, which had allowed players the option of conceding their hand and forfeiting only half their wager whenever the dealer had a possible blackjack, had been one of the few breaks Atlantic City gave blackjack players. If you are interested in *card counting*, Nevada is the only place to play.

NORTHERN NEVADA VS. SOUTHERN NEVADA

Gambling is legal throughout the state of Nevada, and casinos can be found in even the smallest towns, sometimes consisting of just one or two blackjack tables. However, most of the serious gambling occurs in three areas: Las Vegas in southern Nevada, and Reno and Lake Tahoe in the North. When it comes to glitter and glamour, Las Vegas ranks head and shoulders over the other two towns. Reno has long billed itself as "the biggest little city in the world." However, once exposed to Las Vegas, what will hit you about Reno is the "little" part. This is still so despite the massive expansion the town has been going through in recent years with the opening of several new major casinos. Lake Tahoe is even smaller than Reno but offers great natural beauty and such outdoor sports as boating and skiing, if you're into that sort of thing. Personally, I seldom get to see any sunlight when gambling.

GRIND JOINTS VS. LUXURY CASINOS

Gambling casinos can be divided into two categories: those primarily interested in attracting small bettors and those primarily interested in attracting big bettors. In the industry, small bettors are called *grinds* and the casinos that cater to them are called *grind joints*. In Las Vegas, most of the grind joints are located in the downtown area, and most of the clubs catering to high rollers are located on the Strip. However, there are exceptions on both sides. The Golden Nugget is one downtown casino that has had considerable success in attracting high rollers away from the Strip. On the Strip there are a number of casinos that specialize in grind action. The Barbary Coast, the Maxim, and the Frontier are among those that come to mind. The Dunes has the best of both worlds. In its main casino, it caters to its premium customers, while its adjoining, secondary casino, called the Oasis, handles the grind customers.

Grind joints are characterized by lower table minimums and more slot machines. Unlike their more ostentatious neighbors, they often open right onto the street, with wide, doorless entrances to help attract the kind of walk-in business that is of little concern to the high-roller casinos.

Your best bet is to play in casinos where your level of betting is appreciated. If you have a limited bankroll, there is no point in hanging around a casino where you have to wait for an hour to find an opening where you can play because most of the tables have minimum wagers beyond your reach. There is not much enjoyment playing in a place where they act as if you are interfering with their efforts to serve the real gamblers.

On the other hand, if you like to play for high stakes, you shouldn't play in a place where the casino managers immediately start to *sweat* the game as soon as they see a *quarter* (twenty-five-dollar) bet. In these clubs, the management is so scared of a big loss that they congregate around your table with worried looks and agonize over every chip you win as if it were coming out of their own pockets.

It's a common belief that casino executives love to see a big winner because it's great advertising for gambling. This myth is propagated by the casino PR departments and is only believed by people who don't know the industry. Actually, casino executives love to see a big win as long as it happens at someone else's casino; that way they get the benefit of the advertising without the cost. What they really fear is that you will win big in their casino and immediately leave and lose it all next door before they have a chance to win it back. Every casino executive in the world hates to see one of his tables losing. But if you play in a club that is used to big bettors, at least they are likely to take it more philosophically.

LEGAL VS. ILLEGAL CASINOS

Not all the gambling houses in this country are located in Nevada and Atlantic City. In every large city and many small ones, you can find one or more illegal casinos that offer many of the same games found in Las Vegas. What they don't offer is protection for the player. Because these games are not regulated by the government, there is nothing to keep these places from cheating the customers. As a result, many of them do. I can't stress strongly enough that you should never even consider playing in such a place. All the skill, knowledge, and strategy in the world won't help you against sleight of hand or gimmicked dice. If you want a better idea of what can happen to you in one of these *underground joints*, I suggest you read my previous book, *Gambling Scams* (New York: Dodd, Mead & Co., 1984). If that doesn't cure you of any desire to play in these places, nothing ever will.

CASINO NIGHTS

After the illegal underground gambling houses, the Las Vegas nights that many organizations sponsor to raise funds are undoubtedly the worst possible places to do any serious gambling. Since the proceeds from these events usually go to a worthy cause, it's all right if you want to go and chalk up any losses as a contribution to charity. However, don't delude yourself into thinking they offer a fair test for your gambling skills.

The odds in these places are invariably tilted against the player to an obscene degree—far, far worse than in any casino in Nevada, Atlantic City, the Caribbean, or overseas. At blackjack, many of these places follow the rule that the dealer takes all ties. (In a real casino, the player does not lose his money on a tie.) At craps and roulette, they invariably pay *short odds*.

I have a friend who rents gambling equipment and croupiers to organizations sponsoring such casino nights. Once, upon inspecting one of his roulette tables, I noticed that the game was paying 30 to 1 on single-number bets instead of the customary 35 to 1. The other bets all paid proportionately less also. I asked him how he managed to pay such odds without getting lynched. He told me he had never had a single player even notice the difference. This should give some idea of the caliber of player these places attract. (After reading this book, you will notice the difference!) Forget about these places. If you want to contribute to charity, write them a check and deduct it from your taxes. At least that way you will know in advance how big a contribution you are going to make.

What to Play

What casino game you should play depends on what you want to get out of the experience. If profit is a primary motive, there are only three casino games you should consider. These are blackjack, craps, and baccarat, in that order. The first two take work and study to have a real chance of winning. All the information you need is contained in this book, but you have to provide the effort. Blackjack takes more work than craps but also promises a better chance of beating the game. It is the only casino game in which you can actually tilt the odds in your favor if you are willing to work hard enough to become an expert. However, it is also possible to almost completely nullify the *house edge* and make blackjack an even game with only a moderate amount of study on your part. Baccarat is the only casino game where you have a fighting chance to come out ahead even if you don't know what you are doing. All the other games are deathtraps for the ignorant gambler.

Another consideration is your personality and temperament. Blackjack is a game for intellectual, analytical loners. It's just you against the dealer, and your intellect is your only weapon. If you like chess or computers, blackjack is the game for you. By contrast, craps is a fast-paced, uninhibited, social game. It is for the gregarious, extroverted player who wants to jump and shout when he wins and moan and curse when he loses. Crap players at the same table often develop such an "us versus them" mentality that it almost seems like a team sport. When the table is really hot and everyone is winning, it's a communal experience.

Baccarat is a game drenched in glamour and demanding little of the player other than money. (Table minimums are usually high at baccarat.) If you want to feel like James Bond with very little effort, baccarat is your game.

Roulette, slot machines, and keno are not games for anyone who places a high priority on winning. But then, winning is not the only benefit that gambling can offer. It can be a very enjoyable, relaxing, or exciting pastime that provides enough amusement to more than justify the cost—if you at least learn enough about the games to keep the cost at a reasonable level. Roulette is a very leisurely game that can provide enough intermittent excitement to keep your interest. Keno and slot machines are strictly for dreamers. Their main appeal is the (remote) possibility of a huge winning. Keno demands so little of the player that it is almost a spectator sport. If Friday-night bingo is your idea of excitement, keno is for you.

I confess that the appeal of slot machines has always eluded me. However, even here there is room for intelligent strategy to improve one's chances; we will be discussing that in Chapter IX. Today, with the introduction of giant jackpots that sometimes reach over a million dollars, slot machines are more popular than ever. After all, some people really do win those million-dollar prizes. I guess that's what keeps slot players going. Just remember that all those silver dollars that went into making that million-dollar prize had to come from somewhere. A lot of slot players must have contributed to it without getting much back.

Whatever your preferences, the detailed coverage of each of the casino games in this book will not only further help you decide which one is for you, but it will also give you the best possible chance of winning at whichever one you finally choose.

Money Management

When gambling, how you handle your money is every bit as important as how you play the game. Money management in gambling is an instinct that must be developed through experience. But here are some basic principles to keep in mind.

If you are losing, don't make the common mistake of increasing your bets in an effort to recoup your losses. Gamblers call this *chasing* your money. Smart gamblers know that the harder you chase your money, the faster it runs away. When you are losing, you should cut your bets down to the minimum to conserve your bankroll. Your strategy should be to try to ride out your losing streak. The time to bet big is when you're winning and well ahead of the game. At such times, you should bet aggressively in the hope of making a big killing. Bet big with the house's money; bet small with your own.

Undoubtedly, the most important principle of money management is to decide in advance how much money you are willing to risk—how much you can afford to lose. Having set a limit, you must stick by it. If you lose that amount, leave the table. This kind of discipline is your only protection against being badly hurt by a losing streak. I would go so far as to say that whenever you approach a gaming table, you should be psychologically prepared to accept the possible loss of all your gambling money. Some may think this is defeatist thinking. Nothing could be further from the truth. Losing all your gambling bankroll is always a possibility, and you would be foolish to ignore it. If you can't financially afford to lose the money, you have no business gambling with it. If you can't psychologically accept losing it, you will panic as soon as you find yourself in the hole. The moment that happens, you're dead. Paradoxically, as soon as you can accept the possibility of losing philosophically, you automatically improve your chances of winning.

Here is the money-management plan I suggest. If you are going to spend several days in a gambling resort, divide your playing bankroll equally over the number of days you will be there. Then take each day's playing stake and divide it into four equal "session stakes." If you are just planning a one-day trip to Atlantic City, divide all your playing money into four session stakes. When you begin to play, limit yourself to only one session stake. If you should lose all of the session stake, take a break. Go for a walk or get something to eat. After you have had a chance to relax for at least twenty minutes, you can go back to the tables and start again with your next session stake. If you should lose that, you still have two more stakes to fall back on. But in each case, take a break before starting again. This is important to help you maintain a positive mental attitude and the ability to concentrate, both of which are essential for successful gambling. If you lose all the money you set aside for playing purposes for that day, quit. Don't deviate from this rule under any circumstances.

If you should win, keep playing as long as you keep winning. If you succeed in doubling your session stake, double the size of your bets. Once you are at this level, if your total winnings double again, double your bet size again. When your winnings drop back about 10 percent from their highest point, it is time to quit. Remember, in order to show a profit you have to leave the table. If you stay there long enough, you will end up giving it all back to the house.

How to Behave

When it comes to recreational activities, there are few less formal than casino gambling. Nevertheless, there are some unwritten rules of etiquette that have developed over the years. These are simple matters of courtesy to the other players and the dealers. They are important because they help keep the action moving smoothly. These rules of behavior are not usually known to the novice, and even long-time gamblers sometimes step on others' toes through ignorance. The following tips should help you avoid the most common errors.

BUYING IN

The process of changing cash for betting chips is called the *buy-in*. This is done at the table before you start to play. Don't hand your money to the dealer. Place it on the *layout* but not in one of the betting spaces, or the house may mistake it for a wager. The dealer cannot make change for you until he has finished the hand in progress, so be patient. Remember that whatever amount of money you give the dealer will be returned to you in the form of chips. He cannot return any change in the form of cash, nor can he give you cash in return for chips. That can only be done at the casino *cage*. Casino chips come in standard denominations and colors: one-dollar silver tokens or white chips, five-dollar red chips sometimes referred to as *nickels*, twenty-five-dollar green chips sometimes called quarters, one-hundred-dollar black chips, and five-hundred-dollar and one-thousand-dollar chips whose colors vary with each casino. If at any time you want to exchange some or all of your chips for a different denomination, you can have the dealer do it by following the same procedure as in buying in. These chips also have colored markings along the edges. These are a color coding that the casino uses so it can tell its own chips from those of other casinos even when the chips are in a stack. One casino will not honor chips from another.

Before approaching a table, check the small plaque posted at each table that lists the minimum and maximum bets allowed. Novices sometimes embarrass themselves by trying to buy in for twenty dollars at a table where the minimum single wager is twenty-five dollars. The standard minimums are one dollar, two dollars, five dollars, and twenty-five dollars. Only in Atlantic City are ten-dollar minimums common. At baccarat, twenty-dollar minimums are standard.

The maximums are also posted. I remember once seeing an inexperienced player who was contemplating raising his bet from five to ten dollars. First he timidly asked the dealer if such a high bet was allowed. He turned crimson when he was informed that the maximum bet at that table was five hundred dollars. The most common table maximums are five hundred and a thousand dollars. Some casinos catering to high rollers will have two- or even three-thousand-dollar limits at some tables. These casinos will also set special limits for certain very big money gamblers and will even rope off a table for just one player's use if he is willing to bet high enough. The Horseshoe Club in Vegas is famous for the fact that they have no maximum bet. A high-rolling player can set his own limit in the sense that his first bet becomes his maximum bet. If he starts with a five-thousand-dollar wager, he can bet up to five thousand dollars for the rest of the session. A while back, the Horseshoe got a great deal of publicity from the fact that one player came in with a briefcase full of money and made a single wager of a half-million dollars at a crap table. (He lost.) I suspect that such events will become even rarer in the future with the new Regulation 6A that requires casinos to report to the IRS all transactions involving ten thousand dollars or more. Of the few people who can afford to bet a half-million dollars, many are in businesses where it just wouldn't do to have the federal government too well informed.

CRAPS

Many crap players believe it's bad luck for the dice to hit a player's hand on a roll. It's only a superstition, but you can avoid a lot of ill will by always keeping your hands well clear of the playing area during rolls.

Most crap players look forward to their opportunities to roll the dice. Therefore, they don't appreciate a player who arrives at the table and preempts their turn by positioning himself immediately to the left of the present shooter. When joining a crap table, if there are several empty spots, try to come in somewhere to the right of the shooter so the dice will go around most of the table before your first chance to shoot.

When you wish to give the dealer some chips to have him place a wager for you, put the chips on the layout and tell him what bet you want. Never try to hand chips directly to the dealer. Years ago, some dealers worked out a method of stealing chips from their employers by working with partners who posed as players. Every time the player handed the dealer some five-dollar chips to place a bet, the dealer secretly handed him some hundred-dollar chips he had palmed. Ever since that scam came to light, hand-to-hand transfers between players and dealers have been prohibited.

Finally, when it's your turn to roll the dice, remember to throw them hard enough so they travel across the table and bounce off the far railing. Nothing irritates crap table personnel more than a short roll. This is because they know that a few dice cheats have enough skill to control what numbers come up on the dice as long as they don't bounce off the railing. (A very few have the skill to control them even if they do bounce off the railing, but that's another story.)

BLACKJACK

Don't touch your bet once the dealer starts dealing the cards. If you are playing in a casino where all the players' cards are dealt face up, don't touch your cards at any time. If playing in a casino where the players' first two cards are dealt face down, don't hide your cards behind your hands and don't bend the cards as you're handling them. All these actions will make the dealer jumpy because he will be afraid you may be trying to cheat by changing your bet after seeing your cards or by switching or marking the cards you have been dealt. If you constantly cover your cards, the dealer may instruct you to use only one hand to handle your cards. Actually, there is no such rule; players use both hands to handle the cards all the time. However, dealers say that to players when they figure it's the only way to keep them from hiding their cards. In addition to all his other duties, the dealer has to worry constantly about protecting the game against cheats. Don't add to his headaches. What you may consider harmless toying with the chips or cards can be for him another potential security problem.

When making a bet, don't *barber pole* your chips. In other words, don't mix chips of different denominations haphazardly in one stack. This makes paying off more difficult for the dealer and increases the possibility of an error. When making a bet that involves two different denominations, always place the higher denomination chips on the bottom of the stack and the lower denomination on top. Similarly, when making a second bet for a double down or split, place the second wager next to the first one, never on top of it. If you place one wager on top of another, it becomes impossible for the dealer to verify that you added the correct amount, since he probably didn't know how much you had bet to begin with.

When the dealer comes to your hand, use the standard signals for *hitting* and *standing*. Inexperienced players use all kinds of idiosyncratic signs to indicate how they want to play the hand. Some nod whenever they want another card, and some nod when they want to stand. This sort of thing drives dealers crazy, slows down the game, and leads to dealing errors. In games where the initial cards are dealt face down, the correct way to signal for a hit is to scratch the two cards toward yourself on the layout each time you want another card.

To let the dealer know you want to stand, slip the two cards under your bet. In a face-up game where you are not allowed to touch your cards, you should signal for a hit by scratching toward yourself on the felt with your fingers: To stand, wave your flat, palm-down hand back and forth over your cards.

Finally, the behavior I personally find most offensive is the player who verbally abuses the dealer because the player is losing. I have always felt that one of the most important qualities of a true gambler is the ability to take his losses like a man. Unfortunately, this form of self-discipline is a rare commodity in gambling casinos (among casino executives as well as among players). Try to remember that the dealer is only doing his job and is not responsible for your losses. If you always treat him civilly, you will be showing consideration both for him and for the other players at the table, who couldn't care less whether you win or lose.

SLOT MACHINES

Slot players have a notoriously strong territorial imperative. After having poured a good deal of money down a machine, they feel they have an investment in it and start thinking of it as "their" machine. A slot player who has to leave his or her machine for a few moments will mark it by taking one of the plastic cups the casinos provide slot players to hold their coins and placing it inverted over the handle of the machine, or by asking a nearby player to watch the machine. You should respect this claim unless you want to risk having some irate woman belt you with her purse. Since that purse is probably loaded with Ike silver dollars, it can do a lot of damage. These spurned players get particularly incensed if you should hit a jackpot on their machine. Look at it from their standpoint. Some woman spends a couple of hours pouring fifty or a hundred dollars in silver down some machine's throat. Finally, out of exhaustion, she leaves to go to the ladies' room to rest her weary arm and wash her blackened fingers. Then, before she can get back, some guy waltzes over and hits the five-hundred-dollar jackpot she has been stalking all morning. In a Nevada court, it would probably be considered justifiable homicide.

The worst case of this sort I know of occurred last year in a Las Vegas casino. Two friends had gone out together to gamble. One of them was playing a progressive slot machine. Just as he had inserted a series of coins, his friend came over and pulled the handle before the player could stop him. Five 7s came up on the *pay line*, and the machine awarded a six-figure jackpot. Both men claimed to have won the prize. The Gaming Control Board directed the casino to pay the money to the busybody handle-puller rather than the guy who had been pumping in his hard-earned cash. This is the sort of thing that can strain a friendship.

CASINO PERSONNEL

Experienced casino dealers know their jobs, but even the best dealers make mistakes occasionally. If you think that a dealer has made an unfair decision against you, don't hesitate to speak up. If you don't get satisfaction from the dealer, call over a *floorman* or *pit boss*. They are the unhappy-looking men in business suits who prowl around inside the *pits* peering over the dealers' shoulders. Explain to him what happened. In most cases, you will get satisfaction. If you feel you have been unfairly treated, you can always pick up your chips and walk. At least you can give your business to someone who is willing to give you a fair break.

Anytime you find things not to your liking, don't be afraid to look elsewhere. If you find the dealers surly and unpleasant, you don't have to put up with them. However, don't blame a dealer if he refuses to go along with your efforts to engage in small talk. Many casinos forbid their dealers to engage in any unnecessary conversation with players. (Don't ask me why; it's just another example of casino paranoia.) A common complaint is games that are conducted too fast. If a blackjack dealer deals faster than you can add up your cards, or if a crap table crew keeps the dice moving so fast you can't get down all the bets you want to make between rolls, take your business next door. If more players did that, these few casinos would be forced to drop their bad habits.

TOKING

In gambling casinos, *tokes*, or tips, are a way of life. Everyone has his hand out. The dealers really had it made until the IRS decided that their tips were taxable income and not tax-free gifts as the dealers had maintained. Even so, tokes are still the great attraction of a casino dealer's job. If you knew how low their salaries are, that wouldn't surprise you. In fact, dealers vie for the opportunity to work in the major Las Vegas Strip casinos because the tokes are much higher there. Each dealer's tips are eventually deposited in a communal toke box and later divided among all the dealers in the same pit on that shift.

There are two ways of tipping a dealer. You may simply hand the chips directly to him, or you may make a bet for the dealer. For example, at blackjack you may make a separate wager in your betting spot in front of your own hand. When you do this, inform the dealer that this bet is for him. You may instead place the dealer's bet in front of your betting spot in the area marked for insurance bets. In either case, the dealer will lose his tip if you lose your hand, but he will win twice as much if you win. At craps, making a bet for the dealers is the universally accepted method of tipping.

Some dealers are rather aggressive in encouraging tokes. They will let it be known in more or less subtle ways that a tip would be appreciated. Some will blatantly ask, "How about a bet for the boys?" Most casinos discourage *toke hustling* by dealers since they feel that every dollar you give as a tip is a dollar the house can't win from you. Nevertheless, you may encounter this kind of behavior from time to time—usually when you're winning.

If you are having a great run of luck at the tables and are beginning to feel guilty about not sharing your success with the dealers, just remember this. If you were suffering a losing streak, not one of those dealers would offer you any money to ease the pain.

You are under no obligation to tip, and you will gain nothing tangible from tipping. It won't improve your chances of winning and, personally, I feel that the value of tipping as a way of keeping from being barred if you are a blackjack card counter has been greatly overrated. However, if you are just feeling generous, go right ahead.

I do suggest strongly that you withhold tipping until just before leaving the table. Only then do you really know how much you can spare. Too many players tip liberally and frequently during a temporary winning streak. When their luck turns, they don't have enough of a bankroll to survive. Similarly, many novice card counters walk away from a table thinking they have lost when they have actually handed away their profits through too-frequent tipping.

Gambling casinos provide free drinks to players at the tables. Some also provide free drinks to the slot machine players. Cocktail waitresses circulate among the players taking orders. If you don't see one, you can ask a dealer to call one over for you. Although the drinks are free, you should tip the cocktail waitress when she brings the drink. One last suggestion: Stick to soft drinks when you're gambling. Otherwise, those free drinks may prove extremely costly.

SELF-CONTROL

After sound technical knowledge of the games, self-discipline is the single most important requirement of a successful gambler. Many gamblers will begin by playing intelligently. Yet as the game continues, their play will slowly degenerate, with more poor and emotional moves creeping in until they are playing as badly as rank novices. There are many subtle pressures in any gambling situation that can drive a player into an emotional playing pattern. Some of these pressures are manufactured by the casino, some are inherent in the gambling experience, and some are unwittingly imposed by players upon themselves.

The casino environment itself has been carefully engineered to lead players to act against their own best interests. The betting layouts most prominently feature the proposition bets that offer the least chance of winning. Dealers are instructed to encourage players to wager on these sucker bets. The cocktail waitresses ply big winners with more and more free drinks until their judgment starts to deteriorate. The noises and lights on the slot machines are designed by behavioral engineers not only to attract play but also to subtly condition slot players into continuing play indefinitely.

At craps, herd psychology sometimes takes over, which can easily undermine a player's good judgment. If the table is *cold* and most players have been losing, many will begin to increase the size of their bets in an effort to recoup their losses. When this happens, there is a strong psychological pressure for the other players to follow suit, although that is the worst possible move to make under the circumstances.

The gambling experience itself promotes an emotional state of mind. The euphoria of winning and the depression of losing can both promote impulsive playing maneuvers detrimental to your chances of ending up a winner. Many players unwittingly increase the pressures on themselves by gambling with money they can't afford to lose. Thus, any initial losses trigger a panic that virtually guarantees further losses.

To avoid making the mistakes that put emotional pressures on players and lead them to impulsive, self-destructive play, I recommend you observe the following simple but vital rules:

1. *Never gamble when tired, ill, or depressed.* When gambling, the situation is constantly changing. You have to be attuned to these

changes in order to fully exploit a winning opportunity when it develops. Illness, fatigue, or a negative mental attitude can impair the concentration and judgment that are so necessary for success. For the same reason, you should never drink when gambling.

2. *Always set a prior limit on your losses.* The worst situation a gambler can get into is to lose more money than he intended. Panic sets in, judgment deteriorates, and more losses inevitably follow in the player's frantic effort to get even.

3. *Never set a prior limit on your winnings.* Many players approach the table with the thought, "If I win a thousand dollars, I'll quit." Winning is the worst possible reason for stopping play. Never put a limit on success. Don't stop until the tide turns.

4. *Never play with money you can't afford to lose.* The player who does places an immense emotional burden on himself from the outset. His overwhelming fear of losing almost guarantees that he will. It is a universally accepted truism among professional gamblers that scared money always loses.

5. *Learn as much as you can about your favorite games.* The more you learn about the unbending rules of mathematics that govern every game of chance, the less temptation you'll have to abandon logic in the hope that those longshots will come through "just this once." That's what the rest of this book is about.

II. Gambling, Luck, and Probability

♣ In my experience, there are two types of situations that tend to bring out superstitiousness in people. The first is the situation in which an individual is completely in charge of what is about to happen, has a great deal at stake, and fears he may screw up. He has to produce; the success or failure of the entire event is in his hands. When a big-league baseball pitcher or an actor starring on Broadway steps onto the mound or the stage, he knows that the outcome rests entirely on his shoulders. If he fails to come through, there won't be anyone he can turn to for help. No one can come to the rescue. It's a lonely position to be in and a daunting responsibility to carry. It's little wonder that he may look for some psychological crutch to make him feel that it really isn't all up to him. If he can convince himself that wearing the right shirt or performing the correct little ritual before stepping out in front of the crowd will guarantee success, it will relieve some of the pressure. Ironically, for that reason it may actually promote success. Consequently, it should not be surprising that athletes and stage actors are notorious for their superstitions. Anyone who finds himself in a similar situation, where he has to deliver the goods time after time with serious consequences if he slips up, is likely to fall into the same habit.

Ironically, the other kind of situation that tends to produce superstitious behavior is exactly the opposite, in which the individual has a lot at stake and no control at all over the outcome. This, of course, is the situation with which gamblers are familiar. A crap shooter has a large bet on the *pass line*. He is about to throw the dice, and he knows that no matter how he throws them he can exert no control whatever over what number comes up. This knowledge produces a different kind of anxiety from that of the athlete or actor. Yet it can be relieved in the same way: by believing that some kind of talisman or ritual will give one magical control over the outcome. It doesn't work that way, but it can make one feel a little better—at least until the dice stop rolling.

The problem is that in this latter case, the superstitious behavior won't produce improved performance on the part of the individual. It will almost certainly produce poorer performance. Reliance on "magic" solutions leads gamblers to ignore the elements that really could give them partial control over the results of their gambling: playing knowledge, strategy, money management, and an understanding of the unbending laws of mathematics that rule all gambling games. Gamblers have a saying: "Losers believe in luck; winners believe in skill."

Learning about the smart way to gamble will never eliminate the slight touch of anxiety just as you roll the dice or turn over each card; it will just help you win. But then, that tingle of anxiety is really one of the lures of gambling. The excitement of challenging the unknown when you gamble is second only to the excitement of winning big. Let's look at some of the concepts that can help you do that.

Probability

Probability theory is the branch of mathematics that deals with predicting chance events. That makes probability central to all gambling. Although the science of probability can reach levels of unbelievable complexity, most of the concepts you have to understand in order to be a skillful gambler are fairly simple. The first question that arises is: Just what do we mean when we speak of the probability of an event occurring? Most people would say that it means how often something will happen over a given number of trials. This is true as far as it goes. However, it leads some people to say, "I don't care how often I would lose if I rolled the dice a million times, because I don't intend to play that long. I'm just going to play for a half-hour. And in a half-hour anything can happen." That's why it is important to understand that probability doesn't just tell you what will happen in a million trials, it also tells you how likely something is to happen in a single trial. Actually, there is a good deal of debate among mathematicians and philosophers over exactly what that last statement means. But one thing is clear. Whether you intend to gamble for a half-hour or for a million rolls of the dice, you have a better chance of winning if you take into account the probability of the events you are betting on.

Some gamblers would dispute this point. They prefer to rely on luck, superstition, talismans, hunches, ESP, or half-baked mystical theories. I won't argue the point at length. I will just offer one argument that I feel is conclusive. Every legitimate gambling casino bases its operations squarely on probability theory. Their expectation of profits stems directly from the exploitation of mathematical probability in practical terms. And any one of those casinos earns more money in one year than all the hunch-and-superstition players put together. If you hope to earn some money when you gamble, I suggest you put your trust in the same principles the casinos do. For the remainder of this chapter, we will look at the key probability concepts that affect your chances of winning every time you gamble.

Independent Trials

I have a friend who is a roulette addict. He always approaches the game armed with a pad of paper and a pen. He scrupulously records what color comes up on each spin of the wheel. If he notices that over a period of time red has come up much more often than black, he immediately starts betting on black, convinced that black must soon start coming up more frequently to even things out. Although this system has cost him thousands of dollars, he clings to it with the faith of a religious fanatic.

What my friend and so many other gamblers refuse to recognize is that each spin of the wheel, like each roll of the dice or each flip of a coin, is an independent event. What happened on the previous spins has absolutely no effect on what will happen on the next spin.

Everyone knows that if you flip a coin, the chances of it coming up heads are 50–50. But suppose you flip a coin ten times in a row. And suppose the first nine times it comes up tails. What are the chances of it coming up heads on the tenth flip? The answer is that the chances are still 50–50. The coin, not being a sentient creature, cannot remember it came up tails on the previous tosses. Therefore, those previous tosses cannot possibly influence the next toss.

But doesn't the law of averages say that the more trials of an event you have, the more the results will even out? Doesn't that mean that an excess number of heads has to be followed by an excess number of tails in order for the long-run results to balance off?

The answer to both these questions is no. What laymen call the law of averages and mathematicians call the law of large numbers states that the more times a coin is flipped (to use our example) the closer the ratio of heads to tails will approach the true probability of 50:50. This does not mean that when a run of tails occurs it must be followed by a run of heads to even things out.

For example, after 100 flips of a coin, we might find an imbalance of 70 tails to 30 heads. After another 100 flips, we may have a total of 130 tails to 70 heads. There has been no excess of heads tossed in the second 100 trials to offset the run of tails in the first 100 trials. On the contrary, we have continued to get a larger than average number of tails. However, the ratio of 65:35 after 200 trials is closer to the true 50:50 probability than the 70:30 ratio we had after only 100 trials. That is precisely what probability predicted would happen.

Each flip of the coin is independent. The odds remain the same on the next toss no matter what happened on the previous tosses. Crap players have a saying: "The dice have no memory." We might just as validly say that the roulette wheel, wheel of fortune, and coin have no memory. Therefore, the odds must remain constant on each roll of the dice, spin of the wheel, or toss of the coin, regardless of what happened on the last roll, spin, or toss, or the last one thousand rolls, spins, or tosses.

I plan to remind you of that from time to time, because even gamblers who pay lip service to the "no memory" concept tend to ignore it in practice. That is because it goes against what our instincts tell us must be the case. There is something inside us that insists that if a coin came up tails nine times in a row, the chances of it coming up heads on the next roll must be greater than if we have flipped five heads and four tails on the previous nine tries. This kind of thinking is so prevalent that it has a name. Mathematicians call it "the fallacy of the maturity of chances." It is such a popular belief among gamblers that mathematicians also call it "the gambler's fallacy." It might also be called "the gambler's downfall," because no other myth has been responsible for as many gamblers going broke as this simple misconception. The irony is that so many of them defend their belief as scientific thinking and label it "the law of averages." The real scientific thinking on the point is that every time an independent trial is concluded, the slate is wiped clean. The next trial is a whole new ball-game. To believe otherwise is to believe that there is some kind of metaphysical link that ties every roll, spin, or toss to every one that has gone before it and every one that will come after it. So the next time you head for the roulette table, leave the paper and pen at home. And the next time you see a player make eight straight *passes* at the crap table, don't bet the farm it can't happen a ninth time.

Standard Deviation

The probability of an event is usually given as a decimal number from 0 to 1. A 0 probability would of course mean that the event is impossible, while a probability of 1 means that the event is certain to occur. By definition, the probability of a chance event must be more than 0 and less than 1. When you flip a coin, there is a .5 probability that it will come up heads and a .5 probability that it will come up tails. (One of the basic laws of probability is that the sum of the probabilities of all the possible events in a particular trial must add up to 1, since 1 represents certainty and it is certain that one of these possible events will occur.) That means that, over a series of flips, about half the results will be heads and about half tails. Yet we know from experience that in a short number of trials, ten flips for example, the results will seldom conform exactly to this theoretical norm.

These short-run fluctuations in the expected results are measured by mathematicians as standard deviation. One might say that standard deviation tells us the probability that short-run results will match the predictions of probability. An examination of just how standard deviation is calculated would really be more technical than we need to get for our purposes. It is enough to note that the larger the number of trials, the smaller the standard deviation. In other words, the longer you gamble, the more closely the results will match the predictions of probability. In the short run, the deviations can be very great.

When these short-term fluctuations at the gaming table happen to coincide with the way we are betting, we tend to think of it as a run of good luck. When the fluctuations run against the way we are betting, we conclude that we are experiencing bad luck. These terms are a misnomer since the factors at work are not in any way affected by concerns over our welfare. Still, in our anthropocentric world, the labels are convenient. This, then, is the sense in which the terms "good luck" and "bad luck" will be used in the remainder of this book. But remember the lesson provided by the mathematics of standard deviation. The longer you gamble, the less important luck becomes, and the more important an understanding of basic probability, the mathematics of gambling, becomes.

The House Advantage

When the casinos calculated how much money they would pay a player each time he won a bet, they might have opted to pay in a ratio that exactly reflected the player's chances of winning the bet. In that case, they would have created what mathematicians call a fair game. However, since they do have bills to pay, they elected instead to give themselves a mathematical advantage. This house advantage is the most important factor in determining your chances of winning at any casino game. For that reason, it is the most important concept in gambling. Yet very few players clearly understand what the house advantage is or how it works.

The house advantage on any particular bet is usually expressed as a specific percentage. This percentage reflects the casino's expectation on that particular bet. Similarly, one may speak of the player's disadvantage on the same bet, which is also expressed as a percentage. In almost all cases, the two figures will be the same, except that if it is a positive expectation for one side, it must be a negative expectation for the other. For example, the house advantage on most roulette wagers is 5.26 percent, and the player's disadvantage is − 5.26 percent. This is to be expected because whatever the player loses, the house wins. Actually, there are a very few cases where the house advantage and player disadvantage will differ very slightly for mathematical reasons that need not concern us here. In general, we can speak of the house advantage, also known as the house edge or the P.C., and the player disadvantage interchangeably. These figures allow the player to determine his expectation on any bet he may make. If he wagers on roulette, he can expect to lose five dollars and twenty-six cents out of every one hundred dollars he wagers at the game. Because of standard deviation, his actual results in the short run may differ; but the longer he plays, the closer his financial results will reflect the mathematically predicted results. Remember, however, that even in the short run, the higher the disadvantage you face on a bet, the more likely you are to lose.

The specific techniques a casino uses to grant itself an advantage differ from game to game and wager to wager. However, they all involve giving the player less in winnings than the risk he is taking justifies. Ironically, this means the casino makes its profit every time you win a bet, not when you lose one. An example should make this clear. Suppose you and I start flipping a coin. Each time it comes up heads you pay me a dollar. Each time it comes up tails I pay you a dollar. If we do that nonstop for a week, neither of us will make much of a profit.

Let's try it again. Each time a head is flipped, you pay me a dollar. But each time a tail is flipped I pay you seventy-five cents. The longer we play, the more money I'll make. My profit is the twenty-five cents of your money I keep in my pocket every time you win. That is how the house percentage works. You might say that the casino's profits will take care of themselves as long as you are losing. It is when you win a bet that the house must protect itself. It does so by paying you less than your due. Casinos are very clever about disguising the house percentage. But it is there in every game. It is like an invisible tax levied on you every time you win. And we all know how devastating taxes can be.

Of course, if you are lucky and win an unusually high percentage of your bets, you can show a profit despite the house edge. But if your wins and losses conform to the predictions of probability, you will end up losing because of all the money the casino kept in its pocket each time you won a bet.

For some casino games, calculating the house precentage can be very complex. But for most games and wagers, you can do it very simply by measuring the amount of money the house withholds from you when you win. This merely involves comparing the true odds of winning the wager to the odds the house pays you if you win. Consider an example. An American-style roulette wheel contains thirty-eight numbered slots. Therefore, if you bet on a particular number, your odds of winning are 37 to 1. If the casino paid you thirty-seven dollars on a winning bet of one dollar, it would be a fair game. Instead, it pays you only thirty-five dollars. The other two dollars it keeps in its own pocket. After winning, you should have had a total of thirty-eight dollars—the thirty-seven-dollar payoff plus your original wager.

Two dollars withheld from what should have been a total of thirty-eight dollars gives us a fraction of 2/38. When converted to a percentage, the result is 5.26 percent. That is how much you can expect to lose in the long run from every sum of money you place on this particular wager. By the same process, you can calculate the P.C. on most casino wagers.

The size of the house advantage can vary greatly from one casino game to another. That is why a roulette player can be expected to lose his money at about a five times faster rate than a baccarat player. The house percentage can also vary greatly from one bet to another in the same game. Two people playing side-by-side at the same crap table may face vastly different chances of winning. If the first player is betting the pass line, he faces a very modest 1.4 percent house advantage. If the second player is betting the *big* 8, he is bucking a massive 9.09 percent edge. Because this percentage is seven times greater than on the pass-line bet, the big 8 bettor's prospects for success are seven times worse than the pass-line bettor's.

Bankroll vs. Action

What sometimes puzzles players is how come they end up losing all their money if they face only a 5.26 percent disadvantage. If they started with five hundred dollars, shouldn't they have lost just 5.26 percent of that five hundred dollars? Gamblers use the word *action* to describe gambling activity measured in terms of the amount of money wagered over a period of time. This concept can help explain how the house percentage works. If you approach a roulette table with five hundred dollars, you might make twenty consecutive wagers of twenty-five dollars each. If you lose all twenty bets, you will have given the house five hundred dollars' worth of action, and your five-hundred-dollar bankroll will be gone. However, it is very unlikely that you would lose twenty bets in a row. If you win your first bet, you will probably collect your winnings and bet the original twenty-five dollars again. That gives the 5.26 percent house edge two opportunities to work on the same twenty-five-dollar bet. To put it differently, you have given the house fifty dollars' worth of action, and it is on that fifty dollars that the 5.26 percent house tax is levied. In a typical gambling session, you will both lose wagers and win wagers, with the result that the same money may be bet many times over. Consequently, with a five-hundred-dollar bankroll, you will probably provide the house with far more than five hundred dollars' worth of action. Eventually, 5.26 percent of all your action may equal 100 percent of your bankroll.

A concrete illustration of the difference between bankroll and action is provided by an advertisement that the Vegas World casino on the Las Vegas Strip has been running in a number of magazines lately. The headlines read "LAS VEGAS VACATION virtually FREE." The ad goes on to explain that you can receive two nights' accommodations for two at Vegas World for $254, in return for which the casino will provide you with four hundred dollars' worth of action at their tables. The fine print explains how this works. You receive four hundred dollars in special nonredeemable casino chips, which you can bet at any of the games. If, for example, you make a five-dollar bet with these chips and lose, your bet will, of course, be collected by the house. However, if you make a five-dollar bet and win, the casino will pay you your winnings but will collect your original five-dollar bet. "Wait a minute," you say. "Why should the house collect my original bet if I win?" The answer is that those five dollars in special chips have already given you five dollars' worth of action. If they pay you your winnings every time you win but collect your original bet, win or lose, by the time all your special chips are gone, you will have received four hundred dollars' worth of action, which is all the casino promised you. There is no question of false advertising here, since the casino is making good on its promise and since the advertisement is very clear on just what the vacationer can expect to receive. Still, anyone who just skims over the ad and hastily concludes that Vegas World is going to give him a hotel room and four hundred dollars in return for his paying $254 will be in for a surprise when he arrives at the hotel.

The distinction between bankroll and action is responsible for some paradoxes in gambling. For example, suppose a gambler had five hundred dollars and approached a roulette table with the goal of trying to double his money and with a determination to keep playing until he either succeeds in that goal or loses all his money. He might decide to make continuous twenty-five-dollar wagers on red for every spin of the wheel until he had either worked his bankroll up to a thousand dollars or had no money left. Alternatively, he might decide to put all five hundred dollars down on red as a single wager. With all the money riding on the next spin of the wheel, he would either reach his goal of doubling his money or he would lose it all on that one bet. Either way, he would leave the table after that single wager was settled. Which of these two approaches do you think would offer a greater chance of reaching the goal of doubling the bankroll? Think about it carefully, because the problem provides a good test of the various concepts we have been discussing.

The answer is that the all-or-nothing one-bet strategy offers the greater probability of success. By breaking his bankroll into a series of small wagers and continually betting until the bankroll is either doubled or exhausted, the player only gives the house edge far more opportunity to *grind down* his bankroll. He provides the house with more action, which means that that 5.26 percent house advantage has more to work on until, in all likelihood, the gambler will have exhausted his entire capital.

Yet very few players would opt for the one-bet method. This is because such an approach to gambling provides little satisfaction. This underscores a point that should always be kept in mind when discussing gambling strategy. After suffering a big loss in a short period at the tables, I have often heard gamblers say they didn't mind so much losing the money; they just objected to the fact that they didn't get a run for their money. In other words, they got very little excitement or enjoyment out of their gambling because it was over so quickly. Any sensible person who gambles does so primarily because he enjoys it. This is why many highly successful professional poker players regularly wager, and lose, part of their poker winnings on things like sports betting, where they don't enjoy the expertise they do at poker. To gamble in a casino purely in the hope of profit is foolish in light of the fact that the odds are against you in virtually every game. Even in the case of card counting at blackjack, where the odds favor the expert player, the individual could probably earn as much in some other profession with the same amount of effort. Speaking for myself and every other successful card counter I have ever known, the attraction was as much the appeal of gambling as the profit potential.

There is no point in telling someone that he has a better chance of winning at craps than he does at the slot machines if he hates to play craps and loves playing the slots. The nonmonetary payoffs that gambling can provide in the form of excitement, recreation, and diversion are all perfectly legitimate considerations when deciding what to play and how to play. However, keeping in mind that you should always know how high a price you are paying for your entertainment, and also keeping in mind that winning is more fun than losing, I will concentrate for the remainder of this book on showing you how to maximize your chances of showing a profit when you gamble.

III. Basic Blackjack

♣ Blackjack is my favorite game. A lot of people agree with me. Over the last twenty years, blackjack has grown tremendously in popularity, to the point where it has eclipsed craps as the most popular table game in American gambling casinos. I think that what appeals to most players about the game is the same thing that appeals to me: the fact that it is the only casino game that can truly be called a game of skill. Unfortunately, most blackjack players play very poorly. Too often, the same people who are attracted to the game because of the skill element have no understanding at all of the skillful plays at the game. This is why casinos' earnings at the game keep skyrocketing despite the fact that the game can be beaten by the expert player.

Since the early 1960s, blackjack play has been revolutionized by experts who have anlayzed the game with the aid of computers and who have developed advanced strategies for obtaining a mathematical advantage over the house. Everyone has heard about professional blackjack players who are so good that casinos bar them from playing the game. Such players, called card counters, gain their edge by mentally keeping track of the cards as they are played and making their betting and playing decisions accordingly. Many people figure that only a mathematical genius could achieve such a feat. There is no denying that truly advanced blackjack strategy can reach dizzying levels of complexity. Card counting does not really require great intellect, but it does require great dedication and discipline. For that reason, it is certainly not for everyone. The next chapter, dedicated to the subject of advanced blackjack strategy, should help you decide whether card counting is for you.

However, many people don't realize that the research that has been done in developing advanced and complex blackjack strategies has also produced tremendous insights into the game that can be of great value to the average recreational player. These insights have been codified into what is known as *basic strategy*. Basic strategy can be mastered by any player with only minimal study and can tremendously improve your success at the game. In this chapter, I'm going to concentrate on teaching you basic strategy and, in the process, making a sophisticated blackjack player out of you.

The Basic Game

Almost everyone feels they know how to play blackjack because, at one time or another, they have played at home with friends. However, before you can hope to learn to beat casino blackjack, you have to realize that the game that is played in gambling casinos throughout the world is a very different game from what is played in private among friends. In fact, it is not at all uncommon to encounter people who have been playing blackjack in casinos around the world for many years yet who still do not fully understand how the game is played. They know how to hit and stand, which is all you have to know to be able to sit down at a table and play without disrupting the game. But they may not really understand options like doubling down and splitting that are absolutely essential to beating the game. I want to go over the basics of the game with you both to avoid any confusion and to make sure you understand the procedures of the game well enough to feel completely in control the next time you sit down to play.

Later we will discuss some of the procedures that can vary from one casino to another and how those options can affect your chances of winning.

THE SETUP

Blackjack is played on a table that accommodates either six or, more often, seven seated players and a standing dealer. Unlike in home blackjack games, in a casino the deal does not rotate among the players. The casino provides a permanent dealer who stands behind the table and who is the only one to handle the deck.

Your first step when approaching the table is to buy in, or purchase, chips with which to play, unless you have some from your previous playing. This you do by placing your cash on the table between two of the betting spots marked on the felt layout. Don't place it inside

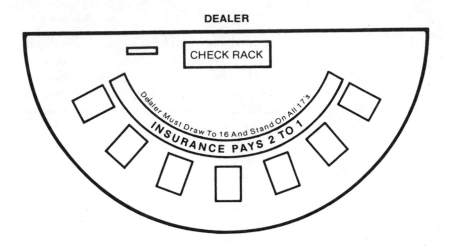

CHECK RACK

Dealer Must Draw To 16 And Stand On All 17's

INSURANCE PAYS 2 TO 1

one of these spots, or the dealer will assume it is a bet. As soon as the dealer finishes the hand in progress, he will count out chips for you from the *check rack* in front of him and place them in front of you. He will then deposit your cash in the drop slot. Remember that a dealer cannot give you any change in cash. Whatever cash amount you put down will all be converted to chips. As soon as you place a bet from among your chips into the betting spot in front of you, the dealer will include you in the next hand.

SHUFFLE, CUT, AND DEAL

When you play blackjack at home, I'm sure you always use a single standard deck of playing cards. Gambling casinos also use standard cards, but they sometimes use more than one deck. Depending on where you play, you may find the game dealt from one deck or from two, four, five, six, or even eight decks shuffled together. In one- and two-deck games, the cards are dealt from the hand in the normal way. However, when more than two decks are used, the dealer will place the cards in an oblong box called a *shoe* after he has shuffled them. The cards are then dealt through an opening in the front of the shoe as the shoe lies on the table to the dealer's left. The only purpose of the shoe is to make the cards more manageable, since the dealer can't hold four or more decks in his hands at once while dealing.

After the dealer shuffles, before beginning the deal, he will offer the cards to a player to cut. If the dealer offers the cards to you for the cut, you should know the correct way to cut them in order to avoid disrupting the game. In a single-deck game, the dealer will place the deck in front of you. You should reach over with one hand only, cut off a group of cards, and place them on the table next to the other cards. Don't reach over with both hands, and don't pick the entire deck up off the table. The dealer has to keep control over the cards at all times in order to protect against cheats. To avoid making him nervous, just cut off a group of cards with one hand and place them on the table. Don't try to give the cards a fancy or complicated cut; you won't impress anyone, and you won't even be allowed to do it. Don't cut very near the bottom or top, or you may be told by the dealer that the cut is invalid and you must cut again. Don't try to complete the cut by placing the bottom cards on the original top half. You're not allowed to do that either. That's part of the dealer's job. Just cut off some cards, put them on the table, and back off.

If you are playing in a multiple-deck shoe game, you have even less contact with the cards when cutting. The dealer will turn the entire block of cards on its side with the back of the cards toward you. Then he will hand you a blank plastic card called the stop card. You should insert the stop card somewhere into the middle of the cards but leave at least half the card protruding. The dealer will then divide the cards at the point at which you inserted the stop card and reassemble the cards so that that point becomes the top of the multiple deck. The plastic card method of cutting is sometimes used in one- and two-deck games also.

After the cut, the dealer will *burn* one or more cards. In a multiple-deck game, the dealer will deal anywhere from one to four or five cards out of the shoe and place them in a discard rack on his left. In a single-deck game, the dealer may employ a discard rack, but more commonly he will place the burn card face up on the bottom of the deck.

Unlike poker and most other card games, blackjack is not a game in which the cards get reshuffled after each hand. In fact, if it wanted to, the casino could keep dealing without reshuffling until all the cards had been used. For reasons that will be discussed later, casinos don't do that anymore. The stop card is usually inserted about two-thirds to three-quarters from the front end of the shoe. The dealer will deal cards from the opening at the front end of the shoe until he reaches the stop card. That is his signal to *break the deck*, or reshuffle, before dealing the next hand. In a game dealt from the hand, the dealer will reshuffle at his own discretion, usually after about two-thirds to three-quarters of the cards have been used. Contrary to widespread belief, the dealer does not have to wait until the stop card is reached to reshuffle. Sometimes you may see a dealer reshuffle sooner, perhaps at the instruction of a supervisor. You may possibly even see him reshuffle after every hand. This is the casino's right.

The dealer begins each hand by checking to make sure that each player has placed a wager in the rectangular or circular betting spot marked on the layout in front of him. He then deals one card to each player and one card face up to himself. He will then deal a second card to each player and a face-down card to himself. In some casinos, both of the players' cards are dealt face down, while in other casinos both cards are dealt face up. It does not matter if the dealer sees your cards, since, as we shall see, he cannot use that information in deciding how to play his own hand. In casinos where the cards are dealt face up, the players are not allowed to touch their cards. This is done to prevent cheating techniques such as palming or marking the cards. This style of dealing is followed by all the casinos in Atlantic City and most overseas casinos, as well as some of those in Nevada.

THE PLAY OF THE HAND

No matter how many people are sitting at a table, blackjack is always a game between two people. The players are not trying to beat each other. Rather, they are each individually trying to beat the dealer. It is irrelevant whether you have a better or poorer hand than the person sitting next to you. If there are seven players sitting at a table, there are in effect seven blackjack games going on simultaneously: a game between the first player and the dealer, an unrelated game between the second player and the dealer, a game between the third player and the dealer, and so on. The only thing all these games have in common is that the dealer plays the same hand in each of them.

In each game between a player and the dealer, the person who wins is the one who comes closer to a total of 21 without going over 21. The way you determine how close to 21 you are is to add up the values of the cards in your hand. Number cards count their numerical value. An 8 of clubs and a 9 of hearts would give you a hand of 17. All *paints*, or picture cards (jacks, queens, and kings), have a value of ten. An ace can count as 1 or as an 11, at the discretion of the player holding the ace. This means you could count an ace and a 4 as 15 or as 5. And you can change the valuation in your own mind as you play the hand. You may begin by counting an ace as an 11. Then, as cards are drawn to your hand, you may decide instead to count the ace as a 1. Typically, a player will count the ace as the highest value he can without going over 21.

At the end of a hand, if you have 18 and the dealer has 17, you win. However, if the dealer has 19, he wins because he is closer to 21. If you are both equally close to 21—you both have the same total—neither of you wins. This situation is called a *push*. The dealer will not pay you any money, but he will not collect your bet either. It is yours to keep to bet again or to take back. When the dealer goes around and settles the bets at the end of the hand, he will signify a push by rapping his knuckles on the table in front of your bet. Unlike home-style blackjack, in a casino the dealer never takes ties.

NATURALS

There is one way that a player can win automatically. That is to receive a total of 21 on the very first two cards he is dealt. This can only happen if one card is an ace and the other is a ten-value card. This type of hand is known as a *natural* or a *blackjack*. When a player receives a natural, he not only wins immediately and automatically, he also wins a bonus payoff. Normally at blackjack, all bets are paid off at even money. But in the case of a natural, the player is paid off at odds of 3 to 2. If he has bet fifty dollars, he will receive a payoff of seventy-five dollars. If you receive a natural, you should turn your two cards face up immediately so the dealer can pay you.

The only time a player can receive a natural yet not get paid off is when the dealer also receives a natural. As observed above, this is a tie, with no money changing hands. However, the only thing that will tie a natural is another natural. That means that, if you receive a queen and an ace and the dealer receives two 7s and draws a third 7, you still win your 3 to 2 payoff, even though you both have totals of 21.

BUSTS

It is also possible for the player to lose automatically. This happens whenever his total goes over 21. This is called *busting* or *breaking*. Whenever it occurs, the player should turn his hand face up, and the dealer will collect his bet and his cards. A busted hand is an automatic loss in the sense that the player loses even if the dealer should also go over 21. Whenever the dealer and a player tie with a total over 21, the player still loses. In fact, a player with a total of 22 loses even if the dealer should end up with a total of 26. When the dealer busts, he loses only to those players who have not busted.

HITTING AND STANDING

The player has four options available in playing his hand to attempt to come closer to 21 than the dealer. These are *standing, hitting, doubling down,* and *splitting.* After the initial cards have been dealt, the dealer will turn to each player in clockwise order to get his decision as to how he will play his hand. A player who is satisfied with his hand will choose to stand. He will signal this to the dealer by sliding his two cards under his bet. In the case of a game where the cards are dealt face up and the player is not allowed to touch them, he will signal a stand by waving his flat, palm-down hand back and forth over the cards.

Alternately, the player may elect to draw more cards. This is known as hitting. This is signaled by the player scratching the two cards on the felt toward himself. In a face-up game, he simply scratches with his fingers. Each time you do this, the dealer will deal you a face-up card. This card is added to your total, and you can keep asking for more cards until either you are satisfied with your total, in which case the dealer will turn to the next player, or you have gone over 21, in which case the dealer will collect your bet and your cards.

DOUBLING DOWN

Normally at blackjack, you must make your bet before any cards are dealt to you. In effect, you don't know what you're betting on. There are, however, a couple of limited situations in which you may bet again or alter your bet after you have received your initial two cards. One of these situations is doubling down. When you look at your first two cards, if you feel that you have a hand that has a very good chance of winning with only one additional card, you may, if you wish, double down. This means that the casino will allow you to make a second bet equal in size to your first bet. In return for this privilege, you must agree to accept one more card on your hand, no more and no less. Thus, you cannot double down and take two hits, and you cannot double down and stand on your initial hand. Also, you cannot double down after you have taken a hit. You are entering into a contract with the casino to be allowed to double your bet after you see your two cards in return for limiting yourself to only one more card. Many casinos will allow you to double down by adding an amount that is less than your original wager, but you should never do this. If the hand is worth doubling down on, it is worth doubling down for the full amount.

The way to let the dealer know that you wish to double down is to turn your two cards face up and place a second wager in the betting spot next to your original wager. Remember, the second bet is placed next to the first one, not on top of it. If you ever try to place more chips on top of your original bet after the deal has begun, the dealer will think you are trying to cheat and get very upset with you. The dealer will give you one card, either face down or face up according to house policy, then move on to the next player. After the dealer has played his hand, your hand will win or lose just like any other hand. If you are closer to 21, your doubled bet will be paid off at even money. If you tie, you keep your money. Otherwise, the dealer collects it.

SPLITTING

Splitting is an option that becomes available to you whenever the first two cards that you are dealt are of the same value, such as an 8 of diamonds and an 8 of hearts or a 10 of clubs and a queen of diamonds. (In Nevada, 10s, jacks, queens, and kings are all considered to be of the same value for splitting purposes. However, in Atlantic City, you must have a matched pair such as two queens in order to split.) If you wish, you can play such a hand just like any other hand, by hitting, standing, or doubling down. Alternatively, you may elect to split the hand. This means that you will actually divide the hand to create two different hands. Each card of the pair becomes the basis for a new hand. Your original wager now applies to only one of these hands. In order to be allowed to split, you must make a second wager, equal in size to the first, which will apply to the second hand.

When you split a pair, you will be dealt a second card to each card of the pair to form two completely separate hands. Each of these two new hands is totally independent of the other. You play out the hand on your right first, hitting or standing as you see fit. When you have finished with the first hand, you play out the second hand. Since the two hands are independent, you may end up winning both hands, you may lose both hands, or you may win one hand and lose the other. If the latter occurs, the dealer will leave both bets undisturbed in front of you, signifying that the loss on one hand cancels out the win on the other.

To let the dealer know you wish to split a pair, turn the two cards face up and separate them. Then place a second wager equal to your first one next to it in the betting spot. The original wager now becomes the bet for one of the two hands, while the new wager becomes the bet for the second hand.

INSURANCE

There is also one situation in blackjack in which you may bet on the dealer's hand instead of your own. It is called an *insurance* bet. Anytime the dealer has an ace as his face-up card, he may have a natural. In such a case, before the dealer allows anyone to play out his hand, he will offer each of the players the chance to make an insurance bet equal to half the size of his original wager. This bet is not placed in the betting spot but is placed instead in a specially marked space that runs across the layout and contains the words "Insurance pays 2 to 1." The dealer then checks his *hole card* to see if he has a natural.

The player who takes insurance will win his insurance bet if the dealer has a ten-value card in the hole—that is, if he does have a natural. In that case, of course, the player will lose his original bet unless he also has a natural. If it turns out that the dealer does not have a ten in the hole, the player will lose his insurance bet and must play out his hand to see whether or not he will win his original bet.

Insurance bets are paid off at 2-to-1 odds. That means that if you win an insurance bet, you will be paid two dollars for every dollar you wagered. Since your insurance bet must equal half your original bet, if you win your insurance bet it will exactly cancel out what you lost on your original bet. In that sense, the bet provides "insurance" against losing your initial bet in case catastrophe strikes in the form of a dealer natural.

In some casinos today, the dealer will not check his hole card to see if he has a natural until the players have finished playing their hands. Insurance bets are then settled at that point. This is an attempt on the part of management to foil cheating dealers who may signal their hole cards to a partner acting as a player. If the dealer is forced to wait until the others have played before checking for a natural, it will be too late for the information to help the players. In casinos that follow this policy, the player only loses his initial bet if the dealer does get a blackjack. This means that, if you double down or split and the dealer turns up a natural at the end, you will be allowed to keep the additional bet you made.

THE DEALER'S HAND

When all the players have finished playing their hands, the dealer turns his hole card face up and plays out his hand. The dealer is not allowed to double down or split; he is not even allowed to decide whether or not to take a hit. Dealers are not allowed to make any decisions at all. Management is afraid that if they allowed dealers to make decisions, they might make stupid decisions, perhaps on purpose to help their brother-in-law win.

Therefore, the rules for playing the dealer's hand are spelled out for him. In fact, they are even spelled out for you, right on the layout. Every blackjack table carries the words "Dealer must draw to sixteen and stand on seventeen." This means that, if the dealer has a total of 16 or less, he must draw a card and continue drawing cards until he has 17 or more. At that point, he must stand. If he has 17 or more from the outset, he must stand. He has no choice in the matter. That is why it does not matter if the dealer sees your hand. Even if every player at the table has a 19 or a 20, if the dealer turns up a 17 in his hand, he must stand. Similarly, if the dealer has a 15 or 16, he must hit even if every player stood on 14 or lower. Although the dealer may already have all his opponents beaten, he must hit until he has at least 17, even though in doing so he risks losing by going over 21.

The only exception to the above rule occurs in some casinos where the dealer is required to hit a *soft* 17 (a 17 consisting of an ace and a 6). In other casinos, he will be required to stand on such a hand.

When the dealer has finished playing his hand, he will go around the table counterclockwise, starting with the player on his right, and either pay or collect each player's bet according to how that player's hand compares with his own.

The Elements of Strategy

Blackjack offers more opportunity for the knowledgeable player to benefit from his knowledge than any other casino game. It is more a game of skill and less a game of chance than any other casino game. In the final analysis, blackjack is the only casino game that can be truly "beaten" without cheating. That is, the skilled player can completely eliminate the house edge at the game, in effect playing for free. With sufficient skill, he can even shift the mathematical edge over to his side. This is because blackjack is different from any other casino game in two important ways.

THE PLAY OF THE HAND

First, blackjack gives the player more opportunity to influence the outcome of each round than any other casino game. In most casino games, the player's job is finished as soon as he has made his bet. In craps, you make your bet, throw the dice, and hope for the best. In roulette, you make your bet and then pray for the right number to come up. In every casino game except blackjack, once you've made your bet you become a passive participant in the game.

In blackjack, after you've made your bet, your job is just beginning. You now get to make a series of decisions that will directly affect the outcome of the hand. You decide whether to hit, stand, split, or double down. Obviously, those decisions can greatly help your chances of success—if they're the correct decisions.

DEPENDENT TRIALS

The second characteristic that makes blackjack different from any other casino game is the fact that it is the only game in which your chances of winning fluctuate significantly from one hand to the next. We learned in Chapter II that most casino games involve independent trials. In roulette, your mathematical likelihood of winning is exactly the same on every spin of the wheel. What happened on the previous spin in no way affects what will happen on the next spin. This is also true of every roll of the dice at craps. It is true of every casino game except blackjack.

In blackjack, what happened on the previous hand does affect what may happen on the next hand. The reason for this is that, after each hand, the cards that were dealt out are removed from play until the deck is reshuffled. If you are dealt a certain card in a hand, you know you cannot possibly be dealt that same card in the next hand or in any subsequent hand until the cards are reshuffled. To take an extreme example, if four aces are dealt out to the players in the first hand of a blackjack game that is dealt from a single deck, you can forget about being dealt a natural in any subsequent hand until the next shuffle. The removal of other cards may have a less dramatic effect, but every card has a measurable impact on your chances of winning when it is removed from play by being dealt out. This may not seem like a very important point, but it is one of the keys to beating the game.

One of the two main factors that determine your chances of winning the next hand is what cards are left in the deck at the start of that hand. (The other factor is how you play the hand.) This is because, as certain cards are removed from the deck, your chances of being dealt various combinations from the remaining cards increases or decreases. This is just as true in a multiple-deck game dealt from a shoe. Since the composition of the deck is constantly changing, your chances of winning are constantly changing. Sometimes the house has a large advantage over the player, sometimes a small advantage. Sometimes the player has a large advantage over the house, sometimes a small advantage.

This is not all just meaningless theory. A real understanding of this point can help you walk away from the table a winner. If you know that your chances of winning the next hand are very high, you make a large wager. If you know that your chances of winning the next hand are very low, you make a small wager. In the long run, you will tend to win primarily large bets and lose primarily small bets. That means that you can come out ahead even if you lose more than half your bets. Knowing your chances of winning before each hand is dealt depends on keeping track of the cards as they are dealt by means of some card-counting system.

The availability of playing options and the constantly changing odds due to constantly changing deck composition are the two factors that set blackjack apart. Basic strategy and card counting are the two techniques that exploit each of these factors in turn to beat the game. In this chapter, we will learn basic strategy; in the next chapter, we will discuss card counting.

THE PLAYER'S EDGE

The nature of the rules of blackjack gives the player certain advantages and the dealer certain advantages. The player has the advantage that he can decide how to play each hand. The dealer doesn't have that freedom. He must draw if he has 16 or less and stand if he has 17 or more. That policy is set by the rules, and the dealer can never deviate from it. His play is predictable; yours need not be.

The player also has the advantage that he can decide how much to wager on each hand. Again, the dealer doesn't have that freedom. He must cover any player's bet, regardless of size, as long as it's within the table limits. The player also has the opportunity, under certain circumstances, of altering the size of his bet by doubling down or splitting. Those options are not available to the dealer.

Finally, the player also has the advantage of an extra-large payoff whenever he receives a natural. In such a case, he is paid off at 3 to 2 odds. The dealer, on the other hand, may win with a natural, but he never receives a bonus payoff from the players.

THE DEALER'S EDGE

By contrast, the dealer has only one advantage over the player, but it is an important one. Given its importance, it's amazing how many players have no idea what that advantage is. Let me ask you a question that I have asked countless blackjack players without ever receiving the correct answer. The question is a simple one: What happens in a blackjack game when the player and the dealer tie on the same total?

The answer I always receive is that the hand is a standoff with no money exchanged. But that is not entirely correct. If the player and the dealer tie on 17, no money changes hands. If they tie on 18, no money changes hands. If they tie on 19, 20, or 21, no money changes hands. But if they tie on 22, 23, 24, or any total over 21, the dealer wins the player's bet even though the hand was a tie. Any time you break, the dealer wins your money even if he subsequently breaks also.

All right, I admit it is a trick question. But if it gets you to understand that the automatic house win on a player bust is the only intrinsic edge the casino has at blackjack, I hope you'll forgive me. Without this one feature of the game, the house could not make a profit against any halfway decent blackjack player, and the blackjack tables would be taken out of every gambling casino in the world.

How Not to Play Blackjack

With a clear understanding of the weapons at your disposal and the weapon at the casino's disposal, you can now start learning how to play blackjack like an expert. But first you have to learn how *not* to play. The sad fact is that most blackjack players lose, not because they get beaten by the house, but because they beat themselves. They follow erroneous playing strategies that rob them of any chance of winning. They virtually give their money to the casino through their poor play.

MIMICKING THE DEALER

There are two extremely bad playing strategies whose popularity has earned untold millions for the casinos. The first is sometimes called "mimicking the dealer." The pattern has been repeated thousands of times. A blackjack player finds that almost every time he plays, he ends up a loser. He realizes that it can't just be a coincidence. He reasons that there must be something the casino is doing differently from him that is responsible for their success. He thinks about it long and hard, and eventually he believes he has found the answer. The dealer always draws to 16 or less and stands on 17 or more. That must be the secret! He figures that if he always does the same, he will at least have an even chance of winning.

The logic is appealing in its simplicity, but it is totally off-base. We have already seen that the important thing the casino is doing differently from the player is not the policy of drawing to 16 and standing on 17. What it is doing differently is automatically collecting the player's bet every time he breaks—even if the dealer also breaks. That is the real reason why the casino is winning. That means that the mimicking-the-dealer theory is based on a faulty <u>causal</u> analysis. Not only does this strategy not affect the source of the casino's advantage, it causes the player to abandon most of his own advantages: the doubling-down and splitting options and the freedom to play the same hand differently under different circumstances.

People who favor this strategy are the type who like simple answers to complex problems. They counter any criticism of their approach with the smug answer, "Well, it works pretty well for the house!" I don't really waste my energy trying to change this kind of person's mind. But I will try to save you before *you* fall prey to this type of thinking. I figure I owe it to you in return for buying the book.

The fact is that the "draw to 16 and stand on all 17s" rule does not work all that well for the house. Casinos could actually make more money if they gave the dealer the freedom to use his own judgment in playing each hand. If the dealer could take into account such factors as how many players have busted, how many small cards are in his hand, how many low and high cards have been dealt in hits, and just how close to 17 he is, in deciding whether to hit or stand he could make a substantially higher profit for the house— assuming that he was both smart and honest.

There is the rub; most dealers are both smart and honest, but not all of them. If the casinos gave their dealers freedom of choice, they would have to start training them in the fine points of the game (something not many casino managers know themselves). They would have to start worrying about how an excess of dumb dealers on the payroll might hurt profits. They would have to worry about the possibility that an epidemic of head colds among their blackjack dealers might produce a rash of poor playing and a consequent unforeseen drop in the bottom line.

Worst of all, they would have created an uncontrollable form of cheating. Few people realize that all the closed-circuit TV cameras, two-way mirrors, and steely-eyed floormen watching for cheating are mainly there to keep the dealers honest. The big problem is the dealer who brings in an accomplice to pose as a player, then cheats to help the accomplice win money from the casino. Later, the two split the profits. If dealers could play their hands any way they wanted, such cheating would become child's play. Instead of needing difficult sleight of hand, the dealer could just engage in bonehead moves, playing each hand as poorly as possible to help his partner win. Therefore, the casinos are willing to forgo the possible profits of allowing dealers freedom of choice in order to obtain the predictability and security of the stand-on-17 rule.

THE NEVER-BUST STRATEGY

Next, we have the player who once actually picked up a book on blackjack. It may even have been this one. But he didn't read far enough. He only read up to the point where it said that the reason the casino wins is because it automatically collects your bet if you bust. He figures the solution is simple: He will make sure he never busts. The only way to ensure that you never bust is never to draw a card to a total of 12 or higher. So that is just what he does. He hopes to turn the tables on the casino by sitting on his low totals and waiting for the dealer to bust.

The only problem is that it doesn't work. Notice again that the player is abandoning his strongest weapons. He never doubles down or splits and, most important, he always plays each hand exactly the same way.

In addition, he is creating a new problem for himself. Since the dealer never stands on less than 17, the only way our friend can win is if he is dealt an excellent hand on his first two cards, if he catches a high card when drawing to a total of less than 12, or if the dealer breaks. None of those things is going to happen often enough to save him. The dealer simply does not bust often enough (only about one-fourth of the time). The player's low totals will lose time after time.

The advantage that either side enjoys in a game is expressed as a percentage. Both the mimicking-the-dealer strategy and the never-bust strategy give the house an edge of over 5 percent. That means that with either of these systems, you will lose more than five cents out of every dollar you wager in the long run. That makes both these approaches sucker strategies.

INSURANCE

Another common pitfall you must learn to avoid is the insurance bet. You will recall we learned that whenever the dealer has an ace as his *up-card*, the player may make a wager equal to half his original bet that the dealer has a natural. This is a very popular bet among most players but one that is always avoided by the expert player.

To find out why, pick up a deck of cards and place an ace face up on the table. This will represent the dealer's up-card. Now sort the rest of the cards into two piles. All the non-ten-value cards should go in the first pile, while all the ten-value cards go in the second pile. Remember, that includes jacks, queens, and kings as well as 10s. You will find that there are thirty-five cards in the first pile. If any of these should turn up as the dealer's hole card, the insurance bet would lose. You should have sixteen cards in the second pile. If any of these should turn up as the dealer's hole card, the insurance bet would win. Thus, these two piles of cards represent the player's chances of winning an insurance bet. Thirty-five non-tens and sixteen tens means that the odds are 35 to 16 against collecting on an insurance bet. (These figures remain essentially valid even for multiple-deck games. Since each deck in the shoe has the same composition, the ratios remain the same.)

In order for insurance to be a fair wager, a player who wins should be paid thirty-five dollars for every sixteen dollars he bets. But the payoff odds on the bet are only 2 to 1. That means that the casino will only pay you thirty-two dollars for every sixteen dollars you bet. The difference between the thirty-five dollars you should receive and the thirty-two dollars you do receive is the reason why insurance is a sucker bet. If you remember what you learned in Chapter II, you should be able to figure out for yourself that the house enjoys a prohibitive 5.88 percent edge on insurance bets.

INSURING A NATURAL

Even many players who do not usually take insurance will do so when the dealer has an ace up and the player is holding a natural blackjack. In fact, the admonition that you should always take insurance if the dealer shows an ace and you hold a natural is the most commonly heard piece of advice on the game. The biggest victims of this fallacy are the blackjack pit bosses, floormen, and dealers themselves; most of them will heatedly argue that this is a smart play.

Most players reason that if the dealer has a natural, they will make a profit because they collect on their insurance bet while their original bet is a standoff. If the dealer does not have a natural, they will still make a profit because, although they lose the insurance bet, they collect 3 to 2 on their original bet. Thus, they argue that insuring a natural is the one situation in blackjack in which the player is assured of a profit. Actually, it is true that you will always make a profit if you insure a natural. It is also true that you will make a greater profit in the long run if you do not.

To see why this is the case, pick up your deck of cards again. Once more, deal an ace face up onto the table to represent the dealer's face-up card. Then deal yourself an ace and a ten-value card to represent your hand. Now divide the rest of the deck into non-tens and tens. This time you will have thirty-four non-ten-value cards in the first pile. If any of these cards should turn up as the dealer's hole card, your insurance bet would lose. You should have fifteen ten-value cards in the second pile. If any of these should turn up as the dealer's hole card, your insurance bet would win. Therefore, the true odds against your winning your insurance bet in this case are 34 to 15. But the casino pays only thirty dollars for every fifteen dollars you wager on insurance. This disparity between the true odds and the payoff odds gives the house an 8.16 percent advantage. That means that taking insurance is an even worse idea when you are holding a natural than when you are not.

Most players just cannot see beyond that guaranteed payoff when insuring a blackjack. It is this that leads to the advice so often given to blackjack players by floormen: "You should always insure a blackjack. That way you can't lose." In fact, when you insure a blackjack you do lose something very important. You lose the opportunity to get a 3 to 2 payoff on your hand if the dealer should prove not to have a blackjack. If you never insure a natural, the profit you make from the 3 to 2 payoff when the dealer doesn't have blackjack will more than offset the money you don't collect when the dealer does have a blackjack. Unless you are an expert card counter, in which case you know the density of tens in the deck at any given moment, the smart approach is never to take insurance, regardless of what hand you are holding.

Basic Strategy

At one time there was no way of knowing what the correct decision should be on any particular blackjack hand. Players had to be guided by instinct and guesswork. But today, through the use of advanced computers to simulate blackjack play, it has become possible for the first time to mathematically calculate the best possible play for any situation a player may face. These optimal playing decisions have been formulated into a simple set of rules known as basic strategy. Yet most players still consider blackjack a guessing game. Should they stand, hit, split, double down? For the expert player, there is no guesswork involved. Blackjack is a game of mathematics in which there is one, and only one, correct play for every possible situation. If you always follow the rules of basic strategy, you can be confident that you are giving yourself every possible chance of winning each time you play. The cards may sometimes beat you, but at least you will never beat yourself through ignorant play. The basic strategy rules I am going to teach you are the same rules that are followed by professional blackjack players in the bulk of their playing. If you learn them, you will never have to guess again.

Most editions of Hoyle state that the player's objective in the game of blackjack is to come as close to 21 as possible. Unfortunately, many people believe them. The player's objective should not be to get 21 or close to it. The player's only legitimate objective in blackjack is to beat the dealer. This is not a hairsplitting point. It is the single most important thing you have to understand to play winning blackjack. Even a 21 won't beat the dealer if he gets 21 also; but a 13 can beat him if the dealer breaks.

As soon as you decide that your only goal is to beat the dealer, the question arises: What factors affect your chances of doing so? If you think about it, you will realize that there are three elements. The first is the hand that you have been dealt. The second is the hand that the dealer has been dealt. And the third factor is the cards that remain in the deck, which determine what you are likely to draw if you hit and what the dealer is likely to draw if he hits. This last factor is exploited in card counting. Basic strategy is concerned with the first two elements, your hand and the dealer's hand.

THE DEALER'S UP-CARD

When I say that I'm going to teach you to evaluate the dealer's hand as well as your own, you may object that the dealer is not about to show you what hand he has. However, he does have to show you one of his first two cards. That one face-up card is a major clue. It can tell you what hand the dealer is likely to end up with. Most important, it can tell you what his chances of breaking are.

Computer studies have shown that when the dealer has a 4, 5, or 6 up, he is very likely to break. When he has a 2 or 3 up, he is only moderately likely to break. And when he has a 7, 8, 9, 10, or ace up, he is not likely to break.

If you think about it, you will realize that makes sense. Remember, there are more ten-value cards in the deck than any other value. Thus, the dealer always has a very good chance of having a ten in the hole. If he does have a ten in the hole, then a 7, 8, 9, 10, or ace up would give him an excellent hand. He would not have to draw any cards, and that means he would not have to run the risk of breaking.

By contrast, a 4, 5, or 6 up would mean a 14, 15, or 16 if he had a ten-value card in the hole. Those are very dangerous hands for the dealer. Since he is under 17, he must draw a card. But unless he draws a small card, he is dead. About half the cards in the deck will bust him, so his chances are not very good.

Finally, a 2 or 3 up would mean a hand of 12 or 13 if the dealer has a ten-value card in the hole. These hands are borderline cases. They might break when the dealer hits, but they have a fair chance of not breaking.

But keep in mind that the reason we know just how likely the dealer is to break on the basis of his up-card is not just by assuming that he may have a ten in the hole. We know because it has been established by extensive computer testing. Get into the habit of thinking of dealer up-cards as falling into three groups: 4, 5, or 6, which mean he is very likely to break; 2 or 3, which mean he is moderately likely to break; and 7, 8, 9, 10, or ace, which mean he is not likely to break.

CLASSIFYING PLAYER HANDS

Every blackjack hand can be classified as either a *soft hand* or a *hard hand*. A soft hand is a hand containing an ace that the player is counting as 11. A hard hand is one that does not contain an ace counted as 11. Either there are no aces in the hand, or any aces contained in the hand are being counted as 1s. If you are dealt an ace, you should always count it as 11 unless doing so would put you over 21. In other words, always play a hand with an ace as a soft hand unless you have no choice. The mathematical properties of hard hands and soft hands are so different that it is necessary to learn two completely different sets of playing guidelines, one for hard hands and one for soft hands.

Our first concern will be to learn the correct way to play hard hands. Every hard hand can be classified as either a *pat hand*, a *breaking hand*, or a *no-bust hand*. A pat hand is a hard total of 17 through 21. This is an excellent hand, one that gives you a very good chance of winning without drawing any cards. While there is always the possibility that a pat hand might become even better if you drew a card, it is not worth the risk. You should always stand when holding a pat hand.

A breaking hand, also known as a *stiff*, is a hard hand totaling 12 through 16. The problem with a stiff is that if you don't draw a card, you are left with a very poor hand. But if you do draw a card, you are likely to bust. If you stand on a stiff, your only chance of winning is if the dealer should break. We have already seen that the dealer's up-card is your guide for determining his likelihood of breaking. So as we will see in a moment, the dealer's up-card will provide the answer to the tricky question of when you should draw to a breaking hand.

A no-bust hand is a hard hand totaling 11 or less. The characteristic that defines no-bust hands is the fact that there is no chance of breaking if you draw one more card. Since there is no risk, you should never stand on a no-bust hand.

HARD HANDS

To make it as easy for you to learn basic strategy as possible, I have broken it down to some simple rules (pp. 63–65). Most of the rules govern the play of hard hands, while others cover soft hands.

Actually, there is more than one version of basic strategy. This is because there is more than one possible set of rules you may encounter when playing in a casino. For example, there is one version of basic strategy specifically designed for games that employ only one deck of cards, and there is another version designed for games that employ four or more decks of cards. However, the differences between the two are very minor, so there is little harm if you learn only one version and use it always, regardless of the number of decks in the game. This is the approach I recommend for the average player. If you are going to learn only one version, it is best to learn the one for games with four or more decks, since this is what you will encounter in the majority of cases. Right now, I am going to teach you multiple-deck basic strategy. Later, I will explain how you can also learn the other version just as easily, if you wish.

First, we will learn the rules governing how to play hard hands. When playing a hard hand, there are three different kinds of decisions you may have to make: whether to hit or stand, whether or not to double down, and whether to split a hard hand composed of a pair.

WHEN TO HIT

Earlier, we divided all dealer up-cards into three groups. Those three groups are the basis for the three rules for hitting or standing on hard hands. If the dealer has a 7, 8, 9, ten, or ace up, he is not likely to bust. And if he does not bust, he will, of course, end up with a hand of 17 or more, since the dealer is not allowed to stand on less than 17. If the dealer gets 17 or better, you have no chance of winning unless you have at least 17. Therefore, our first rule is: *Stand on 17 or higher against a dealer up-card of 7, 8, 9, ten, or ace; otherwise, hit*. If you have less than 17, you must draw against any of those up-cards.

If the dealer has a 4, 5, or 6, he is very likely to bust. But that won't do you any good if you bust also. Therefore, to ensure that you don't bust in such a situation, you should never draw to a stiff. That's why our second rule is: *Stand on 12 or higher against a dealer up-card of 4, 5, or 6; otherwise, hit*.

If the dealer has a 2 or 3 up, he has a good chance of breaking but also a fair chance of making a hand. For that reason, it is worth taking some risk and drawing to a stiff when the dealer has a 2 or 3. The question is: How much of a risk should you be willing to take? At which point should you stand? The exact answer to the question has been established through computer analysis. Our third rule is: *Stand on 13 or higher against a dealer up-card of 2 or 3; otherwise, hit*.

As simple as these three rules are, it will take a little practice for you to learn them well enough that they become an automatic reflex whenever you play blackjack. This is important particularly since, as we go along, you will have more on your mind as you play. To learn these rules, I suggest that you practice two exercises with a deck of cards.

First, pick up the deck and remove the ace through 10 of spades. As soon as you have those ten cards, mix them so they are in an unknown, random order. Now deal the top card of the packet face up. Pretend that this card is the dealer's up-card in a blackjack game. Recite the relevant rule about when to stand against this up-card. For example, if you turned up the 8 of spades, you should say, "Stand on 17 or higher against 7, 8, 9, ten, or ace." Turn over the next card and repeat the process. If this card were a 3, you would say, "Stand on 13 or higher against 2 or 3." Keep going in this same manner until you have dealt through the entire packet, each time pretending that the card you just turned over is the dealer's up-card in a game and stating the rule that applies in that case.

When you have gone through all ten cards, shuffle them again and repeat the process. Keep this book nearby for reference. At first, you will have to go slowly, and you may have to refer to the book from time to time. But before long, you should be able to go through the entire deck without hesitation.

This drill will help you to learn the rules, but it is also important that you be able to apply those rules quickly in a game situation. For that purpose, I suggest the following drill. For this one, you will need all the cards in the deck except the four aces. You should discard the aces before you begin. That will ensure that no soft hands can be dealt, since you have not learned how to handle them yet.

After you have removed the aces, shuffle the remainder of the deck. Then deal the top card about a foot in front of you onto the table. This card will represent the dealer's up-card in a game. Now deal two overlapping cards face up directly in front of you. These two cards will represent your blackjack hand. Now simply state whether you would hit or stand on this hand according to the three rules you have learned. For example, if the up-card is a 5 and your hand consists of a 7 and an 8, you should say "Stand." Remember, the rule is "Stand on 12 or higher against 4, 5, or 6."

As soon as you have announced your decision, deal another face-up card on top of the one that represented the dealer's up-card and two more face-up cards on top of your first hand. Now you have a completely different playing situation facing you—a new dealer up-card and a new hand to play. Again, state whether you would hit or stand. Then continue in the same manner until you have gone through the entire deck. If at any time you are at all uncertain of the correct answer, look it up in this book before going on with the drill.

The most productive approach is to alternate between the two drills. When you can do both drills at a brisk pace without any errors and without consulting the rules in your book, you can feel confident that you have mastered the hard standing rules. Of course, there are many cases where the correct decision is neither hitting nor standing but, rather, splitting or doubling down. We will consider the rules governing those decisions in a moment. However, when those options have been ruled out, the three rules you have just learned should govern the play of hard hands.

WHEN TO DOUBLE DOWN

Doubling down allows you to double the size of your bet after seeing your first two cards but limits you to only one additional card for that hand. Obviously, you don't want to double the size of your bet unless you think you have a very good chance of winning. There are two ways in which you might win if you double down. You will win if you end up with an excellent hand that beats the dealer's hand. You will also win, regardless of your hand, if the dealer busts. The most important consideration in deciding whether to double down is how likely you are to end up with a strong hand if you draw only one more card. The second most important consideration is how likely the dealer is to break, based on his up-card.

Since picture cards count as ten in blackjack, when you double down you are more likely to draw a ten-value card than any other card. Therefore, the best total to double down on is one that would become an excellent hand if you were to draw a ten-value card. Not surprisingly, the only hard hands you will ever double down on are totals of 9, 10, or 11. Eleven is, of course, the best possible hand on which to double down. You should always double down on a total of 11 except when the dealer has an ace up. The next-best hand to draw a ten-value card to is a hand that totals 10. You should always double down on a total of 10 except when the dealer has a ten or ace up. Nine is a borderline case, since even a 19 might lose to a better hand. You should only double down on a total of 9 when the dealer's up-card indicates that he is fairly likely to break. The policy to follow here is to double on 9 only against a dealer up-card of 3, 4, 5, or 6.

The correct doubling-down plays on hard hands can be reduced to the following three rules: *Always double on 11 except against an ace. Always double on ten except against ten or ace. Double on 9 against 3 to 6.* You should always follow these rules without exception. As with all the basic strategy rules I am teaching you, their accuracy has been established through extensive computer testing.

To practice these rules, use the second drill I gave you for learning the hard-hand hitting strategy. Perform the drill exactly as it was taught, dealing an up-card for the dealer and giving yourself two cards, then stating whether you should hit or stand. The only difference now is that, if you turn up a hand that you should double down on according to the three doubling rules, you should say "Double" rather than saying "Hit." For example, if you dealt yourself a 5 and a 6 and the dealer's up-card is a 7, you would say "Double." Don't actually play the hand out; just state how you should play it, then move on to a new hand. If you are in doubt as to the correct answer, check the book. A few practice sessions should be all you need to get the doubling rules, as well as the hitting rules, down pat.

WHEN TO SPLIT

The last thing you have to learn in order to know how to play any hard hand correctly is when to split if you have been dealt a pair.

Intelligently used, splitting can offer you two advantages. First, it sometimes allows you to turn a poor hand into two good hands. Second, it enables you to double your bet when the dealer is likely to bust.

A perfect example of the first advantage occurs when you are dealt a 16. Sixteen is the worst possible blackjack hand you can get. You will lose most of the time if you have a 16, regardless of what the dealer's up-card is. If you hit, you will probably bust; if you don't hit, the dealer will win unless he busts, since the rules say he can't stand on less than 17. However, if your 16 happens to consist of two 8s, you can change that terrible hand into two new hands, both of which are likely to be better than the one you started with. Even if you win one hand and lose the other, you will still be better off than you probably would have been playing out that 16; breaking even is better than losing.

Similarly, a hand of two aces gives you a 12, which is a poor total to draw to. But if you split those aces, you will probably end up with two excellent hands. In fact, regardless of the dealer's up-card, splitting aces is always so advantageous for the player that the casinos limit that advantage by imposing a restriction on split aces. When you split aces, you are given only one card on each ace and are not allowed any further options. You may not draw further cards, double down on either hand, or resplit if you receive a third ace. This limitation applies only to aces, not to any other pair you might split. Also, if you draw a ten-value card to one of your split aces, it counts as 21 but it does not count as a natural blackjack. You will not get a 3 to 2 payoff, and if the dealer gets a three- or four-card total of 21, it will be considered a draw. Yet despite all these limitations, splitting is still the best possible way to play a hand of two aces. Our first splitting rule is: *Always split aces and 8s.*

Of course, if you use the splitting option unwisely, you may trade in a good hand for two poorer ones. For example, a pair of ten-value cards gives you a 20, which is an outstanding hand. If you split them, the likelihood is that neither of your split hands will be as good as the one you started with. The only way your split hands could be as good or better than the hand you now have is to draw ten-value cards or aces to them. The fourteen tens left in the deck (the other two are in your hand) and the four aces give you sixteen chances of this happening. By contrast, there are twenty-four other cards in the deck that, if drawn, will leave you with worse totals than the twenty you started with. Clearly, the majority of the time, splitting ten-value cards means trading in one strong hand for two weaker ones. Splitting tens is one of the most ignorant moves a blackjack player can make. Yet you will see this play pulled by people at casino tables all the time. It is the most graphic evidence one could want that most players are their own worst enemies. Incidentally, if you split tens and catch an ace on one hand this also does not count as blackjack. I mention this only as a point of information; don't split ten-value cards.

Similarly, a pair of 5s gives you a total of 10, which is a great hand for doubling down. Even if you don't double down, it is a very good hand to draw to. But if you split those 5s, you will probably end up with two weak hands, since a 5 is a very poor total to draw to. If, for example, you drew one of those many tens in the deck, you would have a total of 15, one of the most hopeless hands you can receive. The smart thing to do is to keep those 5s together and hope that you do draw a ten-value card. A 4 is also a poor card on which to build a hand. That is why another of our splitting rules is: *Never split 4s, 5s, or tens.*

When you should split other pairs depends on what the dealer's up-card is. The rules have, of course, been worked out so as to give you the best profit potential in each case. As you might expect, you will split most often when the dealer's up-card indicates that he is likely to bust.

The six basic strategy rules for splitting are:

1. *Always split aces and 8s.*
2. *Split 2s and 3s against a dealer up-card of 4 to 7.*
3. *Never split 4s, 5s, or tens.*
4. *Split 6s against a dealer up-card of 3 to 6.*
5. *Split 7s against a dealer up-card of 7 or less.*
6. *Always split 9s, except against a dealer up-card of 7, ten, or ace.*

Once you have split a pair and have received a second card on one of the split cards, you should play the hand just as you would play any two-card hand you were dealt. Just apply the hitting and doubling-down rules you have learned.

Sometimes you may find it desirable to double down on one of the hands that has resulted from the split. Suppose the dealer has a 3 up and you have been dealt a pair of 6s. You split your 6s just as the splitting rules say you should. You draw a 4 to one of those 6s, giving you a total of 10. The doubling rules say that you should double down when you have a 10 and the dealer has a 3 up. Many casinos will not allow you to double down on a hand that has resulted from a split. Other casinos, however, will allow it. If you are allowed to double down after splitting, it becomes profitable to split a pair in certain situations in which you otherwise would not do so. When playing in a casino that does allow doubling after splitting, you can gain a slight additional advantage by following a more liberal splitting policy. The optimal splitting rules for such a situation are listed in the two Basic Strategy Tables under the heading "Splitting (Double)." Although they are almost the same as the rules I have just given you, there are a few differences.

After you have become experienced at strategy play, you can, if you wish, learn to use these more liberal rules when playing in a casino that allows doubling after splitting. But don't worry about that now. Just learn the rules given above and use them in any casino you play in. Even if you never learn the other splitting rules but always use the ones I just gave you, you will do well. The more ambitious who want to take advantage of every possible refinement will want to learn both sets of rules eventually, but not until after all other aspects of blackjack strategy have been completely mastered.

To learn the splitting rules, you should use two drills, one to teach you the rules and one to help you apply them in a game situation. Take your deck of cards and remove the ace through 10 of spades. These are the only cards you will need for the first drill. Shuffle these ten cards, then deal the first one face up on the table. If it is a 7, pretend that you have been dealt of pair of 7s, and say the relevant splitting rule for this pair. In our example, the rule would be "Split 7s against 7 or less."

Then turn over the next card. If it is a 5, state the rule that governs the splitting of 5s, which is "Never split 4s, 5s, or tens." Continue in this manner until you have dealt through all ten cards, giving the correct rule for each pair. At first, you will have to consult the book often to check the correct answer. When you can go through all ten cards rapidly, reciting the proper rules from memory, you will be ready to go on to the next drill.

For this one, you will need the entire deck. Shuffle the pack and deal a card face up. This will represent the dealer's up-card. Then deal a second card face up nearer to yourself. This second card will represent a pair that you have been dealt in a blackjack game. Thus, if the first card is a 10 and the second card is a 9, pretend that you have been dealt a pair of 9s against a dealer up-card of 10. Just state whether or not you would split in this situation. In the example I just gave of a pair of 9s against 10, the correct answer is "Don't split."

Continue by dealing another card onto the first card you dealt, to represent a new dealer up-card. Then deal another card onto the second card you dealt—the one near you. This card represents a new pair that you have been dealt. Again, simply state whether the correct play would be to split or not to split. Keep going in this manner until the entire deck has been dealt into two piles. At that point, you will have had a chance to practice twenty-six playing decisions involving splitting. It would take you many hours of actual playing to get that much practice in splitting pairs, and even then, some of the pair situations would still not have come up. This is the strength of the drills; they concentrate the playing experience and focus it on just what you want to practice and learn at that particular point.

An effective way to practice is to alternate between the two splitting drills. When you can perform both of them at a fairly rapid pace, without any pauses, without having to consult the book, and without making any mistakes, you can feel confident that you have mastered the splitting rules.

HOW TO PRACTICE

Before we go on, I want to discuss a little further the proper way to perform the various drills. These drills for learning the various aspects of blackjack strategy are among the most valuable information I can give you on blackjack. All the information in the world about how to play correctly won't do you any good unless you can actually do it under fire in a casino. These drills will enable you to do so. Also, I am sure you want to learn proper blackjack strategy as quickly as you can. These drills provide the fastest possible method of learning to be a skillful player. But in order to obtain the fullest benefit from these drills, you must perform them correctly.

Never guess when practicing the drills. If you are not certain of the correct answer to a particular problem, stop the drill and immediately go to the book and look up the answer. Don't guess, and don't wait until the drill is over before checking the answer. Stop cold right in the middle of the drill and go to the book. This procedure will help impress the correct answer on your mind.

Always practice in a quiet place where there are no distractions and where you can be sure you won't be interrupted. You need this atmosphere in order to concentrate completely on the drills. Complete concentration when drilling will not only help you learn the strategy rules faster, it will also help you to concentrate later on, when you are playing in a casino where you do have to cope with distractions.

For the same reason, after you have gained proficiency with the drills, you should strive to do them more rapidly. In fact, you should do them as fast as you can without making mistakes. This speed forces you to concentrate completely on the drills. It makes the learning experience more intense so that you learn faster.

In all the basic strategy drills, you make the decisions as to how to play each hand, but you don't actually go through the motions of playing out the hand. You may be tempted to do so out of curiosity. It's fun to see whether you would have won or lost. But don't give in to the temptation. It would just waste time that could be used for learning. The educational benefit comes from making the decision, not from the mechanical process of playing the hand. Also, playing out the hand would dissipate the intensity of the drill.

SOFT HANDS

The only thing you have yet to learn about basic strategy is how to play a soft hand, a hand containing an ace counted as 11. Whenever you hold a hand with an ace in it, you should count the ace as 11 unless doing so would put you over 21.

Keep in mind that a hand with an ace is only considered soft as long as you are counting the ace as 11. If you were holding a hand consisting of an ace, a 5, and a 10, you would have to count the ace as 1 in order to avoid going over 21. In this case, the hand would be considered a hard hand despite the presence of the ace. Therefore, you would play the hand according to the rules you have already learned. That means that you may begin by playing a certain hand according to the soft-hand rules and finish by playing it according to the hard-hand rules. Incidentally, the dealer will also count any ace he may have as 11 unless doing so would put him over 21.

WHY SOFT HANDS ARE DIFFERENT

The reason that we need a separate set of rules for soft hands is that the mathematical characteristics of soft hands are completely different from those of hard hands. This becomes clear if we consider a specific example. Compare a hand consisting of a 10 and a 7 with one consisting of an ace and a 6. If you were trying to decide whether to draw a card to the hard 17, you would have to consider the fact that there are only sixteen cards in the deck that would improve your hand.

These are the four 4s, the four 3s, the four 2s, and the four aces. Any one of the other thirty-four cards in the deck would break you. In other words, two-thirds of the cards you might draw would mean an automatic loss. With odds like that, it would be very foolish to take a card. That is why under the hard-hand rules you learned never to draw to 17.

But consider the situation with that ace-6 combination, the soft 17. There are only fifteen cards that would help: those same four 4s, four 3s, four 2s, and the three remaining aces. But there are another sixteen cards that won't help but also won't hurt you: the sixteen ten-value cards. If you draw a ten, you will still have a total of 17. You will have lost nothing by taking the gamble. That leaves only nineteen bad draws in the deck. By contrast, there were thirty-four bad draws on the hard 17. And even that is not the whole story. A bad draw on a soft 17 would just convert your hand to a low hard total. At that point, you would have a possibility of getting a good hand by drawing again if you thought it wise. Unlike the case with the hard 17, you cannot break when drawing to a soft hand. That is why it is always foolish to draw to a hard 17, but it is always wise to draw to a soft 17. This is just one example of why we need a separate set of rules for playing soft hands.

STANDING ON SOFT HANDS

We have already touched on the first soft hitting and standing rule: *Never stand on soft 17 or less.* However, you should always stand on a soft 19 or 20. Eighteen is a borderline case. You should only hit a soft 18 against a dealer up-card of 9, ten, or ace, and stand against 2, 7, or 8. In a moment you will learn how to play a soft 18 if the dealer has a 3, 4, 5, or 6. But first, remember these rules:

1. *Always stand on soft 19 or 20.*

2. *Stand on soft 18 against 9, ten, or ace and hit against 2, 7, or 8.*

3. *Never stand on soft 17 or less.*

DOUBLING ON SOFT HANDS

When I say you should never stand on a soft 17 or less, I don't mean you should always hit. Sometimes you should double down. If the dealer's up-card indicates he is likely to break, it may pay for you to increase your bet by doubling down. As you would expect, you double down most often against the poorest dealer up-cards. The rules for doubling down on soft hands are:

1. *Double on soft 17 or 18 against a dealer up-card of 3 to 6.*
2. *Double on a soft 15 or 16 against a dealer up-card of 4 to 6.*
3. *Double on a soft 13 and 14 against a dealer up-card of 5 or 6.*

As soon as you learn these rules, you will know the correct way to play any blackjack hand you can possibly be dealt. There are two drills you should use to learn the soft-hand rules. As with all the basic strategy drills, the first one is designed to help you learn the rules, while the second one will teach you how to apply the rules in a game situation.

For the first drill, remove the ace through 9 of spades and discard the rest of the deck. Place the ace face up on the table in front of you. Now shuffle the other eight cards. Then deal the top card of the packet onto the table next to the ace. That creates a soft hand. Just state the rule or rules that govern the play of this hand. For example, if you have a soft 15, you should say "Never stand on soft 17 or less" and also "Double on soft 15 or 16 against 4 to 6."

Then deal the next card from the packet onto the previous card next to the ace. This creates a new soft hand. State the rules that apply to this new hand. Continue in this manner until the entire packet has been exhausted. Keep at it until you can perform the entire drill completely from memory. At that point, you should add the second drill.

For the second drill, you should start with the entire deck. Remove one ace and place it face up in front of you. Discard eight ten-value cards from the deck, then shuffle the rest of the cards. Deal a card face up in the center of the table to represent the dealer's up-card. Deal another card face up next to the ace to form a soft hand. Now just state the correct way to play this hand, whether you should hit, stand, or double down.

Then deal another card onto the one that represented the dealer's up-card and another one onto the card next to the ace. Now you have a completely new situation: a different soft hand against a different dealer up-card. Now you should announce how this new hand should be played. Continue this way until you have dealt the entire deck into two piles. Sometimes you will get a hand of a pair of aces. Then, of course, the correct decision is to split.

With this drill, you will deal yourself a lot of naturals. Don't let it go to your head. That is why you discard half the ten-value cards at the outset—to reduce the number of naturals that will come up.

As with the other drills, the most effective approach is to alternate between the two soft-hand drills until you can do both without hesitation or error. At that point, you will have completely mastered basic strategy. With that information, you will have a better chance of winning when playing blackjack than you could ever achieve in any other casino game.

FOUR-DECK BASIC STRATEGY

The Hard Hands

HARD STANDING RULES

Stand on 13 against 2 or 3.
Stand on 12 against 4 to 6.
Stand on 17 against 7 to ace.

HARD DOUBLE-DOWN RULES

Always double on 11 *except* against an ace.
Always double on ten *except* against ten or ace.
Double on 9 against 3 to 6.

SPLITTING RULES (DOUBLE)

Always split aces and 8s.
Split 2s or 3s against 7 or less.
Split 4s against 5 or 6.
Never split 5s or tens.
Split 6s and 7s against 7 or less.
Always split 9s *except* against 7, ten, or ace.

SPLITTING RULES (NO DOUBLE)

Always split aces and 8s.
Split 2s or 3s against 4 to 7.
Never split 4s, 5s, or tens.
Split 6s against 3 to 6.
Split 7s against 7 or less.
Always split 9s except against 7, ten, or ace.

The Soft Hands

SOFT STANDING RULES

Always stand on soft 19 or 20.
Hit soft 18 against 9, ten, or ace (stand against 2, 7, or 8).
Never stand on soft 17 or less.

SOFT DOUBLE-DOWN RULES

Double on soft 17 or 18 against 3 to 6.
Double on soft 15 or 16 against 4 to 6.
Double on soft 13 or 14 against 5 or 6.

ONE-DECK BASIC STRATEGY

The Hard Hands

HARD STANDING RULES

Stand on 13 against 2 or 3.
Stand on 12 against 4 to 6.
Stand on 17 against 7 to ace.

HARD DOUBLE-DOWN RULES

Always double on 11.
Always double on ten *except* against ten or ace.
Double on 9 against 6 or less.
Double on 8 against 5 or 6.

SPLITTING RULES (DOUBLE)

Always split aces and 8s.
Split 2s against 7 or less.
Split 3s against 4 to 7.
Split 4s against 4, 5, or 6.
Never split 5s or tens.
Split 6s against 6 or less.
Split 7s against 8 or less.
Always split 9s *except* against 7, tens, or ace.

SPLITTING RULES (NO DOUBLE)

Always split aces and 8s.
Split 2s against 3 to 7.
Split 3s against 4 to 7.
Never split 4s, 5s, or tens.
Split 6s against 6 or less.
Split 7s against 7 or less.
Always split 9s except against 7, ten, or ace.

The Soft Hands

SOFT STANDING RULES

Always stand on soft 19 or 20.
Hit soft 18 against 9, ten, or ace (stand against 2, 7, or 8).
Never stand on soft 17 or less.

SOFT DOUBLE-DOWN RULES

Double on soft 17 or 18 against 3 to 6.
Double on soft 15 or 16 against 4 to 6.
Double on soft 13 or 14 against 5 or 6.

Fine Points

BASIC STRATEGY VARIATIONS

The basic strategy rules I have taught you are designed particularly for games employing four or more decks of cards. They give you the optimal decisions for any situation that can possibly arise. If you use these rules for games employing one or two decks, you will also do well in the long run, since these rules come very close to the optimal decisions for such games.

However, if you are going to play primarily in games employing only one deck, you can gain a slight additional advantage by using the basic strategy rules that have been specifically designed for single-deck games. These are very similar to what you have already learned, differing in only a couple of instances. You will find the rules for one-deck basic strategy in the second Basic Strategy Table. Of course, you can learn any variation of basic strategy by using the same drills we have already covered.

There is certainly no need to memorize all the basic strategy variations simultaneously. If you really want to maximize your chances, you should find out in advance whether the casino you are planning to play in deals a one-deck game or a multiple-deck game and whether or not they allow doubling down after splitting. Then, just before going down to play, drill on the rules that apply to that specific situation.

STAYING IN PRACTICE

Even after you have mastered basic strategy, you will still have to drill from time to time to stay in shape. It really won't take much. But unless you play blackjack constantly, an occasional brush-up is necessary. A little practice time before each trip to Vegas or A.C. will do the job.

After you have mastered basic strategy, it will not be necessary to practice all the drills we have covered in order to stay in practice.

Here is a drill that is perfect for review purposes. Remove eight of the ten-value cards from the deck and discard them. Add four extra aces from another deck. Shuffle this forty-eight-card deck. Deal one card face up to represent the dealer's up-card. Deal yourself two cards face up. State how you would play this situation. Deal a new card on top of the original dealer's up-card, and deal yourself a new hand on top of your original hand. State how you would play this new situation. Repeat until all the cards have been exhausted.

The purpose of removing some tens and adding more aces to the deck is to make for fewer easy hands (like 20s) and more difficult hands (like soft hands). A few run-throughs with this drill, always checking the book when in doubt, will provide you with a perfect refresher on basic strategy.

Playing Conditions

RULE VARIATIONS

Playing basic strategy will place you on an essentially even basis with the casino, with no significant advantage on either their side or your side. There are, however, a number of different variables that can slightly shift the balance one way or the other. The most important of these are the specific playing rules that are followed in the casino in which you are playing. Although all the major rules are fairly uniform, small differences occur between casinos in different countries, between different cities in the same country, and sometimes even between different casinos in the same city. These differences are important because, although seemingly minor, they can affect your chances of winning.

That's why it is important to scout the opposition. Although many casinos print free booklets describing the games they offer, these are usually too superficial to be of much help to the serious player. Certain casinos such as those of Atlantic City, London, and Puerto Rico, will also have the key rules prominently displayed at the tables. However, the most reliable method to find out the rules in a particular casino before you go there is to phone and ask to speak to someone in the blackjack pit. If you haven't taken the trouble to find out in advance, at least ask the dealer before you do any serious gambling.

To comparison shop intelligently, you must understand how the different rule variations affect your chances of winning. Mathematically, the impact of a rule variation on your profits is expressed as a percentage, just as the overall house edge is.

THE NUMBER OF DECKS

The single most important variation to consider from one casino to another is the number of decks employed. The rule of thumb is, the fewer decks the better. Almost all gambling casinos in the Caribbean and overseas deal from a four-deck shoe. In Atlantic City, all the games presently use either eight decks or six decks. In Las Vegas, you may encounter single-deck and double-deck games dealt from the hand, and shoe games using four or more decks. Sometimes you find both at different tables in the same casino. For some reason, many people seem to think that single-deck blackjack games are a thing of the past. Actually, in Nevada there are plenty of such games to be found. In Las Vegas, about a third of the casinos offer single-deck games on at least some of their tables. Many others have two-deck games, which is almost as good. In Reno and Lake Tahoe, most of the games are single-deckers. If you learn the four-deck basic strategy that I have taught you, the use of four decks will hurt your chances of winnng by only .54 percent. However, if you decide to tackle card counting, the number of decks used will have other implications, which we will discuss next chapter.

SOFT 17

Another variable of casino practice is the policy concerning dealer hands of soft 17. In most downtown Las Vegas casinos and most clubs in Reno and Lake Tahoe, the dealer must draw a card when holding a soft 17. In Atlantic City, the dealer must stand when holding a soft 17, just as he would if he were holding a hard 17. This is also the policy in most Las Vegas Strip casinos, but there are exceptions. There is no point in mentioning specific gambling houses because these policies change from time to time. Generally, it is the few grind joints on the Strip that have the dealer hit soft 17.

In analyzing basic strategy, we saw that it is really a sucker move to stand on soft 17. As a selfish player, you want the dealer to do the stupid thing—to stand on soft 17. Casinos that follow the hitting policy will only hurt your chances of winning by .2 percent. This is certainly not very significant, but if added to other unfavorable rules in a particular casino, it may be enough reason for you to take your action elsewhere.

DOUBLING-DOWN RESTRICTIONS

A casino can also hurt your chances of winning by limiting the options available to you in playing your hand. If you were to play blackjack in any of the clubs in London, you would find the house rules prominently displayed on a plaque at each table. One of the rules would inform you that the player may only double down on totals of 9, 10, or 11. In discussing soft hands, we saw that there are a number of situations in which it is desirable to double down on a soft total. Because the British casinos do not allow soft doubling down, your chances of winning would be cut by .14 percent.

If you found this limitation frustrating, you might decide to go elsewhere on your next vacation. You might decide to combine your gambling with some skiing and pick Lake Tahoe, Nevada. Unfortunately, matters are worse there. These clubs limit doubling down to totals of 10 or 11. You would not only lose a .14 percent edge by not being able to double on soft hands, but you would also suffer an additional .14 percent loss by losing the right to double on a 9. Most of the clubs in nearby Reno follow the same policy.

A little Caribbean sun and fun sound good? Don't pick Puerto Rico if you also intend to play blackjack. Here you would encounter the most restrictive doubling down rules of all. The Puerto Rican casinos allow doubling down only on a total of 11. That's a loss of .14 percent due to no soft doubling, and another loss of .14 percent due to no doubling on 9. But now you can also tack on another .56 percent disadvantage because of the loss of the right to double on 10, a very favorable play for the player. The cumulative difference between a casino that allows unrestricted doubling down and one that limits you to doubling on 11 only is .84 percent. In a game of small edges like blackjack, this is very significant. Fortunately, all the casinos in both Las Vegas and Atlantic City do allow you to double down on any total. When you consider that Las Vegas also offers many single-deck games while Puerto Rico deals from a four-deck shoe (remember, that costs you .54 percent), you can start to see how where you play blackjack really can make a big difference.

SPLITTING AFTER DOUBLING

As I mentioned earlier, some casinos allow you to double down on a hand that results from splitting a pair. Other casinos allow you to split or to double down, but they do not allow you to do both in the same round. As a knowledgeable player, you want all the freedom you can get. It is to your advantage to be allowed to double down after splitting, particularly if you have taken the trouble to learn the more liberal splitting rules for casinos that do allow this option. Since use of these rules will enhance your chances of winning by only .1 percent, it is for you to decide whether they are worth the extra work to learn. However, being allowed to double down after splitting is to your advantage, regardless of which set of basic strategy rules you play by.

RESPLITTING

Some casinos also restrict your right to resplit pairs. If, for example, you were dealt a pair of 8s, you should split them. If you drew a third 8 to one of those split 8s, the intelligent play would be to split again. If you were playing in Las Vegas, you would be allowed to do so; if you were playing in Atlantic City, you would not be allowed. This restriction hurts your chances of winning, but its impact is minimal. You suffer only a .05 percent disadvantage.

CHECKING HOLE CARDS

Finally, here is a dealing variation that does not affect your chances of winning at all. However, I want you to understand it clearly; otherwise, you might find it rather confusing the first time you encounter it. In the traditional style of dealing blackjack, the dealer deals one card to each player and one card face up to himself. He then deals a second card to each player and a second card to himself, this time face down. The dealer's face-down card is called his hole card. Normally, the dealer does not look at his hole card until all the players have finished playing their hands. The one exception is when the dealer has an ace or a ten-value card showing. In this case, he will check his hole card to see if he has blackjack before allowing the players to hit, split, or double down. If the dealer sees that he does have a natural, he will bring the game to an end at that point, collecting the bets of all the players except those who also have blackjack. The purpose of this practice is to avoid wasting time. There is no point in allowing players to hit, split, or double down when the dealer has them beat from the outset.

However, the practice of the dealer checking his hole card on a possible natural has led to a persistent cheating problem for the casinos. Some dealers will secretly signal their hole cards in this situation to a partner who is posing as a player. If the dealer does not have a natural, the partner now knows with certainty the best way to play his hand. In this way, the two can defraud the casino and split the profit later. In addition, by means of a technique called spooking, cheats can sometimes catch a glimpse of the dealer's hole card as he looks at it without the dealer's knowledge.

In order to foil these practices, most casinos outside the United States follow the practice of the dealer not giving himself a hole card. In other words, at the end of the initial deal, the dealer's hand will consist of only a single face-up card. Only after each player has finished playing his hand does the dealer give himself a second card. This is dealt face-up, and the hand is then played out according to the stand-on-17 rule.

When Atlantic City first opened up, the casinos adopted a kind of compromise policy. The dealer takes a hole card but does not look at it until the players finish—even if he has a possible natural. Although this slows down the game slightly, it also helps protect the game. The dealer cannot signal his hole card if he doesn't know what it is. In the last couple of years, a number of Las Vegas casinos have adopted the policy of letting the dealer check his hole card only when he has an ace showing, not when he has a ten showing. Whether the game is dealt European-style or Atlantic City–style, the players can still take insurance when the dealer shows an ace, but they must wait until all the hands have been played to find out whether they have won or lost the bet.

Most of the time, this style of dealing will have little impact on your game. However, keep in mind that with this approach, you may end up doubling down or splitting when you would not have if you had known from the outset that the dealer had blackjack. When this happens in any American casino, you will lose only your original bet. The house will not take the additional money you put out for the split or double. Therefore, your chances of winning are not affected. If you play in a casino overseas where the dealer collects both bets in this situation, it will cut your chances of winning by .13 percent.

SEATING POSITION

One of the questions I am most often asked by blackjack players is what seat at the table gives the player the best chance of winning. The answer is that it doesn't matter. The cards have been thoroughly shuffled. No one knows what order they are going to come out in. So just grab a seat and start playing.

Recently, after one of my lectures, a member of the audience came up and told me a sad story about how he had lost a great deal of money at blackjack because of another player's ignorance. It seems that this player, who was sitting in the last seat at the dealer's right, insisted on drawing cards that should have gone to the dealer, instead of standing pat and letting the dealer bust. No doubt he expected me to commiserate. Instead, I tried to make him realize that he was placing the blame on the wrong person.

One of the most persistent of the many myths that flourish in gambling is the belief that the *third-base* player in blackjack (the one in the last seat) controls the game. Again and again, one will hear the other players berate this unfortunate soul for drawing a card that would have busted the dealer if the player had stood on his hand.

Losing gamblers are always on the lookout for a scapegoat, and the third-base man is often it. Similarly, gamblers who think they are skilled players will sometimes seek out the last seat in the belief that their superior strategy will bring the dealer to ruin. I have known people who will not play blackjack if they cannot have the third-base seat. Invariably, these players are so ignorant of proper strategy that their fetish saved them money only because it restricted their playing opportunities. The less often they played, the less money they lost.

Followers of the third-base theory usually defend their beliefs with more passion than logic. When the last player draws a card that would have helped the dealer, nobody notices. But when he draws a card that would have busted the dealer, this is immediately cited as proof of the special importance of the last seat.

The third-base seat is not different from any other seat at the blackjack table for the simple reason that no one can possibly know what card is going to come out of the shoe next. Therefore, the last player's hitting and standing decisions are a purely random factor with no predictive impact on the dealer's hand. In other words, it doesn't make any difference.

Look at it this way. Suppose that each time the dealer hit his hand, instead of taking the top card, he randomly pulled a card from the middle of the deck or shoe. Would this affect his chances of winning? Of course not—not as long as the cards had been randomly shuffled and the card randomly selected. When the last player elects to hit, it means that the dealer gets the second card instead of the first. It is no different if the dealer randomly pulls out the second card or the fifth or the tenth or any other card.

The next time you play blackjack, concentrate on playing your own hand and let the other players play their hands. If you should find yourself in the third-base seat, remember that your best chance of winning lies in playing your hands exactly as you would if you were in any other seat, following the strategy advice in this book. If you get any heat from other players, remind them that it is your money riding on your hand. Unless they are willing to reimburse you for any losses you suffer, you should have no interest in their opinions.

If you should go on to become a card counter (explained in Chapter IV), I recommend that you select a seat near the center of the table for two reasons. First, this position provides a better view of the other players' cards. Second, the players in the first and last seats tend to get closer scrutiny from the house because they know these are the two positions favored by cheats, who prefer to be at the periphery of the dealer's field of vision.

FREE ADVICE

While on the subject of other players offering you advice, let me stress again that most such suggestions are pathetically misguided. The more eager a player is to help you, the more likely he is not to know what he is talking about. For some reason, the free advice syndrome is more prevalent in blackjack than in any other game.

One of the worst examples of this that I ever saw occurred once when I was playing blackjack at the Flamingo in Las Vegas next to a very attractive young woman. She had obviously studied the game; she was playing perfect basic strategy and winning. Her boyfriend standing behind her insisted on continually giving her playing advice in a condescending manner. Unfortunately, his "help" was about as misguided as possible. He provided such gems as, "Good, you got two tens; you should split those."

I guess she figured his ego was too fragile for her just to say, "Look, if you don't understand the game, at least be quiet so I can concentrate. In fact, here are a few quarters. Go play the slot machines; I'll pick you up when I finish here." Instead, she had to rely on coy comments like, "I'm sure you're right that I should hit, dear, but I just have this hunch that the dealer is going to bust." I felt like telling her I had a hunch she should drop this loser. But I make it a policy not to offer advice when not asked.

The high point came when she had a hand of four small cards, and he told her she should take another hit and try for Five-Card Charlie. Even the dealer had a hard time keeping a straight face on that one. Five-Card Charlie is a rule played only in home and barroom games whereby a player who gets five cards without busting gets a bonus payoff. There isn't a casino in the world that recognizes this rule. Don't ask the dealer for your Five-Card Charlie bonus unless you want to blow your Nick the Greek image right away. You might as well ask him where you can find the high-stakes Go Fish tables.

If you have absorbed the information covered in this chapter and practiced the drills, you will be able to play every hand dealt to you optimally according to the most extensive computer tests. No one will really be able to give you any better advice on how to play your hand. You will already be playing the game better than ninety-five percent of the people sitting at those tables, including most thousand-dollar-a-hand high rollers, professional pit bosses, floormen, and blackjack dealers. The only way you could possibly play better would be to learn how to count cards. If you are interested, check out the next chapter.

IV. Advanced Blackjack

The Card-Counting Revolution

♣ Ever since Edward Thorp, the mathematics professor who pioneered modern card counting, published his classic book *Beat the Dealer* in 1962, both gambling casino operators and the general public have become increasingly aware of the fact that blackjack is the one casino game that can be consistently beaten by the skilled player. It is the one game where the player can gain a mathematical edge over the house. Over the years, a number of professional blackjack players have succeeded in utilizing card-counting techniques to earn steady and substantial profits at the game.

The casinos have responded by adding more decks of cards to their games and instructing dealers to shuffle the cards earlier, with a substantial number of cards still remaining undealt. However, these measures, designed to make counting more difficult and less profitable, have been paralleled by continuing refinements and improvements in card-counting techniques that have made expert players increasingly effective. The casinos have been left with only one final line of defense: *barring* suspected counters from play. The casino industry has taken the position that anyone can play at its tables as long as he doesn't know enough about the game to stand a real chance of winning. However, anyone whose skill raises him above the level of a guaranteed victim runs the risk of being 86'd by the house. Using one's God-given intelligence to help you win at gambling is no crime, but the casinos go as far as the law allows in treating card counters like criminals.

This cynical policy has led to numerous lawsuits challenging the legality of barring players who have done nothing dishonest. In Nevada, these suits have been uniformly unsuccessful and will probably continue to be so until someone succeeds in getting jurisdiction in another state so that the case may be heard outside the Nevada courts. In Atlantic City, card counter Ken Uston eventually prevailed in his lawsuit. The New Jersey Supreme Court ruled that the casinos had to allow counters to play. The casinos retaliated by shifting from four-deck games to the present use of eight decks in each shoe. They also eliminated the early-surrender rule, which had been a very favorable option available to New Jersey blackjack players. Finding even these defensive measures inadequate protection, they also adopted the practice of *shuffling up* on suspected card counters. When casino supervisors think they have spotted a card counter at one of their tables, they instruct the dealer to shuffle after every hand. This practice, which effectively eliminates the value of counting, is continued until the player leaves in disgust.

Before you start feeling sorry for the beleaguered casinos, keep in mind that in recent years blackjack has grown to become the most profitable table game offered by casinos in this country precisely be-cause players have been attracted by all the publicity surroundng card counting. For every player who has successfully mastered a count system and won money from the casinos, there are hundreds of others who optimistically concluded that, if blackjack can be beaten, they could do it without any real preparation and who succeeded only in swelling the casinos' coffers. Consequently, the casinos themselves have been the biggest financial beneficiaries of card counting. The fact is that the casino industry has profited so much from the publicity generated by card counting that they can easily allow the few successful counters to play at their tables and write it off as an advertising expense.

Pros and Cons

If you are considering learning a count strategy, you should guard against unrealistic expectations. The astronomical sums reportedly won by counters have been won largely by professionals playing in teams. As a recreational gambler playing alone, you cannot expect results anywhere near this range. Neither can you expect that you will win every time you play blackjack simply because you count. The short-run fluctuations that affect all gambling plague card counters also. They are not immune to losing streaks. Mastering a count strategy will only provide you with the comfort of knowing that you have the best possible chance of winning and that, if you play frequently enough, you will show a long-term profit.

In addition, the increasing paranoia of casinos against card counters has meant that counters have had to avoid the more flamboyant moves, such as big jumps in bet size, that may get them spotted and 86'd from the casino. This has further curtailed the profit margin. About fifteen years ago, when I first started playing blackjack professionally, conditions were much looser, and it was far easier to make money at the game. Eventually, I reached the point where I had been barred from enough places to make counting less profitable; I have not played blackjack for serious money for the last seven years. The field is not what it was when I began in it, and I would not recommend to anyone that they consider blackjack as a profession today. However, I do feel that card counting can be a valuable skill for the serious amateur who plays the game frequently. If you are going to play anyway, you may as well give yourself the best possible chance of winning.

Whether the profit you can hope to achieve through counting is enough to justify the work involved depends on just how much of a chore you find it to master card counting and apply it when you play. If you find the whole thing a lot of drudgery, I suggest you just skim through this chapter for background knowledge and stick to basic strategy when you play, secure in the knowledge that the level of your play will be far above the average. However, if you are an analytically minded individual who enjoys playing blackjack and also enjoys a challenge, I think you will find card counting valuable as much for the additional pleasure you will derive from the game as for the increased profits.

Of the many blackjack players who have tried to learn card counting in recent years, the large majority have failed, often losing large sums of money in the process. There are many pitfalls that can prevent you from becoming a successful counter. The most common error is trying to learn how to count before having thoroughly mastered basic strategy. Even after you become an expert card counter, you will still make most of your playing decisions according to basic strategy. Those decisions must be made instantaneously and automatically so you can devote all your attention to keeping an accurate count. You can't concentrate properly on the count if you have to hesitate even a moment in recalling the correct way to play your hand. If you feel at all weak in this area, now is the time to go back to those basic strategy drills before delving further into this chapter.

The field of card counting is far too large to allow comprehensive treatment in one chapter. However, in this chapter you will learn enough about what is involved to be able to intelligently decide whether it is for you. At the end of the chapter, I have listed several books that I recommend for anyone who wants to pursue the subject further.

I am forever having people come up to me after my lectures and seminars to tell me that they count cards whenever they play blackjack. When I ask them what system they use, they usually say something like, "Oh, I don't use any particular system. I just keep track of the cards in my head as the game progresses and take it into account as I play each hand." The bizarre notion that you can card count without a system, just by relying on some vague instinct, is ridiculous and is no doubt largely responsible for much of the increased casino profits from blackjack that I mentioned earlier. It just underscores how little the public understands about the subject, despite all the publicity. I don't think a person can really understand what card counting is all about just from reading a general discussion of it, any more than one can understand what baseball is all about by reading theoretical discussions of the game. To understand baseball, you have to get out on the field and play it at least a couple of times. To understand card counting, you have to learn a counting system. That is why I am going to devote the bulk of this chapter to teaching you a simple but effective card-counting strategy called the *plus-minus system*.

Learning to Count

THE THEORY OF CARD COUNTING

The principle behind card counting, or *casing the deck*, is simple. We saw in the previous chapter that, unlike other casino games, in blackjack the percentages fluctuate from one hand to the next. Sometimes the odds are in the player's favor. Sometimes they are in the casino's favor. Obviously, the most effective way to bet your money would be to bet more when your chances of winning are high and less when your chances are low. That way, when you win, you will mostly win large bets, and when you lose, you will mostly lose small bets. You could lose more than half your bets and still show a good profit.

The trick is knowing when the odds are in your favor and when they are against you. We have already seen that what determines your chances of winning the next hand is the composition of the cards remaining undealt. An overabundance of high cards remaining will improve your chances of winning, while an overabundance of low cards will hurt them. If you had some way of knowing the ratio of high cards to low cards remaining in the deck at any given moment, you could size your bets accordingly.

THE COUNT

Most people think that in order to accomplish this you would have to memorize every card as it's played. Fortunately, there is a much simpler way. It requires no memorization at all—just some very simple arithmetic. The key is to assign a plus or minus value to each card in the deck, then to total those values as each card is dealt. All the cards from the 2s to the 6s hurt your chances of winning. It is to your advantage to have those cards removed. For that reason, we will assign a $+1$ value to each of these cards and add $+1$ to our count each time one of these cards goes out of play by being dealt to someone's hand. This reflects the fact that each time one of these cards is eliminated, it is a plus for your chances of winning the next hand.

The tens and aces are the cards most favorable to the player. Each time one is removed, your chances of winning the next hand suffer. Therefore, we will assign every ten and ace a -1 value and add -1 to our count each time one of these cards is dealt. The remaining cards, 7s, 8s, and 9s, have so little impact on your chances of winning that we will assign them a value of zero. You can simply ignore these cards in your count when you see them. Thus, the point values you have to remember for this count system are as follows:

2	3	4	5	6	7	8	9	10	A
+1	+1	+1	+1	+1	0	0	0	−1	−1

Throughout the game, you keep a running computation of each card as it is dealt. Your count begins at zero before any cards have been dealt from the deck or shoe. If the first card dealt is, for example, a 4, you count $+1$, since that is the value assigned to 4s in your count strategy. If the next card is a 3, your count goes to $+2$. If the next card is a queen, your count goes down to $+1$ again. This reflects the fact that the elimination of the undesirable 3 a moment ago has been counterbalanced by the loss of a desirable ten-value card. Of course, all this calculation is done silently in your mind. This is known as keeping a *running count*.

To make sure you understand exactly how to keep a running count, I suggest you pick up a deck of cards and try it once. Deal through the entire deck, card by card, counting each one. Go as slowly as you need to, and refer to the point values in the chart above whenever necessary.

If you did that correctly, your count should have ended at zero after going through all fifty-two cards. This is because there are exactly as many desirable − 1 cards in the deck as there are undesirable + 1 cards. If you came up with any number other than zero at the end, you either made a mistake in your count or you need to buy a new deck of cards because there is a card missing.

You started at zero and ended at zero, but in between you saw the count fluctuate between plus and minus figures. Each of those plus or minus figures represented an imbalance in the deck between high cards and low cards. Whenever the count was higher than plus one, the odds of winning a blackjack hand dealt at that moment were in your favor. Whenever the count was minus, the odds were against you. In a real game, you would have gauged the size of each of your bets accordingly.

COUNTING DRILLS

Card counting won't be of any value to you unless you can do it quickly and accurately. If you make mistakes in your count and then use it to guide your betting, you will be throwing your money away. To help you master the technique of keeping a fast, accurate count, I am going to give you three drills to master.

For the first drill, take your deck of cards and shuffle it thoroughly. Then remove one card and place it aside without looking at it. You are now going to deal through the entire deck, dealing the cards one at a time into a face-up pile on the table. As you do so, keep a running count just as you did a moment ago. Don't refer to the point-value chart unless you have to.

If you do this correctly, when you finish going through the fifty-one cards, your count will either be + 1, − 1, or zero. This final count should tell you what card you placed aside at the outset. It won't tell you the exact identity, but it will tell you whether it was a high card, a low card, or a middle-value card. Since a complete deck count should end in zero, a count of +1 means the remaining card must have a −1 value; it must be a high card. An ending count of −1 would mean that the missing card was a low one. A count of zero would mean that it was a neutral 7, 8, or 9.

The card placed aside at the beginning of the drill is your method for checking the accuracy of your count. If your count did not correctly predict what that card was, you must have made a mistake somewhere along the line. Also, if your count ended at plus or minus 2 or 3, you made an error in your running count.

In practicing the drill, go as slowly as you need to in order to avoid errors. Once you get to the point where you never make a mistake, you can begin to work for speed. Practice for a short while each day. When you have attained both speed and accuracy, you will have taken the first step to becoming a successful blackjack counter.

When you reach that stage, there are two more drills you should begin to practice. These will help you keep an accurate count even in a fast-paced game. This next drill is performed exactly like the previous one, with only one difference. You shuffle the cards just as before, and you place one aside just as before. But this time you deal through the cards in pairs. Deal through the entire deck two at a time. Each pair should be dealt overlapping so that you can see the faces of both at once. As you do this, keep a running count on all the cards as they appear. The last will be a single. Count that one too. As before, the card you placed aside at the outset is your check against error.

The final drill is performed exactly like the other two, except that this time you turn the cards over three at a time. With a little practice, you should be able to count all three at a glance. If you stick with it, before long you will be able to do all three drills accurately almost as fast as you can turn over the cards.

BETTING THE COUNT

The ideal way to bet when you count at blackjack is to bet in exact proportion to the count. Whenever the count is negative, 0, or +1, you would not bet at all but instead sit out the hand. However, if the odds are higher than +1, the odds are in your favor. In such a case, you would ideally bet a number of units equal to the plus count. If the count were +2, you would bet two units. If the count were + 5, you would bet five units. This would mean that the greater your advantage on the next hand, the bigger your bet would be.

While that is the ideal, you just can't do it that way in a real casino. The house is not going to let you sit there taking up space during all the negative counts. Furthermore, betting in the above style would immediately brand you as a counter and get you barred. In order to be a successful card counter, you must learn how to disguise your strategy.

Surprising as it may seem, most casino personnel do not know how to count at blackjack. In fact, most have a very poor understanding of all aspects of blackjack strategy. A few casinos do employ *counter catchers*, people who can count cards themselves and thereby tell if a suspected card counter's playing pattern actually coincides with the count of the deck. However, this is the exception rather than the rule. The reason some card counters get barred is because they are obvious about what they are doing. I have actually on several occasions seen card counters sitting at a blackjack table moving their lips as they kept the count. Others dart their eyes back and forth across the table, studying all the face-up cards as if their life depended on it, while still others practically sweat blood from concentration.

I can assure you from extensive experience, however, that it is possible to successfully count at blackjack without being nailed if you employ the proper camouflage. In Atlantic City, for the first two years after casino gambling was legalized, the three casinos then in operation—Resorts International, the Boardwalk Regency, and Bally— were about as paranoid about counters as any gambling house I have ever seen. Players were being barred left and right. On many occasions, these players were innocent victims, noncounters who had made the mistake of getting too lucky at the blackjack tables and who consequently were tossed out by incompetent and overzealous casino personnel.

On two occasions playing blackjack, I was counting the cards and winning, when another player at the table was barred from play. Both times these were obvious, incompetent counters. I actually liked playing with these guys around because their antics drew the heat off me.

After one of these episodes, I innocently asked the floorman what the commotion was about. He patiently and somewhat condescendingly explained to me that there were some blackjack players who could actually keep track of all the cards being played and use that information to beat the house. He assured me, however, that he could always spot such players and that he immediately ejected them. I acted properly impressed and resumed my game. I remember that was a particularly lucrative session for me.

As a card counter, the most important part of camouflaging your play consists of disguising your betting pattern. The most important thing to avoid is making large changes in bet size from one hand to the next. There is nothing suspicious about changing the size of your bet from one hand to the next. Many people do that from time to time. But anyone who goes from a five-dollar bet to a fifty-dollar bet is bound to attract unwanted attention.

In fact, if you want to impress your gambling buddies with the fact that you are such a skilled blackjack player that the casinos are afraid of you, just engage in such radical bet changes. Don't even bother to count the cards, just jump your bets around. It won't be long before you are shown the door. A few blackjack-system sellers have done just that to gain publicity for their systems.

If, instead, you would rather make some money as a counter, there are four guidelines you should adopt in your betting. First, *No matter how much the count improves from one hand to the next, never bet more than double what you bet on the previous hand.* If your last bet was ten dollars, your next bet should not exceed twenty dollars. Second, *No matter how much the count worsens from one hand to the next, never bet less than half of what you bet on the previous hand.* If your last bet was ten dollars, your next bet should not be less than five dollars.

The third rule is, *Never change the size of your bet after a tie.* The cards that are dealt after a tie hand may alter the count and lead you to want to change your bet before the next hand, but don't do it. Such a move would differ from what virtually all other players would do in that situation. There is simply no reason to change your bet after a push—unless you are counting. To do so only advertises that you are counting.

The fourth rule, and one of the most important to keep in mind to disguise your betting strategy, is *Never hesitate when making a bet.* Fumbling, pausing, or changing a bet after you have made it are all tipoffs to be avoided. Don't let your thinking show. Don't even touch your chips until you have calculated how much you should bet on the next hand.

If you follow these rules, you will cut your mathematical advantage slightly, but you will still be betting more when the odds are in your favor and less when the odds are against you. And you will be able to do it safely even under the scrutiny of the casino's pit personnel.

COUNTING IN A GAME

It is always important to follow exactly the same procedure when counting each hand in a game. Otherwise, you will begin to make mistakes. The exact procedure to follow depends on whether you are playing in a *head-up game,* in a game with other players where the cards are dealt face up, or in a game with other players where the cards are dealt face down.

Let's consider the head-up game first. If you are the only player at the table, begin counting as soon as the dealer finishes dealing. First, you count the dealer's up-card and your own two cards. The third drill I taught you should enable you to count all three cards together at a glance. Then, each time you draw a card you count it. When you finish playing your hand, the dealer will turn his hole card face up. Count it as soon as he does so. Then count each card that the dealer draws. You count each card as soon as it is exposed to you. The head-up game is the easiest one in which to count. For that reason, you may wish to seek out head-up games whenever possible. The availability of such games depends on how much you are betting and what time of day you are playing.

The procedure for counting when there are other players at the table varies depending on whether all the cards are dealt face up or whether the players' first two cards are dealt face down. First, let's take the example of a face-up game. As soon as the dealer finishes dealing, you should turn your attention to the first player's hand. Count his two cards along with the dealer's up-card. Each time that player draws a card, count it. When the first player is finished and the dealer turns his attention to the next player, you should do the same. Count this player's two cards, then count each card he draws. Continue in this same manner with each subsequent player's hand, including your own. When the dealer turns his hole card up, count it. Then count each card the dealer draws.

In a game where the player's first two cards are dealt face down, follow the same procedure, with only one difference. Since the first two cards that each player holds are not exposed to you, you cannot count them at the outset. Instead, count each pair of cards as they are turned up by the dealer at the end as he pays off and collects bets. If a player should bust, you should count his two down-cards as soon as they are turned face up. If a player should receive a natural, count it as soon as the dealer pays it and collects the cards. If you have faithfully practiced your second counting drill, you should have no trouble counting all the cards in pairs as they are turned face up at the conclusion of each round.

ADDING YOUR HAND

As you can see, when counting your mind must be free at all times to concentrate on keeping the count. That means that any other thinking you have to do should be as automatic as possible. Even as simple a thing as adding up your hand can be a distraction when counting unless you can do it almost automatically. In fact, if you improve your ability to add up your hand quickly, you will find it much easier to count at blackjack. For that reason, I am going to give you three drills to improve your ability at totaling your hand.

For the first drill, you should begin by shuffling your deck of cards. Then start dealing the cards into a face-up pile. Each time you deal a new card, announce the cumulative total. For example, if the first card is a 7 and the second card is a 4, you should say "Eleven" as soon as that second card is dealt. If the next card is a 5, you should say "Sixteen" as soon as you deal it. As soon as the total reaches 17 or more, push the cards aside and begin a new pile. In other words, you don't draw another card once you reach 17 or more, just as you would never draw another card in a game once you had reached 17. If your total goes over 21, just say "Over." Continue this way until you have gone through the entire deck. As with all the drills, accuracy is the most important thing, but as you get better you should concentrate on speed also.

For the second drill, begin by removing seven ten-value cards from the deck and discarding them. Shuffle the rest of the cards. This time, turn the cards face up three at a time in a spread condition so that you can see all three at the same time. Try to add the three cards as soon as you see them and announce the total. If the three cards total over 21, just say "Over." Keep dealing through the deck in groups of three and announcing the total of each three-card spread as rapidly as you can. However, if you are unsure of the total, check it over slowly. The reason for removing the seven ten-value cards at the outset is to make the drill more of a challenge, since the tens are the easiest cards to add. Also, removing seven cards will leave you with a number of cards that is exactly divisible by three.

These two drills should greatly improve your ability to add up your hand quickly and accurately. They are similar to the drills that apprentice blackjack dealers use to perfect their skills. At first, you will probably find that soft hands are the most difficult to total. You can overcome this by using another trick employed by blackjack dealers. Eleven is an awkward number to add. So instead, whenever you have an ace in your hand, add the cards counting the ace as 1, then add 10 to your total. This simple technique will greatly simplify matters and speed up the whole process.

When you have mastered these two drills, there is one final drill you should use to help you become a good card counter. This one will take a little more work than the others, but it can be tremendously useful in improving your performance in the casino. I call it the count-and-add drill, because that is exactly what you are going to do. You are going to keep a running count and add up your hand at the same time.

Shuffle the deck and place a card aside without looking at it. Then start to deal the cards into a face-up pile one at a time. As you do this, you should simultaneously maintain a running count and add the cumulative total of the cards. For example, if the first card is a 5, say "Plus one." If the next card is a 6, "Plus two, eleven." That means that the running count is +2 while the total of your hand is 11. If the next card is a ten, you should say "Plus one, twenty-one." In other words, the count is now +1, and the total of your hand is 21.

As soon as the hand reaches 17 or more, you should push it aside and start dealing a new pile. If the total goes over 21, just say "Over" rather than announcing the exact total. Your total begins anew with each pile, but the running count is carried over from one hand to the next. At the end, your count should tell you whether the card you placed aside is a high card, a low card, or a neutral card. As with all the count drills, the card you place aside acts as a check on the accuracy of your count. In this drill, you are doing exactly what you must do when playing your hand in a casino. You are adding up your hand while still maintaining the count. That is why the drill is such valuable practice for anyone who seriously wants to master card counting.

THE TRUE COUNT

There is only one more thing you have to learn in order to master the count system: how to adapt the strategy to a multiple-deck game. For example, it should be obvious that removing a ten from a four-deck shoe will have only one-fourth as much impact on your chances of winning as removing a ten from a single-deck game. For that reason, early in a four-deck game you would have to divide your running count by four in order to see what that count really signified.

Here is how it's done. In a multiple-deck game, you keep a running count in exactly the same way I taught you to do in a single-deck game. However, before deciding how much to bet on a hand, you must convert that running count into what is known as a *true count*. You do this by dividing the running count by the approximate number of decks still undealt. You look at the shoe and estimate about how many decks of cards are left in it. Alternatively, you could look at the *discard rack* to get an idea of about how many decks must be left in the shoe. Either way, you use the number of decks to divide your running count number. The total you arrive at is the true count. You use this number to determine the size of your bet, just as I explained earlier. Thus, if the true count were $+3$, you would want to bet as close to three units as circumstances permit.

Notice that what matters is not the total number of decks in the game, only the number of decks left undealt at the time you are about to make your bet. A rough estimate will suffice; you will get better at estimating with time. Also, it doesn't matter for this purpose at what point the dealer has inserted the stop card. Take into account all the cards left in the shoe in your estimate. When you divide, just round off to the nearest whole number.

Actually, you don't have to go through this process before every bet. It is only necessary if you have a positive running count of more than $+1$. If your running count is negative, 0, or $+1$, you know that you should bet only one unit, so there is no need to convert to a running count.

An important point to remember is that as soon as you have used the true count to figure out your bet size, you must return to your running count to take account of the new cards being dealt out. The true count is used to determine your bet and nothing else. Let's take an example. Your running count at the end of a hand is +4, and there are about two decks left in the shoe. So you divide by two to arrive at a true count of +2, and you bet two units. But as soon as the dealer begins to deal the next hand, you have to pick up your running count again at +4 and continue counting from that point. In other words, as soon as you have used the true count to determine your bet, you forget it and go back to your running count.

You are now ready to start applying the count system in a casino game. Before long, you should be playing like an expert. But remember, don't act like an expert at the table. Don't offer the other players free advice, and don't flaunt your knowledge before casino personnel. Attribute all your success to luck. You should be interested in winning, not in showing off. No matter how much money you win, the casinos will let you play forever as long as they are convinced you are an idiot.

Refinements

You have already learned much more about expert blackjack play than you probably ever suspected existed. Yet the field of advanced blackjack strategy has become so sophisticated in recent years that we have really only scratched the surface. For the reader who wants to learn everything he can about the subject, I am going to recommend several books at the end of the chapter for further study. It's impossible for me in this limited space to cover all the nuances of this subject with the thoroughness of these books that are devoted solely to the game of blackjack. To give you an idea of the kinds of further refinements that are possible at blackjack and that are analyzed in these books, I want to touch on some key areas.

PLAYING STRATEGY

I have taught you how to use the count to guide your betting decisions at blackjack. This is the most important aspect of card-counting strategy. However, it is possible to improve your profits still further by also using the count to guide your playing decisions. There are times when, because of the composition of the deck as indicated by the count, you should play a hand differently from what basic strategy dictates. These situations do not arise very often, but you can make more money at blackjack by recognizing them when they do occur. In order to know when to depart from basic strategy, you must memorize strategy tables geared to your count system. This means more hard work, study, and drilling. As with every other aspect of advanced blackjack strategy, only you can decide if the additional work is worth it. However, if you aspire to become a true expert player, you will want to eventually master playing strategy based on the count. The books I am going to recommend to you will show you how to go about doing so.

OTHER SYSTEMS

The system I have just taught you is the most basic version of card counting. It is called a plus-minus or *high-low system*. It is a *level-one system*, which means that the point values assigned to the various cards do not go beyond $+1$, 0, or -1. Many other systems have been devised by card counters, some far more complex than the plus-minus. Some are level-two systems, which means that while some cards are valued at $+1$, 0, and -1, as in our system, other cards are assigned values of $+2$ or -2. Still other systems fall into the level-three and level-four categories. Such a system may involve as many as seven different point valuations assigned to different cards. In some cases, these systems succeed in providing more detailed information about the cards remaining in the deck at any given time due to the greater variety and precision made possible through the use of a greater spectrum of card valuations. Needless to say, these systems are also far more difficult to master and apply in a casino.

Once you have thoroughly mastered the plus-minus count and have had considerable experience using it in games, you may want to experiment with some of these more advanced strategies. But please keep the following points in mind: 1. How well you master a system is far more important than which system you choose to master. 2. The price of a system is not necessarily an indication of the value of the system. 3. Most important, the complexity of a system is not necessarily an indication of its value. Many players make the mistake of tackling a very difficult strategy beyond their capabilities. They then make so many errors in playing the strategy as to completely nullify its value. A good, simple system played well will produce far better results than a complex system played inaccurately.

If you do eventually decide to move on to a more advanced system, you will find that the time you invested in mastering the plus-minus count was not wasted. Learning a more complex strategy will come much easier as a result of having first thoroughly mastered a basic count. In fact, one reason why many would-be counters fail is that they attempt to master an advanced strategy without having first established a firm foundation of basic blackjack skills. My own recommendation is to stick to the plus-minus count even if you do decide to move on to more advanced playing techniques. The plus-minus will provide you with all the strength you need from a count. Instead of flitting from system to system, you can improve your abilities as a counter by concentrating on developing such counting-related skills as the ability to camouflage your playing and the ability to distinguish between profitable and unprofitable games.

CAMOUFLAGE

We have already discussed the problem of casinos barring card counters or shuffling up on them. One of the most important requirements for winning money as a card counter is getting the casino to let you play. This means concealing the fact that you are a counter. The first step in concealing your counting is to learn to do it well enough to be able to do it with no visible strain. The next step is to camouflage your betting, as I have already suggested. However, for the counter who plans to play very extensively, further refinements are needed. He has to learn how casino personnel think, what their stereotypical image of a card counter is, and what their stereotypical image of a losing know-nothing player is. He can then fashion his play to avoid the former image and reflect the latter. Card counters call this developing an *act*. A good act can only come with considerable playing experience, as well as study of the blackjack literature. But once you've got one, you are on your way to real blackjack profits.

SELECTING A GAME

Not all blackjack games hold the same profit potential for the counter. The number of decks employed, the percentage of those cards dealt out by the dealer, the house rules on such matters as doubling down, and that particular casino's tolerance for bet variation by the player are all factors that determine how much money you can hope to take out of a particular game. One of the most important improvements in blackjack strategy in recent years has been the development of methods of measuring the cumulative impact of these factors. My friend blackjack expert Arnold Snyder has been in the forefront of exploring this aspect of advanced play. Here again, if you wish to reach the higher echelons of blackjack skill, you will have to study the literature.

RECOMMENDED READING

There are many really fine works available on advanced blackjack strategy, as well as some worthless books that are merely attempting to cash in on the public's interest in the subject. I am going to recommend the three books that I think will be of the greatest value to you as the next step after mastering what I have taught you: *Professional Blackjack* by Stanford Wong, *Blackbelt in Blackjack* by Arnold Snyder, and *Turning the Tables on Las Vegas* by Ian Anderson. Each of these books concentrates on what is really important in winning at blackjack without getting bogged down in overly technical issues that won't make you any money. There are other books you should study too, and even some fine newsletters devoted solely to helping card counters. However, if your interest in the subject continues to grow, I am sure you will discover these other works in time. The three I have recommended should keep you busy for a long time. If you have trouble finding these in your bookstore, you can order them—and just about any other gambling book in print—from the Gambler's Book Club, P.O. Box 4115, Las Vegas, NV 89127. Write and ask them to send you their catalog.

Even if you decide not to tackle card counting, please learn basic strategy. You will be a better player than the vast majority of people who sit down at the blackjack tables each year. You will win more often, and you will enjoy the game more too. Playing blackjack without using basic strategy is simply giving your money away to the casino.

V. Craps

♣ Craps is probably the single most frightening casino game for the beginner. The complex layout, the many betting options, and the speed at which the game is played all combine to create a confusing and intimidating picture for the novice. What is even worse, everyone else standing around the table seems to understand exactly what is going on and what is expected of them. None of us wants to be the one dunce at the table with everyone else staring at us. The result is that the game is avoided by many people who are new to casino gaming, and even by some who are experienced at other games, because they are intimidated by it.

This is a pity, because craps is not only the most exciting of all casino games, it is second only to blackjack when it comes to giving the knowledgeable player a chance to come out a winner. Much of the fear of playing craps can be dispelled by gaining a clear understanding of what you can expect to encounter before first stepping up to the table. If you take the trouble to become thoroughly familiar in advance with every aspect of procedure at craps, once you start playing you will find that the alien will quickly become the familiar. Before long, you will be playing with as much confidence as all the veteran players crowded around the table. What is much more important, if you follow my advice on strategy, you will also be playing far more intelligently than even most veterans, and you will walk away a winner far more often than they do.

The Elements of the Game

THE PERSONNEL

The first requirement in removing the mystery from the game is an understanding of the duties of each member of the crap-table team. A crap game is conducted by a crew of four dealers, only three of whom are on duty at any given time. In addition, a supervisor called the *boxman* sits at the center of the table on the casino's side of the pit and oversees the game, guarding against any errors or irregularities. He is the final arbiter of any dispute at the table. He is easy to identify, since he is the only casino employee at the table who is seated and also the only one wearing a suit rather than a dealer's uniform. In some casinos, if a table is very busy they will have two men sit box, one to watch the left half of the layout and the other to watch the right half. In this case, the two men will sit side by side.

Two dealers are stationed on the inside (pit side) of the table, one on either side of the boxman. Each of these two dealers is in charge of collecting and paying all bets on his half of the layout. Since the left half of a crap layout is identical to the right half, both dealers have exactly the same job. The only reason for having two dealers and two duplicated layout patterns is that no player will have to stretch all the way across the table to place his bet. These two dealers also have the job of changing cash into chips for the players. When you buy in, place your cash on the layout in front of you. The dealer will pass the money over to the boxman, who will count it and announce the total to the dealer. The dealer will then count out the proper amount in chips and pass them over to you. Finally, the boxman will deposit your cash in the drop slot in front of him. You may also have the dealer change your chips to those of a different denomination.

Standing on the players' side of the table at the center, opposite the boxman, is a third dealer, who plays the role of the *stickman*. He is in charge of the dice. He has a long wooden stick curved at the outer end that he uses to gather in the dice after each roll and push them to the *shooter* for the next roll. It is also his job to announce the number that is rolled on the dice each time. This is for the benefit not only of the players but also of the two dealers, since they are not supposed to take their eyes off the layout at any time. They must rely on the stickman's call to know how to settle the bets.

The stickman also helps the boxman oversee the game. When bets are paid and collected, he watches the dealer at the end of the table at which the dice have to come to rest, while the boxman watches the dealer at the other end of the table. Finally, the stickman is also in charge of the proposition bets, which are on the central part of the layout directly in front of him. When a player wants to make one of these bets, he places his chips in front of the stickman and indicates the bet he wants. Later, the stickman will instruct the other dealers on taking or paying these bets. He will tell them the amount of each payoff and which player to give it to.

Each crap-table crew also contains a fourth dealer. The dealers rotate, each taking his turn at the stick and at each of the two ends of the layout. Since there are only three dealer positions, this always leaves one dealer free to take a break in the dealer's room. Craps is the most difficult of all casino games to learn to deal and the most grueling one to conduct. Crap dealers are recognized as the most skilled of all casino dealers. If you think it's confusing for you, imagine how demanding it is for a dealer, who has to simultaneously keep track of the progress of the game and the bets of a half-dozen players, many of them having several wagers going at once, while simultaneously watching for cheating. When you consider how costly a mistake on a dealer's part may be, you can realize how much pressure the crap-table crew is under. Taking frequent breaks is necessary for dealers to maintain the required level of concentration.

The complexities of dealing craps and the many opportunities for error are also the reasons why there is more extensive supervision of craps than any of the other games. In addition to the one or two boxmen, there is also a floorman inside the pit, who typically has two crap tables assigned to him to watch. While the management of the game is generally left in the hands of the table crew, the floorman can and, if necessary will, overrule any decisions in the course of the game.

Most of the time when playing you need only be concerned with two of these people, the stickman who will offer you the dice each time it is your turn to bet, and the dealer on your side of the layout, who will pay off and collect your bets. Don't worry about the proposition bets; they are strictly for suckers. You will be staying away from them.

THE EQUIPMENT

The Table   Craps is played on a large table surrounded by a railing that serves to keep the dice from rolling off the table when they are thrown. The railing also helps keep the game honest. When rolling the dice, you will be expected to throw them hard enough so that they bounce off *the rail* at the opposite end of the table. This rail is lined with ribbed rubber. Bouncing the dice off the rail helps ensure that the roll will be completely random, beyond the control of the shooter. If you fail to bounce the dice, you will be warned by a dealer or the boxman to throw harder. If you repeatedly fail to hit the rail, you may lose your turn to shoot.

The top of the rail contains two grooves for you to keep your chips in. Keep your hands up there also when not betting. If you have your hand down on the table when the dice are rolled and one of the dice hits your hand, it can upset the shooter. If he didn't get the number he was hoping for, he may blame you for affecting the outcome. The crap-table crew may also get upset, fearing that you may have been trying to "past post" (make an illegal bet after the deadline).

The Dice   The dice used at casino craps are quite different from the ones you use at home to play Monopoly. Each one has the casino logo and a serial number imprinted on it, to make it more difficult for a cheat to counterfeit. It is transparent, to make it more difficult for a cheat to load, and larger, to make it more difficult for a cheat to palm. The standard sizes used in casino games are ¾ inch and ⅝ inch. And I mean <u>exactly</u>; these dice have been measured by caliper to ensure that there is no more than a one-ten-thousandth-of-an-inch difference between any of the sides. The spots on these dice have been filled, so they are flush with the surface of the die. The material that the spots are made of has the same specific gravity as the material that the dice themselves are made of, so each die is perfectly balanced even though it has more spots on some sides than on others. Those dice you use at home are slightly imbalanced by the fact that they have six little holes on one side and only one hole on the opposite side. Finally, casino dice have sharp edges and corners, which are more precise than the rounded ones found on cheap dice. This means that the dice must be changed frequently to avoid imbalances caused by chipped corners and edges. In other words, the casinos spare no expense to ensure that their dice are the perfect instruments for arriving at a random number from 2 to 12.

Although only two dice are used in the game, the stickman has a set of from five to eight dice. When it is your turn to shoot the dice, he will push all of these dice over to you with his stick. Pick out any two you want to use. You will use these two dice as long as it is your turn to roll. The stickman will then drop the other dice into a small semicircular wooden bowl called a *dice boat* that he keeps in front of him.

The Stick   The stickman's wooden stick serves two purposes. It allows him to retrieve the dice from any part of the table without undue stretching. It also helps protect the players from cheating. The most common method used by crooked gambling houses to cheat the patrons at craps involves the stickman periodically switching the dice for various kinds of crooked dice by sleight of hand. To do that, he must pick up the dice with his hand. Use of the stick keeps the dealer's hand from coming into contact with the dice. You won't have to worry about this kind of cheating in any major casino in places like Las Vegas, Reno, Lake Tahoe, Atlantic City, or Puerto Rico. However, if you should ever find yourself in a casino crap game where the stickman follows the practice of picking the dice up with his hand to toss them back to the shooter, pick up your money with your hand and leave immediately.

The Buck   The last piece of equipment you will find on the crap table is the *dice buck*. This is a round piece of black and white plastic that looks a little like an Eskimo Pie. On one side it bears the word ON and on the other side it bears the word OFF. There are two of these, one on each side of the layout. The two dealers use the buck to help the players keep track of what is happening in the game at any given moment. This is done by placing it with the proper word up and positioning it on the correct spot on the layout.

The Layout   The surface of the crap table is usually green, although sometimes it is blue or even red. On it is an elaborate pattern of boxes, words, numbers, and drawings of dice that is called the layout. The crap layout acts as a roadmap to the game.

Initially, this layout may appear confusing. Actually, the crap layout is only half as complicated as it appears to be, since the right side of the layout is a duplicate of the left side. Each player only has to concern himself with the half nearest him. The central portion of the layout consists entirely of sucker bets carrying prohibitive house

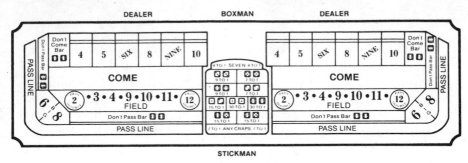

LAS VEGAS-STYLE LAYOUT

percentages. If you completely ignore this central portion, it will not only simplify matters for you, but it will also save you money.

The exact position of each wager on the layout identifies what the player is betting on, which player made the bet, and what the status of the bet is at that point in the game. Some of these bets are placed on the layout by the dealers, some are placed by the player, and some are placed by the player and later moved to a different part of the layout by a dealer when the status of the bet changes.

ROLLING THE DICE

Let's assume you have just made a pass-line bet and it is your turn to shoot the dice. The stickman has offered five dice to you, and you have selected the two you wish to use. You throw the dice so they bounce off the rail at the opposite side of the table. When throwing the dice, all rolls count, except where one or both dice go off the table or land on top of the rail, in the dice boat, in the *checks* (chips) that are in front of the boxman, or in the vertical check racks in front of one of the dealers. If a die lands *cocked*, leaning against some chips or the railing, the roll still counts. The stickman will determine which side of the die is closest to being on top and will announce the total of the dice accordingly.

After each roll, the stickman will pull the dice with his stick over to the center of the table in front of the boxman. He will wait until the dealers have collected or paid any wagers that have been settled by that roll and until the players have made any new wagers they wish. He will then push the dice back to the shooter.

The first roll of the dice of each round of play is called the *come-out* roll. It is possible to win or lose on this first roll, although more often it will take several rolls to determine whether you have won or lost. You will win automatically if you roll a total of 7 or 11 on the come-out roll; this is known as throwing a *natural*. You will lose automatically if you roll a total of 2, 3, or 12; this is known as throwing *craps*. (Players also refer to a total of 2 as *snake eyes*, while a total of 12 is called *boxcars*.)

The other possible totals you may roll are 4, 5, 6, 8, 9, or 10. These are sometimes called the *box numbers* because they are the numbers that are contained within a row of boxes along the top of the layout. If any of these numbers comes up, it becomes your *point*. When this happens, each dealer will place his buck with the ON side uppermost onto the numbered box on the layout that corresponds to your point number. This keeps the players from forgetting what the point number is as the game progresses.

You must now continue rolling to determine whether you will win or lose. From this point on, only two numbers are relevant to determining whether you win or lose: your point number and 7. If you succeed in rolling your point number before rolling a 7, you win. If you roll a 7 before rolling your point, known as *sevening-out*, you lose. In either event, each dealer will remove his dice buck from the numbered box and place it with the OFF side uppermost in the *don't-come* space of the layout.

Any number other than 7 or your point number that may be rolled while trying to repeat your point is irrelevant as far as determining whether you win or lose. For example, suppose you roll a 9 on the come-out. You then roll the following series of numbers: 2, 4, 6, 12, 4, 9. You win because the 9 reappeared before a 7 turned up. This is called *making your point*. By contrast, suppose you roll a 5 on the come-out. You then roll the following: 6, 11, 3, 9, 7. As soon as the 7 turns up, you lose. You can see that 7 is the pivotal number at craps. If it appears on the come-out roll, you win. However, if it appears on a subsequent roll, you lose. In fact, every bet at craps either wins or loses when 7 is rolled, so every roll of 7 clears the layout of all wagers.

As long as you keep winning, the above sequence is repeated. You start all over again with a new come-out roll. As long as you are winning, you can keep rolling the dice indefinitely. If you lose by rolling craps (2, 3, or 12) on the come-out, you still retain control of the dice. But if you lose by sevening-out, your turn as shooter is over. The dealer will then offer the dice to the player on your left.

In this manner, the dice are continually traveling around the table in a clockwise direction. The entire series of rolls from the shooter's first roll to the time he sevens-out is called his *hand* or *shoot*.

You do not have to roll the dice when it is your turn. If you prefer, you may decline, and they will be offered to the next shooter. Also, if you wish, you may relinquish the dice before your hand is over. In that case, the next player will finish your hand, then begin his own. However, since rolling the dice is a key part of the excitement of craps, there is really no reason to do either.

Although, in the above description, I assumed that you had made a pass-line bet, there are many other kinds of bets you could make at craps instead of, or in addition to, a pass-line bet. However, in order to be eligible to roll the dice, you must make either a pass-line bet or a *don't-pass* bet.

The Right Bettor

In craps, players who bet that the shooter will beat the house (by analogy, this includes come bettors) are known as *right bettors* or *do bettors*. Those who wager that the shooter (or come bettors) will lose are known as *wrong bettors* or *don't bettors*. These are just the terms that are used; they don't imply that wrong bettors are actually doing anything wrong or that right bettors are in any way superior to them.

THE PASS-LINE BET

The pass-line bet is the basic wager at the game of craps. It is a bet that says the shooter will win through one of the means explained above, throwing a natural on the come-out or making his point. You do not have to be the shooter to make a pass-line bet. Any player who wishes to can bet on the shooter by making a pass-line wager. This is why you will often see the other players at a crap table cheering when the shooter wins. It's not out of any altruistic feelings. Their fortunes were riding with him because they all had pass-line bets down.

The proper way to make a pass-line wager is to place the chips you wish to bet within the strip marked PASS that circles the outer part of the layout. Because of the position of the pass line on the layout, these wagers are also called *front-line* bets. The appropriate time to make the bet is immediately before a come-out roll. Pass-line bets are paid at even money. The dealer will place your winnings on the pass line next to your original bet. You must collect this money before the next roll, or it will count as a new pass-line bet. When you bet the pass line, the house enjoys a 1.414 percent edge. In the long run, you will lose about a dollar and forty-one cents out of every one hundred dollars you wager on the pass line.

COME BETS

When betting the pass line, it will often take several rolls to determine whether you win or lose. On the average, it takes 3.4 rolls of the dice to settle each pass-line bet. For many players, this is too long a wait. They want to win or lose bets more frequently, perhaps even on every single roll. Craps offers many choices for the player who is looking for such fast-paced action.

For the player who favors pass-line bets, the most obvious way to increase the tempo of the game is to also make *come bets*. A come bet works exactly like a pass bet. The only difference is that you don't have to wait until the come-out roll to make it. You can bet on the come before any roll. When you do, for the purposes of that bet, the next roll is a come-out. For example, the shooter may be trying to make his point. You then make a come bet, and the shooter throws a 7 on the very next roll. All the players with pass-line bets lose because the shooter sevened-out. However, your come bet wins because, for you, that roll was a come-out and the shooter rolled a natural. By contrast, if the shooter should roll a 4, 5, 6, 8, 9, or 10 on the roll directly after you make your come bet, that number becomes your *come-point*. If he then succeeds in repeating that number before rolling a 7, your come bet will win. However, if he rolls a 7 before repeating the come-point, your bet will lose.

I realize this concept is a little difficult to grasp at first. To understand it, make sure you clearly follow the winning and losing shooting sequences that were explained in the section on betting the pass line. Now imagine that the shooters' rolls of the dice are a never-ending stream of numbers. One could, in effect, cut into that stream at any point, designate the next roll as the come-out, and pick up the play at that point. That is exactly what the player making a come bet does. He is using the same numbers as the other players, but his game is slightly out of sync. In effect, he is sharing the same numbers as the other players but using them to play a different crap game.

The reason many players do this is that they do not want to have to wait for the next come-out roll to make another bet. With the come bet, the player can make several wagers before the next come-out. He might even make a new come bet on every roll. This style of play is used by some crap players when they see that the shooter is really *hot*—rolling for a very long time without sevening-out. In such a case, the player making continuous come bets might win a bet on almost every roll of the dice. However, if the shooter rolls a 7, every come bet will lose except the one made immediately before the roll. For that one bet, the 7 is a natural. For all the other come bets, the 7 represents a seven-out.

To make a come bet, place the chips you wish to wager in front of you in the large space on the layout marked COME. You may make a come bet at any point except before the come-out roll. If you wish to bet before the come-out roll, you should make a pass-line bet instead. Like the pass-line bet, which it parallels, the come bet also pays even money and faces a 1.414 percent edge.

When making a come bet, if the shooter throws a natural on the next roll, the dealer will place your winnings in front of you. If, instead, he rolls a point number, the dealer will move your come bet to the numbered box on the layout corresponding to your come-point. If the shooter should succeed in repeating the come-point before rolling a 7, the dealer will place your bet and your winnings in the COME box in front of you. You must collect this money before the next roll of the dice, or it will count as a new come bet. Anytime the shooter rolls a 7, the dealer will collect all the come bets that have been moved onto numbers but pay those come bets that are still on the come line.

The Wrong Bettor

THE DON'T-PASS BET

One of the appealing things about casino craps is that you can bet either with the shooter or against him. When wagering against the shooter you are, in effect, betting with the house. When they win, you win. To bet against the shooter, you would make a don't-pass bet. It would seem that the casino could not allow players to bet both with and against the shooter without giving the edge to one or the other group of bettors. After all, if the odds are against the pass bettor, they must be in favor of the don't-pass bettor. On the other hand, if the odds are against the don't-pass bettor, they must favor the pass bettor. One way or the other, somebody must be getting an advantage over the house.

As a matter of fact, the odds are slightly against the shooter. We have already seen that when a player makes a pass-line bet, the house enjoys a 1.414 percent edge. However, the casino is not about to hand over that 1.414 percent advantage to the don't-pass bettor. If it did, it would be in the charity business, operating the game as a public service.

The reason the house allows players to make don't-pass bets is that it has an ingenious trick up its sleeve. You will see it printed on the line where don't-pass bets are made. It is in the form of the word BAR, followed by a picture of two dice showing 6–6. This means that when the shooter rolls a 12 crap on the come-out, the pass bettor loses, but the don't-pass bettor does not win. It is considered a standoff. The wrong bettor does not lose his bet; the bet simply remains on the line, to be decided by the next series of rolls. In other words, for the don't-pass bettor, when a 6–6 is rolled, it is as if the roll had never occurred.

Since the bettor does not actually lose his bet on the 12-crap roll, many players find it difficult to understand why the bar 6–6 gives the house an edge. Remember what we learned in Chapter II: The casino makes its profit when you win a bet, not when you lose. It does so by putting part of your winnings in its own pocket. In this case, it goes further. If you're betting against the shooter, when 6–6 comes up you should win, but the casino puts all your winnings in its pocket. Even though your original bet remains untouched, you've just lost some money. The result of this maneuver is that instead of reaping the benefit of the 1.414 percent edge against the shooter, the wrong bettor now suffers a 1.402 percent disadvantage himself. This Machiavellian maneuver allows the house to *book* both right bets and wrong bets and enjoy an almost identical advantage on both sets of bets. (You will occasionally see a book cite the house edge on wrong bets as 1.38 percent. This difference is only a matter of definition. Some mathematicians count rolls of 6–6, not as a decision on the don't-pass bet, but only as a delay in the action. Calculated this way, the house edge comes up a very slightly different figure.)

Although all the casinos in Las Vegas and Atlantic City bar 6–6, those in northern Nevada bar 1–1 and pay off on 6–6. This does not change anything, since 2 crap is rolled exactly as often as 12 crap. However, beware of any casino crap game where the layout says BAR

1–2. In such a game, the odds are twice as high against you, since 3 crap is rolled twice as often as either 2 crap or 12 crap. (See the discussion of odds below.) You will occasionally encounter such a layout in Las Vegas night charity games and some illegal underground games. Any such game is for suckers only.

To make a don't-pass bet, place your wager in front of you on the don't-pass line. This is the strip marked DON'T PASS that parallels the pass line along the outer border of the layout. Because of the position of the don't-pass line on the layout, these wagers are also called *back-line* bets. The time to make a don't-pass bet is immediately before the come-out. Don't-pass bets are paid at even money. If you win, the dealer will place your payoff on the don't-pass line next to your original bet. You must collect this money before the next roll, or it will count as a new don't-pass bet.

THE DON'T-COME BET

If you have followed the discussion so far, you should have no trouble understanding how don't-come bets work. They are just like don't-pass bets, except that you can make them at any time during the game other than before the come-out. For the purposes of such a bet, the very next roll is considered the come-out roll. The bet is paid off at even money. The don't-come box will say BAR 6–6 or BAR 1–1 just like the don't-pass line. This works exactly the same way that it does on don't-pass bets and is the source of the house's edge on this wager. In fact, on the Reno/Lake Tahoe crap layout, the don't-pass line and the don't-come line are the same line. If you make a wager in this space just prior to the come-out, it counts as a don't-pass bet. A wager made in the same space after the come-out is considered a don't-come bet.

The Las Vegas and Atlantic City layouts contain a don't-come box in which these wagers can be made on any roll after the come-out. If the shooter rolls a point number on the next roll after the bet is made, the dealer will move the bet to the box directly above the numbered box that corresponds to this point. If the number is repeated before a 7, the dealer will collect this bet. Whenever a 7 is rolled, the dealer pays off all the don't-come bets that are in these boxes but collects any don't-come bets that are in the don't-come box. For the don't-come bets in the boxes above the numbers, the 7 represents a seven-out and therefore a win. But for don't-come bets in the don't-come box, the 7 represents a natural and therefore a loss. When a don't-come bet wins, both the player's original bet and his payoff will be placed in the don't-come box by the dealer.

Figuring the Odds

THE BASIC TOOLS

In order to really understand the game of craps, you must be able to calculate the odds of different possible events occurring in the rolls of the dice. In most cases, this is extremely easy to do. The fundamental tool in doing so is a knowledge of how many ways each of the different numbers at craps can be rolled. Although there are eleven possible numbers that can be rolled with two dice (anywhere from a total of 2 to a total of 12), there are actually 36 different possible combinations that can come up on the two dice. This is because each die has six sides and each of the six sides on the first die can come up in combination with any of the six sides on the other die: six times six gives us thirty-six combinations.

The number 2, the lowest total, can only be rolled with one combination (1–1). This is also true of 12, the highest total, which can only be rolled with 6–6. By contrast, the number 3 can be rolled with two combinations (2–1 or 1–2). Similarly, the number 11 can be rolled with two combinations (5–6 or 6–5). The number 4 can be rolled three ways (1–3, 2–2, 3–1), and the number 10 can also be made three ways (4–6, 5–5, 6–4). The number 5 can be rolled with four combinations (1–4, 2–3, 3–2, 4–1), and the number 9 can also be rolled with four combinations (3–6, 4–5, 5–4, 6–3). The number 6 can be made five ways (1–5, 2–4, 3–3, 4–2, 5–1), and the number 8 can also be rolled five ways (2–6, 3–5, 4–4, 5–3, 6–2). Finally, the number 7 can be rolled with any of six different combinations (1–6, 2–5, 3–4, 4–3, 5–2, 6–1). Obviously, the more combinations that a number can be rolled with, the more frequently that number will come up. So it is no accident that the number 7 is the central number at craps. It was chosen because it is the most frequently rolled number.

All of this may seem very simple, and it is. But if you plan to play much craps, I urge you to memorize the contents of the above paragraph. You will constantly use that information in calculating various odds and probabilities in the game. Remember that there are a total of thirty-six possible combinations. Remember how many ways each number can be rolled. Take particular note of the symmetry between the numbers 2 and 12, 3 and 11, 4 and 10, 5 and 9, and 6 and 8. This means that any odds that apply to the number 6 will also apply to the number 8. Similarly, any calculations you make concerning the number 5 will be just as valid for the number 9. This symmetry is graphically illustrated in the illustration below.

You will note that all the paired numbers add up to 14. This is because any two opposite sides of a die always add up to 7. Therefore, any two opposite sides of a pair of dice must always add up to 14. Every time you roll a pair of dice and get a 6 on top of the dice, you have also gotten an 8 on the bottom of the two dice. It follows, therefore, that 8 can be made with exactly the same number of combinations as 6 can. The same is true of 5 and 9, 4 and 10, 3 and 11, and also 2 and 12. As soon as you get accustomed to thinking in terms of these pairings, you will find that you have, in effect, only half as much to remember about the various bets, payoffs, odds, and percentages at craps.

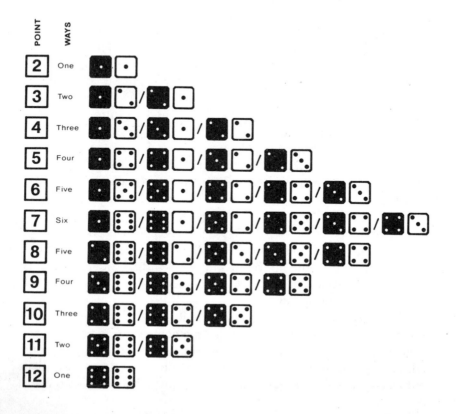

What throws some people is the notion that a combination like 4–3 is different from 3–4. To them, they are the same combination and should not be counted twice. This is an understandable but dangerous fallacy. Someone who thinks this way will believe that 6 can be rolled three ways (1–5, 2–4, 3–3) and that 7 can also be rolled three ways (1–6, 2–5, 3–4). He will therefore believe that a wager that a 6 will be rolled before rolling a 7 is an even-money bet since either number is equally likely to come up. In fact, someone betting that he can roll a 6 before a 7 should be getting 6 to 5 odds in order for the bet to be a fair one (six ways of rolling a 7 versus five ways of rolling a 6). Anyone who takes that bet at even money will soon be bankrupt.

You can prove this to yourself by getting two dice of different colors, for example, one green die and one white die. Start rolling the dice. One time you may roll a 7 with a 4 on the green die and a 3 on the white die. Later you may roll a 7 with a 3 on the green die and 4 on the white die. Clearly, these are two different ways of rolling a 7. The two die faces that combined to produce the first 7 are completely different from the two die faces that combined to make the second 7. They must be counted as two different combinations in order to correctly calculate dice odds. By contrast, you may roll a 6 with a 3 on the green die and a 3 on the white die. This is the single combination that will give you a total of 6 with two 3s. That is why you cannot equate a reversible combination like 3–4 with one like 3–3.

PRESSING AND TAKING DOWN BETS

As soon as you understand the different ways the various numbers can be made, you will be able to analyze why the casino does many of the things it does at craps. For example, a player making a don't-pass or don't-come bet is allowed to rescind his wager at any time after the first roll if he wishes. If you were to bet twenty-five dollars on the don't-pass line and the shooter rolled a 4 on the come-out, if you have second thoughts about the bet you can ask the dealer to return the money to you at any time, as long the shooter has not yet rolled a 7 or repeated his point. This is known as *calling down* or *taking down* your bet. Alternatively, you can ask him to return just part of the bet. The same is true of don't-come bets. In fact, every wager at craps can be called down by the player before a decision has been reached, except for the pass and come bets. This double standard on the part of the house seems illogical and capricious until you study the odds.

When the shooter starts to roll, he has eight ways in which he may win on the first roll by throwing a natural. These are the six ways in which 7 can be made and the two ways 11 can be made. By contrast, he has only four ways he may lose on the first roll, the two ways of rolling a 3, plus the one way of rolling a 2 and the one way of rolling a 12. This means that if the bet should be decided on the first roll, the odds are 2 to 1 that it will go in favor of the right bettor.

However, the situation radically changes after the first roll. If the shooter has rolled a point on the come-out, the odds immediately shift against him. In order to win, he must throw the same number again before rolling a 7. But since there are more ways of making a 7 than any other number, the odds are against the shooter making his point, no matter what that point might be. The casino now has the bettor where it wants him, and it is not about to let him wriggle out of it by taking back his money.

If the casino allowed right bettors to rescind their bets at any time, smart gamblers would take down their bets immediately after the first roll. They would have 2 to 1 odds going for them on every come-out and, if the shooter didn't roll a natural or craps, they would take back their bets and wait until the next come-out. Insisting that the do bettor's wager remain in play until a decision is reached is the only way the casino can get a real shot at the money. And they will be only too happy to allow the bettor to *press* his pass-line or come bet—add more money to it—after the come-out roll when the odds are strongly against him. For the same reason, the casino will allow a player to make a pass-line bet after the come-out roll. At that point, he is getting by far the worst of it.

However, with the wrong bettor, the situation is just the opposite. Suppose the shooter's point is 4. There are 6 ways of rolling a 7, but only 3 ways of rolling a 4. This means that the odds are 6 to 3—or 2 to 1—in favor of the don't-pass bettor. The odds will be in his favor whatever the point number may be.

The only reason the casinos are willing to accept don't-pass bets in the first place is that they have such a good shot at winning them on the come-out roll. The odds on that roll are 8 to 3 against him. Remember, the house bars 12, so the only numbers the don't-pass bettor has going for him on the come-out are 2 and 3.

Whenever the don't-pass bettor is lucky enough to survive the come-out roll, the odds shift in his favor. The casino is now the underdog.

Naturally, if the player is willing to take back his bet at this point, the casino will be relieved to let him do it. He will be letting the house off the hook. They will also let him call the bet *off* for a particular roll. In other words, the bettor can instruct the dealer that the bet should not count for the next roll. In that case, the dealer will mark the bet by placing a small button on it that says OFF. What they will not let him do is press the bet now that he has the upper hand.

To summarize, the house will let you press your pass-line and come bets and make late pass-line bets, none of which you should ever do. They will let you call down or reduce your don't-pass and don't-come bets, but not increase them. They will allow you to either press or call down any other wagers on the layout.

Refinements

TAKING THE ODDS

The most important craps bet from the standpoint of the smart gambler is the *free odds* wager. When you make a pass bet, if the shooter rolls a point number on the come-out, you are allowed to make a second bet, equal in size to the first, called a free odds bet. This is a wager saying that the shooter will make his point. The unique thing about this bet is that it is paid off by the house at true odds. If you make a free odds bet on point 6 or 8 and win, the casino will pay your bet at 6 to 5. These are the correct odds of winning the bet—six ways of rolling a 7 versus five ways of rolling a 6. If the odds bet is on point 5 or 9, it will be paid off at 3 to 2. On the 4 or 10, the payoff is 2 to 1. If you remember what we learned about the ways of making the various numbers, you realize that in every case these payoffs reflect the true odds of winning the bet.

Because the casino is paying off at true odds, it is not making any profit on the bet. That is why it is called a free bet; the house is not charging any secret tax of the kind we discussed in Chapter II. Of course, in order to make a free odds bet, you must first make a line bet. That's where the casino makes its profit. Nevertheless, when you *take the odds*, you reduce the house advantage as it applies to the total amount wagered. If you make a ten-dollar bet on the pass line, the house will enjoy a 1.414 percent edge on those ten dollars. If instead you make a five-dollar line bet, if the shooter rolls a point on the come-out, and if you then make a five-dollar free odds bet, you will still get ten dollars' worth of action, but the edge that the house enjoys on the ten dollars is reduced to only .8 percent. In the long run, your money will last almost twice as long, giving you that much more opportunity to catch a lucky run and perhaps build your bankroll into a real bundle.

The amazing thing is that many players will make a pass-line bet without taking the odds. I can only assume that either they don't understand why the wager is to their advantage or they don't really know how to go about making the bet. At this point, you should understand why the bet is such a smart move, so let me tell you how to make the wager. After making your pass-line bet, if the shooter rolls a point number (4, 5, 6, 8, 9, or 10) on his first roll, you should place your odds bet on the layout outside the pass line but directly behind your first bet. There is no space on the layout designating the free-odds bet. Come to think of it, this may be why many bettors don't take the odds. Because it's not written down anywhere, they may not even know it exists. Because your odds bet goes directly behind your line bet, taking the odds is also called *backing the bet*.

The casino will also allow you to make a free odds bet when you have made a come bet and the shooter rolls a point number on the next roll. It is definitely in your interest to bet the *come odds* since it will reduce the house advantage against you in exactly the same way it does when you back your pass-line bet. When the dealer moves your odds bet to the proper point-number box, place your odds wager in the come box and tell the dealer what bet it relates to. For example, you might say, "Odds on the 9." The dealer will place the odds bet on top of the come bet but offset so that the two can be distinguished. This is called *heeling the bet*. If the come bet wins, the dealer will pay the come bet at even money and the odds bet at true odds. If the shooter rolls a 7 before repeating the come-point, both bets will lose. The odds on come bets are off on the come-out roll. This means that for determining the outcome of the come odds bet, the come-out roll does not count. If the come bet should win or lose on the come-out, the odds bet will simply be returned to you.

Casinos offer free odds only as a way of encouraging players to make more line bets. Since the house makes no profit on the odds bet, it imposes a restriction on how much a player can wager on the odds. In most casinos, your odds bet cannot be larger than your line bet. This limit is called *single odds*. You are allowed to bet less, but it is in your interest to make the largest odds bet permitted by the size of your line bet. This is known as taking *full odds*.

However, except in those few casinos that have twenty-five-cent minimums at their crap tables, the casino will not pay off in less than one-dollar sums. If you had five dollars on the line and the shooter rolled a 4, 6, 8, or 10, this would present no problem. You could take the odds for five dollars and collect ten dollars on the 4 or 10 or twelve dollars on the 6 or 8. However, if the point were 5 or 9, a five-dollar bet would be unacceptable. Since points 5 and 9 pay 3 to 2, the payoff on a five-dollar wager would be an unwieldy seven dollars and fifty cents. Rather than deal with small change, the house will let you bet six dollars on the line to collect nine dollars if you win. Although this can vary some from casino to casino, most clubs will let you bet one unit more than your line bet if it is necessary to allow a round payoff when taking odds on 5 or 9. What constitutes a unit depends on what you are betting. For a five-dollar bet, one dollar is a unit. However, if you are betting in multiples of five dollars with red chips, or multiples of twenty-five dollars with green chips, or multiples of one hundred dollars with black chips, that would be your unit. A fifteen-dollar bet on the pass line would permit you to make a twenty-dollar odds bet if the point were 5 or 9.

The same issue can arise when taking odds on points 6 or 8. Since these numbers pay off at 6 to 5, such a bet must be made in multiples of five to permit a round payoff. Most casinos will permit you to round off up or down to the nearest multiple of five. An eight-dollar wager would permit a ten-dollar odds bet on 6 or 8. However, a seven-dollar wager would permit you to make a five-dollar odds bet on 6 or 8 but not a ten-dollar odds bet, since the nearest multiple of five in this case is five, not ten. The player with a seven-dollar line bet may, if he wishes, bet a full seven dollars on the odds on 6 or 8. However, the casino will only pay the bet at true odds up to the highest multiple of five; anything over that is paid off at even money. Therefore, a winning seven-dollar odds bet on point 6 would collect an eight-dollar payoff: six dollars for the first five dollars of the wager and two dollars (even money) for the remaining two dollars of the wager. This gives the house a large edge on the two-dollar portion of the bet. For that reason, the player should only make odds bets in sums that permit a full payoff at true odds. For points 5 and 9, that means making odds bets in even sums; for points 6 and 8, it means making odds bets in multiples of five units. Since the policy may vary from casino to casino, if you are unsure of the maximum odds wager that your line bet entitles you to, just ask the dealer.

DOUBLE AND TRIPLE ODDS

Some casinos offer free *double odds*. This means that your odds bet can be twice as large as your line bet. This can be very profitable to the player if he knows how to use it. Let's again take the example of the player who is used to making ten-dollar pass-line bets. If he plays at a casino that gives double odds, his wisest course will be to bet three dollars on the line, then take six dollars on the odds whenever the shooter rolls a point on the come-out. This will give him nine dollars of action, almost exactly the same amount he usually wagers. However, because two-thirds of the bet is paid off at true odds, the house advantage on the nine dollars is only .6 percent, compared with a .8 percent edge on the ten dollars if he bets five on the line and five *behind the line* (single odds) or a 1.4 percent edge if he bets all ten dollars on the pass line.

Double odds are offered in a few Las Vegas Strip casinos, most downtown Las Vegas casinos, and most of the casinos in Reno. There are a few casinos that even offer *triple odds*; your free odds bet can be three times as large as your line bet. Our ten-dollar line bettor could now bet three dollars on the line and nine on the odds.

Note that in each case, he would want to keep the sum of the line and odds bets at about that ten-dollar range to get the full benefit of the fact that the odds bet is paid off at correct odds. Many writers on gambling seem to miss this point. They simply advise crap players to make as large an odds bet as the house will allow in proportion to their line bet. This alone accomplishes nothing. A bettor making ten-dollar line bets and taking free double odds will lose his money just as fast as another player making ten-dollar line bets who takes no odds. They are both paying 1.4 percent of ten dollars on each bet. But a third player who bets five dollars on the line and five on the odds can make his money last almost twice as long as either of the first two bettors because half of his ten dollars is riding free. Don't make the mistake of betting more money than you had planned to or more than you feel comfortable wagering just to take full advantage of the odds. Your goal is not to bet as much as possible on the odds but rather to decide how much you want to wager, then figure how to get as large a portion of that total sum behind the line. That is why it is worth the serious crap bettor's while to seek out double- or triple-odds games.

With double and triple odds, you may again be allowed to bet slightly more in order to permit a round payoff. The rule is that you can bet double or triple what would normally be allowed in a single-odds game. Most casinos that permit double or triple odds will post that fact on the plaque that lists the table limits. However, if you are unsure, feel free to ask the dealer.

LAYING THE ODDS

The don't-pass or don't-come bettor can also take advantage of the free odds bet, but in this case he is *laying the odds* rather than taking the odds. This means he is putting up the large part of the bet. He must put up the 6 part of the 6 to 5 wager on points 6 and 8, the 3 part of the 3 to 2 wager on points 5 and 9, and the 2 part of the 2 to 1 wager on points 4 and 10. Once again, these payoff odds accurately reflect his true chances of winning the bet. His odds wager may be as large as need be to ensure that, if he wins, he will win an amount equal to his back-line wager. If he has five dollars on the don't-pass line and the shooter rolls a 10 on the come-out, the don't bettor can wager up to ten dollars on the odds. If he wins, he will receive a five-dollar payoff on his line bet and another five dollars for his odds bet.

If you are a wrong bettor, you should always lay full odds and, when possible, seek out games that offer double or triple odds. Remember, however, that your goal is to reduce your line bet so that the combined total of your line and odds wagers reflects the amount you want to bet against the shooter, rather than increasing the total amount you bet in order to lay the odds. In this manner, the odds bet will decrease the house advantage on your total wager in the same way and to the same extent as explained in connection with taking the odds.

To lay the odds on a don't-pass bet, you should place the appropriate number of chips next to your don't-pass bet. To distinguish this bet from a don't-pass bet, all of the chips except the bottom one should be offset so that they are in a stack half on and half off the bottom chip. To lay the odds on a don't-come bet, you should place the chips in the don't-come box and tell the dealer which don't-come bet they apply to. You may lay the free odds at any time after a point has been established, but it is to your advantage to do so immediately after the roll that establishes the point (or the come-point, in the case of a don't-come bet). In this way, you get the full benefit of this free bet.

RIGHT BETTORS VS. WRONG BETTORS

One of the perennial controversies among crap players is whether a player has a better chance of winning as a right bettor or a wrong bettor. Although the large majority of crap players are right bettors, one can always find a few vocal defenders of wrong betting. As mentioned earlier, right bettors face a house edge of 1.414 percent, while wrong bettors face a 1.402 percent house advantage. The two figures are so close that, for all practical purposes, your chances of winning are the same in both cases. This difference is certainly no basis for choosing one side over the other.

Many crap players will say that your choice of betting right or wrong should be determined by whether the table is hot or *cold*. By this is meant that there are times when the shooters are winning again and again, rolling a lot of numbers and seldom sevening-out; this is known as a hot table. At other times, none of the shooters seems capable of getting a roll started. Sevens come up on almost every roll—except on the come-out; this is a cold table. It is true that you can often tell whether a table is hot or cold as soon as you approach it. Since most crap players *bet with the dice* (right betting), a hot table is usually crowded with enthusiastic players. If you approach a quiet table where the energy level among the players is low, you can be sure the dice are cold.

According to advocates of the hot-and-cold school, all you need to win at craps is to bet with the table. Bet right when the dice are hot and *bet against the dice* when they are cold. This is like saying that the way to win at roulette is to bet on the winning number. You don't know what the winning number is until the ball drops into the slot, and you don't know that a table is still hot until you have won your right bet. When you make a bet, you may be able to say with absolute certainty that the table has been hot (or cold) up until now, but you have no way of knowing that things will continue in the same direction. The moment you make your next bet may be the moment events take a turn. Remember what we learned in Chapter II: The dice have no memory. In any case, much of the time the dice will be neither hot nor cold but rather *chopping*—shooter wins and losses pretty much mixed together.

The hot-and-cold theory may seem to make sense emotionally to many players, but it provides no real guidance as to how to bet. Don't get me wrong—if you have a feeling that the dice are going to keep rolling point number after point number, feel free to bet right. If you feel the ivory cubes are getting so cold they feel like ice cubes, there is nothing wrong with betting the don't-pass and don't-come lines. Since the house edge on both front- and back-line bets is virtually identical, here is one case where you can indulge your hunches with no harm done. But don't delude yourself into thinking that this sort of thing really improves your chances of winning.

Let me suggest another factor to help you decide whether to bet right or wrong in the absence of any overwhelming premonitions. We have already seen that the smart thing to do whether betting do or don't is to back your bets with full odds. For the right bettor, this means putting up the *short end* of the bet. If he wins, he will win more money than he risked. However, the wrong bettor must put up the *long end* of the bet. He must wager the larger amount in hopes of winning the smaller amount. In the long run, this fact does not affect his chances of winning since he faces essentially the same house edge as the right bettor. However, such long-run theoretical analyses always assume that the bettor has an unlimited bankroll. In the real world, all gamblers have to work with finite bankrolls. A constant danger is the risk of being temporarily put out of action by the loss of one's entire bankroll.

Because he has the long end of the bet, the don't-pass bettor has to wager more money faster on the free odds in order to have a chance of making the same profit as a pass-line bettor would with the same amount of luck. When luck turns against him, the money goes out at a faster rate. This is even more true when laying double odds, although the double odds are desirable in cutting down the house advantage.

This is why I advise betting with the shooter. On those occasions when you are losing, the rate of loss will be slower. You will last longer. By being better able to weather the dry spells, you increase your chances of being around to cash in on those occasions when the shooter does catch a *monster hand*.

COVERING THE NUMBERS

We have already seen that the smartest bets at craps are the line bets combined with full odds. However, many players want to get as much action as possible, particularly when they feel the table is hot. They want to win whenever the shooter rolls any of the box numbers (4, 5, 6, 8, 9, or 10) rather than just when he succeeds in repeating his point. To accomplish this, they bet on some or all of these numbers individually so that every time any of the numbers they have covered is rolled before a 7, they win. Of course, if the shooter rolls a 7, all of these bets will lose. The two wagers usually used to accomplish this are *place bets* and *buy bets*.

Because place bets, buy bets, and come bets are all wagers used primarily by pass-line bettors as a means of getting more money riding on the shooter, both place and buy bets, like come odds bets, are always off on the come-out; the come-out roll does not count in determining the outcome of these wagers. If the place bets were working on all rolls, it would mean that, if a 7 were rolled on the come-out, the bettor would win his line bet but lose his place or buy bets. Actually, this would have no long-run effect on his chances of showing a profit. It does, however, create an emotional conflict for the bettor. He wants a 7 on the come-out so he will win his pass-line bet, but he doesn't want a 7 so he won't lose his place or buy bets. Having the place and buy bets off on the come-out helps keep the bettors from getting schizoid. However, if a player wishes, he can inform the dealer that he wants his bets *working* on the come-out. In such a case, the dealer will mark the bet either by placing a small button on it that bears the word ON or by placing the dice buck on the bet.

Admittedly, come bettors will still face this paradoxical situation on come-out rolls. If a 7 appears, they win their pass-line bet but lose any come bets they had up. We have already seen that the house never allows pass-line or come bets to be called off after the first roll where it has the advantage. However, it softens the blow for the come bettor by counting the odds part of the bet off on the come-out unless the player requests otherwise.

PLACE BETS

The most popular method of covering the numbers is with place bets. When you make a place bet, the casino gives itself an advantage by paying off the wager at *house odds* rather than true odds. For example, if you make a place bet on 6 and win, you will be paid off at odds of 7 to 6 although the true odds of a 6 appearing before a 7 are 6 to 5. According to the true odds, a thirty-dollar wager should net you a thirty-six-dollar wager. But at 7 to 6, you would win only thirty-five dollars, giving the house a one-dollar profit. That 1/36 edge, when converted to a percentage, means a house advantage of 1.5 percent. The house enjoys the same advantage on place bets on 8. On 5 and 9, place bets pay 7 to 5 rather than true odds of 3 to 2, for a house edge of 4 percent. On 4 and 10, the payoff is 9 to 5 rather than the correct odds of 2 to 1. By paying 9 to 5 rather than 10 to 5, the house is taking a bite of 1/15 or 6.7 percent.

As I mentioned earlier, casinos don't pay off in loose change. To get the full payoff odds cited above, you must bet in sums that can be paid off to the dollar. For numbers 4, 5, 9, and 10, this means betting in multiples of five dollars. If instead you place twelve dollars on 4 and win, the dealer will pay off ten dollars of your bet at 9 to 5 and then pay the remaining two dollars at even money. You will collect twenty dollars. In casino terminology, this is called "paying to five dollars." Place bets on 6 and 8 pay to six dollars. This means you must make such bets in multiples of six dollars to keep from being shortchanged on the payoff.

A player may retract his place bet at any time prior to a decision. He may also reduce the size of it or add more money to it. A player may also call a place bet off at any time by informing the dealer. He will then place a small OFF button on the bet. This means that the bet does not count for the subsequent rolls until the player informs the dealer he wants the bet working again. If the place number or a 7 should be rolled while the bet is off, the wager will not be affected. As mentioned earlier, place bets are off on the come-out unless the player requests otherwise.

To make a place bet, place your chips in the come box and tell the dealer what number or numbers you want to place. He will place the bet on the line directly above or below the box number being placed. The exact positioning of the bet is determined by the position of the bettor at the table. In Reno and Lake Tahoe, the layout has a box on it specifically for place bets. It is located directly above each box number but under the box in which the don't-come bets go. If your bet wins, the payoff will be placed in front of you, but your original bet will remain on the place number and will count as a new bet unless you ask the dealer to return it. If your place bet wins and you wish to add money to the bet from your winnings, let the dealer know, and he will add the money to the original bet out of your winnings before giving you the rest of the payoff.

If a player wishes to make a place bet on the number that is the shooter's point, he can do so as explained above or he can simply place his bet on the layout so that it straddles the lower borderline of the pass line. If the bet involves more than one chip, it should also be heeled (the top chips half on and half off the bottom chip).

Different bettors prefer different patterns. Some bettors like to cover the number that is the mate of the shooter's point. If the point is 6, they will cover the 8; if the point is 9, they will bet on the 5. Others will bet the numbers in matched pairs, for example, both the 6 and the 8, or both the 5 and the 9, or both the 4 and the 10. When one of these numbers wins, such a player will often add the winnings from that number to the bet on the other number that has not yet hit. Some bettors always cover all the *outside numbers*, 4, 5, 9, and 10. Others cover the *inside numbers*, 5, 6, 8, and 9. Still others prefer to place all the numbers except the point number, which they already have covered with a line bet. Many players will simply cover all the numbers *across the board*. When you hear a bettor confidently tell the dealer that he wants 32 *across* (five dollars each on 4, 5, 9, and 10, and six dollars each on 6 and 8) or 15 *across* (three dollars on every number except the point) you might assume that he must really know what he is doing. He doesn't. With the exception of the 6 and 8, the place numbers carry too high a price tag to be considered smart bets.

BUY BETS

Another way to cover a number is to "buy" the bet. When you make a buy bet, the casino pays off the wager at true odds, but it charges a 5 percent commission on the bet. Thus, if you make a twenty-dollar buy bet you must pay the casino an additional one dollar as commission. This is known as the *vig*, *vigorish*, or *juice*. If your bet wins, your twenty dollars will be paid off at correct odds.

The 5 percent commission provides the casino with its profit on buy bets. Most players assume that a 5 percent commission means the house has a 5 percent house edge on these bets, but that is not quite correct. Since you are losing one dollar out of every twenty-one dollars wagered, the house percentage on this bet is 1/21, which is expressed as a percentage as 4.7 percent. In the long run, you will lose four dollars and seventy-six cents out of every one hundred dollars wagered on buy bets.

The house will charge 5 percent on each multiple of twenty or portion thereof. If you bet twenty dollars, you will be charged a one-dollar commission. If you bet ten dollars, you will still be charged a one-dollar commission. If you bet forty dollars, you will be charged a two-dollar commission. But if you bet thirty dollars, you will still be charged a two-dollar commission. Therefore, it is obviously in the player's interest to make buy bets only in multiples of twenty dollars in order to avoid being overcharged. Many casinos give the bettor a break in one situation. They charge only a one-dollar commission on wagers of twenty-five dollars. This is a concession to the green check player who would find it a hassle to convert his chips into a lower denomination just to make this one bet. This reduces the house edge to 3.8 percent.

If you wish to make a buy bet, place your chips, including the commission, in the come box and tell the dealer what number you want to buy. He will remove the commission and place the rest of the chips inside the box of the number you are betting on and will mark it by placing a small button on it bearing the word BUY. This will distinguish the bet from any come bets in the same box. Like place bets, buy bets are off on the come-out unless the player informs the dealer that he wants the bet working on all rolls. The bet can also be called off on any roll. Like all craps wagers except pass and come bets, a buy bet may be called down by the player anytime prior to a decision being reached on the bet. In that case, the dealer will return the commission charge along with the bet.

THE BEST WAY TO COVER THE NUMBERS

As you can see by comparing the various house percentages on the place bets to the 4.7 percent edge on buy bets, it may be less costly for you to place the bet or buy it depending on the number you are betting. Numbers 5, 6, 8, and 9 are better placed than bought. Numbers 4 and 10 are cheaper if bought, as long as you can afford to make a twenty-unit bet rather than the five-unit minimum bet required to place the bet.

You don't really have to remember all that. The house edge on 4, 5, 9, and 10 is so high, whether you place or buy, that the matter is only of theoretical interest. The percentage is simply too high to buck. I strongly advise you to avoid both place and buy bets on all numbers except 6 and 8. In these two cases, the house edge of 1.5 percent is almost identical to the 1.4 percent you face on line bets, making this a reasonable wager.

However, there is still a better approach. The smart bettor achieves essentially the same result as the place or buy bettor at a fraction of the cost by exploiting the come line. When you make a come bet, if the shooter rolls a number—as opposed to craps or a natural—you will have that number covered for a repeat. If the table is hot, with many numbers being rolled and few 7s, you will soon have most of the numbers covered and at only a 1.4 percent edge, which is better than any place or buy bet can offer. More important, when you make a come bet, you can also take free odds on the come point, which cuts the percentage against you still further, to only .8 percent.

Some crap players reject this argument by saying that a number only has to come up once to win if the number was placed or bought but must come up twice before a come bet will win. This reasoning would make sense if you really had some way of knowing that a particular number was going to be rolled soon. Of course, place and buy bettors don't have any such knowledge. They are merely hoping that the shooter will hold on to the dice for a long time. If that should prove to be the case, you will make more money with come bets and odds than with place or buy bets. Keep in mind that it is no more difficult to win the come bet than a place or buy bet, because you are not betting that a number will come up twice. You are only betting that it will come up once after it has already come up on the first roll. The conclusive argument is simply that the P.C. on a come bet is far lower than that on place or buy bets. Remember, the casino places all its faith on the percentages, and that strategy certainly seems to have paid off for them. I suggest you do the same.

When the come bet was first introduced to casino craps, many of the smart-money gamblers predicted that place and buy bets would soon become obsolete. But they reckoned without that breed of animal of which there is one born every minute.

LAY BETS

For the wrong bettor who wants to cover the numbers, there is the *lay bet*. This is essentially the reverse of a buy bet. The bettor is, of course, putting up the *long end* of the bet. The wager is paid off at true odds, but you must first pay a commission. In this case, the commission is computed as 5 percent of what the bet will pay if it wins. If you lay the 4 for forty dollars, you must hand the dealer an additional one dollar as the commission. One dollar is 5 percent of twenty dollars, which is what the bet will pay if it wins. The wager will win if a 7 is rolled before a 4, and it will lose if a 4 is rolled before a 7. The house edge on lay bets on the 4 or 10 is 2.4 percent. On the 5 and 9, the edge is 3.3 percent. On the 6 and 8, it is 4 percent. Since the house charges full commission on every multiple of twenty or every portion thereof that it pays on lay bets, these wagers should be made in the following sizes to avoid excessive commission charges: multiples of forty for numbers 4 and 10, multiples of thirty for numbers 5 and 9, and multiples of twenty-four for numbers 6 and 8.

To make a lay wager, place your chips, including the commission, in the come box and tell the dealer what number you want to lay. He will remove the commission and place the bet above the proper box number in the box where the don't-come bets go. A small BUY button will be placed on the bet to distinguish it from the don't-come bets. The bet can also be called down, in which case the dealer will refund the commission charge. For the reasons explained a moment ago, you would be better off making don't-come bets and laying full odds.

Sucker Traps

At this point, you know how every important bet at craps works. You could play a sharp, sophisticated game with a strong chance of winning strictly on the basis of exploiting the bets you already know about without bothering to learn anything about the many other bets that are available at craps. In fact, you might be better off not knowing anything about the other bets since, without exception, these other wagers are all strictly sucker bait.

Payoffs and Percentages at Craps Wagers

BET	PAYOFF	P.C.
PASS or COME	1 to 1	1.414
PASS or COME (SINGLE ODDS)	1 to 1 plus true odds	.8
PASS or COME (DOUBLE ODDS)	1 to 1 plus true odds	.6

PASS or COME (TRIPLE ODDS)	1 to 1 plus true odds	.4
DON'T-PASS or COME	1 to 1	1.402
DON'T-PASS or COME (SINGLE ODDS)	1 to 1 plus true odds	.8
DON'T-PASS or COME (DOUBLE ODDS)	1 to 1 plus true odds	.6
DON'T-PASS or COME (TRIPLE ODDS)	1 to 1 plus true odds	.4
PLACE 6 or 8	7 to 6	1.5
PLACE 5 or 9	7 to 5	4
PLACE 4 or 10	9 to 5	6.7
BUY BET	true odds minus 5 percent charge	4.7
LAY 6 or 8	5 to 6 minus 5 percent charge	4
LAY 5 or 9	2 to 3 minus 5 percent charge	3.2
LAY 4 or 10	1 to 2 minus 5 percent charge	2.4
THE FIELD	1 to 1 (double on 2 and 12)	5.5
	1 to 1 (double on 2, triple on 12)	2.7
BIG 6/BIG 8	1 to 1	9.09
HARDWAY 6 or 8	9 to 1	9.09
HARDWAY 4 or 10	7 to 1	11.1
ANY-SEVEN	4 to 1	16.7
ANY-CRAPS	7 to 1	11.1
2 or 12	30 to 1	13.9
	29 to 1	16.7
3 or 11	15 to 1	11.1
	14 to 1	16.7
HARDWAY HOP	30 to 1	13.9
	29 to 1	16.7
OTHER HOPS	15 to 1	11.1
	14 to 1	16.7

I am going to tell you about the other craps bets for only two reasons. First, I promised you this book would be a complete guide to the casino games. You therefore have a right to expect that all craps bets will be discussed. Second, if I leave you in ignorance about these bets, you might be tempted sometime to try your hand. By providing a brief description of the proposition bets, I am hoping that, if the urge ever comes over you to make one of these wagers, you will take a cold shower, look up the analysis of the bet in this section of the book to find out why it is a sucker proposition, and go back to being a smart bettor.

In each case, I have provided the house edge for the bet. You can check the accuracy of these figures for yourself by using the information we covered earlier on possible combinations with two dice and the method of calculating house advantage I taught you in Chapter II.

While the free odds bet is not marked anywhere on the craps layout, the proposition bets are prominently featured on the layout. This is in accordance with the general rule of thumb that the more conspicuously the casino displays a bet on a layout, the worse the bet is likely to be.

In citing the payoff odds for these bets, I have given the most favorable odds that are available in any casino. Some gambling houses, primarily the major Las Vegas Strip casinos, offer payoffs on some of the propositions that are slightly lower, making these wagers even more blatantly sucker bets. In general, the poorer odds are found in casinos catering to high rollers. These clubs pay one unit less than what I have listed on the 2, 3, 11, and 12 wagers. The better odds are found in casinos catering to grind action. Both sets of payoff odds and percentages are listed in the "Payoffs and Percentages at Craps Wagers" table on pages 119–120.

THE FIELD

The large box on either side of the layout containing the numbers 2, 3, 4, 9, 10, 11, and 12 is for the *field bet*. Wagers are made by placing the chips in this box, and winnings are paid off in the same space. That means that they must be claimed before the next roll, or both the original bet and the payoff will count as a new field bet. A player who bets the field is wagering that one of these numbers will come up on the very next roll. If it does, he will be paid off. If the number is a 2 or a 12, he will be paid off at 2 to 1. All the other numbers pay even money. However, if a 5, 6, 7, or 8 is rolled, the bet will be lost.

This wager is deceptively appealing to the novice because there are many numbers on which he can win, but only a few on which he can lose. If you remember what I taught you about the ways in which each number can be made, you should have noticed that the few numbers that lose for the field bettor are those that are rolled most often. In fact, there are more ways of rolling those few numbers than there are ways of rolling all the winning numbers. Number 7 can be rolled six ways. Numbers 6 and 8 can each be rolled five ways. Number 5 can be rolled four ways. Since there are only thirty-six combinations that can be rolled with two dice, this gives the house twenty ways to win against the player's sixteen ways. Even though you get paid double on 2 and 12, that still means twenty units lost for every eighteen won. This gives the house an edge of 5.5 percent, far too high for you to have a real chance of winning over the long run.

In the northern Nevada and downtown Vegas clubs, the 2, or in some cases the 12, pays 3 to 1 instead of double. Whatever payoff policy the casino follows will be marked off on the layout with a circle around each field number that pays more than even money and a notation around the circle stating the payoff odds. With a triple payoff on 2 or 12, the house edge is cut to only 2.7 percent. This is a big improvement. Nevertheless, it is still more than three times as high as the low edge you face on line bets with odds.

BIG 6 AND BIG 8

A *big* 6 or *big* 8 bet is made by placing your wager in the large boxed-off 6 or 8 at either corner of the layout. Winnings are paid off in the same box. If you don't claim them before the next roll, both the original bet and the payoff will count as a new bet. Both of these bets work the same way. If you bet on the big 6, you are wagering that a 6 will be rolled before a 7. The big 8 bet pays if an 8 comes up before a 7. If this sounds familiar, it is because this kind of bet works exactly the same way as either a place bet or a buy bet on 6 or 8. The difference is that the big 6 and big 8 pay only even money, while the place bet pays 7 to 6 and the buy bet pays 6 to 5 minus the 5 percent charge.

The even-money payoff on a bet where true odds are 6 to 5 gives the house a massive 9.09 percent advantage. Compare that with the 1.5 percent edge on the place bet and the 4.7 percent on the buy bet. This is like having an identical product on sale at the supermarket at three different prices. Only a masochist would buy it at the highest price. If you want to cover the 6 or 8, the smart way to do it is with a place bet. The big 6 and big 8 cost over six times as much as a place bet on the same number. To make a big 6 or big 8 bet at a crap table is to immediately brand yourself a sucker in the eyes of the crap dealers and knowledgeable players.

In Atlantic City, the big 6 and big 8 pay off at 7 to 6 just like the place bet, as long as you bet in multiples of six dollars. In these casinos, there is really no difference at all between the two kinds of bet. Even there, I would advise you to place the bet rather than put your money on the big 6 or big 8, just for the sake of your image.

PROPOSITION BETS

The wagers in the central part of the layout in front of the stickman are called *proposition bets*. To make any of these bets, you would place your chips on the center of the layout and announce to the stickman both the amount of the wager and the type of bet you want to make. For example, you might say, "Twenty on the hard eight." When one of these bets wins, the stickman instructs one of the dealers how much to pay and which player to give the winnings to. The dealer will place the payoffs directly in front of the winning player. However, the original bet remains on the layout and counts as a bet for the next roll. Proposition bets are never returned to the player unless he asks the stickman to do so.

I am telling you all this just for the record. These bets represent the worst gambles available at craps. If you insist on making any of the proposition bets, do me a favor and don't tell anyone you read my book. To satisfy your morbid curiosity, I am going to tell you just what these bets consist of.

Hardways When a number is rolled by getting the same number on each of the two dice, this is known as making the number *the hard way*. Obviously, the only point numbers that can be made this way are 4 (2–2), 6 (3–3), 8 (4–4), and 10 (5–5). Any other way of rolling one of these four numbers is called making the number *the easy way*. When a player bets a particular number the hard way, he is wagering that this number will be rolled the hard way before it is rolled the easy way and also before a 7 appears. If either the 7 or one of the easy combinations of that number is rolled first, the bet will lose.

Since both 4 and 10 can be rolled by the same number of combinations, the hardway 4 and hardway 10 bets both have the same payoff odds of 7 to 1. True odds are 8 to 1. The eight losing combinations are the six ways a 7 can be rolled plus the two easy ways the 4 (or 10) can be rolled. By holding out one unit in what should be a nine-unit pot, the casino gives itself an advantage of 1/9 or 11.1 percent.

The 6 and 8 can also be rolled by the same number of combinations, so they also have the same payoff of 9 to 1. True odds are 10 to 1. The resulting house edge is 9.09 percent. With percentages like this against the player, making *hardway bets* can only be considered a sign of a self-destructive personality.

Any-Seven   This and the remaining proposition bets are all one-roll bets. This means that you are betting on what will happen on the very next roll. Of the bets we have covered so far, only the field bet also falls into this category.

An *any-seven* wager means that you are betting that a 7 will come up on the next roll. There are six different ways of making a 7. If any of the other thirty possible combinations comes up on the next roll, you lose. Clearly, your chances of winning are 30 to 6, which can be simplified to 5 to 1. The house pays 4 to 1. You pay 16.7 percent of the money you wager. If you bet this long enough, that should come to all your money.

Any-Craps   You win if the shooter throws 2, 3, or 12 on the next roll. You have four combinations going for you, and the remaining thirty-two against you. That works out to 8 to 1 correct odds. The house pays 7 to 1, for a 11.1 percent edge.

2 or 12   These are two different bets, but they work the same way. If you bet on the 2, you have one way of winning and thirty-five ways of losing. The house pays 30 to 1. Doesn't sound fair, does it? The bite is 13.9 percent. A bet on 12 works the same way and costs just as much.

3 or 11   Once again, these two bets work the same way. (Remember, 3 and 11 are symmetrical pairs). If you think 3 will be thrown on the next roll, you have two chances to win and thirty-four to lose. That means true odds of 17 to 1. The casino will pay you 15 to 1 if you are crazy enough to take this proposition and lucky enough to win. The house advantage works out to 11.1 percent. The same bad news applies to a bet on 11.

The Hardway Hop   This bet appears on the Lake Tahoe/Reno layout but not on the Las Vegas/Atlantic City layout. However, in their eagerness to cover any suicidal bet a player is willing to make, many casinos will allow you to make this wager even if it does not appear on the layout. If you think the shooter will make a hardway 4 on the next roll, you can make such a bet by placing your chips in front of the stickman and telling him you want to bet a hardway 4 on the *hop*. (A hop is a wager that a particular combination will appear on the dice on the very next roll.) He will leave the bet on the unmarked part of the layout beneath the section on which the proposition bets are marked and will acknowledge the bet by stating the amount and nature of the bet. The same bet can be made on the hard 6, 8, or 10. This kind of bet is also known as a *hardway on the turn* or a *one-roll hardway*.

The house will give you 30 to 1 odds. If you want to know how this breaks down mathematically, look at the analysis of the 2 and 12 bets above. Although the numbers are different, the math is the same because in each case you are talking about only one winning combination out of thirty-six possibilities.

The house edge is 13.9 percent. This is true whether you bet the hard 4, 6, 8, or 10. The number you are betting on changes, but both the true odds and the payoff odds remain the same. Therefore, the house edge is the same.

Other Hops You can make the same kind of one-roll bet on any easy combination for any total. For example, you may wager that an 8 will be thrown as 5–3 on the next roll. Simply tell the stickman you want to bet the 5–3 on the hop. The bet will be handled by the stickman exactly as explained in regard to hardway hops that do not appear on the layout. Since this time you have two possible winning combinations (5–3 and 3–5), the house pays 15 to 1 on this bet, for an edge of 11.1 percent. This is exactly analogous to the 3 and 11 bets discussed above.

The Horn The *horn bet* is one wager that will be new to some who have done all their crap playing in Las Vegas. The horn is not listed on the Las Vegas Strip layout but is prominently displayed on the layouts used in Reno, Lake Tahoe, and Atlantic City. When a player bets the horn, he is wagering that either a 2, 3, 11, or 12 will appear on the next roll.

The horn bet must always be made in multiples of four units, since the player is, in effect, betting one unit on each of four different numbers. If a 2 or 12 appears on the next roll after the player makes his bet, one-quarter of his wager will be paid off at 30 to 1 odds, and the remainder of the wager is forfeited. If a 3 or 11 appears, one-quarter of the player's wager will be paid off at 15 to 1, while the rest of the bet is forfeited. Of course, if neither a 2, 3, 11, or 12 appears, the entire wager is lost.

Some players figure that there are six ways of making a 2, 3, 11, or 12 and thirty ways of making any other number. They conclude, therefore, that they have a 5 to 1 chance of winning the bet and convince themselves it is a pretty good gamble. The fallacy of this kind of thinking is that the horn bet is really four different wagers. Remember, only one out of every four units bet will be paid off if a 2, 3, 11, or 12 appears.

The true odds against a 2 appearing in one roll are 35 to 1. These odds also apply to your chances of getting a 3 in one roll. But the casino pays only 30 to 1 on either of these numbers. The true odds against rolling a 3 are 17 to 1. The 17 to 1 figure also applies to your chances of making an 11 in one roll. But the casino pays only 15 to 1 on these two numbers. Thus, the house is giving itself a massive 13.9 percent edge on the 2 and 12 and 11.1 percent edge on the 3 and 11. In the long run, you figure to lose about twelve dollars and fifty cents out of every hundred dollars bet on the horn.

The Horn High   A common variation of the horn is called the *horn high* bet. In this case, the wager must be made in multiples of five units rather than four units. One unit is bet on each of the four numbers 2, 3, 11, and 12, plus an additional unit wagered on whichever of the four numbers the player chooses. A bettor might, for example, hand the stickman five dollars and say, "Horn high eleven." The 11 will be covered with two dollars, and the 2, 3, and 12 will be covered with one dollar each. Needless to say, this bizarre variation does not make the wager any better.

Basically, the horn and horn high bets are a casino gimmick to get players to make four different sucker bets at the same time.

Craps-Eleven   Also referred to as the C & E for short, the *craps-eleven* bet is a wager that either a craps (2, 3, or 12) or an 11 will appear on the next roll. If a craps is rolled, the bet pays 3 to 1; if 11 is rolled, it pays 7 to 1. This is exactly the same as making two equal bets, one on any craps and one on 11. Both of these wagers were discussed above.

Other Split Bets There are many other proposition bets that, in effect, consist of the bettor making one wager that is divided over two or more different one-roll bets. One example is the *three-way craps*. Unlike the *any-craps* bet, this is a three-unit bet that is equally divided between the 2 bet, the 3 bet, and the 12 bet. Other split bets include 11 and 12 split; the *high-low* bet (pays on 12 or 2); the ace-deuce and 11 bet (pays on 3 or 11); the aces and ace-deuce bet (pays on 2 or 3); and the ace-deuce and any-craps (pays on 2 or 12, and extra on the 3). There is really no point in analyzing each of these bets separately, since the individual components have all been discussed above. They are all strictly for suckers; I mention them only for the sake of completeness.

"To" vs. "For" Throughout this book I have followed the format of citing odds as "X to Y." This is also the more common format used by gambling casinos in listing odds on their layouts. However, you will also encounter crap layouts where the odds are listed as "X for Y." Don't make the mistake of thinking this means the same thing as "X to Y."

Here is what really happens. Let's assume you are making one-dollar bets. If the layout says the bet pays 5 to 1, it means that if you win, the house will give you five dollars in addition to letting you keep the one dollar you bet. However, if the layout says the bet pays 5 for 1, it means that if you win, the casino will take your one-dollar bet and give you five dollars in exchange for it. It gives you 5 for your 1. A little reflection will show you that changing the word from "to" to "for" costs you one dollar.

Frankly, I feel this "for" double-talk is just misleading advertising. If you don't spot the difference in terminology or don't understand what it means, you may assume a casino is giving you better odds than at other clubs you have played in. For example, an unsophisticated player seeing that this layout pays 6 for 1 on the any-seven bet may assume he is getting a better deal here than at a casino that pays 5 to 1. In fact, both games are giving exactly the same odds.

Alternately, the "for" ploy may give the impression that the house is offering the same odds as the competition when in fact it is actually giving short odds. A wager like the 12 bet may be listed as 30 for 1 instead of the standard 30 to 1. To the uninformed player, this looks like the same odds he is used to seeing on the layout. In fact, the house has boosted the already-prohibitive 13.9 percent house edge to a grotesque 16.7 percent. If you remember that 10 for 1 means the same thing as 9 to 1, you won't be misled.

INSURING BETS

Considering how bad the proposition bets are for players, the question arises: Why do they get so much play? One reason is that the high payoff odds are attractive to some bettors, particularly those who have been losing heavily and are desperate for any chance to recoup quickly. Another reason is that during a hot hand, players want to get as much money as possible down on the point numbers. To some unthinking gamblers, the hardway bets seem like just one more way of doing this.

However, the most common, and the silliest, reason for making proposition bets is to try to reduce the risks involved in your line bets. The one-roll bets in the center of the layout all pertain to the five nonpoint numbers, 2, 3, 7, 11, and 12. These propositions receive play mainly on the come-out roll. A player who is betting the pass line may find that he is losing because the shooter is crapping out too often. As a result, he decides to protect his line bet by making an any-craps wager on the come-out.

Similarly, a wrong bettor may realize that the odds favor the wrong bettor after the come-out. He knows that he faces his greatest chance of losing on the come-out because of the high probability of the shooter rolling a natural. He decides to eliminate that risk by making an any-seven bet or both an any-seven and an 11 bet on each come-out. He figures that, if the shooter throws a natural, the profit from the proposition bet will more than compensate for his loss on his don't-pass bet. Gamblers refer to such strategies as "betting both sides of the table." Another good description is betting against yourself.

Still another wrong bettor may have read somewhere that the reason the house has an advantage over wrong bettors is because it bars the 6–6 roll. By making a 12 bet on every come-out in addition to a don't-pass bet, he figures to make a profit every time the shooter loses and thereby outsmart the casino.

All these approaches are efforts to insure the line bet against a loss on the come-out. They sound good if you don't think about them too hard. In fact, some players actually succeed in convincing themselves that they have come up with a foolproof system for beating the house with these betting combinations. The myriad bets offered by craps makes it possible for a bettor to succeed in confusing himself with a combination of contradictory bets and to delude himself into thinking he has somehow swung the percentages in his favor.

A little reflection will show this is impossible. Every single wager available at craps has a negative expectation for the player. Anyone who has had high-school math knows that you cannot add two or more negatives and end up with a positive, no matter how you combine them. The best you can do at craps is to stick to those bets that have the smallest negatives attached to them. All you accomplish by attempting to protect a line bet with a proposition bet is to impose a drain on your line bet profits every time the proposition bet doesn't win. Trying to protect a wager that has only a -1.4 percent expectation with another wager that has a massive 11.1 percent disadvantage does not make sense. Gambling will always involve risk. Misguided efforts to "insure" against losing will remove the risk only to the extent that they help ensure that you end up a loser.

PROTECTING YOUR BETS

Misplaced Bets   It is your responsibility at the crap table to protect your money at all times. This means understanding the layout well enough to make sure that when you put down a bet, it is actually the kind of wager you intend to make. It also means watching the dealer to make sure that he does not make a mistake in placing your bets. The rule at craps is that "the bet plays as it lays." This means that a wager will always count as what it is on the layout, and not necessarily as what you wanted it to be—even if the error was the dealer's fault. If a dealer makes a mistake in positioning your bet, you must point out the error before the next roll of the dice; otherwise the bet will count as he made it.

You will note with experience that in placing each bet in the proper box, the dealer positions it in relation to the bettor's location at the table. This makes it possible for him to keep track of what bet belongs to which player. It also makes it easier for you to keep track of your bets.

If you follow a consistent pattern in your betting, the dealer will pick up on this pattern before long. He will know that you always take the free odds, or that you want your bets working on the come-out, or that you always take down a place bet after a win. He will then be able to handle your bets correctly with a minimum of instruction from you. However, if you decide to change your betting pattern suddenly, you must be sure to make this clear to him.

Winnings   It is also your job to get your money off the layout when you are paid. Otherwise, it may count as a bet you didn't want to make. For example, come bets are paid off in the come box. If you don't collect your winnings before the next roll, they become a new come bet.

Sleeper Bets   Another danger to your bankroll is the *claim bet artist*. A player with a large number of bets working at the same time can easily lose track of some of them, particularly at a crowded table. Sometimes he will win a wager without even realizing it and leave the winnings unclaimed on the layout. Crap dealers are familiar with this phenomenon and call them sleeper bets. Sometimes a dealer will notice what has happened and call your attention to your forgotten bet, but you can't count on this. Small-time cheats are constantly on the lookout for this situation and will move in to collect unclaimed bets as their own. If caught, they brush the incident off as an accident.

Some crooks will go so far as to steal a few of a player's chips directly from the rail as he is playing. Players can become so caught up in the game and so engrossed in watching the dice, particularly on a hot roll, that such thievery becomes child's play. If you are not alert against such scams, you can end up a loser even after a winning session of play.

The Game Plan

PREGAME PRACTICE

If you have never played casino craps before, your first task should be to become thoroughly familiar with the game and comfortable at a crap table. You have to be able to play at the table with complete confidence, without any fear of looking foolish or making a mistake, before you can even start thinking about making money at the game. If you follow the advice I am going to give you, you will be able to look, act, and feel like a pro at craps in no time.

The first step is to read through the sections on The Basic Game and Refinements several times. Really study them. Don't worry about the material on Sucker Traps at this stage. Once you have assimilated all the information in the first two sections, you should start practicing the following three simple drills.

First, get a pair of dice and start rolling them. After each roll, call out the number that pairs with the number you just rolled, as explained in the section on The Basic Tools under Figuring the Odds. For example, if you roll a 9, call out 5; if you roll a 3, call out 11. As soon as you have these pairings set in your mind and understand what they mean as I explained earlier, you will find that the information you have to know to understand the game of craps becomes much more manageable.

For the second exercise, start rolling the dice again. This time announce the number of ways in which each number you roll can be made. This was also explained in the section Figuring the Odds. If you roll a 6, call out "Five ways"; for a 10, you should announce "Three ways." Keep this up until you can do it without the slightest hesitation. The number of ways a number at craps can be made is the basic information underlying all the mathematics of the game. To be able to play effectively, this knowledge has got to be second nature to you. You won't have time to figure it out in your head in the middle of a hectic crap game.

Finally, for the last exercise, start rolling the dice again. This time, every time you roll a 2, 3, or 12, announce "Craps." Every time you roll a 7 or an 11, announce "Natural." Every time you roll a point number, 4, 5, 6, 8, 9, or 10, announce the true odds of repeating that point before rolling a 7 (6 to 5 for the 6 and 8, 3 to 2 for the 5 and 9, and 2 to 1 for the 4 and 10). The reason you must have this latter information at your fingertips is that you will be using it constantly when making free odds bets. Having the information from these three drills at your command instantly is important, not only so you can make your bets without fumbling and looking like an amateur, but also so that your mind will be free to concentrate on the other matters it has to deal with during an actual game.

YOUR FIRST TIME

Once you have read and drilled sufficiently to feel confident in your mastery of the information, you are ready to approach the tables. Pick a crap table that has few players. This is not only less intimidating than a crowded table, it also means that the game is likely to proceed at a slower tempo, which will make things easier for you as a beginner. Stick to making pass-line bets on each come-out and nothing else. Your goal at this point is to familiarize yourself with table procedures. Watch the dealers and the other players and try to understand why they do what they do. If anything is unclear to you, try to remember it so that you can check it out in this book when you get back to your room.

Throughout this chapter I have gone to great pains to explain to you how each bet works, how it is handled, and why everything is done in the way it is. With this background, things should begin to fall into place for you at the table in a very short time. A couple of sessions during your first day at the casino should be all you need for this phase. By the end, you should feel confident enough to start making odds bets to back your pass-line bets and also an occasional come bet with odds. When you feel totally comfortable with these right bets, try betting the don't-pass and don't-come with odds. Although I have recommended right betting, you should have enough flexibility to know how to bet the wrong side of the table should you want to. Finally, go back and read the section on sucker traps. By the next day, you should be ready for some serious playing.

PLAYING STYLE

Regardless of what some gambling writers may lead you to believe, there is no magic formula that will make you a winner at craps, no special progression or combination of bets that will ensure a profit. However, there are certain principles that will maximize your chances of coming out a winner. The most important of these is, *Stick to wagers that have the lowest house percentage.* Pass-line bets, come bets, don't-pass bets, don't-come bets, and place bets on 6 and 8 have low enough house edges to make them permissible for the smart bettor. Of these, the 6 and 8 place bets have the highest percentage, and they can be avoided by using come bets to cover the numbers.

The second principle is, *Exploit the free odds bet to the fullest.*

This means always taking full odds and playing in casinos that offer double odds or triple odds whenever possible. It also means understanding how to use the odds to best advantage. Remember, the key here is to decide how much you want to bet on the shooter each time, using the principles explained in Chapter I, then determining how to get as much of that sum as possible behind the line. Although there is no ultimate sense in which right betting is better than wrong betting or vice versa, as I explained earlier, it becomes a lot less painful to fully exploit the free odds when you bet right.

The next important principle that should govern your style of play is, *Use come bets properly*. Come bets provide more action for the bettor than pass-line bets alone can provide and at no higher cost in terms of house percentage. When making come bets, you should always take full odds if the shooter rolls a come point. Although it is possible to make a come bet on every roll other than the come-out, I don't advise this. You can lose a good deal of money on one roll if the shooter throws a 7. In addition, having this many bets out is very difficult for even experienced players to keep track of and tends to give rise to some of the errors discussed earlier.

I recommend keeping two come bets working at all times. In other words, if you make a come bet and the shooter rolls a natural or a craps on that roll, make another come bet immediately. Keep this up until you have two come bets on numbers as well as your line bet, all with odds. Make no more bets until one or more of these wagers is settled. At that point, start betting again until you are back in the same position, a line bet and two come bets. This betting pattern should provide you with enough action to keep things interesting and a chance to make some real money if the table should heat up. At the same time, it keeps the number of bets and the amount of money at risk at any one time to a manageable level.

BETTING PATTERN

The basic money-management principle underlying all smart gambling is to bet more when you're winning and less when you're losing. At craps, if you are betting right, you also want to bet more when the table is hot. If you follow the betting pattern recommended above, both goals should coincide automatically. You will start making more money when the table is hot.

When you note that your bankroll has started to increase rapidly in a short time, increase the size of your bets by about fifty percent. As long as you keep winning, keep increasing your bets. As soon as things level off after a hot winning streak, pick up your money and take a break from the tables. This betting approach won't guarantee a profit, but it will allow you to take the fullest advantage of a lucky streak when it does come along.

VI. Baccarat

♣ The casinos go to considerable trouble to imbue baccarat with an aura of glamour and elegance. The game is not played on the main casino floor but is set off in a quiet corner behind a railing or cordon. One immediately gets the feeling that something very special is happening behind that rail. Most casinos have only one or two baccarat tables, further adding to the feeling of exclusivity. The table and chairs are far more plush than those found at the other games. The dealers conducting the game wear tuxedos rather than the standard casino uniforms. The house may even hire beautiful, expensively dressed women to act as *shills* at the game. That means that they will play with house money at an otherwise empty table to make the game look lively and attract players; many people dislike being the only player at a table. If the table starts to fill up, the shills will discreetly leave to make room for paying customers. With all the attention to ambience the casino lavishes on the game, just sitting down to play can make you feel like James Bond.

Despite the European flavor surrounding baccarat, the game as played in Nevada and Atlantic City is an American invention, different in many ways from the European game from which it is derived. Basically, the American casinos have retained the trappings of the game while simplifying it to remove any strategy considerations and also turning it into a game in which players bet against the house rather than against each other, as in the original version. Baccarat was first introduced at the Dunes in Las Vegas in 1959. Since that time, it has grown slowly but steadily to the point where it can now be found in every major casino, and some of the lesser ones as well.

Many people are intimidated by the exclusive and glamorous atmosphere surrounding baccarat. This is a pity because the game offers one of the lowest house advantages of any casino game. That means it offers you one of the best chances of coming out a winner. It is also an extremely easy game to learn to play, by far the easiest of all the table games. In fact, I suspect that one of the reasons the casinos go so far to cloak the game in ritual and mystique is to disguise how little substance there is to the game itself.

Baccarat is a game that involves high table limits. It is certainly too expensive for some players. If playing would put a strain on your bankroll, that is a very good reason to avoid it. But if you can afford it, there is no reason why you can't be playing like a pro soon after studying this chapter.

The Basic Game

THE EQUIPMENT

Baccarat is played on a large table around which the players are seated. Most baccarat tables are designed to seat fourteen players, although some seat only twelve. Each seating position is numbered on the layout in front of the seat. On a fourteen-player table, the seats are numbered 1 to 15; the number 13 is omitted in deference to superstitious players. The table layout also contains numbered betting spaces corresponding to the seat numbers, so each player may bet in his own space without danger of different players' bets being confused. Similarly, in front of the two dealers are small boxes that are also numbered to correspond to the players' seats. These boxes are used by the dealers to keep track of how much commission each player owes the house.

Baccarat is played with eight decks of cards dealt from a shoe. The cards are shuffled by the dealers but dealt by the players.

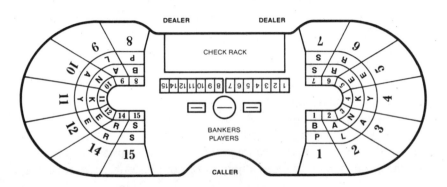

THE DEALERS

The game is conducted by three dealers. Two of these dealers are seated together at the center of the table. It is their job to collect losing wagers, pay off winning wagers, and keep a record of the commissions owed by the players in the numbered commission boxes in front of them. Each of these two dealers is responsible for half the table. One dealer takes care of bets made by the seven players seated on the left side of the table while the other dealer takes care of the bets made by the seven players on the right side of the table.

Standing on the other side of the table opposite these two dealers is the *caller*, who supervises the game, announcing the various hands, directing the players in dealing the cards, and announcing the winning hand. Seated off to the side beyond one end of the table on a high chair is the *ladder man*. He takes no active part in the game. It is his job to oversee the game and protect against irregularities in the same way the floorman does at the other table games. He is the final judge on any disputes that might develop at the table.

THE BASIC CONCEPT

Baccarat has been called blackjack for idiots. While this is an overly harsh judgment, it is true that baccarat is somewhat analogous to the game of blackjack but without any of the complexities of strategy or player options. While the underlying concept of the game is like a simplified version of blackjack, the way in which the game is conducted is more analogous to craps. There are two dealers and a caller, whose duties roughly correspond to the two dealers and stickman at craps. The dealing shoe circulates around the table from player to player in much the same way the dice do at craps. The player with the shoe can keep dealing until he deals a losing bank hand, comparable to sevening-out at craps. The two basic bets at baccarat, *bank hand* and *player hand*, correspond to the two line bets at craps, pass and don't-pass.

Regardless of the number of players at the table, there are always only two hands dealt in the game. These are called the player hand and the bank hand. These names are a holdover from the original European version of the game, in which one player takes the role of the bank and all other players bet against him. In American-style baccarat, these names have no real significance since anyone can bet on either hand. The names are just an arbitrary way of distinguishing the two hands. Each player makes a bet on either the player hand or the bank hand before any cards are dealt for that round.

Between these two hands, the one that wins is the one that comes closer to a total of 9. It is impossible to go over 9 because, in totaling the values of the cards, tens are always canceled out. Therefore, if the cards totaled 17, this would be considered a 7. If they totaled 24, this would count as 4. In adding the cards, each card counts as its numerical value, except 10s and picture cards, which count as zero. Another way of looking at this is that the cards have the same values as they do in blackjack, with the 10s and picture cards counting as ten. However, since tens are canceled out in baccarat, ten and zero are synonymous. As we shall see, 10s and picture cards do count as ten for purposes of burning cards. A couple of examples of totaling hands should clarify the process. A hand consisting of a 5 and a 3 counts as 8. A hand consisting of a 6 and a queen counts as six. A hand consisting of a 5, an 8, and a jack counts as 3. A hand consisting of a king, a 5, and a 9 counts as 4.

Initially, each hand consists of two cards. However, depending on the total, one or both hands may draw an additional card in an effort to improve the total. However, unlike in blackjack, in baccarat the players have no choice of whether to draw a card. House rules stipulate when a card must be drawn and when one cannot be drawn. In no case is more than one card ever drawn to a hand.

Once the two hands have been dealt and have received any draw they may have coming, the two totals determine the winner. Which-ever hand—player hand or bank hand—is closer to 9 wins. Players who had bet on that hand are paid off at even money and those betting on the other hand lose their wagers. If the bank hand wins, the house will charge a 5 percent *commission* on the winnings. No commission is charged on winning bets on the player hand. If both hands end up with the same total, this is considered a tie and no money changes hands. Each player keeps his original bet and is free to wager all or part of it again or to take the money back.

THE DEAL

After the cards have been shuffled by the dealers, they are offered to a player to cut, using a plastic card that he inserts into the deck at the point where he wishes it cut. A dealer then places the cards into the dealing shoe and inserts the plastic card into the deck at some point near the end of the shoe. Later, when this plastic card turns up during the deal, it will notify the dealers that the cards should again be shuffled. Finally, before beginning the first round of play, the first few cards are burned by a dealer. This is done as follows. The top card is dealt out and turned face up. The value of this card determines how many cards will be burned. For example, if the card is a 7 of spades, the 7 will be discarded along with the next seven cards. These cards are dropped into the discard slot in the table, as are all used cards as the game progresses.

The cards are dealt by the players themselves under the direction of the caller. Every player has the right to deal as long as he has a bet on either the bank hand or the player hand. Most of the time, the dealer handling the shoe bets on the bank hand because the player with the shoe in effect represents the bank and most players are psychologically uncomfortable "betting against themselves." However, the dealing player does have the choice of betting on either hand and can change his betting from one hand to the other whenever he wishes.

The dealing shoe travels counterclockwise from player to player. In other words, it travels in numerical order in accordance with the numbering of the players' seats on the layout. A player who does not wish to deal can simply pass the shoe on to the next player on his right. Once a player begins to deal, he may keep dealing as long as the bank hand continues to win. As soon as the player hand wins, the shoe passes to the next player. A player may also voluntarily surrender the shoe at the end of any hand.

The caller begins each round by announcing "Cards." This is the signal to the player with the shoe to begin dealing. He deals a hand to the caller to represent the player hand and one to himself to represent the bank hand. First he deals a card to the caller, then a card to himself, which he slips under one of the front corners of the shoe. This should be the corner away from the caller so it won't get in the way as subsequent cards are dealt. He then deals a second card to the caller and a second card to himself, which is also slipped under his previous card at the corner of the shoe. All cards are dealt face down.

The two cards dealt to the caller constitute the player hand. The caller passes this hand on to whichever player, other than the one dealing, has the largest wager on the player hand. This player turns the cards face up and tosses them back to the caller, who places them face up in front of himself and announces their value. If no one has bet on the player hand, the caller will turn the hand up himself.

The player who dealt then turns his two cards face up and tosses them to the caller. These two cards, the ones from under the corner of the shoe, represent the bank hand. The caller places these cards face up in front of himself on the spot on the layout marked BANK HAND and announces the value of the hand.

Depending on the value of the two hands, one or both of them may be entitled to one more card. If so, the caller will direct the player dealing to deal accordingly. He may announce "Card for the player," in which case the player dealing deals a card to the caller, who turns it face up, adds it to the player hand, and announces the new total. Instead, or in addition, he may announce "Card for the bank," in which case the same procedure is followed for the bank hand. The rules governing this process of drawing cards are covered in detail below.

Once both hands have been completed, the caller announces the winning hand, player or bank, and the two dealers take and pay bets accordingly. The used cards are inserted into the discard slot, and the next hand commences. If the previous round was won by the bank hand, the same player deals. If the round was won by the player hand, the deal moves to the next player on the right.

When the plastic card appears during a hand, the hand in progress is completed. Then the cards are once again shuffled by the dealers and the entire process starts again. After the shuffle, the shoe will revert back to the same player if the bank hand won the last round before the shuffle. If the player hand won the last round, the shoe moves to the next player. When a particular player keeps the shoe for a long time until finally the plastic card appears, this is known as *running the shoe.*

DRAWING CARDS

As mentioned earlier, the players have no discretion as to whether or not a card will be drawn to either hand. This is spelled out by the rules of the game. Sometimes a hand must stand pat; other times it must receive an additional card. In no case is more than one card ever drawn to a single hand. The rules that govern when a card is to be drawn to either the player hand or the bank hand are uniform from casino to casino and are printed on cards available to the players at the table. On these cards the rules are given in the form of the following chart:

Player Rules

HAVING
1–2–3–4–5–10	DRAWS A CARD
6–7	STANDS
8–9	NATURAL. Bank cannot draw.

Bank Rules

HAVING	DRAWS WHEN GIVING	DOES NOT DRAW WHEN GIVING
3	1–2–3–4–5–6–7–9–10	8
4	2–3–4–5–6–7	1–8–9–10
5	4–5–6–7	1–2–3–8–9–10
6	6–7	1–2–3–4–5–8–9–10
7	STANDS	
8–9	NATURAL. Player cannot draw.	

This chart requires a little explaining. The first thing to note is that a hand consisting of a total of 8 or 9 on its initial two cards is termed a *natural*. When either the player hand or the bank hand receives a natural, neither hand may draw a card; the natural wins automatically. If both hands have naturals, the higher natural wins; a 9 beats an 8. If both hands have totals of 8 or totals of 9, the hand is a tie.

Assuming neither hand consists of a natural, the first determination to be made is whether the player hand draws a card. The drawing rules for the player hand are simple. Any total other than 6, 7, 8, or 9 draws a card. If the player hand does not draw, the bank hand is governed by the same rules as the player hand. No card will be drawn if the total is 6, 7, 8, or 9. In any other case, a card will be drawn. This last point is not stated in the table of rules but is universally followed.

If the player hand does draw a card, the rules governing whether a card will be drawn to the bank hand become a little more complex, because the decision rests both on what total the bank hand has and on what card the player hand has drawn. These rules are listed in the chart above under "Bank Rules." A couple of examples should clarify how to read the chart. If the bank hand has a total of 3 and the player hand has drawn any card except an 8, the bank hand must draw a card. By contrast, if the bank hand totals 6, it will draw only if the card drawn by the player hand was a 6 or a 7. If the card to the player hand was any other value, the bank hand must stand. Another point that is not mentioned in the printed rules is that the bank hand always draws when holding a total of 0, 1, or 2, unless the player hand has a natural. Incidentally, we have already seen that in baccarat 0 and 10 are synonymous. That is why on some rule cards you will see references to the value 10, while on others the same section will refer to 0.

The decision whether or not to draw a card to the bank hand depends entirely on the value of the card drawn to the player hand, not on the value of the player hand itself. This can create some unusual and, for bank-hand bettors, agonizing situations. It will sometimes happen that, after the player hand has drawn a card, the bank hand will already have a better total than the player hand, yet it will still have to draw a card according to the rules of the game. In drawing a card, the bank hand may end up with a poorer total and lose to the player hand. This is analogous to the situation a blackjack dealer in a face-up game finds himself in when he turns up a 16 and must draw a card even if his 16 is good enough to beat every player's hand. He realizes that in drawing a card he may bust and lose to hands that he already had beaten, but he has no choice.

The reason for this paradoxical situation in baccarat is historical. In the original French version of the game, the player handling the player hand did not have to show his original two cards until the end of the hand. While these two cards remained hidden, the draw card was dealt face up. In deciding whether to draw a card, the banker had to make his decision based purely on the value of the player's visible draw card and on speculation as to what the player's two face-down cards might consist of. What developed was an optimal strategy based on the value of the banker's hand and the player's draw card. This is similar to basic strategy at blackjack in which the player makes his decision as to whether to stand or hit based on the value of his hand and the dealer's up-card. The bank-hand drawing rules followed in American baccarat consist of that optimal strategy. Although the player's hand is no longer hidden, the same rules are enforced. Just as a blackjack player might sometimes want to vary from basic strategy if he happened to catch sight of the dealer's hole card, the baccarat player handling the bank hand might want to vary from his drawing rules because he can see the entire player's hand. Nevertheless, he must, in effect, pretend that his opponent's first two cards are hidden.

There is no need to memorize the rules governing drawing cards since the caller has memorized them and will instruct you as to whether to deal an additional card to either hand. In fact, most baccarat players don't have the rules completely memorized and just do what the caller tells them to. However, I think you will find it enhances your enjoyment of the game if you do learn them so you can follow along more easily. If you review them from time to time before playing, you will find that they will soon be committed to memory.

BETS AND PAYOFFS

All bets at baccarat must be made before any cards are dealt. If the player wishes to bet on the player hand, he placed his wager in the space in front of him marked PLAYERS. If he wishes to bet on the bank hand, he bets in the space beyond that one, which is marked either BANK or BANKERS. These spaces are subdivided and numbered to correspond to the players' seating positions in order to identify each player's bet. Sometimes the section for player bets is not subdivided. In that case, the player places the wager in the portion of the betting space that is directly in front of him.

The standard table limits at baccarat are twenty dollars to two thousand dollars. The use of twenty dollars as a minimum bet rather than the twenty-five dollars used at most other games is unusual but results from the history of baccarat in this country. When the game was first introduced in Nevada, it was played with cash rather than chips. This was part of the effort by the casinos to imbue the game with an atmosphere of glamour and wealth. The large sums of currency regularly changing hands were one of the appeals of the game. Unlike casino chips, U.S. currency does not come in twenty-five-dollar denominations, but it does come in twenty-dollar bills. Hence, it was more convenient to make twenty dollars the minimum bet.

The Nevada Gaming Commission eventually forced the casinos to switch from using currency to using chips in order to permit tighter accounting procedures. Chips are also used in Atlantic City. However, the twenty-dollar minimums remained, partly because it is more convenient to charge a 5 percent commission out of twenty dollars—a round one-dollar charge—than it is out of twenty-five dollars, which comes to a cumbersome dollar twenty-five. Some smaller casinos have five-dollar minimums. In line with the typical pattern in Atlantic City, the table minimum there is usually higher than in Nevada, most commonly forty dollars or some other multiple of twenty dollars.

In American baccarat, the house books all bets. Players do not bet against each other as in the European version of the game; they bet against the casino. Naturally, the casino is not going to cover any bets unless it has the advantage on the wager. This happens automatically when people bet on the player hand, because the player hand will win slightly less than half the time. Since the house pays even money, it is guaranteed a long-term profit. Since the bank hand wins slightly more than half the time, the casino could not show a profit if it paid this bet off at even money. The technique it uses to solve this problem is to charge a 5 percent commission on all winning bank-hand bets. In effect, it pays ninety-five cents for every dollar bet on the bank hand rather than paying dollar for dollar.

Counting out payoffs in ninety-five-cent sums can become quite cumbersome, so the house uses a simple bookkeeping process to simplify matters. In front of the two seated dealers on the layout is a small row of numbered boxes. Each box corresponds to one of the seat numbers. Every time a player wins a bank-hand bet, he is paid at even money, but a record is made of the amount of commission money the player owes the house. If the player in seat number 8 wins a one-hundred-dollar bet, the dealer will place a five-dollar commission marker—a flat button bearing the words FIVE DOLLARS on it—in the small box marked number 8. At any given moment, these numbered boxes provide the house with a record of how much commission each player owes the casino.

The more the player wins on bank-hand bets, the more his commissions mount up. These commissions give the house its edge on this bet and are a particularly clear example of the point made in Chapter II, that the house makes its profit every time you win a bet, not when you lose a bet. Of course, if a player has a lucky streak and wins more hands than probability dictates, he will show a profit. But if he wins exactly the number of hands dictated by the laws of probability, it is the house that will end up ahead, not the player, due to the 5 percent commission.

The casino can demand payment of these commissions due at any time it wishes. In practice, commissions are collected at the end of each shoe while the cards are being shuffled. If a player leaves the game before the shoe is finished, he must pay his commissions before leaving.

The Mathematics

HOUSE PERCENTAGES

If both the player hand and bank hand followed the same rules to determine whether or not an additional card is to be drawn, baccarat would be an even game with no advantage on either side. It would be no different from flipping a coin and betting on either heads or tails. However, because the rules for drawing to the bank hand are slightly more advantageous than those for drawing to the player hand, the bank hand will win slightly more often than the player hand. Determining the exact percentage against the player hand is a complex process that involves isolating each of the differences in drawing rules and determining the impact it has on each hand's chances of winning. The calculation reveals that the player hand wins 49.32 percent of the time and the bank wins 50.68 percent of the time. If you subtract the first figure from the second, you will find that the player hand faces a 1.36 percent disadvantage. Since player-hand bets are booked by the house, when someone bets on the player hand, he is giving the casino a 1.36 percent edge.

We have already seen that when someone bets on the bank hand, the casino gives itself an edge by charging a 5 percent commission on any winnings paid on the bet. Don't make the very common mistake of assuming that this means that the house has a 5 percent edge on the bet. First, you must keep in mind that the 5 percent is charged only on winnings. It is not charged on the wager itself, like the 5 percent charge the house makes on buy bets at craps. This, in effect, means that the 5 percent is only charged on half the money involved in the transaction. This cuts the casino edge in half, from 5 percent to only 2.5 percent.

However, even this figure does not tell the whole story. You must remember that, without the commission charge, the bank hand would enjoy an advantage of 1.36 percent over the player hand. This figure has to be subtracted from the 2.5 percent cut the house is giving itself to arrive at a net house advantage of 1.14 percent. This figure is very close to the actual house percentage, but one more adjustment has to be made. In converting the 5 percent commission to a 2.5 percent edge, we assumed that the bank hand would win half the time. Yet we have already seen that it wins very slightly more than half the time due to the difference in drawing rules. This means that the 5 percent commission is charged very slightly more than half the time, increasing the house edge very slightly. When this factor is taken into account, we find that, instead of 1.14 percent, the casino ends up with an advantage on the bank-hand bet of 1.17 percent.

This can be calculated as follows. The bank-hand bettor wins 50.68 hands out of every one hundred played but receives only 95 cents for each dollar bet. Therefore, the gross profit from one hundred one-dollar wagers would be 50.68 × $.95 = $48.15. Since the bank-hand bettor loses 49.32 hands out of every one hundred played, the gross loss for one hundred one-dollar wagers is $49.32. If you subtract the profit of $48.15 from the loss of $49.32, you arrive at 1.17, which is the house P.C. on the bank-hand bet.

A disadvantage of 1.17 percent on the bank hand and 1.36 percent on the player hand makes baccarat one of the best games for the player to be found in the casino. It is a smaller percentage than that faced at line bets and 6 and 8 place bets at craps, far smaller than the edge at all other craps wagers and all wagers at roulette. Only pass-line craps bets with full odds and blackjack with proper strategy offer the player a better break than baccarat.

Although the bank hand retains a very slight edge over the player hand, the two figures are so close that for all practical purposes it can be considered that the two bets offer virtually identical chances of winning. So if a baccarat player asks, "Which hand should I bet on, player or bank?" the answer is, "It doesn't much matter." One may as well ask whether it is better to bet heads or tails when flipping a coin.

Baccarat is a game of pure chance. There is no element of strategy either in the play of the hands, which is dictated by the rules, or in deciding which hand to bet on. This is one situation in which you can safely rely on hunches, ESP, the I Ching, or any other arcane system you wish for deciding on which hand to bet next. I don't for a moment think these techniques will help you win, but they won't hurt either. As long as you don't make the mistake of thinking that your particular method of determining which hand to bet on offers an unbeatable system—a delusion that might lead you to wager money you can't afford to lose—there will be no harm done. Follow any whim you wish in deciding whether to place your money on the player hand or on the bank hand, because it is bound to be as good as any other method of deciding.

The opposite side of the card that the casino provides that lists the drawing rules for player and bank hands is a scorecard designed for the player to keep track of whether player or bank hand wins each round. This is for those players who like to look for trends or believe that eventually the wins and losses on the two hands have to even up. We have already discussed the fallacy of the maturity of chances enough for you to realize how silly this kind of scorekeeping is. It is true that, strictly speaking, baccarat is not a completely independent-trials process because, as the game proceeds, the shoe becomes depleted of different value cards at different rates. Therefore, there is a sense in which what happened on previous hands can have an impact on what happens on subsequent hands. However, which hands have won earlier in the shoe, player or banker, does not act as any kind of an indicator of what is happening to the composition of the cards remaining in the shoe. In other words, previous hands have no predictive value for subsequent wins. Personally, I think following your hunches on what hand will win next is better than trying to detect any pattern from a scorecard. Both methods are equally unreliable, but at least the hunch method is less tedious and more fun when it does work.

CARD COUNTING

Mention of card depletion at baccarat might lead you to wonder whether a card-counting system like those used at blackjack could be developed for beating the game of baccarat. Just about every serious blackjack card counter has wondered the same thing at one time or another. Several of the world's leading blackjack theoreticians have investigated the possibility. All have concluded that it can't be done. In fact, no less an authority than Dr. Edward Thorp, the man who revolutionized blackjack play through the introduction of card counting, has stated unequivocally that it is impossible to develop a card-counting system for the player and bank hands at baccarat that would give the bettor an edge.

A couple of years ago, two authors wrote a book that did purport to offer a card-counting strategy for baccarat. Unfortunately, unlike card counting at blackjack, this system did not give the player an edge over the house. It only cut the house edge slightly. Considering the great amount of work required to keep the count during the game, most gamblers concluded that it was not worth the trouble.

Mini-Baccarat

When baccarat was first introduced in Nevada, the casinos did everything they could to surround the game with an aura of wealth and luxury in the hope of attracting high rollers. They proved highly successful in that goal. Then they started worrying about all the grind action they might be missing out on from small bettors who were potential baccarat players but couldn't handle the high table limits. Similarly, those casinos that catered to small bettors were interested in making the game available to their clientele. The answer they eventually settled on was mini-baccarat. Mini-baccarat was first introduced at the Silver Slipper Casino in Las Vegas in 1974. Today it can be found in a number of casinos in Nevada and Atlantic City.

Mini-baccarat is the game of baccarat with all the fancy trappings stripped away. It is played on a table that resembles a blackjack table. In fact, the similarity is so close that players often mistake mini-baccarat tables for blackjack tables. Like a blackjack table, it seats seven players. In front of the players' seats are betting spots like those found on blackjack tables. However, in this case there are two spots in front of each player. One is marked for bets on the player hand; the other one is for bank-hand bets.

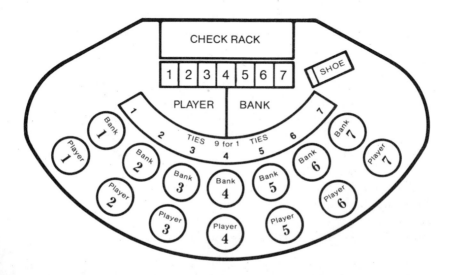

As in blackjack, the game is conducted by a single dealer who stands behind the table. The dealer is the only person to touch the cards. He deals them from a shoe at his left, dealing the player hand to the spot marked PLAYER on the layout at his right and the bank hand to the spot marked BANK on the layout at his left. All the cards are dealt face up. After the initial hands have been dealt, the dealer draws cards as required to each hand, following the same rules as for regular baccarat. In fact, all the rules for mini-baccarat are identical to those for regular baccarat. Only the style of dealing differs—that and the table limits, which are always either a five-dollar or two-dollar minimum and a five-hundred-dollar maximum.

When playing off bank-hand bets, the dealer records the 5 percent commission due the house in the small numbered boxes on the layout in front of the check rack. Because of the lower minimums, a good supply of small change is kept at the table both for recording the commissions and for making change for players when they pay the commissions at the end of each shoe. The commission on a five-dollar bet is a quarter, while on a two-dollar bet the commission is a dime.

Since the rules for standing and drawing at mini-baccarat are the same as at the regular game and since the same 5 percent commission is charged on bank-hand winnings, the house P.C. remains the same as at the original game. What does change is the tempo of the game. Many more hands can be dealt per hour at mini-baccarat than at regular baccarat because of eliminating the time-wasting procedure of having the players handle the cards. This means that the house percentage, although still small, gets to act on your money more often.

Mini-baccarat is a good training ground for anyone who wants to try his hand at baccarat but wants to familiarize himself with the game before tackling the big table with its big bets. It is also a good game for anyone who is attracted to blackjack but doesn't want to put in the effort to learn basic blackjack strategy.

If you enjoy gambling but can't be bothered with learning strategy and don't want to take a chance on making any embarrassing errors, then baccarat is the game for you. It is a game that offers glamour, excellent odds, and almost no room for either brilliant maneuvers or dumb mistakes.

VII. Roulette

♣ Roulette has never attained the kind of popularity in this country that it enjoys in Europe, where it is the number-one casino game. Since the house edge at roulette is quite high, I cannot recommend this game for serious gambling. Yet it does have its virtues. It can provide an enjoyable and relaxing evening of gambling for those who find the other table games too hectic. There is certainly no harm in this as long as bets are kept low to minimize losses. Fortunately, most roulette games in this country do have low table minimums.

Although the game looks complicated to the beginner, it is actually very easily mastered. In all, there are eleven different types of bets that can be made on a roulette layout. You can bet on the numbers in groups of one, two, three, four, five, six, twelve, or eighteen. This variety is more apparent than real. Unlike craps, all the wagers work pretty much the same way, all except one face the same house edge, and every bet is decided on each spin of the wheel.

There are two different versions of roulette, the American style and the European style—which uses a different wheel and a different way of dealing the game. I will first teach you the American form of the game, which is played in Nevada, Atlantic City, and the Caribbean. Then I will explain the differences you can expect to encounter if you should find yourself in a casino overseas. If you want to learn how to play roulette, study the material in this chapter, and I guarantee that within a few minutes of sitting down at the table for the first time, you will be playing as well as the most seasoned veteran.

Equipment and Personnel

THE WHEEL

Roulette is played at a large table surrounded by chairs for the players. The wheel, which is inset at one end of the table, is about three feet in diameter. The outer stationary frame is called the *backtrack*. This contains the groove in which the ball is spun. Sloping inward and downward from the backtrack is the *bottom track*, down which the ball slides in reaching the numbers. This bottom track is studded with eight brass barriers spaced at equal distances, alternately vertical and horizontal, to help give the ball a random bounce as it descends. The central portion of the wheel, called the *wheel head*, is the only part that actually spins. It contains thirty-eight numbered slots: the numbers 1 to 36, half of which are in red slots and half in black, and the numbers 0 and 00, in green slots.

At first glance, the order of the numbers on the roulette wheel seems random. Actually, it represents an attempt to distribute low, high, red, black, even, and odd numbers in as balanced a fashion as possible. The 0 and 00 are directly opposite each other, with eighteen numbers on each side. The colors alternate. Directly across from each odd number is the next higher even number. (One is opposite 2, 3 is opposite 4, and so on.) Pairs of odd numbers alternate with pairs of even numbers, with exceptions occurring just before the 0 and 00. Thus, numbers that are near each other on the layout and might be covered by a single bet are actually far apart on the wheel.

The wheel is spun counterclockwise and the ball is spun clockwise in the backtrack. As it loses momentum, the ball begins to descend along the bottom track, and it eventually settles into one of the numbered slots of the wheel head.

One of the most persistent myths in gambling is the belief that some croupiers, through years of experience, have learned how to control the spins of the wheel and ball so as to cause certain numbers to win or prevent certain numbers from winning. Everyone seems to have a friend whose cousin has a friend who knows someone who is a croupier and can do this.

In a lifetime of involvement with gambling, I have never encountered a dealer who could exert the slightest control over the winning number when using a regulation wheel and spinning it in the manner required by legitimate casinos. I have never even met anyone in the gambling field who has ever seen it done or who even has a friend whose cousin has a friend who knows someone who can do it. This is one fantasy that is limited strictly to laymen who don't know the gambling business.

Admittedly, just about every break-in roulette dealer goes through a period in which he tries to see if he can learn to control the wheel. It helps break the boredom on those long shifts. But they all discover before long that it can't be done. The fact that the ball and the wheel are traveling in opposite directions at two different speeds, combined with the metal obstacles in the bottom track and the balanced distribution of the numbers on the wheel, makes it impossible for anyone to exert any influence over what number wins.

THE CHIPS

Although roulette may be bet with standard casino chips, each roulette table also sells special chips that are different from the casino's regular chips. These roulette chips, also known as *wheel chips*, come in six different colors. They are always sold in groups of twenty, called *stacks*. You can buy roulette chips either with cash or with regular casino chips.

When you purchase your chips, you are assigned a color that no other player may use until you leave the game. This system is designed to avoid uncertainty over the ownership of bets. At a crowded table with chips piled all over the layout, it would be easy for confusion to arise over whose bet was whose when payoff time came.

Roulette chips have no monetary value printed on them. When you purchase them, you must tell the croupier what you wish to have your chips valued at. This may be any amount from the table minimum to the table maximum.

The croupier records the value of your chips by placing a coin or a numbered marker button on top of a corresponding color chip on the rim of the wheel. If you buy your chips for the table minimum, the dealer will not bother to mark the value.

The only record of what your roulette chips are worth is at the table at which you are playing. That is why players are not allowed to leave the roulette table with wheel chips in their possession. If you should start to do so, the croupier will stop you. This is for your own good. If you were to attempt to cash in these chips at the cashier's cage, they would have no idea how much money you were entitled to. The croupier will convert your wheel chips to regular casino chips when you finish playing. Remember, if you should accidentally leave the table unnoticed with your chips, the casino will refuse to redeem them for cash. Those wheel chips can make expensive souvenirs.

THE LAYOUT

The roulette layout lists all thirty-eight numbers that appear on the wheel. These are listed in numerical order, with the 0 and 00 side by side on top and the remaining thirty-six numbers appearing in twelve rows of three, creating three columns of numbers. The numbers appear on the layout in the same color as they appear on the wheel; the numbers are equally divided between red and black except for the 0 and 00, which are green. In addition, there is a series of boxes on one side of the numbers and at one end to accommodate specific wagers.

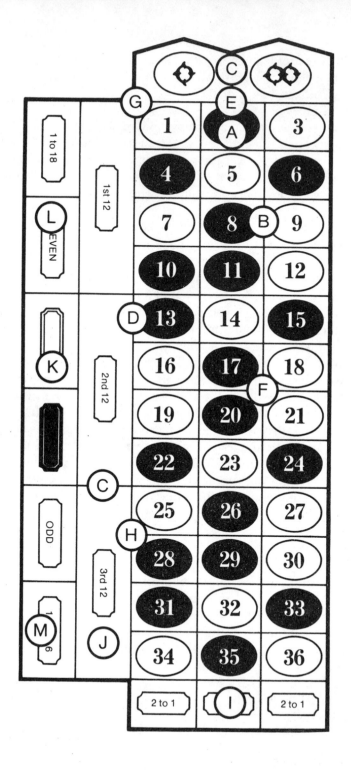

THE DEALERS

In this country, roulette is usually conducted by one dealer, although at a busy table a second dealer will be assigned to help. In casino parlance, the primary dealer is called the *wheel roller*, while his assistant is called the *check racker*. The wheel roller conducts the entire game, selling chips to players, spinning the wheel and the ball, announcing the winning number, and taking and paying bets. The check racker assists by counting out chips for the payoffs and sorting the losing chips by color into stacks of twenty.

In this country, most roulette dealers are blackjack dealers who double on *the wheel*. The roulette wheel is most often found in the blackjack pit, sealing off one of the ends. In Europe, where roulette is a much bigger game, the roulette croupiers are specialists in that game.

Wagers

If you are going to play roulette, it is vital that you familiarize yourself with the various bets available at the game and particularly with the correct payoff on each one. Dealers do make errors on these payoffs from time to time. If you don't know how much you have coming to you, you have no way of protecting yourself in such a situation. It is also extremely important that you understand the correct way to make each bet on the layout. A placement of your chips an inch off from where they should have been can mean that you end up making a wager completely different from the one you intended.

Roulette wagers are divided into two broad categories: *inside bets* and *outside bets*. The inside bets are those that are made on the numbered central portion of the layout. Every time you wager on a single number or on a combination of two, three, four, five, or six numbers, you are making an inside bet.

The outside bets are those that are made in the boxes on the periphery of the layout. These wagers can be further subdivided into those that pay 2 to 1 odds and those that pay even money. All outside bets lose whenever 0 or 00 comes up.

INSIDE BETS

The Straight-Up Bet This is a wager that one of the thirty-eight possible numbers on the wheel will come up on the next spin. It pays

35 to 1. This bet is made by placing one's chips directly on a particular number. The 0 and 00 may be bet just like any of the other numbers. In the layout illustration, A is a wager that number 2 will win.

The Split Bet   This is a wager that either of two numbers will come up on the next spin. It pays 17 to 1. This bet is made by placing one's chips on the line separating any two adjoining numbers. In the layout illustration, B is a wager that either 8 or 9 will win.

Zero and double zero can also be wagered as a split bet. This is the only wager that can be made at two completely different points on the layout. It can be bet by placing one's chips so they overlap the two numbers. However, as a convenience to players who are sitting too far to reach that point, it can also be wagered by placing one's chips on the line separating the second twelve box from the third twelve box. In the layout illustration, the two bets marked C are both split bets on 0 and 00.

The Street Bet   This is a wager that one of three numbers will come up on the next spin. It pays 11 to 1. This bet is made by placing one's chips on the outside border of the numbers at the end of the row of three numbers one wishes to bet on. In the layout illustration, D represents a bet that either 13, 14, or 15 will win.

There are three different three-number bets that include 0 and/or 00. These are the bets on 0–1–2, on 0–00–2, and on 00–2–3. These wagers are made by placing one's chips so they overlap all three desired numbers. In the layout illustration, E represents a wager on numbers 0, 00, and 2.

The Corner Bet   This is a wager that any of four numbers will come up on the next spin. The bet pays 8 to 1. One may only make a corner bet on four numbers that are in a square formation. For that reason the wager is also called a *square bet*. It is also known as a *quarter bet*. The bet is made by placing one's chips at the point where the corners of all four numbers meet. In the layout illustration, F represents a wager that either 17, 18, 20, or 21 will win.

The Five-Number Bet   Also known as the *house special*, this wager is unique in roulette for two reasons. First, there is only one five-number bet that can be made. This is a wager on 0, 00, 1, 2, and 3. The second reason why the five-number bet is unique is that it is the worst wager in the game. Unlike all other roulette bets that face an identical house percentage, the five-number bet, with its 6 to 1 payoff, gives the house an edge that is fifty percent higher.

The five-number bet is made by placing one's chips at the corner where the line separating the 0 from the number 3 meets the outer border of the numbered section of the layout. In the layout illustration, G is a wager on the house special. However, this is one roulette wager that should never be made by a knowledgeable player.

The Line Bet   This is a wager that one of six different numbers will come up on the next spin. It pays 5 to 1. This bet is made by placing one's chips on the outside border of the numbers at the point where it is intercepted by one of the lines separating two rows of numbers. These two rows of three numbers each are the numbers on which the player is betting. In the layout illustration, H represents a wager that either 25, 26, 27, 28, 29, or 30 will win.

OUTSIDE BETS

The Column Bet   This is a wager that one of the twelve numbers the player is betting on will come up on the next spin. It pays 2 to 1. There are three different columns the player may bet on. The bet is made by placing one's chips in the box marked 2 TO 1 at the base of the column one wishes to bet on. In the layout illustration, I is a wager on the middle column. It will win if any of the following numbers comes up: 2, 5, 8, 11, 14, 17, 20, 23, 26, 29, 32, or 35. Numbers 0 and 00 are not considered part of the three columns.

The Dozen Bet   This is a wager that one of twelve consecutive numbers will come up on the next spin. Like the column bet, it also pays 2 to 1. There are three different dozen bets one may make: numbers 1 to 12, called the first twelve; numbers 13 to 24, called the second twelve; and numbers 25 to 36, called the third twelve. The bet is made by placing one's chips in the box at the side of the layout that parallels the twelve numbers one wishes to bet on. In the layout illustration, J is a wager that any one of the numbers 25 to 36 will win.

Red and Black Bets   This is a wager that a number of a particular color, either red or black, will win. The bet pays even money. It is made by placing one's chips in the box at the side of the layout that is marked with the appropriate color. In the layout illustration, K is a wager that the winning number will be a red one.

The red or black bet is one of three wagers at roulette that pays even money. Because each of these even-money bets loses if either of the green numbers (0 and 00) comes up, they each give the player eighteen ways to win and twenty ways to lose. The Atlantic City casinos offer a feature on the even-money bets that cuts the players' losses in half. This will be discussed in the next section under the heading En Prison.

Odd and Even Bets   This is a wager that one of the eighteen odd numbers (or one of the eighteen even numbers) will come up on the next spin. This bet also pays even money. The wager is made by placing one's chips in the appropriately marked box at the side of the layout. In the layout illustration, L is a bet that the winning number will be an even one.

1 to 18 and 19 to 36 Bets   This is a wager that one of the eighteen low numbers (or one of the eighteen high numbers) will come up on the next spin. It is the last of the three even-money bets at roulette. The wager is made by placing one's chips in the appropriately marked box at the side of the layout at either end. In the layout illustration, M is a bet that the winning number will be a high one (from 19 to 36).

Play

BETTING

As mentioned earlier, roulette can be bet either with standard casino chips or special wheel chips. Aside from avoiding confusion, another advantage of using wheel chips is that the lowest denomination of wheel chips is usually less than the lowest denomination of casino chips. With its high house edge, roulette is a game to be played for fun, not profit. So you may as well play as cheaply as you can. The most common minimum for wheel chips is twenty-five cents, but you will find games with ten-cent denomination chips and also games with higher minimums, particularly in Atlantic City.

You may begin making bets on the layout as soon as the bets from the previous spin have been collected and paid off. If you cannot reach the part of the layout on which you wish to wager, slide your chips over to the dealer and tell him what bet you want to make. He will position the bet for you. The dealer will roll the wheel in one direction, then spin the ball on the backtrack in the opposite direction. It takes the ball a little while to lose momentum sufficiently to start its descent toward the numbered bowl. You can continue betting until the ball begins to descend and the dealer calls "No more bets." If you make a bet too late, it will simply be returned to you whether the bet wins or loses.

As soon as the ball lands in a numbered slot, the dealer will announce the winning number and point to it on the layout. He may also mark it on the layout by placing a transparent plastic tube on the number. He will then gather in all the losing bets and, finally, pay off the winning bets. The outside bets are paid off first, then the inside bets. The dealer pays off the outside bets in the boxes in which they were made. He will then calculate the total payoff for all of a player's winning inside bets—for example, a player may have both a straight bet and a street bet that covered the winning number—and place the sum of his winnings in front of him. However, the winning bets themselves are left on the layout. It is the player's job to collect these bets from the layout, as well as the payoffs from any winning outside bets, before the dealer calls "No more bets" again. Otherwise, they will count as wagers on the next spin.

Each player is paid off in the same kind of wheel chips he is using to wager with. In cases of a large win, the dealer may use regular casino chips for the payoff since he has only a limited number of wheel chips for each player.

MINIMUMS

There are two kinds of table minimums at roulette, a chip minimum and a table minimum. The chip minimum is the lowest amount at which you can value each chip. The table minimum, which is always higher than the chip minimum, is the lowest amount you can wager. With a twenty-five-cent chip minimum, the usual betting minimum is one dollar. This minimum works differently for the outside bets from how it works for the inside bets. For the outside bets, the table minimum is the lowest amount you can wager on any one bet.

However, for the inside bets, the table minimum is the lowest aggregate amount you can have wagered. If the table minimum is one dollar, the total of all your inside bets must be at least one dollar, but each individual bet need not be one dollar. You may, for example, make two different straight bets for twenty-five cents each plus one line bet for fifty cents. If the minimums are not posted at the table or if you are unsure how to interpret them, ask the dealer before you begin to play.

The Odds

THE HOUSE PERCENTAGE

The house percentage on any roulette wager is very easy to figure. Let's take the straight-up bet as an example. You are wagering on one number out of thirty-eight possibilities, so the correct odds are 37 to 1. The house pays 35 to 1. Therefore, two units are being held out of the pot by the house. This means that the house advantage is 2/38, which, when converted to a percentage, yields 5.26 percent as the house edge. In plain terms, you can expect to lose two dollars out of every thirty-eight dollars you bet.

Let's try the split bet. This time you are covering two numbers out of 38 for true odds of 36 to 2. The house pays 17 to 1, which is the same as 34 to 2. The casino's profit margin is two units out of 38, which we have already figured out is 2/38 or 5.26 percent. In fact, although there are eleven different wagers offered at roulette, you do not have to remember eleven different house percentages. The house advantages for straight-up, split, line, corner, street, column, dozen, red/black, odd/even, and high/low bets are all 5.26 percent. You can easily check this for yourself using the same process I applied in the above two examples.

There is also another simple way to calculate the house edge at roulette. Simply figure out what your net loss would be if you made a particular bet thirty-eight times in a row and each of the thirty-eight possible results came up once. For example, assume that you made a line bet on numbers 1, 2, and 3 thirty-eight times and that each number came up once. (This is exactly what you can expect will happen in the long run.) Let's further assume that each bet consisted of one chip, for a total investment of thirty-eight chips. The number

1 would come up once, giving you a profit of eleven units plus returning your original one-chip bet. Number 2 would come up once for another return of twelve units. The one time number 3 came up would give you another twelve units. All your other bets would lose. In the end you would have thirty-six chips left after having wagered thirty-eight chips, for a net loss of two chips. By now, I don't have to tell you that the loss of those two chips means 2/38 or 5.26 percent.

This percentage—5.26 percent—is a pretty bad edge to have to buck. It is more than five times as high as what you will face at either blackjack or craps if you play the way I've taught you. And there is no getting away from it, because it is everywhere on the layout. In fact, there is only one wager you can make at roulette that does not face this 5.26 percent bite. That is the five-number bet. Don't get your hopes up. This one is even worse. The house percentage is a huge 7.89 percent. You will lose your money 50 percent faster on this wager than on any other roulette wager. Instead of losing two dollars out of every thirty-eight, you will lose three dollars out of every thirty-eight dollars wagered on the five-number bet. To make a five-number bet at roulette is to prove that you know nothing about the game. The best thing you can do is to forget that this bet even exists.

ZERO AND DOUBLE ZERO

The American-style roulette wheel contains the numbers 1 through 36 in red and black plus 0 and 00 in green. If the zeros did not exist, a player betting on red would have just as much chance of winning as the casino since half the numbers are red and half black. The same would hold true for anyone betting on odd or even, high or low. The reason the house makes a profit on all these wagers is that they all automatically lose whenever 0 or 00 comes up. It is also true that if the zeros were eliminated, there would be no house advantage on the inside bets, assuming the payoff odds remained unchanged. For example, the 35 to 1 payoff on a single-number bet would reflect the player's actual chances of winning. On the column and dozen bets, the 2 to 1 payoff would accurately reflect the 24 to 12 odds the bettor faced. If the house eliminated the 0 and 00 from the wheel and maintained the same payoffs, it would be paying true odds. Only the five-number bet would still give the house an edge.

Many players have heard that the reason the house wins at roulette is the presence of the 0 and 00. Unfortunately, most of them don't really understand what that means. Some feel that by betting on 0 and 00, they are somehow betting with the house and have a better chance of winning. There are four different ways you can cover the 0 and 00: by making straight bets on them, by making a split bet on them, by making a three-number bet on 0, 00, and 2, or by making a five-number bet. None of these wagers offer any advantage over the other bets you could make at roulette. For example, since there are thirty-eight possible outcomes on each spin of the wheel, the true odds on a split bet on 0 or 00 are 18 to 1. The casino pays only 17 to 1, which still gives them a 5.26 percent edge.

Sometimes a player making an even-money bet such as wagering on red will try to use the 0 and 00 split as an insurance bet. This is also futile. The player's losses on the split bet will whittle away at his profits when red is hitting, while his losses on red will cut into his profits when the zeros come up. Finally, his losses will be greater when black comes up since both bets will go down the drain. Every single wager at roulette has a negative expectation for the player, including those on 0 and 00. Any way you look at it, two negatives don't add up to a positive.

Variations

THE SINGLE-ZERO WHEEL

Many roulette players are under the misconception that the double-zero roulette wheel is an American innovation. Actually, the wheel used in this country is the original European wheel, complete with 0 and 00. In 1840, when gambling entrepreneur Francois Blanc opened a gambling casino at Hesse-Homburg in Germany, he realized that he would need some gimmick to attract players. He eliminated the 00 from the wheel in hopes of luring customers because of the better odds so created. Because the removal of the 00 resulted in two red numbers side by side, the order of the numbers was also changed. The ploy was so successful that the single-zero wheel eventually became standard throughout Europe. This type of wheel has come to be known as the *French wheel*. Today, this style of wheel is used in virtually every casino in the world except those in the United States and the Caribbean.

Since the payoff odds on the various bets are the same in Europe as in this country, use of a wheel with only thirty-seven slots rather than thirty-eight cuts the player's disadvantage almost in half. On a straight-up bet, the house pays 35 to 1, while the true odds are 36 to 1. The player loses only one out of every thirty-seven dollars wagered instead of two out of every thirty-eight. That 1/37 edge means a house advantage of only 2.70 percent instead of the 5.26 percent you face in Las Vegas. The elimination of the 00 also means there is no five-number bet on the European layout. Since this is the worst bet in the game, European players are getting another break since even an ignorant player can't hurt himself by making this bet.

Many writers on gambling have suggested that the reason that roulette has never really caught on in this country as opposed to its great popularity in Europe is that the house edge against the player is so much higher here than on the French wheel. They usually end by recommending that the Nevada and Atlantic City casinos switch to the single-zero wheel to stimulate more play.

I wish I could believe that gamblers are really that perceptive about recognizing their own advantage. Unfortunately, I can't agree with this analysis. From time to time, some Las Vegas casino will experiment with introducing single-zero wheels. They usually eliminate them after discovering that they are no more popular than their previous wheels. The house is not going to give up part of its edge without getting something in return. Several years ago, one casino opened a roulette table with a single-zero wheel right next to another table with an American double-zero wheel. They eventually closed down the French wheel after finding that both tables got equal play.

At present, the Las Vegas Hilton is offering single-zero roulette. In northern Nevada, both the Cal-Neva Club and the Nevada Club have single-zero wheels. If you enjoy playing roulette, it would be worth your while to patronize these casinos when in the area.

Nevertheless, I don't think these clubs are going to spark any great growth in player interest in the game. I think the real reason why roulette gets little action in this country is that it is a slow, relaxing game. Americans seem to want excitement from their gambling rather than relaxation. A single-zero wheel is not going to change that.

EN PRISON

The overseas gambling houses give their bettors another break in addition to the single-zero wheel. When the ball lands on 0, those players betting on the even-money wagers (red/black, odd/even, 1–18/19–36) do not lose their bets, as they would in this country. Instead, they lose only half the wager. Alternatively, the bet may be held *en prison* (in prison) until the next spin of the wheel. The wager is moved by the dealer onto the outside line of the betting space to distinguish it from the new bets. If the bet should lose on the next spin, the house collects it. However, if the bet wins on this next spin, it is returned to the player. He does not receive a payoff on the bet, but he gets a reprieve from his loss.

Both of these variations have the same effect. The player betting on even-money wagers loses only half as much when 0 comes up. This has the effect of cutting the house edge—already lower than in the American game—in half. Instead of a 2.70 percent edge, the player making any of the three even-money bets faces only a very reasonable 1.35 percent house advantage.

This practice was adopted by the Casino Control Commission in New Jersey when gambling was first legalized in Atlantic City. Bettors who lost on the even-money wagers were given a choice of either forfeiting half their bet when 0 or 00 came up or of leaving the bet in prison for the next roll. Experience showed that most players were just confused by the choice, so the procedure was later modified to entail an automatic loss of half the bet whenever either of the green numbers came up. Since mathematically both procedures have the same effect on the players' long-run profits, this modification did no harm.

Atlantic City uses the American-style double-zero wheel, so even-money bettors still do not fare as well there as in Europe, but they do face only a 2.63 percent house edge. This is only half as high as the percentage on any of the other bets, and it is the best bargain that can be found on any roulette wheel in this country.

THE EUROPEAN STYLE OF DEALING

The design of the European layout is also slightly different, but anyone familiar with the American version of the game should have no trouble interpreting it. In Europe, the croupiers use a rake, a long wooden stick with a crosspiece at the end, to drag in losing bets and push out winnings. (That's where we get the phrase "raking in the chips.") Inside bets as well as outside bets are paid off on the layout rather than in front of the winning player.

The European gambling casinos do not follow the practice of using special wheel chips and assigning a different color to each player, as is done in this country. Instead, all the players bet with standard casino chips. This can create confusion when there is a large profusion of bets on the layout. The problem is made worse by the fact that the game attracts many more players overseas. Confusion can easily arise as to who owns what winning bet. In such disputes, Americans are usually at a disadvantage due to the language barrier. In some European countries, the croupiers have a reputation for being notably unsympathetic to the claims of American players.

Systems

Roulette is synonymous with gambling systems. Roulette has always been the favorite game of system players. This is partially because it allows so many betting options that all kinds of exotic combinations become possible and partially because the game proceeds at a slow enough pace to permit system players to make any abstruse calculations their system may require before putting down the next bet. In fact, what little popularity the game does enjoy in this country is due in part to the activities of system players.

No less a mathematical authority than Albert Einstein has said, "No one can possibly win at roulette unless he steals money from the table while the croupier isn't looking." However, just in case you have a friend who thinks he knows better, I'll try to show you why these systems don't work before you mortgage your house to finance your friend's scheme.

BIASED WHEEL PLAY

The theory behind this strategy is that, with extensive wear, wheels develop imperfections that favor certain numbers over others. If one records all the numbers rolled on a particular wheel over a period of time and studies the results, he may be able to pinpoint what numbers that wheel favors and exploit this information in his betting as long as the same wheel remains in play.

At one time this theory worked, and a number of gamblers did succeed in making substantial profits by *clocking* roulette wheels. Today, the casinos are wise to this danger and have realized that a little money spent on maintenance can save a lot of money in lost bets. The wheels are examined frequently and changed regularly. You will not find a biased wheel in operation in any major gambling casino in the United States.

THE THIRD-COLUMN SYSTEM

This system is probably as old as the game of roulette itself, but it still surfaces with depressing regularity. Each time it does, it is touted as a revolutionary "new" method guaranteed to beat the tables. Just a couple of years ago, a system seller out of Texas was pitching it through the mail for twenty-five dollars. As soon as the episode fades from the memories of all the customers who got burned, some new system pitchman (or the same guy under a new alias) will start peddling it again.

The system is based on the fact that the third column on the roulette layout contains eight red numbers and only four black numbers. For some reason, this has struck some misguided individuals as some kind of mathematical flaw in the layout that can be exploited by the player. The way they try to do that is to bet one unit on the third column and two units on black every spin. The fact that they have the eighteen black numbers going for them and, on the column bet, have twice as many reds working for them as blacks is somehow supposed to mean that they have pulled a fast one on the casinos.

You can put this one through a trial run very easily. Get hold of a bunch of pennies and go through the process of betting three pennies, as explained above for thirty-eight consecutive spins. Assume that each of the thirty-eight numbers comes up one time. You can use the drawings of the roulette layout and wheel in this book to work this out. If you have the perseverance to follow this through, you will find that you end up with six pennies less than you started with. Since you put a total of 114 pennies into action (3 × 38), this means a loss of 6/114, which comes to 5.26 percent. For a lengthier discussion of this startling coincidence, check the section on Multiple Betting Systems in the next chapter.

ROULETTE COMPUTERS

It has often been said, quite rightly, that no mathematical system ever has been devised nor ever will be devised to beat the game of roulette. However, in my previous book, *Gambling Scams*, I explained that a group of scientists had devised a method for successfully beating the wheel using physics rather than mathematics. I revealed that a few computer scientists had succeeded in devising a covert microcomputer that could be worn hidden under one's clothing for beating roulette. The computer measured the speed of the wheel and the speed of the ball and projected what sector of the wheel the ball would fall in sufficiently in advance to allow the operators to get down bets before the ball dropped. The calculations utilized the same theories that are used to predict the decaying orbit of a satellite circling the earth. By utilizing such a computer, a player could shift his expectation at the game from − 5.26 percent to an advantage of about 44 percent in his favor.

Gambling Scams was the first book to publicly reveal that this technique had been developed and tried against the Las Vegas casinos. About a year after the publication of my book, a book by Thomas Bass entitled *The Eudaemonic Pie* appeared. Bass is one of the physicists from the University of California at Santa Cruz who developed the computer strategy. In his book, he details how the system was developed, how it works, and how it fared against the Las Vegas tables.

Once they learned of it, the state of Nevada wasted little time in responding to this new threat to their tax coffers. On May 30, 1985, Nevada Governor Richard Bryan signed a law making it a felony for any person in a gambling casino to "use, or possess with intent to use, any device" for projecting the outcome of any game or analyzing the probabilities or "the strategy for playing or betting to be used in the game." The law imposes a penalty of one to ten years imprisonment or a fine of up to $10,000.

Although the bill had originally been aimed at the use of covert blackjack computers by card counters, the Nevada Gaming Control Board successfully lobbied for the removal of the phrase "played with cards" from the bill so as to cover devices like roulette computers. The prime mover behind passage of the law was the management of the Harrah's casinos. The bill was signed into law less than three weeks after it was introduced into the legislature, which gives you some idea of how fast the casino interests can get their way in Nevada.

So there is a system that can beat roulette after all. Unfortunately, it is illegal. If anyone wants to sell you a covert computer for beating roulette, blackjack, or any other game at a cheap price, don't even consider it. Just the possession of such a device in a Nevada casino can get you into very serious trouble.

OTHER SYSTEMS

There are countless other systems that have been devised in a futile effort to beat the roulette wheel. In fact, almost every single system used today at craps and baccarat was originally utilized in the eighteenth or nineteenth century for the game of roulette. However, since these systems have since spread to the other casino games, they will be considered separately in the next chapter.

VIII. Gambling Systems

Mail-Order System Sellers

♣ The ad in my mail said, "Make money on every roll of the dice." The writer promised that his gambling system would make every casino my private bank. I don't know what I did that first got my name on the sucker lists that mail-order system peddlers use and trade among each other. But in the last several years, I have received countless offers in the mail to make my winnings "pile up astronomically."

Browsing through these advertising brochures, I find one that guarantees I can win five hundred dollars a day playing blackjack. In another, a craps system seller challenges, "I defy anyone to use my system without winning." A more modest roulette system peddler promises merely that I will win 90 percent of the time. In each case, the writer claims that he has devised a system for beating some casino game or another. (A few even claim that their system will work against any casino game.) All I have to do to own this miraculous secret is to send in the purchase price, which can vary anywhere from two dollars to two hundred dollars.

If you were to receive one of these pitches in the mail, your first thought would probably be, "If the system is so great, why is this guy willing to part with it? Why doesn't he make money by playing the system instead of selling it?" That question occurs to every potential customer. That's why the pitchman is ready with an answer. One system seller explains that he has been sickened by the sight of so many innocent people losing their money to heartless casino owners. He wants to avenge all those losers by teaching them how to fight back. Another one says he is suffering from a crippling disease that keeps him from the gaming tables. Still another explains his motives this way: "There's no greater reward than knowing you've helped many toward a better life." (Such altruism notwithstanding, he still won't send me his winning system until I mail him forty bucks.) My all-time favorite, however, is the pitchman who gives the following reason for parting with his cherished craps system:

> I am a married man with four dependents. If the Good Lord should see fit for me to seven-out tomorrow, there would be no income for them to finish their educations and for my dear wife's support. I've tried to get her interested in learning the [gambling system], but the slots is as far as she wants to go. I finally had to give up. She can, however, run my little mail-order business. It has gotten to where it will pay the bills and keep the wolf from the door until the kids get through school.

Okay, pull yourself together so we can go on. At the risk of being accused of persecuting crusaders, cripples, widows, and orphans, I have to tell you that these systems are all ripoffs. They sound good because the sellers are experts at making these things sound good. They are not gambling experts; they are direct-mail selling experts.

One convincing ploy that they use extensively is testimonial letters from purchasers of these systems describing how much money they have won. The system sellers don't forge these letters only because they don't have to. Before you get too impressed by these testimonials, consider this. Around the turn of the century, the sale of patent medicines was one of the most thriving businesses in this country. Every patent medicine seller used testimonials in his advertising and had reams of testimonial letters in his files to back them up. These glowing endorsements from customers praised the healing benefits of products that consisted of nothing but water, coloring, and alcohol.

Patent medicines received testimonials because, when a large number of people are sick, some of them will recuperate no matter what they do. If they happen to be taking a patent medicine at the time, they attribute their cure to it. Worthless gambling systems receive testimonials because, when a large number of people are gambling, some of them will win no matter how stupidly they play. If they happen to be using some silly system at the time, they attribute their success to it. Later, when luck turns on these same players and they lose what they had won plus much more, they may write another letter to the system seller, but that one won't be quoted in the promotional material.

The most clever ploy I have seen was used by one of the most successful system pitchmen in this country in a recent campaign. His advertising carried a photograph of his previous year's income tax return, showing a gross revenue of over a million dollars. This was accompanied by a notarized statement from his accountant to the effect that the tax information was completely accurate. This seemed like impressive support for the money-making power of his gambling system. What was not explained was that the million dollars was earned, not from gambling, but from the guy's huge mail-order system-selling empire.

All these system ads feature a money-back guarantee. Most of the sellers don't honor them, but a few do. They know that most people won't bother to ask for their money back even after they realize they have been burned. In any case, the real financial loss from these systems is not the purchase price but the often-large sums the buyer loses when he applies the system in a casino.

Keep in mind also that the purchase price asked is absolutely no indicator of the worth of these systems. Some hucksters charge high prices because they prefer to get a few large checks. Others charge modest sums because they prefer to get a great many small checks. Some system sellers get the best of both worlds. First, they offer their system for sale at a hundred dollars. After a few months have passed and they figure that that market is played out, they write again to everyone who didn't buy the first time offering the system "for a limited time only" for twenty-five dollars. After that has been mined for all it's worth, they write one last time to the remaining holdouts, offering to sell the same system for only five dollars.

The advertising material for these systems is always multicolored and expensively produced. But if you purchase the system, you receive two or three pages of cheaply mineographed instructions. All the money and ingenuity went into the advertising. From the seller's standpoint, the system itself is the least important element in his business.

Recently, I received an ad from a company that specializes in renting mailing lists of gamblers to system sellers. (I don't understand it; I'm on the suckers mailing list and on the scamsters mailing list, too.) The novel feature is that this same company will also sell me a system booklet that I can sell to my victims. They offer either a craps system or a horse-race system in lots of one hundred booklets each. They charge substantially for use of their mailing lists but only ask two dollars apiece for the system booklets. Anyone who is good at writing persuasive pitches can rent the list and sell these babies at twenty dollars apiece for a thousand percent markup.

By now, you are probably wondering what the systems themselves are like. Although they are always described as new and revolutionary or the result of "twenty-six years of research" on the author's part, every one of these mail-order systems is simply one or the other of the many gambling systems first used in the nineteenth century by European gentlemen of leisure in a futile effort to beat the tables at Monte Carlo or Baden-Baden. People would often spend months at a time at these spas, taking the waters by day and squandering their inherited incomes by night at roulette or *trente et quarante*. They had a lot of time on their hands to devise ingenious systems to test at the tables. All these systems have one thing in common: They don't work.

Yet these same systems still succeed today in luring countless gamblers because they really seem to make sense—to anyone who doesn't really understand the nature of gambling, and that includes most gamblers. They also succeed because, down deep, we all want to believe that there is some miraculous secret way of beating the casinos. The worst victims of this wishful thinking are the many players who become system addicts. No matter how much money they lose or how many different systems fail them, they are always ready to fall for the next one. They are continually tinkering with various systems, modifying them and twisting them around in hopes of eliminating the fatal flaw. Like medieval alchemists searching for the formula to turn lead into gold, they prefer to believe that the secret lies in some small change in the ingredients rather than face the fact that the entire premise is fallacious.

In an effort to save you money, I am going to explain to you exactly what these systems are and why they don't work. When you encounter one of these systems, it will probably have a different name. The names constantly change, but the systems stay the same. I have purposely used the historical names for these systems to give you an idea of just how old they really are.

I suggest you study this chapter carefully. You may consider yourself too sophisticated to fall for any magazine ads offering to show you how to "win more than you ever dreamed possible," how to "own your own private money machine," or "make every day payday" at the casinos. However, there is an even more insidious way these systems seduce people. It happens when some friend of yours—someone whose judgment you really respect—tells you that somebody passed along to him a system for beating Las Vegas that really works. He has tried it eight or nine times and won every single time. He doesn't want to sell you the system; he just wants to share it out of friendship. This is difficult to resist when you know that your friend is a person of integrity.

What I have just described happens all the time. These people mean well, but they can do a great deal of unintentional harm. I am going to explain to you why your friend's system is a loser (and also why he won with it eight or nine times). Whatever his radical, secret, new system is, you will find it in this chapter. He may have some minor variation or a hybrid of two or more systems. But if you understand what I am going to teach you, you will realize why those can't work either. Most important, you will understand the one vital axiom of all system playing: any system can win if you get lucky; every system will lose in the long run.

The Martingale System

The *Martingale* is the granddaddy of all gambling systems. It is probably the oldest, easily the most popular, and definitely the most dangerous of all gambling systems. The source of the name is uncertain. The most plausible theory is that it was named after Henry Martindale, a West End London gambling house operator during the late 1700s. With time, the word became altered to Martingale. The system is known to every casino employee in the world, all of whom consider playing it a sign of a true amateur. It is also known as the *double-up system*.

The Martingale first became famous when Charles Wells used it in 1891 to win forty thousand pounds in three days of play in Monte Carlo, starting with a stake of only four hundred pounds. Wells's fame spread when his achievement was immortalized in "The Man Who Broke the Bank at Monte Carlo," a popular song at the turn of the century. Whatever Monte Carlo lost to Wells, it and other casinos throughout the world have won it back many times over from other gamblers who have tried to emulate his success with the Martingale system.

Most system peddlers lead their customers to believe that their system is specifically designed for one particular game. In reality, most of them can be applied to any even-money wager. Systems are most often used at the even-money bets at roulette, at baccarat, and on the field bet at craps. The Martingale has been applied by naïve players to every one of these, as well as to blackjack and the line bets at craps.

The system can be summarized in one sentence: Double the size of your bet every time you lose. Let's apply the system to the field bet at a crap table. You start by betting the table minimum, $2. If you lose, you double the bet, wagering $4. If you lose the $4, you bet $8. Even if you lose again, you're not in trouble. The next time, you bet $16. If you win this time, it wipes out your previous losses, plus giving you a $2 profit. This is the appeal of the system. You have to win a bet eventually. By doubling your bet, you ensure that, no matter how many wagers in a row you lose, a single wager will wipe out all your losses plus giving you a net profit equal to whatever the initial bet of the sequence was. In our example, your profit is $2 because you began with a $2 bet. After each win you start all over again with another $2 bet.

There is one little hitch; every casino table has both a table minimum and a table maximum. Let's take the example of a $2 to $500 table, the most common limits found on the Las Vegas Strip. Here is what happens if you hit a long losing streak while playing the Martingale. If you suffer eight straight losses, your betting will go as follows: you start with the $2 minimum. Then you wager $4, $8, $16, $32, $64, $128, and finally $256. This is a total loss of $510. The system dictates that you now wager $512. But such a bet would exceed the table limit of $500. That leaves you with no way of recouping your $510. That's a pretty awesome loss to incur while chasing a $2 profit. If neither your money nor your nerve has run out at this point, you may decide to wager the table maximum of $500 on the next bet. If you win that one, you are still in the hole ten dollars. If you lose it, you are really in desperate trouble with a deficit of over a thousand dollars. And remember, your chances of losing that $500 bet are better than fifty-fifty.

"Okay, but how often are you going to hit eight straight losses?" you ask. Not very often, but often enough to invalidate the system. With the Martingale, when you win, you win small. When you lose, you lose big: $2 wins versus $510 losses, in our example. It would take 255 winning sequences to nullify a single sequence of eight straight losses.

Probability theory dictates that, in an even game, the likelihood of experiencing eight losses in a row is $\frac{1}{2} \times \frac{1}{2} \times \frac{1}{2} \times \frac{1}{2} \times \frac{1}{2} \times \frac{1}{2} \times \frac{1}{2} \times \frac{1}{2}$. If you take the trouble to work that out, you will find it comes to 255 to 1. Therefore, if you are playing the Martingale and being paid off at true odds, your losses will exactly equal your winnings in the long run. This is true even if you are playing at a table with different limits from the one in the above example. The exact figures will change, but the final result is the same.

Of course, no casino ever pays off at true odds. On the craps field bet, the house gives itself an edge of 5.5 percent. No system of varying bet size can alter that fact of life.

While the Martingale system does not affect your long-run chances of winning, it does tend to redistribute the pattern of wins and losses. You will experience many small wins combined with a few very large losses. The many small wins are what convince the system player that he is on to something. However, those small profits coming in by dribs and drabs are usually too insignificant to provide any real benefit to the player. When the occasional large loss comes, it can be financially devastating. Many vacations to Las Vegas and other casino resorts have been ruined when a Martingale player has gotten financially wiped out on the first day of play.

A good player wants to capitalize on winning streaks and ride out losing streaks. The Martingale system handicaps you during winning streaks by limiting you to small wagers. But during a losing streak, it forces you to dramatically increase your bets so that even a short spell of bad luck can prove disastrous. It is this system more than any other that is responsible for the gamblers' proverb, "All system players die broke."

Other Progressions

Instead of a straight doubling sequence, gamblers sometimes use other mathematical progressions to increase their bet after each loss. A popular one is the *Grand Martingale* system. In this case, each time you lose a bet you double your last wager plus one unit. One unit is whatever the first bet of the sequence was. At a two-dollar table, a series of losing bets would go as follows: $2, $6, $14, $30, $62. When you finally win, you not only wipe out your losses plus one unit, but also show a profit of one unit for every previously lost bet. If your $62 bet wins, you make a ten-dollar profit, five two-dollar units, because you had to go through five bets to hit a winner.

Presumably this was developed by some Martingale player who got tired of going through a harrowing series of losses just to show a measly two bucks' profit when he finally won. The system does have an advantage over the Martingale in that regard. But it also has an undesirable side effect. During a losing streak, your bets balloon at a much faster rate. Therefore, you will hit the wall much faster by running out of capital or reaching the table limit in a shorter series of losses. At a $2 to $500 table, you would hit the maximum limit after seven losses instead of the eight losses required with the standard Martingale. This is an inescapable feature of all *negative progression* systems (those where you bet more after a loss). You always have a trade-off between high profits and low risk.

Gamblers have tried countless other number progressions to try to beat this dilemma. One that has enjoyed some popularity is the Fibonacci sequence, named after the mathematician who invented it in the thirteenth century. It consists of always adding the previous two numbers in the sequence to arrive at the next number: 1, 1, 2, 3, 5, 8, 13, 21, 34, and so on. This series has a number of intriguing characteristics that have long fascinated number freaks. The ability to beat the casinos is not one of them. You can test this system and any other negative progression betting strategy you may ever run across the same way we already have the Martingale and Grand Martingale. You will find that, in each case, you must choose between a low profit margin or a high probability of getting stopped by the table limit or running out of money. Even the low profit margin wouldn't be so bad if it were not for the massive loss that always comes sooner or later and always more than counterbalances all the small wins.

The Labouchere System

The last time I heard about this one was when a friend of mind confided to me that he had a foolproof system for winning at roulette. My friend, a well-educated professional man, explained earnestly that the system had been invented a couple of years ago by a Canadian acquaintance of his. He said that he had tried it out himself at home and it definitely worked. The only problem was that it involved writing down and crossing out numbers as you played, and he knew, of course, that the casinos would bar him as soon as they saw him writing things down as he bet.

At this point, I could have told my friend exactly what his system was, but I didn't want to rob him of the pleasure of explaining it. As I expected, it proved to be a version of the *Labouchere system*. My friend had been wrong only about every single thing he had said. The system was not invented a few years ago. It was not created by a Canadian. It does not work. And for that reason, the casinos will not bar you just because they see you writing things down as you play.

Gambling casinos are quite used to seeing system players with their little note pads and pencils, particularly at roulette and baccarat. European gambling houses even provide their roulette patrons with preprinted scorecards that have a full-color picture of a roulette wheel so that players can see what numbers are next to each other on the wheel; this bit of arcana figures in some systems. American casinos are less accommodating. You have to bring your own stationery supplies. But as long as your record-keeping doesn't slow down the game, the management won't object. (The one exception is blackjack. The pit personnel are so paranoid about card counting that anything might set them off if you are winning big.)

My friend's system was first popularized by Henry Labouchere, an English world traveler, member of Parliament, and gambler. Since Labouchere died in 1912, this is hardly a new system. However, it actually goes back much further. It was invented by a French mathematician, the Marquis de Cordorcet, who died in 1794. So you can see my friend was a bit off on the system's date and country of origin.

Here is how the system works. The player writes down a row of three or four numbers, such as 1–2–3–4. It doesn't really matter what numbers are used or even how many, although everyone who plays the system thinks there is something mystical about the sequence he uses. Also, some players write the numbers in a column rather than a row. That doesn't matter either. The first bet consists of the totals of the first and last numbers in the row. In our example, it would be five units. Each time you lose a bet, you write the amount of that bet at the end of the row. Each time you win, you cross out the first and last numbers in the row. For this reason, the system is also called the *cancellation system*.

The next bet is always the total of the first and last uncanceled numbers in the row. When you succeed in crossing out all the numbers, you will have a net profit equaling the total of your original row of numbers. In our example, you would earn ten units. At that point, you start the whole thing over again with a new 1–2–3–4 row.

The true believer will tell you that you will always succeed in crossing out all the numbers because you cancel two numbers each time you win and add only one number each time you lose. You can lose more than half your bets and still show a profit. That is what lulls the naïve player into thinking that he has really stumbled onto something.

What he won't tell you, because he hasn't discovered it yet, is what happens when you have a bad session and keep hitting more losers than winners. Your bets steadily escalate until the required bet exceeds the table limit, leaving you with a very long row of numbers and no way to recoup your losses.

Some cancellation players think they have an answer for that too. When their losses on one sequence get too high, for example fifty units, they abandon that sequence and make several new number sequences that come to the same total. In our example, we might make five 1–2–3–4 sequences to total fifty units. Now we play the first sequence until it has been canceled, then move on to the second one, the third one, the fourth one, and finally the fifth one.

This approach decreases the size of your bets, but increases the number of wins required. Now you need to hit an exceptionally long series of winners, or you'll be there all night. Suppose you do hit that long string of winners and succeed in canceling all five series. What will you have to show for your fantastic run of luck? A lousy ten units' profit.

Among the ploys that system sellers use to make their products sound appealing are claims that the system has been extensively computer tested. These hucksters know that many people have heard about legitimate blackjack strategies developed with the aid of computers. For that reason, "computer tested" and "computer developed" have become magic words that continually pop up in these ads. The only thing most of these guys ever use a computer for is to organize their mailing lists. However, if any of these systems really has been through a computer and passed the test, it only illustrates the computer specialists' proverb: garbage in, garbage out.

I do know of one legitimate computer testing of a cancellation-type system. The test was conducted by Julian Braun of IBM. Braun is one of the world's leading experts on computer simulation of games of chance and the man who did most of the early computer work that led to the development of modern blackjack card-counting systems. Braun chose for his test a Labouchere system that was being marketed for roulette a couple of years ago at twenty-five dollars. The system involved the goal of winning thirty units every time a sequence was successfully completed by crossing out all the numbers.

After testing the system against a simulated 160,000 spins using the more favorable single-zero French roulette wheel, Braun found that the system actually succeeded in winning the target thirty units twenty out of every twenty-one times the player used it. Unfortunately, those twenty winning sequences produced a gross profit of only 600 units, while the single losing experience out of every twenty-one tries produced an average loss of 1,012 units, giving the player a net loss of 412 units.

This explains a great deal about the appeal of systems. As long as the player is experiencing those twenty winning sequences, or either more or less due to standard deviation, he is convinced that he has found the road to riches. He is only too happy to write testimonial letters to the system seller and try to convert his friends. When the day of reckoning finally comes, he is devastated. Remember the sales pitch I cited earlier that promised the system would win 90 percent of the time. The claim may be true, and yet the system may still be a ripoff. The system Braun analyzed worked 95.2 percent of the time and still lost money.

That is the greatest danger in this kind of system. Most of the time, the player wins a succession of small profits. This sets him up for the inevitable disastrous losing streak, in which he drops all the money he won the previous times and then some. Like the Martingale, this system puts you in the position of risking large sums while chasing small profits.

The d'Alembert System

This one is named after Jean Le Rond d'Alembert, an eighteenth-century French mathematician best known for formulating the law of equilibrium. This system holds that when two events have an equal chance of occurring, if one begins to happen more frequently than the other, the alternative event must eventually begin to occur more often in order to achieve equilibrium. Equilibrium is the situation that exists when both events have occurred the same number of times. D'Alembert believed that nature always seeks equilibrium.

This concept is the basis of the d'Alembert system. The player begins by betting one unit. One unit is simply whatever amount he wishes his basic bet to be. Every time he loses, he increases his bet by one unit. Every time he wins, he decreases the bet by one unit. His bets may seesaw up and down quite a bit, but eventually he will find himself back at the basic bet of one unit. This occurs whenever equilibrium is reached. His losses have been balanced off by an equal number of wins. Therefore, his one-unit increases have been balanced off by an equal number of one-unit decreases, bringing him back to his starting point. The amazing thing is that, when that happens, he will find he has won a net profit of one unit for every win in the sequence. Although he lost as many as he won, instead of breaking even, he has made a profit.

A superficial criticism that might be made of this system is that you never know at what point the results start to get out of equilibrium, so you don't know what will constitute a return to equilibrium. In other words, it is possible that just before you walked up to the roulette table, the color red came up an abnormally high number of times. Not knowing this, you start betting red, using the d'Alembert system. Naturally, a long string of blacks comes up as the wheel seeks to achieve equilibrium. This leaves you in the hole for a bundle, hoping that enough reds will come up to achieve equilibrium and give you a profit. What you don't know is that equilibrium has just been achieved due to what had happened before you even started playing.

However, the real problem with this system is that this whole equilibrium business is just nonsense. The "law" of equilibrium is actually the fallacy of the maturity of chances that we discussed in Chapter II. The wheel doesn't have a memory, so the previous spins won't affect the subsequent ones. It is only the ratio of the difference between the number of red spins and the number of black spins that becomes smaller as the number of trials increases, just as the Law of Large Numbers dictates. The absolute difference between red trials and black trials will actually keep getting larger as the number of trials increases. Nature is actually moving away from equilibrium, in the sense in which d'Alembert used the term.

The d'Alembert is not as dangerous a system as the Martingale, because it does not involve as steep a progression. However, it still forces the player to increase his bets when he is losing and will still leave him stuck on occasions when either his bankroll runs out or the table limit is reached as his bets increase. With this system, it's usually the bankroll that gives out first.

About five years ago, a guy in the Las Vegas area was advertising in the local newspapers and magazines, offering a personal lesson in a foolproof blackjack system for five hundred dollars. What his students got for their money was a lesson in standard basic strategy for playing their hands combined with the d'Alembert system for determining their bets. I taught you basic strategy in Chapter III, and I have just taught you the d'Alembert system, so you could say I've saved you five hundred dollars. I can save you even more money if you will take this advice: Stay away from the d'Alembert system.

The Patience System

Like most systems, the *patience system* comes in many forms, but the underlying concept is always the same. Let's consider how a crap player might use it. He knows that the odds of a shooter making a psss at craps are about 50–50. But the odds against a shooter making three passes in a row are only about 7 to 1. Therefore, he figures that if he waits until the shooter makes two consecutive passes and then bets against him, he will have the odds working for him to the tune of 7 to 1.

It is true that the odds against three straight passes are about 7 to 1. But you are not betting against three consecutive passes; you are betting against another pass after the first two have occurred. The odds on the <u>next</u> roll always remain the same because the dice, not being sentient creatures, do not remember what they did on the previous rolls. (I know I've mentioned that before, but it's important.) Your odds of winning that next don't-pass bet are still slightly less than 50–50.

Keep in mind also that even if the shooter fails to make three straight passes, you will not necessarily win. If he rolls a 12 on the come-out, it is a loss for the shooter, but it only counts as a standoff on your don't-pass bet. That feature gives the house the edge no matter how many consecutive passes you wait for before betting.

Consider an analogy. The chances of a wild elephant charging down the sidewalk in front of your house and then trampling you to death are probably less than a million to one. (I don't know your neighborhood, so I can't calculate the exact odds.) But if you should ever see an elephant charging down the street, I suggest that you don't stand in his path just because you're willing to risk million-to-one odds. Even if the odds against two events happening in sequence are very high, once the first event has occurred, the odds against the second one happening also are not so high.

If you still insist on trying this strategy at a casino, pick a crap table that is not too busy. Otherwise, while you are waiting for your two straight passes before betting, the dealer might ask you to leave the table to make room for paying customers.

The Gagnante Marche System

The above is the historical French name for this system; present-day gamblers know it as the *hot and cold system*. Gamblers are fond of saying that gambling is all a matter of streaks. There are times when it seems the shooter at a crap table will go on forever without sevening-out; at other times, none of the shooters can make a point. At baccarat, sometimes the bank wins time after time after time; sometimes the player hand is the one that can't lose. If one could always latch on to these streaks from the beginning and bet them to the end, making money gambling would be a cinch. The problem is that too often the player finds he is on the wrong side of the streak, betting with the shooter when the crap table is cold and betting against him when the table is hot. By the time he realizes which way the wind is blowing, the streak is almost over and he is lucky if he can switch sides soon enough just to recoup what he has already lost.

The hot and cold system promises to ensure that the bettor will always catch such streaks from the very beginning. It makes good on that promise too. The trick is to always bet on whichever side won last. If red came up at the roulette table last time, bet red the next time. If black comes up instead, immediately switch over and bet black. Sooner or later a streak will develop and when it does, you will be on it from the very beginning.

The problem with this system is what happens while you are waiting for the streak to come along. When there is no streak, the dice, cards, or wheel will be chopping. That means that wins on both sides will be occurring mixed together. With the hot and cold system, you will be chopped up into little pieces during these periods. In the end, you will win no more and no less with this system than if you relied on pure guessing to decide which side to bet on next.

Multiple Betting Systems

Over two thousand years ago, the Greek philosopher Demosthenes said, "What we wish, that we readily believe." That man knew human nature. We all want to believe that there must be some way to beat the house. Gambling games that offer a large variety of betting options, like craps or roulette, make it easier for us to convince ourselves that it's true. The various bets can be mixed together in so many confusing ways that, if we really try, we can use them to blind ourselves to reality.

Multiple betting systems are all based on the premise that different wagers in a game can be combined so that each eliminates the weakness of the other. If bet simultaneously, the correct combination of bets is supposed to yield an edge over the house. There are many versions of this approach. Let's analyze one of the most popular variations, a craps system that involves betting three units on the field every roll, six units each on the place bets on 6 and 8, and five units on the 5 place bet. This means that the system player must have twenty units riding on every roll. The bettor figures that, since he has every number covered except 7, he will win money on every roll of the dice except for the occasional 7, which certainly isn't going to come up often enough to spoil things.

For the sake of analysis, we will use the standard Las Vegas Strip layout that pays double on the field on 2 or 12 and even money on 3, 4, 9, 10, or 11. If 5, 6, 7, or 8 is rolled, the field bet loses. We know that in the long run, every one of the thirty-six possible two-dice combinations will come up an equal number of times. To test the system, we will assume that each of these thirty-six combinations comes up once in thirty-six consecutive rolls. Number 3 will come up twice, 4 will come up three times, 9 will come up four times, 10 will come up three times, and 11 will come up twice. On each of those fourteen rolls, the bettor wins his three-unit field bet for a profit of forty-two units. Numbers 2 and 12 will each come up once, paying 2 to 1, to bring the field bet profit up to fifty-four units.

Number 5 will come up four times. This pays a total of twenty-eight units. But each time the 5 place bet wins, the field bet loses three units. Therefore, the net profit on the 5 place bet is only sixteen units. This brings our profit total up to seventy units.

Number 6 will come up five times, paying a total of thirty-five units. When you subtract the fifteen units lost on the field during those five rolls, you have a profit of twenty units on the 6 place bet. That brings the profit total up to ninety units.

The 8 place bet will work the same way. Number 8 will also come up five times, paying a total of thirty-five units. When you subtract the fifteen units lost on the field during those five rolls, you have a profit of twenty units on the 8 place bet. That brings the profit total up to 110 units.

So far, this sounds so good I'm almost tempted to play this system myself. But now let's see what happens on the rolls when 7 comes up. Number 7 will be rolled exactly six times. Each of those times, the player will lose every bet he has out. We saw at the beginning that the player has to have twenty units riding at all times. Twenty times six gives us a loss of 120 units. Subtract the 110-unit profit from the 120-unit loss, and you arrive at a net loss of ten units. On second thought, I don't think I will play this system after all, and I hope you won't either.

Right now, I can hear some diehard system fanatic saying that the way to plug the hole in the above system is to bet the any-seven proposition on every roll. I'll let you work that one out for yourself. In fact, you can test any multiple betting system the same way we just tested the field bet system. It may be a tedious process, but it's less tedious than trying to get a second mortgage on your home if you try playing one of these things without testing it first. If you check out enough of them, you will eventually learn the one fundamental truth about all multiple bet systems. All multiple betting systems lose at a rate equal to the house P.C. on each individual bet being made. In other words, they don't change a thing mathematically. In practice, because they involve wagering so much money at once and so often involve making sucker bets like the field and various proposition wagers, they can grind down your bankroll with dizzying speed.

Reverse Systems

The reverse gambling system idea has got to be the most perversely ingenious of all. The system addict says, "All right, you've convinced me. That system doesn't work. It has to lose money. But I know how to make money from it. Since, by following the system, I have to lose, I'll do exactly the opposite of what the system calls for. That way I have to win."

The reverse concept can be applied to most of the systems we have looked at. A reverse Martingale or other progression would require increasing your bet after each win and cutting back after a loss. A reverse d'Alembert would involve increasing your bet one unit after a win and going down a unit after a loss. A reverse Labouchere means crossing off the two outer numbers each time you lose and adding the size of your bet to the end of the row each time you win. A reverse hot and cold system calls for betting do or don't exactly the opposite of the way the dice came up last time.

What the reverse system advocate doesn't realize is that the system he was following is not what caused his losses. The system may rearrange the pattern of losses as we have seen. But in an ultimate sense, any system is irrelevant to a player's long-run losses. Those losses are caused not by the gambling system but by the house percentage. Over an extended period of time, a system player's net losses will be exactly what they would have been if he had made uniform-size bets on the same wagers for the same total amount. The loss is simply a function of the amount wagered and the negative expectation of the bet (the house edge).

Because the system is ultimately irrelevant to the player's losses, reversing the system will be just as irrelevant. It may again alter the pattern of losses—perhaps a large number of small losses combined with a few large wins—but it won't guarantee a net profit.

One important thing can be said in favor of reverse versions of the various betting progressions. Because they involve wagering more money when you are winning, they are far better than systems like the Martingale that force you to wager more when you are losing. Betting progressions, positive or negative, will not alter the long-term results of your gambling, but they can have dramatic short-term results. We have already seen that, with any variation of the Martingale, those results can be disastrous. With a progressive betting scheme that involves betting more after a win, the results can be quite favorable because a lucky streak can make your winnings mount up very rapidly. I don't recommend a particular positive progression because there is no magical sequence that offers special advantages, despite what some advocates of these systems believe. If you follow the money-management and betting advice given in Chapter I, you will be betting more when winning without any dependence on any special progression.

The Problem with Systems

I remember as a youngster of eight or nine once trying to settle a dispute with a friend by means of a wager. My friend offered to bet ten dollars that he was right. I pointed out that he didn't have ten dollars. His answer was, "That's all right. I don't need ten dollars, because I'm not going to lose." I wasn't won over by this logic, so we ended up betting a punch in the arm. This is the kind of thing kids do; at least, they did in my neighborhood. I expect that my friend still carries the mark of my knuckles on his upper arm to this day.

I often think of my childhood friend's reasoning when watching system players. The greatest risk of gambling systems is that they often lead people to bet money they can't afford to lose. Like my friend, they think it doesn't matter because they are not going to lose. Blackjack is the only casino game where a system can give a player an advantage over the house. Yet every time a card counter sits down to play, he must face the possibility that he may have a losing session because of random short-term fluctuations in the probabilities. Don't ever let your faith in any magical gambling system, no matter how appealing its simple-minded logic, lull you into thinking you can't possibly lose. The moment you start thinking that way, you are guaranteed to end up a loser.

IX. Slot Machines

♣Blackjack, baccarat, and roulette were invented by the French. Keno was originated by the Chinese. Although craps is an American invention, it is closely based on the ancient English game of hazard. Slot machines, invented in 1887 by Charles Fey in San Francisco and first introduced as a diversion for patrons in that city's bars, are the only truly American casino game. It is perhaps fitting, therefore, that they are the most popular casino game in this country. Gross slot revenues in Nevada and Atlantic City are higher than those for all the *table games* (blackjack, craps, roulette, and baccarat) combined.

In Nevada, machines can be found not only in the casinos but also in supermarkets, laundromats, and countless other business establishments large and small. The state boasts about one machine for every ten residents. The things are almost impossible to get away from. They are the first thing the visitor sees when he arrives and the last thing he sees as he leaves, since banks of slot machines can be found both in McCarran Airport in Las Vegas and in Reno Airport. Many a departing tourist has found that the most expensive flight delay of his life occurred in Nevada.

The Appeal of Slots

Whatever some gambling snobs may think of them, slot machines have a large and ever-growing following that is fiercely loyal to this form of gambling. You can spot hardcore slot players by the blackened hands they get after a long period of handling those dirty coins. Traditionally, the large majority of slot players have been women. The casino stereotype is that slot machines are what the wife or girlfriend plays while her man goes off to the crap table or blackjack pit. Women slot players still outnumber men, but not to quite as great an extent, particularly since the introduction of *video poker*. Slots are not only popular among tourists but are also very popular among the locals in Nevada and New Jersey. In fact, some of the smaller Las Vegas casinos that rely heavily on slot action cater almost exclusively to locals, making little attempt to attract tourist trade. When Atlantic City first legalized gambling, the craps and blackjack tables were so crowded that one often had to wait for hours for an opportunity to play. Many people found that the slot machines were the only games they could get anywhere near. As a result, not only did the slot machines become enormous moneymakers for the casinos, but a great many people in the area were turned into slot fans and still prefer that form of gambling even now that the table games are more accessible.

Slot machines have four qualities that make them appealing to many people. First, there are almost no rules to learn and there is no human contact involved in playing. Consequently, many who find games like craps and blackjack intimidating feel comfortable playing the slots. There is no need to fear making a mistake in front of a machine. Second, slots require a very small financial investment. Most are either one-dollar, quarter, or nickel denomination. There are a couple of casinos on Fremont Street in Las Vegas that even offer penny slot machines. Third, slots offer the possibility of a very large payoff. Only keno comes close in the amount that can be won compared with the investment. Slot machines are the only casino game in which a player can aspire to win a million dollars, as several-dollar progressive slot machine players have already done. Finally, slot machines can become almost addictive. They are a perfect example of operant conditioning. Behavioral scientists have found that the most effective way to reinforce a certain form of behavior is with a random reward schedule. Instead of giving a reward every time the desired behavior occurs, it is provided sporadically. The uncertainty of whether or not this will be one of the times the reward materializes becomes one of the motivations for repeating the behavior. This is exactly what happens every time a slot player pulls the handle. Every pull doesn't provide a reward, but enough of them do, even if it's only a small payoff, to keep encouraging the player to pull the handle again.

The Changing Slot Scene

Slot players have traditionally received a lot of bad press from writers on gambling. They criticize the lack of playing skill required by slots and the small chance of coming out a winner. In the last several years, however, some important changes have occurred to alter the picture. Casinos have come to appreciate more than ever the importance of slot machine revenues to their profits and have attempted to court slot players more aggressively. All of this has been to the benefit of slot fans. Two technological innovations have particularly contributed to the change, the introduction of *progressive jackpots* and the invention of *video poker* machines. Today, the slot player has a much greater variety of machines to choose from and a greater degree of influence over the final results.

Since slot players are not high rollers, they have benefited from the gambling industry trend in recent years to cater more to the small-money bettor. It is in those casinos that concentrate on grind action that the slot player can expect the best break. Downtown Las Vegas clubs like the El Cortez have flourished by concentrating almost exclusively on slot action. In fact, some small casinos in Vegas are nothing but *slot arcades*. They offer no other games except rows and rows of slot machines, finding them a great source of revenue with minimal labor costs and overhead.

One sign of the increased awareness on the part of casinos of the importance of the slot players' action is a new program just instituted by Harrah's Marina in Atlantic City. A group of five hundred slots in the casino have been designated the Captain's Circle. Players who join the Captain's Circle receive a special card similar to a credit card. When the player plays any of these machines, he inserts his card, and the machine keeps track of how much action the player gives the house. The casino then employs this information to grant the player various complimentary items in proportion to the amount he gambles. This is the first major attempt by a casino to recognize big-spending slot players with the same kind of privileges that have always been accorded high rollers at the table games.

Slot players have also benefited from the effects of competition. For many years, Bally Manufacturing had a virtual monopoly on slot manufacture. This is the same company that owns Bally Park Place in Atlantic City. While Bally is still the giant in the field, in the last few years a new company, IGT (International Game Technology), has made inroads as a pioneer in *video slots*.

All this means that there are more winning opportunities today for the slot player but also more to know if he wants to give himself every chance of winning. All slot machines are definitely not created equal. The most important key to success is learning how to tell them apart.

The Cash Flow

I have stressed before that money management is one of the most important elements in gambling. At the slot machines, money management can be a literal problem; those piles of coins can get heavy and unwieldy. When you first arrive, you can convert your paper money into coins either through one of the *change girls* who regularly circulate through the *slot floor* or at the slot cashier's booth. They can also supply you with one of the plastic or cardboard cups the casino provides for storing your coins while playing. Anytime you need change during play, you can summon a change girl by pressing a button on your machine that turns on a light on top of the machine.

Whenever you insert a coin into a slot machine, it goes into the machine's payoff hopper. However, when the hopper is filled, the overflow goes into the drop bucket inside the stand on which the machine rests. These buckets are collected at regular intervals by casino personnel. Consequently, the machine itself does not contain enough coin reserves to pay off the larger jackpots. When you hit one of these, part of the payoff will come out of the machine; the rest will be given to you by a change girl while a slot floorman supervises the accuracy of the payoff.

When you finish playing, you can convert your coins back into currency by taking them to the slot cashier's booth. There the coins will be counted automatically by machine and the cashier will give you the appropriate sum in paper money.

If you get lucky, you may reach the point where you decide to play just a few more coins and then leave with the rest of your profits. If this happens, I strongly urge you to first convert all your coins into currency except for the few you intend to keep playing with. If you don't take this precaution, you may find that the temptation to keep feeding coins into the machine is too strong. Before you know it, you may have given all your profits back to the house. Remember, slot playing is habit forming. For most players, the only thing that breaks it off is running out of money. If you force yourself to get into the counterbalancing habit of periodically taking a break to convert profits into paper money before continuing to play, you will have a great advantage over most other slot players. This is one of the most important tips I can give you to help you beat the slots.

Mechanics and Mathematics

TYPES OF MECHANISMS

In order to understand what your chances of winning are on a particular slot machine, you have to understand how these machines work. Slot machines fall into three categories: mechanical, electromechanical, and electronic. These days, the only place you are likely to find a mechanical slot machine, the kind that is operated purely by cogs and gears, is in an antique collection or some small out-of-the-way casino. All the machines found in major casinos in this country are either electromechanical—traditional machinery, electrically powered—or electronic. These latter resemble video games more than traditional slot machines. Cathode ray tubes replace spinning reels, and instead of pictures drawn on the reels you see computer graphic images of cherries and lemons projected onto the screen. The entire working of the machine is controlled by computer chips.

The electromechanical machines each have three, four, or five *reels* side by side. Each of these reels bears anywhere from twenty to thirty symbols. When the coin is inserted and the handle pulled or button pushed, the individual reels spin randomly and independently and, if you are very lucky, they may come to rest with enough identical symbols next to each other to win you some money.

REEL PSYCHOLOGY

On a three-reel machine, you would need to get three of one particular symbol—for example, three bars—to line up in order to win the largest prize. What happens agonizingly often is that the first reel stops on a bar, the second reel then stops on a bar, and finally the last reel stops on a . . . lemon. The disappointed player feels that he just missed by a hair and is encouraged to try again. What most players don't suspect is that they are victims of a clever psychological ploy on the part of slot manufacturers. The first two reels contain more of the winning symbol than the last reel does. It is relatively easy to get that bar on the first two reels but very difficult to get it to come up on the last reel.

This kind of subtle psychological encouragement is also the reason the manufacturers build the *reel window* large enough for the player to see three rows of symbols even though only the center line pays off. When the player sees a winning combination on the row of symbols directly above the pay line or on the one below the pay line, it makes him feel that he just missed winning by the skin of his teeth, and this gives him the impetus to keep playing. The same effect occurs when he succeeds in lining up two winning symbols on the pay line and sees the third needed symbol on the row just above it or just below it.

SLOT PERCENTAGES

The process the casino must go through in order to determine just how much profit each machine will earn for it is a very easy one to understand. The first matter it must determine is exactly how many different combinations of symbols the machine is capable of producing. For example, if the machine has three reels and each reel has twenty-five symbols, the total number of possible combinations is 25 × 25 × 25, or 15,625. If it is a dollar machine, the casino can assume that for every 15,625 dollars played on the machine, each combination of three symbols will on the average come up one time. On some machines, certain of the *stops* on each reel contain no symbol. These blanks are called *ghosts*. For purposes of this discussion, the blank itself can be considered just another kind of symbol.

The casino now has two variables that it can adjust to determine its profit margin, the number of winning symbols it decides to place on each reel and the amount of money it decides to pay off on each winning combination. It is primarily by manipulating the number of winning symbols on each reel that the house sets the profit margin. The total number of symbols on each reel, the number of winning symbols on each reel (which in turn determines the number of ways those winnings symbols can combine), and the payout on each winning combination allow the casino to determine exactly how many of those 15,625 dollars it will return to the players in the form of payoffs. It may, for example, decide to return 85 percent of the money taken in, which would give the house a 15 percent edge on that machine. In Atlantic City, the maximum amount that a machine can retain is set by law at 17 percent, but in Nevada the casinos have complete freedom in setting the machines to earn as much profit as they wish. Keep in mind that these figures only hold true in the long run. In the short run, a machine may earn more or less than it is supposed to because certain winning combinations may come up either more or less often than expected due to random fluctuations. Neither the casino nor anyone else can affect that. But over hundreds of thousands of pulls of the handle, the machine can be expected to earn very close to what probability dictates.

The important point to understand is that it is what symbols appear on the reels that determines how lucrative the machine will be for the player or the house. This simple point is understood by very few slot players, and even many writers on gambling seem to be misinformed on this point.

A machine that withholds a very small percentage of the money it takes in as profit for the casino is termed a *loose machine*, while one that keeps a large portion of what it takes in is called a *tight machine*. Both players and casino personnel speak of a casino tightening or loosening its slots. Unfortunately, many players take this image literally. They think there is some little screw inside the machine that can be tightened or loosened by the casino to determine how generous the machine will be. This has given rise to the myth that some casinos loosen their machines during the week and tighten them up on weekends when the big crowds come in. When you realize what a major operation it is to tighten or loosen a machine—changing the very *reel strips* themselves—you can appreciate that this is not something lightly or frequently undertaken by the house.

OVERDUE MACHINES

The fact that it is the symbols on the reels and therefore the number of combinations of symbols possible that determines a machine's generosity also shows the fallacy in another very common belief among slot players. Many players think that, if a particular machine has received a great deal of play without paying off, that the machine is "due" for a payoff and is therefore a particularly good one to play. Similarly, almost all players believe that a machine that has just paid a jackpot is not worth playing because it won't pay off again for a long time. This is just the fallacy of the maturity of chances discussed in Chapter II cropping up again in a different guise. Each spin of the reels on a slot machine is a random process, just like each throw of the dice or spin of the roulette wheel. A machine that hasn't paid off in a long time may merely be a very tight machine that is not likely to pay off for a long time more. By contrast, a machine that came up four 7s five minutes ago is every bit as likely to come up four 7s on the very next play. Certainly, the fact that it paid a jackpot recently does not diminish the chances of it happening on the next try. Slot machines don't have any more memory than dice do.

In fact, dice provide a very good analogy to how a slot machine works. If the machine has three reels, it is like throwing three dice. If each reel bears twenty-five symbols, it is just like rolling a die that has twenty-five sides. Admittedly, a die large enough to have twenty-five sides would be a little unwieldy. But if we could construct such dice and paint symbols on three of them that exactly corresponded to the symbols on our three slot machine reels, then tossing those three dice would be mathematically identical to pulling the handle on the machine. If you have learned anything from the mathematical discussion in Chapter II and the coverage of craps in Chapter V, it should be that rolling two 6s on one throw of a pair of dice has no effect on your chances of rolling two 6s on the next throw. That principle is just as applicable to twenty-five-sided dice or to slot machines.

The mathematical principles underlying electronic machines (video slots) are identical to those relating to the electromechanical ones. The only difference is that with computer graphics it is possible to get anywhere from 63 to 253 symbols on each reel. Even using only 63 symbols, that would make for 15,752,961 possible combinations on a four-reel slot.

Straight Slot Machines

Slot machines can be categorized according to the type of jackpot as *straight slots* and *progressive slots*. The straight slot machine is the traditional style characterized by a jackpot amount that is preset and unvarying. Most of these machines permit multiple-coin play. However, this feature does not really affect the house's advantage or the player's chances of ending up a winner. It only increases the total volume of money the machine is likely to receive in play over a given period.

MULTIPLE-COIN PLAY

Multiple-coin machines work in one of two ways. For example, a particular quarter machine may accept from one to four quarters each play. A player who decides to play two quarters on each pull will receive twice as large a payoff every time he wins. If he plays three quarters per play, he will receive three times as large a payoff and four quarters will bring payoffs four times as large as those for single-quarter play. Because the payoffs increase in exact proportion to the increase in the amount wagered, the house edge remains the same regardless of how many coins the player inserts. It is only a question of how much money the player is willing to risk.

An alternative style of multiple-coin machine allows play on more than one line. If a player inserts one quarter, he will only win if a payoff combination comes up on the center line. If he inserts two coins, a winning combination on either the center line or the top line will pay off. Three quarters played on each pull means that a win on any of the three visible lines—top, center, or bottom—will result in a payoff for the player. Some even pay off on diagonal lines. This type of machine is a psychological ploy on the part of the casinos to increase the amount the player wagers. A player who sees that he hit a jackpot on the bottom line but does not get paid because he only played one quarter may be encouraged to play three quarters from then on, thereby tripling the casino's profits. Once again, the percentage advantage the house enjoys does not change, but the amount of profit will increase if the casino succeeds in its attempt to get the player to, in effect, play three slot machines at one time.

DIFFERENT DENOMINATIONS

The three standard denominations for slot machines are nickels, quarters, and dollars. Generally, the nickel machines are the tightest and the dollar machines are the loosest, with the quarter machines in between. The casinos follow this policy for two reasons. First, the casino is not simply concerned with profit percentages but also with dollars-and-cents profits. A nickel machine takes up as much floorspace as a quarter or dollar machine. In order for a lower-denomination machine to earn its keep, it has to withhold a larger percentage of the money played in it. In addition, the house wants to encourage slot players to patronize the higher-denomination machines. By providing a higher return on the players' investment on those machines, it hopes to provide the incentive for people to upgrade their play. Usually, the five-cent machines are set to withhold anywhere from 15 to 25 percent of the money played. By contrast, dollar machines may be set to withhold as little as 2.6 percent of the players' money.

DOLLAR CAROUSEL SLOTS

The low-percentage dollar slot machines are a relatively recent innovation in the casino industry. They are often placed in groups of about a dozen in the form of an oval known as a *carousel*, served by one change person on an elevated ramp in the center. These one-dollar machines were an innovation not only because of the increase in denomination and the low house percentage but also because, in an effort to convert slot players to dollar action, the casinos for the first time started to advertise the house edge on slot machines. Casino marquees now carry statements like "Up to 97% returned on dollar slots" right under the plug for the dollar-ninety-eight breakfast, one-dollar shrimp cocktail, or champagne brunch. Similar statements appear in newspaper advertisements.

The words "up to" mean that not all their machines are that generous. The casino's concern is with the average amount withheld by its machines. Even machines of the same denomination and type within a single casino will not have the same percentage. Some will be higher and others lower than the average percentage the house wishes to withhold. Many casinos alternate tight and loose machines in order to exploit the habit of many slot players to simultaneously play two adjacent machines. The many payoffs on the loose machine hold the player's interest while the tight machine increases the casino's profits. Each casino develops its own *slot mix* that it finds the most profitable.

FINDING A LOOSE MACHINE

Although you can never be sure what the house percentage is on any particular machine, there are a number of simple steps you can take to improve your chances of getting a loose machine. First of all, play in places that cater to slot players. This means avoiding those casinos that concentrate on high-roller action and consider the small bettor a nuisance. Generally, you can expect a much better deal in downtown Las Vegas than on the Strip. The single best indicator that a casino offers the slot player a good deal is the presence of many players at the machines. If a casino has tight slots, any player who tackles their machines will soon become discouraged and move elsewhere. If a place is doing good business at their slots, it is because the players have found from experience that they are getting a fair deal.

Above all, restrict your playing to gambling casinos. Don't bother with places like supermarkets, restaurants, and drugstores that offer a few slot machines as a sideline. These establishments rely on impulse play. They are not concerned with trying to build up a clientele of steady, repeat business, so they have no incentive to keep their percentages low. Invariably, they offer the worst gamble you can find in Nevada. The airport slots are notoriously tight. The operators know they have a captive audience, so they can afford to be greedy.

Because the higher-denomination machines are looser, instead of playing five nickels simultaneously on a multiple-coin five-cent machine, you would be much better off playing one quarter on a quarter machine. If you can afford to play four quarters at a time on a quarter machine, you would be wiser to play one dollar at a time on a 97.4 percent machine. Since even machines of the same denomination may have different percentages, you should try to find out which machine of your denomination is the loosest. There is no surefire way of doing this, but one good approach is to ask a change girl or other slot attendant. From daily observation, they usually have a good idea which machines pay the best. If a casino offers 97.4 percent dollar machines, ask them which ones they are. There is no reason why they shouldn't tell you.

Progressive Slot Machines

A progressive slot machine differs from a straight slot because the giant jackpot is not a set amount. Instead, the jackpot is continually growing as the machine is being played. For example, on a dollar progressive, the giant jackpot may increase five cents for every dollar that is played in the machine. All the lesser payoffs on the machine will be preset, as with straight slots.

TYPES OF PROGRESSIVES

Each machine has a *progressive meter*, an LED number at the top of the machine that records the amount of the jackpot and that changes with each play to reflect the slight increase in the prize. Progressive machines are often in *banks* of twelve machines, each hooked up to the same large meter, which stands above the entire row of machines. Every coin played in any one of the twelve machines contributes to the progressive jackpot, and the first machine to hit the jackpot wins the entire amount for that player.

Another style of machine is the *double-progressive*. In this case, the machine has two giant jackpots, which are shown on two meters at the top of the machine. A lit arrow points to each jackpot alternately on alternate plays of the machine. On the first pull you are playing for one jackpot, on the next pull you are playing for the other one. Each jackpot grows on the play in which it is activated. Depending on when each jackpot last paid off, one may be very large while the other one is small. The concept behind this type of machine is that, even after one giant jackpot has been paid, players still have a motivation to keep playing the machine to win the other one. In trying to do so, they will build up the small jackpot, since it is impractical to play the machine just on alternate trials. Who would be dumb enough to alternate with you and play only for the small jackpot? If you want to win the big one, you have to play through—and contribute to—the small jackpot.

JACKPOT SIZE

Giant progressive jackpots can reach awesome sums, since the amount keeps growing until someone wins it. At that point, the jackpot reverts to whatever amount the casino sets as the minumum. In fact, the Nevada casinos are prohibited by law from reducing the size of a progressive jackpot before anyone has won it. Some casinos do, however, place a ceiling on the jackpot and, when it reaches huge proportions, some pay it off over a period of several years in the same way as is usually done with large state lottery payoffs.

A number of million-dollar jackpots have been awarded in the last couple of years. The Flamingo Hilton in particular, with its very aggressive slot program, has garnered a great deal of publicity because of the huge jackpots it has paid out. At present, there are seven casinos in Las Vegas offering dollar progressive machines with jackpots in the million-dollar range. Sooner or later, every one of them will have to be won by someone. When a progressive jackpot reaches these levels, it is not unusual to find people waiting on line for an opportunity to play the machine. Local residents sometimes team up to play such a machine in shifts around the clock.

Progressive slots in the lower-denomination coins are also popular and offer proportionately large payoffs. At the moment, the Western Casino in downtown Las Vegas has a bank of penny progressive machines on which the jackpot has reached $70,000. In order to be eligible for the giant prize, the player must play three cents simultaneously.

MULTIPLE-COIN PLAY

The multiple-coin feature is found on all progressive machines. Although these machines will accept single-coin play and these single coins do contribute to the growth of the giant jackpot, the player will not be eligible to win that jackpot unless he plays the maximum number of coins the machine accepts—usually three, four, or five. Anyone who plays fewer coins will only win the lesser, set payoffs, even if the giant jackpot combination should come up on the reels.

Naturally, the odds against hitting the giant jackpot on one of these machines are very high. Most progressive machines have either four or five reels, and the winning symbol, usually the number 7, must line up on all the reels to win the grand prize. Most of these machines have twenty-five stops per reel and only one number 7 on each reel. This means that, on a four-reel machine, you have one chance in 390,625 (25 × 25 × 25 × 25) to win; on a five-reel machine, the chances are one in 9,765,625 (25 × 25 × 25 × 25 × 25).

Although progressive slots do give lesser payoffs in addition to the giant jackpot, they are much tighter on these payoffs than straight machines. Disregarding the progressive prize, the percentage faced by the player on these machines is typically 20 percent. This is much higher than on most nonprogressives. That means that the only reason to play these machines is to try to win the giant prize. Therefore, when playing a progressive machine, you should always play the highest number of coins the machine accepts; this is the only way you can qualify for the progressive jackpot. It could well sour the rest of your life to see four 7s line up on the pay line and receive only three hundred dollars when you could have had a quarter-million dollars if you had played four coins instead of three. If you don't feel you can afford to play the full number of coins, then play a straight machine instead. Your chances of showing a profit will be much higher. Also, when playing progressives, make sure that you play for the highest jackpot available in that casino for that particular denomination coin. It doesn't make sense to settle for less, yet players often do because they don't take the trouble to look around before they settle down to play.

Video Poker

Video poker represents the fastest growing segment of slot machine play, not only in Nevada and Atlantic City but throughout the nation. The FBI estimates that there are approximately 250,000 illegal video poker machines in bars and clubs around the country earning about two billion dollars a year for organized crime. Even aside from legal and ethical considerations, you are better off playing these machines in legal casinos, because they provide a better return. Many casino machines return the player's bet if he scores a pair of jacks or better; most illegal machines require a pair of aces or better before returning your bet.

BASIC PLAY

When the player inserts his money and presses the button marked DEAL, a five-card poker hand appears on the screen. This hand is randomly generated by the machine's computer in a manner reflecting the composition of a fifty-two-card deck. In other words, the result is the same as if one were dealt five cards from a shuffled, standard deck of cards. As in draw poker, the player may keep as many of these cards as he wishes and draw to replace the others. Beneath each card there is a button marked HOLD. The player presses the button of each card he wishes to retain. (On some machines, these buttons say DISCARD. Make sure to check before you start to play, or you may end up throwing away precisely the cards you wanted to keep. If you do make a mistake in your selection, press the button marked CANCEL and begin the draw process over again.) After making his choices, the player hits another button marked DRAW. When he does that, the cards he elected not to retain are replaced by other random cards chosen from the forty-seven cards remaining in the electronic "deck."

Alternatively, the player may wish to stand pat. In that case he presses the button marked STAND. Some machines don't have a stand button. In this case the player must press hold under each of the five cards and then hit the draw button.

The final hand the player receives determines his payoff, if any, according to the payoff schedule posted on the machine. These payoffs reflect the rank of hands in the game of poker. A full house pays more than a flush, just as a full house beats a flush in a real poker game.

PAYOFFS

Like regular slots, video poker machines come in both straight and progressive versions. Most accept anywhere from one to five coins. The payoffs are in proportion to the number of coins played. A person playing four coins will receive four times as large a payoff as would a person who played only one coin and received the same hand. The one exception is the royal flush. This is the payoff the house uses to encourage players to play the maximum number of coins. A royal flush pays 250, 500, 750, or 1,000 coins for play of one, two, three, or four coins respectively. But a person playing five coins receives a disproportionately high payoff of 4,000 coins on a straight machine.

On a progressive machine, the royal flush is the hand that wins the giant progressive jackpot—but only if the player plays five coins. These progressive jackpots work exactly as explained earlier, with several machines in a bank all attached to the same progressive meter.

The most common payoff schedule for a nonprogressive machine is as follows:

Poker Hand	Payoff (per coin played)
royal flush	250
straight flush	50
four of a kind	25
full house	9
flush	6
straight	4
three of a kind	3
two pair	2
pair of jacks or better	1

You should not play on any straight machine that offers lower payoffs than these. Progressive machines typically follow the same schedule, except that they pay only 8 units for a full house and 5 units for a flush. Never play a progressive machine without playing the maximum number of coins. Otherwise, you will be ineligible for the giant jackpot and will be putting up with lower payoffs on flushes and full houses for no reason. Machines with the above payoffs give the house a reasonable edge of only about 2 to 5 percent or even less, depending on the progressive jackpot and the intelligence of the player's drawing strategy.

Video Keno

The great success of video poker machines has led slot machine manufacturers to try to come up with other kinds of slots that are patterned after familiar games and that require the kind of active player involvement that has made video poker so appealing to players. One result is *video keno*. A keno card with numbers 1 to 80 appears on the video screen, and the player may mark off anywhere from one to ten spots using the light pen provided with each machine. If he changes his mind, he can start again by pressing a button marked ERASE. Once he is satisfied, he presses a button marked START. At that point, the machine selects twenty numbers at random. The number of hits the player gets, if any, compared with the total numbers he had marked off, determines his payoff.

Video keno machines also come in progressive versions. In order to win the jackpot, you must play five coins and you must pick ten numbers on your card and hit on all ten of them. The odds of doing this are 9 million to 1.

The game carries a house percentage of 15 percent, which comes close to the worst deal found on regular slot machines. Admittedly, it is better than the house percentage on real keno, which is about 25 percent. However, video keno is still more deadly than real keno because of the frequency of play. At keno, you get a game every seven or eight minutes; at video keno, you can play a game every seven or eight seconds or less. Consequently, your money will get eaten up infinitely faster at the machines. If you like slot machines and if you also like to play keno, my advice is to stick to regular slots or video poker and fill out an occasional keno ticket while you tackle the machines.

If You Win

Hitting a jackpot at the slot machines is difficult enough. If you do succeed in doing so, you don't want to lose out because of a simple error. Here are some common mistakes to avoid.

PAYOFFS

Remember that on large payoffs, the machine may only pay part of the prize. The rest of it will be paid to you by an attendant, so be sure you don't leave the machine before you have gotten all the money you have coming to you. When the first casinos opened in Atlantic City, this happened so often that some hustlers started hanging around the slot machines. Whenever a player hit a jackpot and ignorantly left without collecting the remaining portion from the slot attendant, the hustler would move over to the machine and turn on the call light. When the attendant came over, he would collect the money as if he had hit the jackpot. Every machine has a button on it to press to call over a slot attendant. When you call an attendant over for a payoff, don't touch the machine until he gets there. If you play the machine again, he will have no way of verifying your win, since the reels will have moved off the payoff combination, and you won't get your money.

The above advice is designed to ensure that you get what is coming to you. Unfortunately, the casino is also determined to get what is coming to it. It will sometimes happen that, due to a malfunction, a machine will pay out more than it is supposed to. If that happens and a slot attendant sees it, he will give you the money you legitimately won and take back the rest. It's irritating, but the law is on his side.

MALFUNCTIONS

Sometimes, in the middle of a payoff, a machine may black out and shut off. The machines are programmed to black out under certain circumstances as a security measure against slot cheats. However, due to poor maintenance, they sometimes black out for no discernible reason. Don't walk away from a machine if this happens; you probably have more money coming to you. Press the button to call over a slot attendant. He will reactivate the machine, at which point it will spit out the remainder of your payoff. Keep in mind that, on a large payoff, you can get a check from the casino to avoid having to carry around a large amount of cash.

On some machines, you will see a sign that says MACHINE PAYS OFF ONLY ON LIT LINES. You will also note that all or only some of the payoff lines on the reel window are lit. The unlit ones may be out of commission because of any of a number of malfunctions. The sign means what it says. If you play two coins, that might normally mean that, on this machine, you would win if a payoff combination came up on either the center or top line. But if the top line is unlit, you will not receive a payoff on that line, even if a winning combination comes up on it. They won't even refund your second coin. Study the machine and make sure you are not throwing away money on a gamble you cannot win. In fact, all slot machine strategy boils down to studying the machines, getting to know the different kinds, how they work, and how their working affects your chances of winning. Picking a good machine is the best you can do, because once you insert your coin, it's all luck.

X. Keno

♣ Keno is presently not among the games permitted by the Casino Control Commission in Atlantic City. It is, however, found in almost every casino in Nevada. It can be argued that this makes New Jersey gamblers more fortunate than Nevada players, since the advantage the house enjoys at keno is higher than at any other casino game. At about 25 percent, the house P.C. is so high that I cannot possibly recommend this game for serious gambling. However, because keno offers the possibility of such large winnings in return for such a small investment, it will always be popular among some players. The kind of person who can't resist playing the state lottery at home is going to play keno when he vacations in Las Vegas. The lure of a $50,000 payoff is just too great for some people to resist. That is just what the casinos are counting on. It has helped to make some of these casinos among the most luxurious edifices found anywhere in the world.

I can't help you win at keno. Only an extraordinary amount of luck can do that. All I can do is help you understand the correct way to play so that, if you insist on playing, you won't ruin your (slim) chances of winning through some technical error. Then again, for some of you, just reading about keno may be enough to satisfy your curiosity so that you can pass the game by the next time you are in Nevada. You will be the really lucky ones.

The Basic Game

THE TICKET

The essence of the game of keno is as simple as one could possibly wish. The player selects anywhere from one to fifteen numbers on a piece of paper marked with the numbers 1 to 80. Later, the casino conducts a drawing in which it selects twenty different numbers from 1 to 80. If the player has succeeded in picking any of the choices among the numbers he marked on his *ticket,* he may win some money, depending on how many numbers he had marked all together and how many of those were drawn by the casino.

The center of keno play is the *keno lounge.* This is an area of the casino containing rows of seats with writing-surface armrests of the kind found in college lecture halls where players can fill out their tickets and then watch the winning numbers as they are drawn. Throughout the lounge, the player will find blank keno tickets and crayons for use in filling them out. The keno ticket consists of the numbers 1 to 80 printed in sequence on a square of cheap paper in eight rows of ten numbers each.

To play the game, the player marks off any numbers of his choice by drawing an X through each one. He may select anywhere from one to fifteen different numbers in this manner. Each number so marked is called a *spot.* The player then writes the number of spots he has played in the right margin of the ticket and notes the amount of money he wishes to wager in the box in the upper-right-hand corner of the ticket. Finally, he takes the ticket to one of the windows at the *keno counter* at the front of the lounge. There one of the *keno writers* will collect the ticket along with the wager. The bet can be in the form of either cash or casino chips, although payoffs are always made in cash. The writer will also issue the player a *duplicate ticket* on which he has marked with a brush and ink the same numbers the player selected on the *original ticket.* In casino parlance, the original ticket, which the casino retains, is called the *inside ticket,* while the duplicate, which the player retains, is called the *outside ticket.* The duplicate ticket given to the player acts as his receipt for the bet and also his record of what numbers he bet on.

The keno writer will stamp both the original ticket and the duplicate with the date, the number of that particular game—all keno games conducted throughout the day are sequentially numbered—and a serial number unique to that ticket. All tickets are sequentially numbered as they are accepted by the house, and the last number issued is recorded prior to each drawing. This stamping is a security measure to prevent various kinds of fraud that are sometimes attempted at this game. A ticket that has not been properly stamped cannot be redeemed for a payoff.

Within a few minutes of turning in one's ticket, the drawing for that game will begin. Twenty numbers ranging from 1 to 80 will be randomly selected. These twenty numbers determine whether the player is entitled to a payoff and, if so, how much.

THE DRAWING

The drawing of the winning numbers is conducted by a casino employee known as the *caller*, who sits on an elevated platform behind the keno counter. These numbers are chosen by means of a device sometimes called a *goose*. In the early days of the game, the goose was a wooden, globe-shaped container with a long neck. Numbered wooden balls were shaken within the device, then were allowed to slide down the neck into the caller's hand. The design of the mechanism suggested the shape of a goose. Although the device used in the game today is very different in construction and design, the name has stuck.

The modern goose is a round, clear plastic container containing eighty ping-pong balls numbered from 1 to 80 to correspond to the numbers on the tickets. When a *blower* at the bottom of the goose is turned on, a current of air mixes the balls by bouncing them around. Some casinos use a rotating mesh-wire cage to mix the balls instead of a blower. Eventually, balls are randomly forced into the two glass *rabbit ears* (tubes) at the top of the goose. Each of these rabbit ears holds ten balls. These twenty balls supply the winning numbers for the drawing.

As each ball is selected, the caller announces the number over the public address system that covers the keno lounge. The numbers also light up on the electronic *keno board* at the front of the keno lounge. This board contains the numbers 1 to 80 in order just as they appear on each keno ticket, and it also shows the number of the game being called; this is the same number that is stamped on each player's ticket.

As each winning number is called, a casino employee punches the number out of a book of blank tickets so that the tickets are left with holes where the winning numbers should be. These punched tickets are known as *draw tickets*. One of these tickets is put on file as a permanent casino record of the drawing. The others are distributed to the writers and *keno runners*.

COLLECTING WINNINGS

These draw tickets are used by the keno writers to check all the inside tickets for that game. By placing the draw ticket over an inside ticket and using it as a grid, the writer can see how many winning numbers have been marked on the ticket. In this way, he can quickly identify winning tickets. He marks each of the draw numbers with a slash mark, removes the draw ticket, calculates the payoff, and writes the amount on the ticket. They are then placed aside to await the players' coming to collect their winnings.

During the drawing, each player has followed along on his duplicate ticket to determine whether he has succeeded in picking enough winners to qualify for a payoff. In the event that he does, he presents the duplicate to one of the keno writers at the counter. The writer will verify the winning numbers on the duplicate ticket by means of a draw ticket and calculate the payoff. He will then call out the number stamped on the ticket to his supervisor. The supervisor checks the inside ticket and tells him the amount of the payoff. This should coincide with the calculation just made by the writer on the outside ticket and acts as a safeguard against error or fraud. Assuming no discrepancies are found, the writer pays the player his winnings. In case of any discrepancy between the two tickets, it is the inside ticket, the one originally filled out by the player, that determines the payoff. Therefore, it is important that, in initially turning in your ticket before the game, you check to make sure that the writer has not made an error in filling out the duplicate—that it is marked in exactly the same way as the original you turned in. Otherwise, it is possible that you might win a payoff and not know it because you have been misled by an incorrectly marked duplicate.

If the player's win is a large one, a casino executive will be called over to verify the payoff. He will check the player's ticket and the inside ticket. In some casinos each inside ticket is recorded on microfilm and this will also be checked by the casino executive. He will verify the numbers on the balls contained in the rabbit ears of the keno goose and may even replay the videotape that is always made during the calling of each game. In many casinos, instead of videotaping, the drawing is photographed. The camera is activated by the starting and stopping of the blower. One photograph is taken as the machine starts, showing the rabbit ears empty. Then another photograph is taken at the end showing the twenty numbers in the rabbit ears. A clock, a calendar, and a sign showing the number of the game are kept close enough to the goose that they will show in the photograph. These pictures are stored on microfilm. In the case of a large payoff, the player may have to wait until the microfilm is developed and checked by the casino executive. This involved procedure is usually followed for payoffs of $2,500 or more. The entire process may take as much as thirty minutes, but a payoff of that size is worth the wait. However, if any irregularity should be discovered during the verification process, it may result in the suspension of all payoffs on that game until the Gaming Control Board rules on the matter.

The casino is required by law to report all large keno payoffs to the Internal Revenue Service. For this reason, they will request your Social Security number and identification if you should win a large prize.

The most important point to remember about payoffs is that they must be collected as soon as the game has been called, or the ticket will be disqualified. If you have a winner, don't waste time before presenting it. If you do, your $50,000 winner may turn into a worthless piece of paper.

RUNNERS

Although the game of keno is conducted in the keno lounge, you do not have to go to the lounge to play. The casino provides blank keno tickets in its restaurants, bars, and various lounge areas. These areas are patrolled by attractive young ladies in very short dresses who are known as runners. If you want to play, simply fill out a ticket and call over a runner when you see one, or have any casino employee call one for you. The runner can also provide you with blank tickets and a crayon if need be. She will take your ticket and your bet to the keno lounge and register the ticket for you. A couple of minutes later, she will bring you the duplicate ticket.

These same lounge areas contain electronic boards, just like the one in the keno lounge, that flash the winning numbers as they are drawn. After the drawing, the runner will come around again on her rounds. If you have won, she will verify the win for you using her draw ticket, and she will even take your duplicate ticket down to the counter, collect your winnings, and bring them back to you. This makes keno the only casino game you can play while simultaneously engaging in some other activity, such as having a snack in the coffee shop or trying to pick up a young lady at the bar.

However, note the disclaimer that appears in small print on each keno ticket: "Keno runners are available for your convenience. We are not responsible if tickets are too late for current game." The keno runner will do her best to get your ticket in before the next drawing begins. If she fails, she will return your ticket and your money when she comes back on her rounds. At that point, you will have the option of either having her play the ticket for the next game or forgetting about the whole thing. However, if your numbers have come up on the game you missed, you can't sue the casino. If you have had a religious revelation that your numbers are going to hit on the very next game, you had better run down to the keno lounge and play the ticket yourself.

FREQUENCY OF GAMES

Casinos run keno games continuously, twenty-four hours a day. There is no exact time limit. About eight to ten games are conducted each hour, so that two hundred or more games are played in each casino each day, each one running six to eight minutes. Tickets are accepted on these games at all times, except during each drawing, which takes about two minutes. A supervisor sitting behind the keno writers decides when to close each game. At that point, the word CLOSE is lit up on the keno board and no more bets can be made for that particular game. As soon as the drawing is concluded, tickets may be submitted for the next game.

PAYOFFS

The exact pay schedule employed at keno is rather complex and differs from casino to casino. Each casino's policy is detailed in a brochure that can be found in the keno lounge and wherever else blank keno tickets are available. There are three factors that determine the amount of money a winning ticket receives: the number of spots the player played on the ticket, the number of those spots that came up on the drawing, and the amount wagered on the ticket. Every possible payoff based on these three elements is listed in the brochure. Since the player may mark anywhere from one to fifteen spots, *catch* any number of them, and wager three or four different amounts on the ticket, the pay schedule is a pretty complex affair. The only practical way to present this information is in the form of the printed charts that appear in the brochure. The brochure contains fifteen charts in all, one for each type of card, from a one-spot ticket to a fifteen-spot ticket. The player consults the particular chart for the number of spots he played and checks along the top of the chart for the column that relates to his size bet. Then he looks down the side of the chart for the number of spots he caught. The point at which the correct column and row meet gives him the amount he won. For example, the brochure I have in front of me right now is from a major Strip casino. It lists the following payoffs for a six-spot ticket:

Mark Six Spots

CATCH	BET $1.00	BET $1.40	BET $5.00	BET $10.00
3 Win	1.00	1.20	5.00	10.00
4 Win	4.00	6.60	20.00	40.00
5 Win	85.00	120.00	425.00	850.00
6 Win	1,480.00	2,200.00	7,400.00	14,800.00

You will note that most of the three-catch payoffs consist of winning back the exact cost of the ticket. In some casinos, these payoffs will say "free play." Instead of returning your money, the casino will allow you to play another ticket of the same price at no cost.

BETTING LIMITS

Most casinos have a minimum bet of either seventy cents or one dollar. They will also allow bets at two or three other fixed increments. This is indicated by the chart above, which allows wagers at one dollar, one dollar and forty cents, five dollars, and ten dollars. For the specific sums allowed as wagers in a particular casino, you must consult its keno brochure.

Although there is a maximum bet allowed on a single straight ticket, this does not function as a limit in the same manner as the table maximum at other games. A player who wanted to circumvent the limit could simply fill out several identical tickets and take each one to a different keno writer, betting the limit on each one. For that reason, the casino employs a different kind of maximum limit at keno. On each keno ticket, you will find a small-print statement to the effect that the house pays "$50,000 limit to aggregate players each game." What this grammatical monstrosity is supposed to mean is that the casino is not about to pay out more than $50,000 in winnings on any one keno game, no matter what happens. If the total amount won on the game exceeds this sum, the house will prorate the $50,000 among all the big winners. For example, if two players were to win the $50,000 prize, they would each receive half of it—$25,000. If one player were to qualify for the $50,000 prize and two players were to qualify for $25,000 payoffs, the big winner would receive $25,000 while the two lesser winners would receive $12,500 each. In this way, the house protects itself from a catastrophic loss on any one game just as it does at the table games—by imposing maximum limits on individual bets.

However, the house very seldom has to invoke the *aggregate limit* rule. In most games, the total amount paid out comes nowhere near the $50,000 limit. On those occasions when the aggregate limit does have to be applied, it affects only the large payoffs; the small payoffs are always paid in full.

Some smaller casinos have a $25,000 limit, while a few larger ones have $100,000 limits. In each case, the betting limits are adjusted accordingly. However, $50,000 is the norm found in most casinos.

Types of Tickets

REPLAY TICKETS

Many keno players have favorite numbers or combinations that they pick every time they play the game. If you are one of those people, there is no need to fill out a new ticket each time. After the first time you play the ticket, if you wish to bet the same combination again, simply take your duplicate ticket and turn it in to the keno writer with a new wager. He will accept this *replay ticket* as an original ticket for the next game and will issue you a new duplicate, on which he will mark the same numbers but which he will stamp with the number of the next game. You can repeat this process as often as you wish. It is simply a labor-saving device for the player. In fact, every time a player comes to the window to collect a payoff, after receiving his winnings he will be asked by the writer if he wishes to play the ticket again. Even when a player wins, the casino does whatever little it can to get some of the money back.

STRAIGHT TICKETS

The type of ticket we have been discussing so far is known as a *straight ticket* or a *basic ticket*. It is the most commonly played kind of ticket. Since the player may mark anywhere from one to fifteen spots on such a ticket, there are fifteen different kinds of straight tickets. The most popular ones are the six-spot and the eight-spot tickets. The illustration below shows an eight-spot ticket in which the player has bet on numbers 9, 12, 15, 33, 36, 37, 55, and 78. Note that in addition to marking the desired numbers with Xs, the player has written the number of spots marked in the right margin of the ticket and has also written the amount wagered in the box in the upper-right corner. Dollar and cent signs are not used in writing the amount wagered. Instead, the cents are distinguished by being written smaller and being underlined.

The casino's pay schedule printed in the brochure contains only the payoffs on straight tickets. This is because, strictly speaking, a straight ticket is the only kind of wager that a player can make. However, he may play as many different straight tickets as he wishes in each game. What makes things interesting—and sometimes complicated—is that he can indicate each of these different wagers on the same ticket.

In its simplest form, this might involve playing three different three-spots on the same ticket. To do this, the player would mark the first three numbers he wishes to play and draw a circle around them. He would repeat the process with the second group of three he wished to bet on, and then again with the third group, so that he would end with three circled groups of numbers, each of which contained three marked numbers. (Any unmarked numbers that happened to fall within the circles would be ignored.) To let the keno writer know that this ticket was intended as three different three-spot tickets, the player would write the fraction $^3/_3$ in the right margin of the ticket. Below this, he would mark the amount he wished to bet on each of these three-number combinations. This amount would have to be one of the sums accepted by the house as indicated in the keno brochure. (If the player wished to bet different amounts on each group, he would have to go to the trouble of writing three different straight tickets.) Finally, in the box on the upper-right corner he would write the total amount he was wagering, which would, of course, be triple the sum he wished to wager on each three-spot.

However, it sometimes happens that a player wishes to make several wagers by combining several different groups of numbers in different ways. While no different in principle from the kinds of bets we have discussed so far, the details of such bets can become very complex. These types of wagers fall into two categories, *way tickets* and *combination tickets*.

WAY TICKETS

Suppose a player wished to make several six-spot bets. Instead of filling out a number of different tickets or circling different six-number groups on the same ticket, he might proceed as follows. He circles three different three-number groups. He then indicates that he wishes to bet each of these groups in combination with each of the others to form every possible six-spot bet. He does this by writing the fraction $^3/_6$ in the margin. The denominator of the fraction means that he wants to play six-spot bets, while the numerator indicates that the groups he has circled may be combined in three different ways to form six-spot tickets: the first group combined with the second group, the first group combined with the third group, and the second group combined with the third group. Below the fraction he writes the amount he wishes to wager on each of these ways. In our example, this amount is seventy cents. Finally, he writes the total amount wagered in the box. This comes to two dollars and ten cents, seventy cents on each of the three ways. This kind of ticket is illustrated on the facing page.

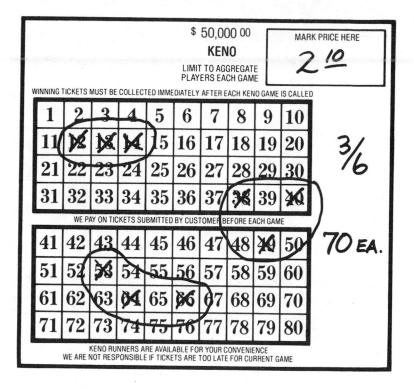

Way tickets can become far more elaborate—and expensive—than the one just described. For example, if the player had circled five different groups of numbers, he would be betting on ten ways. If he circled nine groups, he would be betting on thirty-six ways. Players really do make such complicated bets. In fact, one popular way ticket involves betting on 190 eight-spot combinations. This is done by marking off every single one of the twenty four-number columns into a different group and then playing every one of these groups combined with every other group to form 190 eight-spot bets.

When playing a way ticket, you must wager on every possible way, or the ticket will be invalid. For example, on a ticket that permitted fifteen, if you only wagered on fourteen ways, the house would have no way of knowing which combination you wanted to exclude. If they were to allow such equivocation, it could be used by unscrupulous players who would decide after the drawing which ways they wanted covered.

When more than three groups have been circled, it is far from obvious how many different ways these groups can be combined to achieve the desired bet. A simple formula can be used for calculating all the possible bets on a way ticket. Let's assume you have circled four three-number groups to form a nine-spot way ticket. The fact that there are four groups and the fact that those groups must be taken three at a time to form a way provide the information you need to calculate all the possible ways. You are going to construct a fraction. The denominator of the fraction will be: $1 \times 2 \times 3$. You stop multiplying at 3 because that is the number of groups needed to form each way. The numerator must have the same number of factors as the denominator. You will begin with the number 4 because that is the number of groups you have circled on the ticket. Your denominator will be $4 \times 3 \times 2$. When this is all multiplied out, you will be left with the fraction $^{24}/_6$, which can be simplified to the number 4. You now know that you have constructed a four-way nine-spot ticket.

One more quick example should clarify the process. This time we will assume that you have constructed an eight-spot way ticket by circling five four-number groups. The calculation would be: $5 \times 4/1 \times 2 = 10$. Your ticket is a ten-way eight-spot.

COMBINATION TICKETS

Instead of playing them as three six-spot bets, the three groups of three numbers marked in the illustration on page 215 could be played as three separate three-spot bets or one single nine-spot bet. In fact, the player could do all of those things at the same time. To indicate his intention, he would write $^3/_3$ in the margin. Beneath that fraction, he would write $^3/_6$, and beneath that he would write $^1/_9$. He would be making seven different wagers (the sum of the numerators of all the fractions) simultaneously. This is known as a combination ticket. As in the way bet, he is making several bets on the same ticket. Unlike a way ticket, he is combining several different kinds of bets. A way ticket may comprise many bets, but they are all of the same kind—for instance, all six-spot bets or all eight-spot bets. A combination ticket combines different kinds of bets—for instance, three-spot bets, six-spot bets, and nine-spot bets, as in the example given above.

Each fraction in the margin of a keno ticket represents a different type of bet and is known as a *condition*. The process of calculating the different combinations and noting them in the margin is called *conditioning*. Another way to distinguish between way tickets and combination tickets is to say that a way ticket contains several bets but only one condition, while a combination ticket contains more than one condition as well as more than one bet. To reduce it to the simplest terms, a way ticket will have only one fraction in the margin, while a combination ticket will have more than one fraction.

Naturally, the number of possible combinations can be increased by circling more groups. The variety of kinds of combinations can be increased by circling different-size groups of numbers. Indeed, most combination tickets involve combining different-size groups of numbers. Such tickets can become extremely complicated.

An example of this kind of ticket is given in the illustration below. With a group of two numbers, a group of three numbers, and two groups of four numbers, the following combinations become possible: one two-spot bet, one three-spot bet, two four-spot bets, one five-spot bet, two six-spot bets, two seven-spot bets, one eight-spot bet, two nine-spot bets, one ten-spot bet, one eleven-spot bet, and one thirteen-spot bet. A player who wished to play all these combinations would make the following notations in the margin: $\frac{1}{2}$, $\frac{1}{3}$, $\frac{2}{4}$, $\frac{1}{5}$, $\frac{2}{6}$, $\frac{2}{7}$, $\frac{1}{8}$, $\frac{2}{9}$, $\frac{1}{10}$, $\frac{1}{11}$, $\frac{1}{13}$.

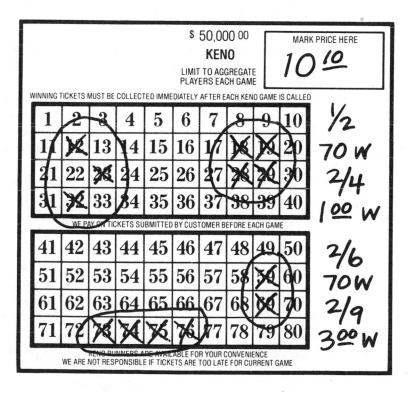

Note, however, that it is not necessary for the player to bet every one of these possible combinations simply because he has circled those four particular groups of numbers. If you check the margin of the ticket on page 217, you will note that the player has chosen to play only four of the eleven different possible types of tickets. He is playing seven different combinations (the sum of the numerators of the four fractions) but only four types of tickets (the total number of fractions).

It is, however, necessary for the player to bet on every combination of any particular type he chooses to cover. Therefore, since the above ticket allows two possible nine-spot bets, the player may not wager on only one of these nine-spot combinations, since the house would have no way of knowing which nine-spot was being bet on and which was not. A player's ticket must be unequivocal. If there is more than one way to interpret what he has written, the ticket is invalid. The casino is certainly not going to let you tell them what you really meant after the game has been called.

All of this points up the fact that simply circling desired numbers on a keno ticket is not enough. It is impossible to know how to interpret a way or combination ticket merely by noting what numbers have been circled. Reference must be made to the notations in the margin of the ticket to know what the player's intentions are in making the bet. Great care must be taken in conditioning any way or combination ticket. Otherwise, you may end up making a bet that is different from what you had intended, or you may design a ticket that is invalid.

Another point to remember is that all the groups of numbers you circle on a way or combination ticket must be mutually exclusive. Although it is theoretically possible to construct a functional ticket using intersecting circles, so that the same marked number is included in two or more groups, such tickets are not permitted by the house.

It is not necessary to wager the same amount on each type of bet on a combination ticket. In our example, the player has chosen to wager a different amount on each. He indicates this fact by writing a different price under each fraction. The W next to each amount stands for "way"; the player is betting that sum on each way the numbers can be combined to form the kind of bet listed directly above it. If he had chosen to bet the same amount on each one, he would have indicated by writing ".70 ea.," for example, under the entire column of fractions. The figure in the box at the upper-right corner represents the sum of all the amounts being wagered on all the various combinations the player is covering. When the same amount is being wagered on every combination, this total can be figured by multiplying the amount of each wager by the sum of the numerators of all the fractions. When a different amount is being wagered on each type of combination, it becomes necessary to multiply the numerator of each fraction by the amount being wagered on that type of bet, then adding up each of the totals arrived at.

The minimum betting limit the house imposes applies not to the total sum bet on a way or combination ticket but rather to each individual way or combination that is covered. In other words, every separate bet, as indicated by the sum of the numerators of all of the conditioning fractions, must meet the house minimum. You can see that, when wagering combinations, the amount of money involved can become substantial. Some casinos soften the blow by lowering the minimum bet required on way and combination tickets. Some cut the minimum in half; others lower it still further. You must ask a keno writer or a runner in order to find out the policy in that particular casino.

KING TICKETS

A *king number* is a single number circled so that it forms a "group" by itself. Any ticket containing one or more king numbers is called a *king ticket*. Although a king ticket is a kind of combination ticket essentially like those we have already examined, it contains enough unique features to merit separate discussion. The simplest king ticket is one in which several numbers have been marked by the player, only one of which is circled. The circled number is the king number, while the uncircled numbers form the *field*. Each number within that field is called a *pawn*. If the ticket contained nine marked numbers, one of which was circled, it would represent an eight-spot bet on all the uncircled numbers plus a nine-spot bet on all the marked numbers including the king. When several groups are circled, one of which is a king, the king number is intended to play in every possible combination with the other groups.

A king number never plays by itself, only in combinations. A ticket may contain more than one king number. In fact, one may play an *all-king ticket*, which consists only of circled individual numbers, each of which is intended to be played in every possible combination with the other king numbers. Such tickets can become mind-bogglingly complex. Just for the record, in order to determine how to correctly condition an all-king ticket, you would have to apply the formula given earlier for calculating way tickets. For example, if you have a ticket composed of five king numbers, you would use the formula to determine all the two-spot combinations possible with this ticket. Then you would employ the formula again to determine all the three-spot combinations, and one final time to determine all the possible four-spot combinations. Obviously, there is only one possible five-spot combination on the ticket.

There is almost no limit to the variations that can be worked out on keno tickets through the use of different-size groups and different numbers of groups played in combination. (Groups fewer than five numbers are usually circled, while those of five numbers or more are separated by means of straight lines.) Some combination tickets favored by many players actually incorporate all eighty numbers on the ticket, separated into different groups and played in combination with each other.

When you turn in your ticket, the writer will go over it carefully to check for errors. Nevertheless, you should do your part to make sure it is correctly conditioned before you submit it. If you find that the tickets you are writing are too confusing for you, there is a simple solution: Stick to less complicated tickets. As we shall see, complex tickets may be intriguing, but they offer no mathematical advantage over even the simplest straight ticket.

HOUSE TICKETS

Almost every casino offers one or more special types of combination tickets with unique payoffs not available in any other casino. Such tickets are known in the business as *house tickets*, although each casino dreams up some catchy name for its particular house ticket. These tickets don't offer the player any significant break in the massive house percentage found in keno, but they may offer advantages of emotional significance. For example, often these tickets will give the player a shot at the $50,000 grand prize for a smaller bet than do any of the standard tickets. They make up for this by offering smaller payoffs for lesser numbers of catches (winning numbers). However, since most keno players are primarily attracted to the game by the hope of a major win, this advantage of the house ticket will make it worth playing for many people. The house tickets offered by each casino will be found listed in their keno brochure.

Strategy

THE HOUSE PERCENTAGE

Calculating the house percentage on each kind of keno ticket is a long and complex process. It first involves calculating the odds of hitting every possible payoff combination for that ticket. This must be multiplied against all the payoffs offered by the house for this ticket. Finally, it is necessary to calculate how much it would cost to play every possible ticket of that particular type (for example, all possible eight-spot tickets), and this cost must be compared to the previously calculated payoff total. This process has to be repeated for each of the fifteen possible straight tickets. Finally, since each casino has its own payoff schedule, this process would have to be repeated at each casino you play in. It's not exactly the kind of thing you work out in your head while filling out your ticket in the keno lounge.

Those who have taken the trouble to perform these calculations (with the help of computers) have all agreed that, as so often happens in gambling, the variety offered by different kinds of keno tickets and different payoff schedules is more apparent than real. All keno tickets in virtually all casinos have a house percentage of just around 25 percent. To put this in perspective, this is about five times as high as the percentage one faces when he makes a bet at the roulette table and about eighteen times as high as the percentage on a line bet at craps. Admittedly, the player would make many bets at roulette or craps in the time it would take to play one keno ticket. This means that the percentages at those other games are applied repeatedly far more often, which gives them that much more opportunity to grind down the player's bankroll. This does not change the fact that a 25 percent edge makes keno as bad a game as one will encounter in a casino.

That 25 percent figure is the most important thing you must always remember about keno. It is far more relevant to your chances of success than all the esoterica about exotic combination tickets. It makes it clear that the best strategy one can ever hope to fashion for keno is to stay away from the game. The next-best strategy is to risk as little money at it as possible. If you feel you have to play the game at all, you should stick to small wagers. Fortunately, the low minimums at the game make this possible.

SELECTING THE NUMBERS

The answer to the often-asked question, what are the best numbers to bet on, is: it doesn't matter. Every number has the same chance of coming up as every other number. If you don't buy that claim, go back and read the section on the fallacy of the maturity of chances in Chapter II. Add to what we have already learned about the mnemonic powers of dice and roulette wheels the following simple but profound truth: ping-pong balls have no memory.

TYPES OF TICKETS

We have taken a brief look at the vast variety of tickets possible at keno. However, in the final analysis, all keno tickets are created equal, except that some are more expensive than others. With a 25 percent house edge, it should be obvious that the cheap tickets are better than the expensive ones. That means that way and combination tickets should be strictly avoided.

I realize that such tickets hold a fascination for many players. Part of this comes from the challenge to one's ingenuity to devise new, intriguing, ever more complex combinations. I have no quarrel with this attitude. Devising keno tickets is no worse an avocation than doing crossword puzzles or fiddling with Rubik's Cube—as long as you don't bet on the things.

Keno players who wager on way and combination tickets are similar to roulette players who try elaborate combinations of bets on the layout, line bets intersecting column bets paralleling street bets enclosing split bets. These things can make really pretty patterns on the layout, but they don't change your chances of winning; they only increase the cost of playing. That's a dangerous thing to do at a game with as great a house advantage as keno.

Players who substitute wishful thinking for rigorous analysis sometimes try to con themselves into believing that, through sufficient experimentation with different keno combinations, they will eventually hit on the magical combination that will give them the edge over the house. If you have really studied this book up to this point, you have too good an understanding of how gambling really works to believe that. You know that adding up a group of minuses (negative expectation bets) won't give you a positive. Remember, playing a combination ticket is no different from filling out a lot of different straight tickets.

All that combination keno tickets accomplish is to increase the amount of money you have to bet on each game, sometimes quite drastically. It will increase the likelihood of winning, but the chances of winning a large payoff remain so small no matter what kind of ticket you play that the difference is almost academic. Most important, you are paying dearly for the opportunity to improve your chances because of the awesome 25 percent house edge.

About the only saving grace that the game of keno has is the chance to win a great deal of money for a very small investment, but as soon as you start playing combination tickets, the investment is no longer so small. My advice to anyone who wants to play keno is to take a philosophical approach. Play the cheapest ticket that will qualify you for a substantial payoff, and just figure that if you are destined to win it, that one little ticket will be enough to do it. If you are not destined to win the big money, all the expensive, convoluted way, combination, and king tickets in the world won't help.

Unlike all the other advice I have given you in this book, this suggestion is not strictly scientific; probability theory does not recognize fate as a factor. The strictly scientific advice would be not to play this game because of the prohibitive house P.C. However, if you are interested in the game of keno at all, you are obviously too much of an optimist to heed such sound advice. So do the next best thing. Stick to small-price tickets. Good luck; you're going to need it in this game.

XI. The Other Games

♣ The games we have covered in previous chapters represent the backbone of casino gambling and are the only ones that should be considered for serious gambling. In this chapter, we are going to look at some of the peripheral games you will sometimes encounter in a casino. I will explain how they work primarily to satisfy your curiosity, since most of the games in this chapter have too high a house advantage to be recommended. You won't find these games in every casino, but will occasionally encounter them in Nevada. In Atlantic City, the only ones you will find are the wheel of fortune and the gambling tournaments.

The Wheel of Fortune

The *wheel of fortune* is really a carnival game that has somehow found its way into gambling casinos. The wheel, which is six feet in diameter, stands upright on a post. The entire wheel is divided into nine sections, each of which contains six divisions. (For this reason, it is also called a *big six wheel*.) This gives the wheel a total of fifty-four segments. Each of these segments is marked by a bill of U.S. currency, either a one-, a two-, a five-, a ten-, or a twenty-dollar bill. (For this reason, the game is also called the *money wheel*.) The two exceptions are one segment that is marked with the casino logo and the segment directly opposite, which is marked with a joker. These fifty-four segments are separated from each other at the periphery of the wheel by nail-like protrusions called posts. As the wheel is spun, these posts strike against a leather indicator at the top of the wooden pole that supports the wheel.

A counter in front of the wheel has a betting layout bearing the same bills and symbols that appear on the wheel. Players make their wagers by placing their bets on the layout on the bill or symbol they think will come up on the next spin. After all bets are down, the wheel is spun by a dealer. In some games, the players may continue making bets until the wheel begins to slow down. When it comes to a standstill, the section marked by the leather indicator above the wheel determines the winning bet.

The winning symbol also determines the amount of the payoff. A wager on the one-dollar bill pays even money. A wager on the two-dollar bill pays 2 to 1. A wager on the five-dollar bill pays 5 to 1 odds. The ten-dollar bill pays 10 to 1, and the twenty-dollar bill pays 20 to 1. The joker and casino logo each pay 40 to 1. In Atlantic City, the players get a better break on this last bet; they pay 45 to 1 on the joker and logo. The table below shows the number of times each symbol appears on the wheel as well as the house payoff on each bet. With that information, you would be able to figure out the house percentage yourself using the method I taught you in Chapter II. But I've already done it for you and listed it in the last column of the table. The few places where the Atlantic City wheel or payoff differs from Nevada have been noted in parentheses.

Analysis of the Wheel of Fortune

SYMBOL	NUMBER OF SYMBOLS	PAYOFF	HOUSE P.C.
$1	24 (A.C.: 23)	1 to 1	11.1 (A.C.: 14.8)
$2	15	2 to 1	16.6
$5	7 (A.C.: 8)	5 to 1	22.2 (A.C.: 11.1)
$10	4	10 to 1	18.5
$20	2	20 to 1	22.2
joker	1	40 to 1 (A.C.: 45 to 1)	24.0 (A.C.: 14.8)
logo	1	40 to 1 (A.C.: 45 to 1)	24.0 (A.C.: 14.8)

It is superfluous to talk about strategy at a game that offers such an outlandishly high P.C. In the last few years, a number of sophisticated gamblers have been experimenting with covert computers and other kinds of devices for clocking the wheel. These devices, worn secretly under the player's clothing, could be used to predict what segment of the wheel the indicator is likely to stop at, based on the speed with which the dealer spun the wheel and the starting position of the wheel before it was spun. However, with the recent legislation in Nevada making the use of such devices a felony punishable by up to ten years' imprisonment or a fine of up to ten thousand dollars, I can hardly recommend this technique to anyone planning to head for Las Vegas. The only intelligent strategy for a game like this is to stay away.

Not every Nevada casino has a wheel of fortune, but it can be found in many of them, primarily in the grind joints. Usually, a casino will have one such game either set off to one side or sealing off one end of a blackjack pit. Most of the time, when one passes the game in a Nevada casino, he will see the dealer holding up a *dead table*. But the game does attract some play when the casino is busy. For some reason, the wheel of fortune gets much more action in Atlantic City, although the slightly better odds offered on a couple of the bets hardly justify this greater popularity.

Like slot machines, the wheel of fortune is popular with people who find themselves in a casino for the first time in their lives and are intimidated by what they see happening at the blackjack, craps, roulette, and baccarat tables. When they spot the wheel, they recognize it from their visits to carnivals and figure that here at least is a simple game they can understand. It is not an exciting game, and it is certainly not one that offers the player much chance of winning. Both in terms of odds and enjoyment, the casino has much better to offer.

Sic Bo

The game of Sic Bo, a name that literally means "dice pairs," has been introduced into a number of Nevada casinos over the last decade in an attempt to capture a part of the Far Eastern gambling market. Asians are noted for being reckless and high-rolling gamblers. This ancient Chinese game is presently the most popular game in the Philippines. Despite its Oriental origin, it is actually very similar to an old English game called Grand Hazard.

When you first approach the Sic Bo table, you may think it is some kind of pinball game due to the elaborate table that lights up in a different pattern after each play. Actually, this is just window dressing. It is really a very simple dice game. The dealer shakes three dice after players have made wagers on what totals or combinations they think will come up on the dice.

Players make their wagers by placing their chips on the appropriate

SMALL ARE THE NUMBERS 4 TO 10 — 1 WINS 1 — LOSE IF ANY TRIPLE APPEARS 小 | EACH DOUBLE: 1 WINS 8 | 1 WINS 150 | 1 WINS 24 — ANY TRIPLE | 1 WINS 150 | EACH DOUBLE: 1 WINS 8 | **BIG** ARE THE NUMBERS 11 TO 17 — 1 WINS 1 — LOSE IF ANY TRIPLE APPEARS 大

4	5	6	7	8	9	10	11	12	13	14	15	16	17
1 WINS 50	1 WINS 18	1 WINS 14	1 WINS 12	1 WINS 8	1 WINS 6	1 WINS 6	1 WINS 6	1 WINS 6	1 WINS 8	1 WINS 12	1 WINS 14	1 WINS 18	1 WINS 50

ONE | TWO | THREE | FOUR | FIVE | SIX

1 TO 1 ON ONE DIE   2 TO 1 ON TWO DIE   3 TO 1 ON THREE DIE

space on the elaborate layout, which illustrates various dice combinations by depicting the faces of the dice in different patterns. This layout, which is painted on translucent glass, is a key feature of the game. The dealer then picks up a sealed container holding three dice called a *shaker*. Shaking the dice, he places down the container and notes the results on the dice. The dealer now enters the results of the dice shake into the electronic table bearing the layout. Instantly, all the winning wagers on the layout light up. This facilitates the dealer's job of collecting and paying off bets on the myriad wagering options the game offers. As soon as all bets have been settled—the winner being paid according to the payoff odds marked on the layout—another round of play is started.

With a little study, the layout becomes extremely easy to read, both as to the wagers permitted and the payoffs on each one. There are seven different kinds of bets permitted in the game. We will consider each one in the order they appear from the bottom of the layout to the top. First, one may wager on any one of the six dice faces, 1, 2, 3, 4, 5, or 6. If that number comes up on one of the three dice, the bettor is paid at even money. If two of the dice bear that number, he receives 2 to 1, and if all three dice come up with that number, the payoff is 3 to 1. This is nothing more than the old game of chuck-a-luck (that's the one with three dice in an hourglass cage) incorporated into Sic Bo. The house advantage on this bet is 7.8 percent.

The next wager is a bet that a combination of two particular numbers, for example 1–6 or 3–4, will come up on any two of the three dice. This bet pays 5 to 1, giving the house an edge of 16.6 percent.

Next comes the wager on the total of the three dice. The player can bet on any specific total from 4 to 17. The payoff on this bet can vary from 6 to 1 to 50 to 1, depending on what total the player bets. The following chart lists the payoff on each total, as well as the house percentage on each bet:

Totals Wager at Sic Bo

TOTAL	PAYOFF	HOUSE P.C.
4 (or 17)	50 to 1	29.1
5 (or 16)	18 to 1	47.2
6 (or 15)	14 to 1	30.5
7 (or 14)	12 to 1	9.7
8 (or 13)	8 to 1	12.5
9 (or 12)	6 to 1	18.9
10 (or 11)	6 to 1	12.5

The first thing that strikes one about this table is how tremendously the house percentage varies depending on what total the player bets on. A bet on 5 faces a house edge almost five times as high as a bet on 7. A bet on 10 pays the same 6 to 1 odds as a bet on 9, even though there are twenty-seven ways to make 10 with three dice and only twenty-five ways to make 9 with three dice. The result is that a player wagering on 9 faces a disadvantage almost 50 percent greater than a player wagering on 10, and he is doing it in hopes of earning the same 6 to 1 profit. One is inclined to ask why anyone in their right mind would bet on 9 or 12 instead of making the same wager on 10 or 11. On second thought, one has to wonder why anyone in their right mind would make any of these bets. They are all so bad that comparing one to another is almost academic.

The next type of bet offered is a wager on "small" or "big," to use the terminology found on the layout. The bets might more correctly be labeled "low" and "high." If you bet on small, you are betting that the three dice will total somewhere from 4 to 10. You lose if totals 3, 11, 12, 13, 14, 15, 16, 17, or 18 appear. The bet pays even money. There are 107 ways to make the totals 4 to 10 with three dice. Three dice can make any of 216 combinations. (Each die has six sides; therefore, the number of combinations is 6 × 6 × 6 = 216.) Therefore, there are 109 ways to win and 107 ways to lose. This alone would give the house a slight edge, but the reality is much worse. The fine print under both the small and big bets says, "Lose if any triple appears." So a wager on small loses if the dice come up either

2–2–2, or 3–3–3, even though those totals come within the 4-to-10 boundaries that constitute "small." This means that the player has only 105 ways to win and 111 ways to lose. At even money, this gives the house an edge of 2.7 percent. Not very good, but better than any of the other bets we have analyzed so far. A bet on "big" wins if the dice total 11 through 17 and loses if they total 3, 4, 5, 6, 7, 8, 9, 10, or come up three of a kind. This bet breaks down the same way as the small bet and gives the house the same 2.7 percent advantage.

You can also bet that a particular three-of-a-kind will come up. You might, for example, wager that three 6s will come up on the next shake. This bet pays 150 to 1, regardless of what set of triplets you bet on. True odds are 215 to 1. That gives the house a whopping edge of 30 percent. Remember, that means that you can expect to lose thirty cents out of every dollar you bet on this wager. (A bet on three 1s is the same as a bet on the total 3, and a bet on three 6s is the same as a bet on the total 18. That is why the house does not bother to list 3 and 18 among the "total" wagers we looked at earlier.)

You can also bet that any triplet will come up. If any three-of-a-kind is shaken, you will win 24 to 1. The true odds on this bet are 35 to 1. On this one, you will lose at a rate of 30.5 percent.

Last, you can wager that a particular pair, such as two 5s, will appear on any two of the three dice. The house pays 8 to 1 on this bet. This time you are paying 33.3 percent of everything you wager to the casino's welfare fund.

I spent more time on this game than it is really worth only because I figured you probably wouldn't take the trouble to analyze it yourself and you might be tempted to play just because of the novelty of the game. I could have just told you to stay away from it for your own good, but I said at the outset that I would try not to ask you to take my word for things. Now it should be apparent why this game is the worst sort of sucker trap imaginable. The game of Sic Bo offers the chance to earn big payoffs for small wagers. As usually happens in casino gambling, the price for such an opportunity is obscenely high house percentages that are almost guaranteed to destroy your bankroll and sour your whole outlook on life. Sic Bo is a fast-action game because every wager on the layout is won or lost after each shake of the dice. This just means that your money will disappear that much faster, since the house percentage has so many more opportunities to work on your bankroll than in a game like craps in which most of the bets may require several rolls of the dice to be settled.

The only other thing Sic Bo offers the player is flashing lights. But the casino signs in Las Vegas and Atlantic City are loaded with flashing lights you don't have to pay to look at. If dice appeal to you, stick to the American version, craps. Study Chapter V to learn how to play the game, and you will end up with much more fun and money than you ever would at Sic Bo.

Pai Gow

Like Sic Bo, Pai Gow is an ancient Chinese game first imported into Nevada about ten years ago in an effort to attract the lucrative Asian gambling market. It can presently be found in a few casinos in Las Vegas, Reno, and Lake Tahoe. I doubt that many Occidentals would care to take the considerable trouble required to learn to play this game, but you might want to know enough about it to have an idea what is going on the next time you pass it by in a casino.

Pai Gow is played on a table resembling an oversize version of a blackjack table. Like a blackjack table, it can accommodate up to seven seated players plus a standing dealer. The game is not played with cards but rather with thirty-two special dominoes bearing red and white spots. In fact, the name of the game means "heavenly dominoes." Each hand begins with the dealer shuffling the dominoes. He does this by spreading them face down on the table and pushing them around with his hands in the style that poker players call "scrambling the deck" and casino dealers call "washing the cards."

The dealer then throws three dice to determine which player he will start the deal with. All the players, including the house dealer, take turns playing the part of the bank. Each player including the dealer receives four dominoes, which he examines and then forms into two separate hands, one called the *high hand* and the other called the *low hand*.

I won't go into the complexities of the ranking of the possible hands. Suffice it to say that each player is attempting to come up with two better hands than the bank does. Each player in turn plays the role of the bank. The other players hope to beat the bank by coming up with a high hand that is higher than the bank's high hand and a low hand that is lower than the bank's low hand. If both of a player's hands beat the bank, he wins. If both of his hands lose to the bank, he loses. If one of his hands beats the bank and the other loses, it is considered a tie and no money changes hands. The house makes its profit by charging a 5 percent commission on all winning bets.

It is impossible to calculate a single house percentage in this game because a player's chances of winning depend on his skill in forming his four dominoes into the two best possible hands and also on the skill of the player acting as the bank in forming his two hands. The first question that has to be determined is: What is the optimal strategy for the play of the hands? John Gwynn of California State University has been attempting to answer that question through computer analysis of the game. It may even happen that he will come up with a strategy that can give a player the edge over the house. Until the issue is settled, I suggest you just enjoy Pai Gow as a spectator. That's what I plan to do. Stay tuned for further developments.

Casino Promotions

The casino gambling field is a very competitive business. Casinos are constantly coming up with new promotional ideas in an attempt to lure players away from the competition. Many of these promotions involve the introduction of new gambling games or twists on old games that give the player a break in terms of bonus payoffs or favorable rules. There is no point in analyzing these games in detail since most of them don't stick around very long. Novelty is a big part of their appeal. As soon as one of these promotions has served its purpose, it is dropped, and the casino starts looking for some new angle. I will outline some of the promotional games that have been used recently to give you an idea of what you might encounter.

One casino installed a red light that would go on at random intervals. When it did, all blackjacks and slot jackpots during that period paid double, and certain numbers paid extra on the field bet at craps. One downtown Las Vegas casino celebrates every Christmas by paying 2 to 1 on blackjacks instead of the standard 3 to 2. Unfortunately, only bets of five dollars or less are eligible for this bonus payoff. Some casinos will run a keno promotion in which they give players free tickets. These are special tickets with limited payoffs. You can't win the $50,000 grand prize with one of these tickets. But then, what do you expect for free?

CRAPLESS CRAPS

As I said, the really generous promotions don't usually last very long. What do sometimes last are those promotions that appear to give the player an advantage while actually giving the casino an even bigger edge than usual. An innovator in this area has been Bob Stupak of Vegas World on the Las Vegas Strip. One of his brainstorms was the game of Crapless Craps. The come-on on this one was the advertising claim, "It is impossible to lose on the come-out roll." Since all crap players have countless memories of losing on the come-out roll, this sounds pretty good—until you take a closer look. In Crapless Craps, if you roll a 7 on the come-out, you win. However, if you roll a 2, 3, or 12, instead of losing, that number becomes your point. You must repeat the number before rolling a 7 in order to win. The same is true if you roll 11 on the come-out. Instead of an automatic win, 11 becomes your point, which must be repeated before a 7 in order to win. Incidentally, the game has no don't-pass line, so every player has to bet with the shooter.

Numbers 2 or 12 can only be made one way with a pair of dice, while 3 can only be made two ways. By contrast, 7 can be made six ways. That means that when 2, 3, or 12 is your point, you will seven-out almost every time. In regular craps, when you roll 2, 3, or 12, you automatically lose. In Crapless Craps, when you roll 2, 3, or 12, you will usually lose. That's an improvement, but not much of one.

By contrast, consider what happens if you roll an 11 on the come-out. In regular craps, you would win automatically. In Crapless Craps, 11 becomes your point. Since there are only two ways of making 11 and six ways of making 7, you will almost always seven-out when your point is 11. Therefore, in Crapless Craps, a come-out roll of 11 is changed from an automatic winner to an almost automatic loser. This more than nullifies the slight advantage the player gains by making 2, 3, and 12 into point numbers. Stupak's game also offers slightly better odds on the proposition bets, but these wagers are such sucker traps that they are still not worth considering. Consequently, Crapless Craps is a far worse game for the player than regular craps. Normally at craps, line bets face a 1.4 percent house advantage. At Crapless Craps, the P.C. jumps to 5.38 percent. Nevertheless, the game has had great appeal for those players who don't know how to intelligently analyze a gambling proposition.

DOUBLE EXPOSURE 21

Another Vegas World innovation is the game of Double Exposure 21. This one has proved so popular with players that it has spread under different names to several other casinos throughout Nevada. In this version of blackjack, the dealer gives himself both cards face up. It sounds like a blackjack player's dream! Imagine knowing exactly what the dealer is holding before deciding whether to hit or stand. But as with Crapless Craps, in this game what is given with one hand is taken away with the other. In Double Exposure 21, the dealer takes all ties and pays only even money on blackjacks. These two rules are such a massive handicap for the player that they more than outweigh even the advantage of knowing the dealer's hole card. Even with a basic strategy designed specifically for Double Exposure, the player will face more of a house edge than if he simply plays basic strategy at regular blackjack. The popularity of this game is just another indication of how many casino gamblers there are out there who can't recognize their own best interest.

If you encounter a promotional game or variation the next time you visit a casino, by all means check it out. Some of them are real bargains. Just don't dive in without looking. Try to analyze the proposition mathematically. With some of them, this might really be too complex a job. In such cases, proceed cautiously. Don't mortgage the farm just because a particular casino angle looks good. However, with some of these propositions you may be able to determine whether the "bargain" the casino is offering really is a bargain just by applying what you have learned about gambling from this book.

Gambling Tournaments

By far the most popular new idea of the last few years in casino promotions has been the gambling tournament. Casinos have long followed the practice of sponsoring backgammon tournaments, gin rummy tournaments, poker tournaments, and other kinds of contests as a means of bringing people into the hotel during slow periods. But for some reason, no one ever thought of the obvious idea of a casino sponsoring a tournament built around a casino game. When a firm called International Gaming Promotions started trying to sell the idea, they found it far from easy to interest casino executives. Eventually, the Sahara Hotel agreed to give the concept a try. The first Sahara World Championship of Blackjack in 1978 proved to be the most successful casino promotion in history. The Las Vegas Sahara was booked to 100 percent capacity during what was normally its slowest period of the year, and suddenly it seemed that almost every casino wanted to sponsor a tournament. Today, gambling casinos both in Nevada and Atlantic City regularly sponsor tournaments on blackjack, craps, slot machine play, and even contests that involve participation in more than one type of game.

TOURNAMENT FORMAT

Most of these tournaments follow essentially the same format. Contestants pay a certain entry fee to take part in the tournament. They are then broken up into groups, each of which is assigned its own gaming table; noncontestants are not allowed to play at these tables. The competition is conducted in the form of several elimination rounds. Each round begins with each player buying in for a certain set amount that cannot be supplemented with any subsequent buy-ins during the round. Therefore, each player starts with the same size bankroll. At the end of a certain time period, the player at each table with the largest sum of money advances to the next round. Once the original number of entrants has been reduced to one table of players, the winner of the most money at that table at the end of the stipulated time period is crowned the winner. Prizes, which can reach the $100,000 range for first prize and may also include noncash awards, are awarded to all finalists. Some tournaments incorporate a second-chance contest, in which those eliminated in earlier rounds can compete by paying another entry fee.

THE SKILL FACTOR

Although the competitors in these tournaments are playing standard casino games such as blackjack or craps and are playing by the standard casino rules for these games, it is important to understand that they are really playing a very different kind of game altogether from what usually is played at a blackjack or crap table. Normally, a casino gamer is competing against the house. In a tournament, the player is competing against the other players. This shift in focus radically alters the game.

The difference is best illustrated by an episode that occurred a couple of years ago in the Sahara Summer Blackjack Classic. In the last hand of one of the elimination rounds, a woman was dealt an ace and a ten—a perfect blackjack. Rather than accept the standard 3 to 2 payoff on the hand, she elected to count the ace as a one, giving her a total of 11, and double down on the hand. Normally, no sane person would ever pull such a bizarre play. For a blackjack player to turn down a sure 3 to 2 payoff in the hope of maybe collecting 4 to 2 by means of a double-down ploy would probably result in the floorman calling for a security guard to escort the player to the nearest mental institution. However, in this case, the player realized that collecting 3 to 2 would not be enough to put her ahead of the front-runner at her table. She decided to play a long shot, and it paid off. She won her double-down hand, and in so doing, she edged out the front-runner at the table and went on to the next round in the competition. Her strategy made sense because she was not really playing for the slightly greater profit that a winning double-down hand would give her. She was playing for the immensely greater profit that winning the contest prize money would give her.

Another paradoxical situation occurred a couple of years ago at the "World Championship of Casino Games" at the Sands in Atlantic City. The player who was crowned Blackjack Champion won the title by losing $215 in the final round of play. Losing doesn't sound like much of a reason for awarding a championship, but the casino had no choice. All the other players in the final round had lost even more money!

This player-against-player aspect of gambling tournaments means that traditional gambling skills such as card counting at blackjack and money-management count for very little. Gambling strategy is designed to maximize the player's long-range chances of showing a profit. But the contest gambler must think strictly in short-range terms. The fact is that gambling tournaments are not designed to select the best player in the competition. They are strictly nonskill events that might most closely be compared to lotteries. This is illustrated by the fact that winners of previous tournaments usually fail to survive even the first round when they try again.

EVALUATING A TOURNAMENT

I cannot really recommend entering a casino tournament as a smart gambling proposition. However, as I observed in Chapter I, recreational gambling also offers nonfinancial rewards. In the case of tournaments, the reward is the excitement of the competition. Everyone I have ever spoken to who has competed in such a contest has said they enjoyed it a great deal. Even those who won nothing—which includes the great majority of competitors—have said that the fun was worth the money. If the idea of competing in a casino tournament still sounds appealing to you after what you have learned about them, you should consider whether the cost seems worth it to you. The cost consists of both the entry fee and the buy-in, which can range from several hundred to a couple of thousand dollars per round. Any time you gamble, you must accept the possibility of losing your gambling stake. In a tournament, this prospect becomes even more likely because tournaments tend to encourage an all-or-nothing attitude as the other players turn to long-shot plays in a scrambling effort to overtake the front-runner in the final minutes of play each round.

Still interested? Then there is one final factor for you to consider. There is one sense in which you should definitely evaluate a tournament strictly as a gambling proposition; that is in the aspect of prize money. Casino tournaments are such a popular promotion these days that you can afford to shop around. Consider the percentage of the collected entry fees that the casino is planning to return to the players in the form of prizes. This is easily determined by multiplying the entry fee being charged by the maximum number of players allowed in the competition and comparing it to the total of all prize money being awarded. All the information you need to make this analysis should be included in the promotional material the casino will send you if you inquire about the contest. (Any tournament that does not provide potential competitors with enough information to allow such an analysis should be ruled out on the face of it.)

A new development is the mini-tournament, in which each player pays a small entry fee such as twenty-five dollars and is issued a certain amount in "funny money" (nonnegotiable chips). Prizes are awarded to those winning the most in this make-believe money. In this case, the danger of losing one's buy-in has been eliminated since there is no buy-in. These contests are aimed much more at locals than are the major tournaments. But they are certainly open to tourists and may be evaluated in the same way as other contests by comparing the entry fee to the prizes.

A good tournament from the player's standpoint is one that returns close to 100 percent of the entry fee money to the competitors in the form of prizes. The sponsoring casino will make its profit by virtue of the fact that it fills its hotel rooms and gaming tables at a time when the place would otherwise be dead. For a casino to try to supplement its profits by taking a large cut of the entry fee purse is pure greed. If the casino brings in an outside company to organize and promote the contest, that company should be paid out of the casino's pocket as a promotional expense, not out of the contestants' pockets. Shop around, and you will find good deals in the tournament field. Taking a gamble is one thing; being made a sucker of is another.

Poker

Poker is not really a casino game, since the players do not play against the house but rather against each other. Nevertheless, many of the casinos in Nevada operate cardrooms offering poker games. The casino provides a house dealer who supervises the game and is the only one to shuffle, cut, and deal the cards. This house dealer does not take part in the game. Rather, the casino makes its profit by *raking off* (collecting) 10 percent of each pot. In the past, each casino could set whatever percentage it wished as its rake, and this led to some abuses and complaints on the part of players as to dealers taking excessive rakes. However, the figure has now been standardized to 10 percent by state law. Some cardrooms limit this further by imposing a maximum amount that can be raked from any one pot.

The games offered are *hold'em*—a form of poker first developed in Texas that has grown tremendously in popularity in recent years—seven-card stud, and *razzle*, which is a seven-card-stud version of lowball. Table limits range from one to three dollars all the way up to No Limit. Since the deal does not rotate, a marker button travels clockwise from player to player to represent the last hand of each deal. In this way, each player in turn gets the disadvantages and advantages of being first or last to bet. The tables accommodate up to eight players, the standard maximum for most forms of poker, and the house tries for a full game whenever possible.

Many cardrooms use shills and *props* to help get games going when short of players. Both shills and props are house players, employees of the cardroom. The difference is that a shill plays with house money. He is not really gambling, since any losses go to the house, whose money it already is, and any wins must later be turned in to the house. By contrast, a prop, short for "proposition player," plays with his own money but only in those games he is directed to play in by the cardroom shift boss, and he receives a salary from the house. There is nothing dishonest about the use of shills and props; they simply help keep games going during slow periods. There are, however, gaming regulations in Nevada that govern the use of shills and props. For example, a cardroom may not have more than four house players in any one game, a maximum of two shills and two props. Also, a cardroom is required to identify any house players in a game if requested to do so by a player.

How successful you are at these games depends, of course, on how good a poker player you are. However, there are a couple of things you should keep in mind when playing in a cardroom if you have not had much experience with public games. First, you are paying for the privilege of playing. The rake is a constant financial drain that increases the demands on a player's abilities. In a private game, you have to be good enough to beat your opponents. In a cardroom game, you have to be good enough to beat your opponents and the house rake.

Keep in mind also that these games have their standard rules and procedures that will be familiar to most of your opponents but may differ from what you are used to in home games. Give yourself time to acclimate to their way of doing things.

Another concern is the fact that Las Vegas is home to a number of full-time poker players who survive in large part by beating tourists. I am not speaking here of cheats but rather of good players who have the advantage over most out-of-town players because they play every day, they are familiar with the playing styles of many of the others in the game who are also regulars, and they are used to the Nevada game. Thus, a tourist in one of these games could easily find that he has taken on more than he can handle.

However, the biggest danger in some cardroom games is teams of players who work in collusion to swindle other players by signaling each other's hands and by coordinating their betting to trap other players. (For a detailed discussion of team play, see my book *Gambling Scams*.) This kind of collusion is a constant problem in public poker games, whether in Nevada or elsewhere, and in fact is a danger anytime you are the stranger in a game with other players who regularly play with each other. Some Nevada cardrooms are very diligent about eliminating such collusive teams; others are not. It pays to shop around if you feel uncomfortable with the first game you find yourself in.

Las Vegas can be a great place to play poker. But proceed cautiously at first. Shop around and give yourself a chance to learn the terrain.

XII. Credit, Comps, and Junkets

♣ Brian Molony was one of Caesars Casino's favorite customers. They used to send a jet plane to fly him from his Toronto home to Atlantic City for gambling jaunts. This service was free as were his luxury accommodations, gourmet meals and drinks at the hotel, and such tokens of the casino executives' esteem as an $8,500 Rolex watch. All told, Caesars reported lavishing over $60,000 in food, lodging, transportation, and gifts on Molony over a period of less than two years. You might think that Molony was taking advantage of those indulgent casino bosses—until you learn that during that same period Molony lost over seven million dollars at the gambling tables, two million of that in one two-day period. Since Molony was in the habit of playing baccarat for as much as $75,000 a hand, a single loss was enough to offset all the gifts the casino had bestowed on him. Now you might think that Caesars was taking advantage of Molony—until you learn that Molony financed his gambling by embezzling $10.2 million dollars from his employer, the Canadian Imperial Bank of Commerce. When the New Jersey Casino Control Commission learned that, they concluded that Caesars had not been sufficiently conscientious in determining where its gambling profits were coming from. As penalty for this irresponsible behavior, the commission ordered the casino closed for one day. The punitive closing will take place about a week from when this is being written—November 1985; it is expected that the loss in revenues to Caesars will constitute the largest fine ever imposed on a gambling casino. Molony's punishment will last a little longer. He is now serving ten years in a Canadian prison.

There are probably several lessons to be learned from this bizarre episode. The most important one from our standpoint is the fact that there is often far more than meets the eye in the complex interaction between casinos trying to encourage players to gamble more money and players trying to get as many casino freebies as possible in return for the money they gamble.

BAITING THE HOOK

Casinos use a variety of ingenious techniques to encourage people to gamble longer, more frequently, and for higher stakes. You will never see a clock on the wall in any gambling casino. Management doesn't want you leaving the tables to run off to some appointment, or worrying that you have squandered too much of the day gambling, or feeling that you should pack it in because it's getting near bedtime. Coupled with the lack of windows in the casinos, the absence of clocks helps create an unreal, timeless atmosphere removed from everyday reality, one in which it is only too easy to follow the path of least resistance and keep gambling until your money runs out. This atmosphere is strengthened by the ever-present cocktail waitresses serving free drinks. Alcohol has never been noted for promoting a responsible attitude toward either time or money.

It has been said that the most brilliant invention in the history of casino gambling is the use of chips instead of money for betting. When betting those clay and plastic chips it is easy to forget they represent real money. If betting currency, it's likely that a player would consider more carefully before risking a week's wages on one roll of the dice. The use of chips is one more element contributing to the unreal feeling that so much of the Las Vegas experience has—the atmosphere that prompts one to act without weighing the real-life consequences.

Chips are also used to encourage players to up their bets. When a player is winning substantially, the dealer will start paying him off in higher denomination chips. For example, if a player bets two five-dollar chips on a blackjack hand and gets a natural, the dealer may collect the bet and give him a twenty-five dollar chip in return. This practice is known as *coloring up*. The dealer follows this practice partially to keep his stock of chips from getting too depleted in any one denomination. However, the procedure serves a more subtle purpose. Before long, the winning player who had been betting five dollar chips may find that all his money has been converted to twenty-five dollar chips. The simplest thing to do then is to start betting twenty-five dollar chips. As we have seen, it is generally a good strategy to increase one's bets when winning. However, make sure you're doing it because you want to and not because you have been subtly pressured into it by the house. Remember, you can always ask the dealer to change your chips back to a lower denomination.

No detail is too small for the casinos to consider in their endless quest to win your money. Even the placement of slot machines is carefully thought out. There are always rows of slots within easy reach of the long lines that form as people wait to enter the showroom. If the waiting gets boring, the machines are there to provide a little diversion. Similarly, in many casino coffee shops, if one wants to go to the restroom, he must leave the restaurant and wander through a long maze of slot machines to get there. If the last time you were having a snack in a casino coffee shop, your girlfriend excused herself to go to the ladies room and took forty-five minutes to get back, now you know why.

Of the many strategies both blatant and subtle that casinos use to encourage you to gamble, none is more complex than the granting of complimentary items to players. To get your business, a casino may be willing to give you not only free drinks, but free food, free lodging, free transportation, free shows, free gifts, and even free money in the sense that casino credit to players is interest-free.

Casino Credit

To apply for credit in a casino, go to the cashier's cage and obtain a credit application. The application will request information about your bank accounts including authorization to obtain information about your balance from the bank. It will also ask you how much of a *credit line* you wish. The credit line is the total amount of credit a casino will grant you on any one trip. After you have submitted the application, you will be notified by mail if your credit has been approved.

You may establish a credit line at more than one casino. In fact, once you have credit with one casino, obtaining the same privileges at others will be very easy. Keep in mind, however, that all casino credit transactions are reported to Central Credit, an agency that keeps its member casinos infomed of your credit status at all other casinos. This means that if you have outstanding debts at one casino, you may not be granted credit at others until that debt has been squared away.

If you were to walk into a bank and request a loan, they would naturally want to know what you planned to do with the money. If you told them you intended to gamble it away, that would be the end of the interview. However, gambling casinos insist that you gamble with the money they lend you. The reason is that the mathematical edge the house enjoys at all the games is what provides it with interest on the loan. If you were to obtain credit from a casino and, instead of gambling with it, took the money out of the casino and used it for home improvements or some other personal use—the kind of thing most lending institutions approve of—you would have succeeded in obtaining a short-term interest-free loan. Don't think the idea has never occurred to anyone.

To prevent being taken advantage of in this way, casinos employ some simple controls. First, credit is never given in the form of cash, but rather in the form of casino chips. Second and most importantly, these chips are always provided at one of the tables rather than at the casino cage. This allows pit personnel to watch what you do with the chips. What you had better do with them is gamble them at the table at which they were issued. It's all right for you to change tables after a while, but an alert floorman will keep tabs on your movements to make sure you don't leave the casino with the money.

The procedure for obtaining credit at a table is as follows: Let the dealer know you want a *marker* for a given sum of money. (Five hundred dollars is the minimum sum for which most casinos will write markers.) He will relay the information to the floorman. If you are not known to the floorman, he will ask you for identification. He will then check the computer terminal in the pit to verify that you have unused credit in that amount. In a smaller casino that is not computerized, the floorman will telephone the cage from the podium within the pit. Once he has received verification, he will ask you to sign a marker; this is a simple IOU form. The marker will be deposited in the same drop slot where the dealer or boxman deposits the cash from buy-ins. The floorman will then instruct the dealer to count out the requisite amount in chips and pass them to you.

If you have a substantial amount of chips left at the end of your playing session, you will be expected to redeem your marker before leaving the table. Pit supervisory personnel have to be very careful about this since some players will engage in some nominal amount of playing with the chips they receive and then attempt to slip out the door with the remainder as soon as the floorman's attention is diverted. If you are caught attempting this, you can be sure your credit status at that casino will suffer. When you pay off markers out of your winnings, the floorman will return the markers to you. It is customary—and wise—to tear the marker up as soon as it is returned.

If you lose all the chips, you may take out another marker as long as you have not exhausted your credit line. If you leave the table a loser, you may write a check at the cage to cover your markers or you may have the casino bill you by mail. In this case, you will be expected to pay off the markers within thirty days and certainly before your next trip to that casino. Even if you still have unused credit, you may be denied credit if you have any markers outstanding from your last trip. When you pay by mail, your markers will be mailed back to you by the casino. If you don't pay within thirty days, the casino may present your markers to your bank for payment since these markers are, in effect, counter checks.

If You Don't Pay

What happens if you can't pay? Discuss your problem with the casino's management. They will set up a time-payment plan you can both live with. They will even welcome you back to their tables as long as you keep up your payments.

But suppose you refuse to pay. The common public conception is that a gorilla will materialize on your doorstep and threaten to break your kneecaps. I can assure you that no major legal casino in Nevada or Atlantic City uses such collection techniques today. What they will do is nag the hell out of you by phone and by letter. They will ask you nicely to pay and then not so nicely.

Eventually, they will point out to you that your debt is legally enforceable in a court of law. This is a new development in Nevada. Until a couple of years ago, gambling debts were not legally binding on either a player or a casino. The casinos could not bring legal pressure to bear to collect debts. That all changed with the passage of Nevada Senate Bill No. 335 in 1983. In Atlantic City, gambling debts have been legally enforceable since the inception of legalized gambling there in 1977.

However, it is not the fear of legal action that leads most recalcitrant gamblers to pay up. Rather, it is simply the threat of losing their gambling privileges at that casino. The kind of gambler who is likely to get in over his head on markers is also the kind of gambler who needs constant action. The worst punishment a casino can mete out to him is to "eighty-six" him from the tables. Sooner or later he will pay up just so he can get back into the game.

This kind of pressure works both ways. While depriving the player of action, the casino is also punishing itself. It is depriving itself of revenue from a high-rolling player who is probably a steady *producer* (a consistent and heavy loser). This is why some casinos will allow a player who is delinquent on his debts to continue playing at their tables as long as he plays for cash. They would still rather see him lose his money at their tables than next door.

This is also why one casino will sometimes seek the patronage of a player who has delinquent debts at another casino. On the surface, it would seem strange that one casino would woo a player, welcoming him with open arms and open credit account, when that player has refused to pay his debts at another casino. To understand why this sometimes occurs one must understand the most common bad-debt situation that casinos face. A high roller patronizes the same casino for a number of years, losing forty or fifty thousand dollars each year. One day he has a disastrous session, signing marker after marker in a futile attempt to get even. When he comes to his senses, he finds he owes a hundred thousand dollars. He sees no way he can cover the sum. His panic reaction is to refuse to pay. He may even blame the casino for letting him play beyond his limit. (At the time, he probably begged, cajoled, and threatened in order to persuade them to lift his credit limit.)

The management of another casino that caters to high rollers hears of the situation and thinks only of getting that annual forty- to fifty-thousand-dollar loss for themselves. They know that if they keep a rein on this player's credit limit, he will continue to be good for his debts as he had been for years at the other casino. They care little for their competition's debt collection problems. Therefore, they go all out to try to win him from the other casino, which has already alienated him with their demands for payment.

This dual pressure on the player to get back in the casino's good graces and back to the tables again and on the casino to start once more helping themselves to this steady loser's bankroll means that many large debts are settled by compromising them. The casino and the player agree to settle for his paying part of the bill and forgetting about the rest. Of course, this is only likely to happen with valued long-time customers. Other players can expect to find themselves in court.

Incidentally, be forewarned that under the new Regulation 6A, if you engage in any cash transaction or series of transactions exceeding $10,000 in a casino you will be required to provide the casino with your name, address, and some form of identification. This procedure is demanded by the Treasury Department to help fight against the use of gambling casinos by drug dealers to launder money. It won't affect you if you win $10,000 or if you pay off markers with chips or a check, only if you buy chips or pay off markers with <u>cash</u> over $10,000.

THE PROS AND CONS OF CASINO CREDIT

If the use of chips in betting tends to promote an unrealistic attitude toward money, this is ten times more true when betting with chips obtained on credit. They're just too easy to get. And when they are gone, it's easy to get more. A quick signature and they hand them over. This is the greatest danger of using credit, the reckless behavior it promotes.

Furthermore, while applying for a bank loan is usually the result of careful consideration and calm study, writing markers is often done on the spur of the moment and under intense pressure. When a player has lost a great deal of money, he may get desperate. His only concern is to somehow make up his loss. Too often, the only answer seems to be to write another marker in the hope that his luck will turn. If he has been drinking, his judgment concerning credit will be even less responsible. At the outset of the book, I warned you against drinking while gambling. I can only stress that this advice is even more important if you play on credit.

More often than not, a player, after having signed several markers in the course of an evening, doesn't even know just how much of his credit he has gone through. You can be sure the casino knows, and they expect every penny back. If you play on credit, I strongly urge you to keep a record on a slip of paper every time you draw on your credit and add it up each time you are tempted to ask for more. Of course, you could always check by just having pit personnel call it up on their computer terminal. But the discipline of keeping track yourself with pen and paper can provide the kind of sobering experience needed to keep things in perspective and keep you from making a big mistake.

Admittedly, there is no denying that playing on credit offers certain advantages for the player who can handle it responsibly. It is certainly more convenient than carrying large sums of cash on you. It also makes it easier for the house to keep track of your action, which in turn may help qualify you for some of the freebies I mentioned at the outset.

Junkets

Everyone knows that a *junket* is a free trip that casinos give to players so they can gamble at their tables. Everyone knows that, but it's not quite correct. To really understand how junkets work, the first thing to do is to stop thinking of them as free. A junket is an informal but very real agreement between a gambling casino and a player whereby the casino agrees to pay certain of the player's expenses in return for the player's commitment to gamble a certain sum of money at their tables over a certain period of time.

There was a time when it seemed that the casino business just couldn't lose money. Even incompetent management personnel seemed to flourish due to the automatic moneymaking capabilities of the industry. This tended to produce a rather freewheeling approach to management. Then during the 1970s, Las Vegas experienced reversals that disproved the long-held industry dictum that casino gambling was a recession-proof business. This rude awakening, combined with the trend toward major corporations moving into the casino business and bringing with them modern management and accounting techniques, has led to many policy changes.

JUNKET PRIVILEGES

Nowhere is this more apparent than in the realm of junkets and *comps* (complimentary room, food, and beverages). In the old days, players fell into two categories, comped and uncomped. A player who was comped could expect to receive anything he wanted for free: hotel accommodations, airfare, gourmet meals, champagne sent to his room, and show tickets both for the hotel in which he was staying and for shows in other hotels. All the major Las Vegas Strip casinos followed this policy and they made money, so they figured that was the way to do things. Today, the casinos recognize that, even among premium players, different players are good for different levels of profit; therefore, the level of comps allowed should be gauged to the expected profit potential of each player. Consequently, there are very wide variations in what a junket participant may receive from the casino. He may be booked into a luxury suite or only a room. He may be allowed to bring a companion on the trip or not, and her airfare may be covered or only discounted. He may be granted free meals in the hotel's gourmet dining room or only in the coffee shop, and he may or may not be allowed to bring guests to these meals. He may or may not be provided with free show tickets. Through extensive monitoring of each premium player's action and even the use of computer analyses, every effort is made to match the cost of comps offered to the profit-generating potential of each player.

Most junkets last three to four nights. Players leave on Wednesday or Thursday and return Sunday night. Participants receive free airfare to and from the casino and free accommodations. As indicated above, there is a great deal of variation as far as the availability of other comps. Recent years have seen the development of the *mini-junket*, a junket lasting only one or two nights with very limited comp privileges for the players. An even more restricted version of the junket concept is the *up-and-back*. In this case, players are brought into the casino for a period of eight to twelve hours. They receive limited food and beverage comps and a discount on their airfare. Naturally, accommodations are not included since the players are not in the hotel long enough to need them. In each of these cases, the amount of money the player is expected to gamble is proportional to the amount of money the casino is spending on him.

Casinos have no desire to give anything away free. They are, however, willing to invest money in a player in the form of free transportation, accommodations, food, and beverages if they are convinced that the amount of money they can expect to win from that player will be substantially higher than the cost of these items. As a rough gauge, most casinos are willing to offer a package costing up to 50 percent of what they expect to win from the player. Experience has taught them that they will, on average, win about 20 percent of the amount of money the player puts into action. Therefore, the projected expense of any junket package will usually be about 10 percent of the gambling bankroll required. A thousand-dollar package would require that the player put $10,000 into action.

JUNKET CONTROLS

The casinos use four basic controls to ensure that each player provides that action. The most basic one is the requirement that each junketgoer bring along $10,000 (in our example). The player is not expected to take this cash up to the playing tables with him. When he arrives at the casino, that money is placed in his account at the cashier's cage. This is known as *front money*. Now whenever the player needs money to play with, he writes a marker at the table for the amount of chips he wishes. The chips are then issued to him against his account.

This is the second control. The marker system allows the casinos to check on how much of the player's cash he actually converts into chips in the course of his stay at the hotel. The expectation is that he will write markers for all or almost all of his front money in the course of his stay at the casino.

Some casinos dispense with the use of markers. Instead, as soon as the player has deposited his front money in the cage he is given the equivalent amount in special chips referred to in the industry as *Mickey Mouse chips*. These chips are different from the regular chips used by that casino and, unlike the regular chips, cannot be converted into cash at the casino cage. They are good for only one thing: betting. If you make a wager with these chips and win, you will be paid off with regular chips, which can be converted to cash.

This procedure automatically ensures that each player will wager the entire amount of his front money. Otherwise he will return home with a pile of worthless chips. In fact, the player will have to wager the special chips over and over again, until they have all been lost. This forces the player to provide the house with a very large volume of action in proportion to his front money. For this reason, casino junkets that are operated on this basis are best avoided in favor of those using the marker approach.

However, even if a player takes out all his front money in the form of markers, that doesn't guarantee that the chips will actually be wagered. Here is where the final two casino controls come in. Each player will be evaluated by the average amount of money he wagers on each bet and by the amount of time he spends gambling each day. The casino management will have a very clear notion in their minds as to what is expected from each player in this regard. In the case of our $10,000 front money example, a fifty-dollar minimum wager and four hours playing time per day would be typical. However, these requirements are somewhat dependent on the game the particular junket participant favors.

Casino executives keep very close watch on junket players to determine whether they meet their requirements of minimum bets and playing time. Every time a junketgoer gambles in that casino, a floorman will observe his play and fill out a *rating card*. To give you an idea of the degree of scrutiny the junket gambler is under, here is the information the floorman must record on the rating card each time a junket participant plays: the date, shift (*day, swing,* or *graveyard*), the table played at (for example, "crap 2"), the player's name and credit line or front money, the city of origin of the junket, the time the player begins betting and the time he leaves the table, a record of all markers he signs during the session of play, the size of his first bet, the size of his average bet, his style of play, and the amount of money won or lost.

A new card is made out each time the player approaches a table. The information from all of these cards is eventually entered into the player's master card or as part of the casino's records on its computer. These records are used by casino management to rate the player's value to the casino.

The most common rating system is an A, B, C, D ranking. The A player is the kind of gambler who doesn't have to be told how long he must play; he has to be dragged away from the tables. He spends every free minute gambling and has the money to do it in style. This kind of player will be welcomed at the casino at its expense as often as he wishes to come.

At the other extreme is the D player. In this case, the D stands for "don't invite back." This player has attempted to get a free ride without fulfilling his part of the bargain. He may get away with it once, but never again.

The C player is one who fulfills his playing requirements, just barely, then goes off to enjoy the casino freebies. The B player goes beyond the minimum requirements, but doesn't have the financial resources to gamble at the A player's level. B and C players will be invited back only as room is available. Since *junket masters* are often paid bonuses by the casino for bringing in higher-rated players, they will invite the lower rated ones only when they can't fill the seats more lucratively.

There was a time when casinos were inclined to simply rate each junket overall for profitability. They didn't mind if there were a couple of freeloaders along for the ride as long as there were enough producers in the group to keep the project in the black. Today, every member of the junket is evaluated and expected to justify his expenses. In addition, each participant is evaluated anew on every trip. In the past, some junketgoers got themselves highly rated on their first couple of junkets, then in subsequent junkets they did minimal playing, riding on their reputations. These days, even long-time customers start with a blank slate and are expected to earn their comps on every trip.

JUNKET REQUIREMENTS

My first advice to anyone considering going on a junket is to make absolutely certain he understands what is expected of him. Talk to the junket organizer and get the facts on all four of the casino's criteria. How much front money will be required? How much must you generate in markers? How long must you play and how much must you bet? Be equally specific in determining exactly which of your expenses will be covered by the casino. As I pointed out earlier, there is tremendous variation in the package that different casinos offer to different players.

Of course, all of these features will vary according to the cost of the junket package the casino is offering and how eager they are to attract junket business. For example, a junket from the West Coast to Las Vegas would naturally involve much lower transportation costs for the casino than one from the East Coast and might require only $5,000 in front money, twenty-five dollar bets, and three hours per day playing time. Similarly, a player being offered a suite and allowed to bring a guest will need to provide more action than one coming alone and receiving only a room.

My second piece of advice is that if you do decide to go, you should go with the full intention of meeting your responsibilities under the agreement. For some reason, junkets often bring out the larceny in otherwise law-abiding citizens. They immediately start scheming as to how they can enjoy a free vacation without risking any substantial losses at the tables.

Not long ago, someone came up to me with a master plan for a free Las Vegas vacation. He and a friend were going to team up on a junket. One would bet only the pass line at craps while the other made only don't pass bets. Therefore, whatever one lost, the other would win (except for the bar 6–6 on the don't pass). They would pool their money at the end and split it evenly, keeping their losses at a minimum. This hoary old gag seems to occur to everybody. Sometimes it's betting red and black at roulette; other times it's bank hand and player hand at baccarat. The scam is so well known in the casino industry that it wouldn't have a prayer of fooling anyone. I only mention it to warn you off.

Admittedly, many scams have been successfully pulled off by junketgoers. These have been executed by sophisticated gamblers who were very familiar with casino operations and their loopholes. I won't provide any details because I don't want to put ideas in your head. The chances of the average individual being able to successfully pull the wool over casino executives' eyes is slightly worse than the chances of throwing twenty straight passes at craps.

If you should be caught trying to short-change the casino on a junket, the reaction won't be pleasant. The first step is usually a warning from the junket master that the casino is not happy with your action. The subtlety of the warning will vary with the individual. I know one junketgoer, a heavy gambler, who retired exhausted to his hotel room after playing almost twenty hours straight at various casinos (not including the one that was hosting him). His head had hardly hit the pillow when he was awakened by a pounding on his door and the bellowing of the junket master demanding that he go down to the tables and play.

If a warning isn't enough to get you to mend your ways you can expect to be called into the casino manager's office and handed a bill for your hotel expenses and airfare. The cost of these items will be deducted from the front money you have remaining in the casino cage. In Atlantic City, the casinos are prohibited by law from reneging on promised comps. Nevertheless, the scene won't be very pleasant there either if you are caught playing games with junket requirements. At the very least, you can expect never to be invited back.

Not only should you meet the junket requirements, you should ensure that the casino realizes you met them. As far as front money, bet size, and playing time are concerned, this will happen automatically. Playing style is also a factor in player rating with preference given to loose players and even downright bad players such as crap players who bet the proposition wagers and blackjack players who play their hands badly. However, I cannot recommend that you play poorly just to impress casino personnel that you are good junket material. Keep in mind that it is not necessary for you to lose to get a higher player rating. Casinos are only interested in how much action you give them: how much money bet over what period of time. They know that given sufficient betting volume, the house's profit will take care of itself, so you needn't try to hide your winnings. In fact some

casino executives are more favorably impressed by seeing a big win
by a player than a small one when rating players. They reason (not
necessarily correctly) that a big win indicates a loose, wild playing
style that must eventually lead to big losses when the tide turns.

The trickiest area for making sure casino personnel realize you did
your part is in the writing of markers. There is little problem if you
have a losing trip, since you will have to keep writing markers to
provide a steady flow of playing capital. The problem arises if you
are winning, particularly if you start winning from the very beginning.
It's quite possible that after writing your first marker for, say, one
thousand dollars you won't have to write another one for the entire
trip because you can keep playing off your early winnings. Nonethe-
less, it is advisable to cash in your winnings after each playing session
and write a marker for chips at the beginning of each new session. If
you are really doing well, you may even want to play more, shorter
sessions rather than a few long sessions so as to generate the requisite
amount of *paper* (markers).

ARE JUNKETS FOR YOU?

There is one simple test you should apply in attempting to decide
whether to go the junket route. Ask yourself: Would I normally gamble
at the level required by the junket if I were paying my own way?
Would I normally take along five thousand dollars with which to
play? Would I really bet twenty-five dollars a hand at baccarat for
three hours a day (or whatever the casino is requiring of its junket
participants)? If the answer is yes, then by all means consider partic-
ipating in a junket. After all, if the casino wants to return part of your
expected losses to you in the form of free services, why not let them?
(If you follow the advice in this book, the casino will be overestimating
the amount it can reasonably expect to win from you, which makes
the junket even more appealing.) If you are this kind of player, exploitation of casino junkets can be another tool in your campaign to
show a profit.

However, if meeting the junket requirements means gambling at
a level at which you would not normally play, then junkets are not
for you. The psychological pressure of betting more than you feel
comfortable with or the fatigue of playing longer than you really want
to can place enormous stress on you, which in turn is almost sure to
damage your effectiveness as a player and produce large losses. Your
"free" vacation won't seem such a bargain then. Even aside from the

issue of financial losses, playing under pressure isn't much fun. And enjoyment should be your prime goal on any vacation.

If you really are the type of player the casino is looking for, the next step is getting on your first junket. By contacting the casino manager or credit manager at the different Las Vegas or Atlantic City casinos you can find out who are the junket organizers in your city and also learn what level of play each casino is looking for.

Getting on your first junket may take a little doing. Junket masters are not keen on first timers. They know that every first-time junketgoer is a question mark, a risk, a potential deadbeat. They take only a limited number of first-timers on each trip. You may be placed on a waiting list. If you have a friend who is a regular junketgoer, find out if he would be willing to vouch for you with his junket master. Depending on how much prestige your friend has with the casino, this may considerably expedite matters.

Above all, don't settle for the first casino you contact. Different casinos concentrate on different segments of the player market. For example, Caesars Palace is famous for catering only to the highest of high rollers and may not care to even bother with a lower level player who might be considered a VIP at another casino. Even within the same casino, junket requirements and benefit packages will change with personnel changes, seasonal changes in demand, and the fluctuating financial fortunes of the casino. As with most things, in the junket field, it pays to shop around.

Comps

You don't have to be part of a junket group to enjoy comp privileges from a casino. Everything that is available to junket participants is also provided by casinos to certain individual players whose action is considered high enough to justify the outlay. You might rate anything from an occasional free meal in the coffee shop or complimentary tickets to the dinner show to reimbursement of airfare and full *RFB privileges* (free room, food, and beverages). Valued high rollers also receive invitations to be the house's guests at various promotional parties, sporting events, and other special events that the major casinos host throughout the year.

If you qualify for any comps, they should, in theory, come your way without your making any special effort. It is part of every casino executive's job to be on the lookout for *action players* and approach them with offers of comps to encourage their patronage. In addition to the floormen and pit bosses, all of whom have the *power of the pencil* (the authority to grant comps), casinos also hire *casino hosts* whose sole task it is to develop relationships with high-rolling players. These hosts are often retired show business or sports celebrities. (You may recall that it was accepting this type of job with an Atlantic City casino that resulted in Mickey Mantle being temporarily removed from the Baseball Hall of Fame.) Casino hosts employ liberal comps and other VIP treatment to build a loyal following of gamblers for their employer.

There are several ways you can help casino personnel to notice and to reward your gambling. Playing off markers makes it much easier for the casino bosses to rate your action. If you don't want to establish a credit line, you can still use markers. Just deposit your betting bankroll at the casino cage, letting them know that you intend to write markers at the tables against this front money. This documents the amount of action you are giving the house. Whether you take this approach or not, if you wish to qualify for comps you may approach any floorman or pit boss when you first arrive at the casino and let him know you would like to be rated. He will make sure that every time you play, a rating card is filled out. He will then use that information for making determinations about comps for you.

To qualify for extensive comps you must be at least a quarter (twenty-five dollar) player, while still higher bets may be required to qualify for airfare reimbursements. Such a player will turn in his plane ticket at the cashier's cage when he first arrives at the casino. When he leaves, a determination will be made about reimbursement on the basis of the player's rating cards for that visit. The rule of thumb followed by most casinos is that they will authorize up to five percent of a player's action on a particular trip for airfare.

However, don't feel you have to be a high roller to benefit from comps. Even a five-dollar bettor may qualify for an occasional comped meal in the coffee shop. If a floorman comes over to watch your play after you have been giving the house a fair amount of action ask him about a comp. Don't feel that you are freeloading. Remember, you are paying for these things through your patronage. Get to know the executives at the casinos in which you regularly play. Make sure they know when you are playing so you can receive credit for the action you are giving them. For the moderate bettor, shopping around becomes particularly important. A casino like Caesars Palace that has several regular customers with one-million-dollar credit lines may not be willing to make much of an effort to pursue your business. But another casino that has built its success on attracting moderate bettors may be more forthcoming.

As I said in connection with junkets, if you have to bet more than you normally would in order to qualify for comps, forget about it. The ego boost you may get from receiving the VIP treatment is not worth getting in over your head. However, if your present level of play is high enough, a knowledge of how the casino comp system works can help you get the most for your money. There are only two legitimate reasons to gamble, to enjoy yourself and to show a profit. Properly exploited, casino comps can contribute to both goals.

Glossary

across the board A bet on all the box numbers (4, 5, 6, 8, 9, and 10) at craps.

act A false personality adopted by a blackjack card counter to help disguise from casino personnel the fact that he is a skilled player.

action Gambling activity measured by the amount of money wagered over a period of time.

action player A casino gambler who bets heavily and plays extensively.

aggregate limit The maximum total amount, usually $50,000, that a casino is willing to pay out in winnings for any one keno drawing.

all-king ticket A keno ticket consisting entirely of king numbers: individual numbers circled to indicate that they are to be played in every possible combination with each other.

any-craps A wager at craps that the shooter will roll a total of 2, 3, or 12 on the next roll.

any-seven A wager at craps that the shooter will roll a total of 7 on the next roll.

back line The space on a crap layout where a player places his bet if he wishes to wager that the shooter will lose.

back the bet To make a free odds bet at craps.

backtrack The stationary, outer rim of a roulette wheel on which the ball is spun.

bank 1. Whoever covers all bets in a gambling game. 2. A row of slot machines linked together.

bank hand The second of the two hands dealt at baccarat.

bar For a casino to ban someone from playing at its tables; the same as 86.

barber pole A bet consisting of a stack of chips of two or more denominations mixed together.

basic strategy A system providing the optimal way of playing any blackjack hand based on the value of one's hand and the dealer's up-card.

basic ticket A keno ticket that contains only one wager and that involves the selection of anywhere from one to fifteen numbers; the same as a *straight ticket*.

behind the line The money wagered on the free odds bet, which is placed behind one's pass-line bet.

bet against the dice To bet that the shooter at craps will lose.

bet with the dice To bet that the shooter at craps will win.

big 6/big 8 A wager at craps that wins if the shooter rolls a total of 6 (or 8) before rolling a 7.

big six wheel A carnival-type game employing a large vertical wheel marked with

U.S. currency around its border; the same as a *money wheel* or a *wheel of fortune*.

black bet   A wager at roulette that one of the eighteen black numbers will win.

blackjack   A perfect blackjack hand consisting of an ace and a ten-value card; the same as a *natural*.

blacks   Casino chips valued at one hundred dollars each.

blower   An air-blowing device used in some casinos for mixing the numbered ping-pong balls and selecting the twenty balls for the drawing at keno.

book   To cover a bet someone wishes to make.

bottom track   The stationary, slanting inner surface of a roulette wheel down which the ball slides to reach the numbers slots.

boxcars   The total 12 at craps.

boxman   The casino supervisor who sits at the center of a crap table and oversees the game.

box numbers   The totals at craps that constitute potential point numbers (4, 5, 6, 8, 9, and 10) and that are contained in a row of boxes along the top of a crap layout.

break   To go over a total of 21 in the game of blackjack; the same as *bust*.

break the deck   For a blackjack dealer to reshuffle the cards before continuing play.

burn   For a blackjack or baccarat dealer to discard one or more cards before beginning to deal from a freshly shuffled deck.

bust   To go over a total of 21 in the game of blackjack; the same as *break*.

buy bet   A right bet on a box number at craps that the house pays off at true odds after first charging a 5 percent commission.

buy-in   1. The process of purchasing chips at a gaming table prior to playing. 2. The amount of chips purchased at the start of play.

cage   The cashier's section of a casino where players may exchange chips for cash.

call bet   A bet made verbally without placing any money on the table.

call down   To retract a wager (usually at craps) before it has come to a decision; the same as *take down*.

caller   1. In baccarat: the dealer in charge of conducting the game and directing the activities of the players. 2. In keno: the casino employee who announces the twenty selected numbers as they are drawn.

cancellation system   A betting system that involves adding to a written series of numbers after each loss and crossing out numbers in the series after each win; the same as the *Labouchere system*.

C&E   A wager at craps that combines the any-craps bet with a bet on the total 11; the same as *craps-eleven*.

card counting   A blackjack strategy that is based on keeping track of what cards have been played in previous hands; the same as *casing the deck*.

carousel   A group of several slot machines linked together in the form of an oval and usually serviced by one cashier located on an elevated ramp in the center.

casing the deck   A blackjack strategy that is based on keeping track of what cards have been played in previous hands; the same as *card counting*.

casino host   A casino executive whose job it is to cater to high-rolling gamblers, providing complimentary services and VIP treatment in order to encourage them to bring their business to that particular casino.

casino manager   The chief casino executive who is responsible for the conduct of all games on all shifts in the casino.

catch   A number marked on a player's keno ticket that coincides with one of the numbers drawn by the house on that particular game.

change girl   A casino employee who patrols the slot machine area providing players with change to play the machines.

chase   For a player to increase his bets in an effort to recoup his losses.

check rack   The tray in front of a dealer that holds his supply of chips.

check racker   The dealer who assists the wheel roller in operating the roulette table if the game is busy.

checks   The name that casino personnel use for betting chips.

chop   A series of wins and losses on a betting proposition with no one side predominating.

clocking   Keeping track of the outcomes in any casino game.

cocked dice   The condition when one or both dice at craps land so that they are leaning against some object at an angle rather than flat on the table.

cold   Said of a player who is experiencing a losing streak; also said of a table, a deck of cards, or dice that keep losing for the players.

column bet   A bet at roulette that one of twelve numbers in a row on the layout will win.

combination ticket   A type of keno ticket on which a player makes several simultaneous bets, all of more than one type; for example, both six-spot bets and nine-spot bets.

come bet   A bet at craps made after the come-out that the shooter will win if the next roll is considered a come-out roll.

come odds   A wager on the come-point at craps that can be made by any player with a come bet and that is paid by the house at true odds.

come-out   The first in a sequence of dice rolls at craps that determines the outcome of the pass-line bets.

come-point   The number (either 4, 5, 6, 8, 9, or 10) that the shooter must repeat in order for a come bet to win.

commission   The 5 percent charge imposed by the house on all winnings paid on the bank hand at baccarat.

comp   Short for "complimentary," meaning a hotel service such as accommodations or meals offered free to a player in return for his patronage.

condition   The type of wager made on a keno ticket as indicated by the notations in the right margin.

conditioning   The process of making notations in the right margin of a keno ticket to indicate the types of wagers the player wishes to make.

corner bet   A bet at roulette that one of four particular numbers will win; the same as a *square bet* or a *quarter bet*.

counter   A blackjack player whose strategy is based on keeping track of what cards have been played in previous hands.

counter catcher   Someone adept at card counting at blackjack who is hired by a casino for the express purpose of identifying counters so they can be barred from play.

Crapless Craps   A version of craps introduced at Vegas World in which totals 2, 3, 11, and 12 count as point numbers.

craps   The totals 2, 3, and 12, which, when rolled on the come-out in a crap game, cause the pass line to lose.

craps-eleven A wager at craps that combines the any-craps bet with a bet on the total 11; the same as the *C&E*.

credit line The maximum amount a particular player is entitled to receive in credit from a casino.

d'Alembert system A betting system that involves increasing one's wager by one unit after each loss and decreasing it by one unit after each win.

day shift The work shift in a casino that runs from 10 A.M. to 6 P.M.

dead table A gaming table that is staffed by dealers and open for business but that has no players.

desperado A reckless gambler.

dice boat A receptacle, somewhat resembling an ashtray, in which the stickman at craps keeps those dice that are not being used by the shooter.

dice buck The large round marker, bearing the word "on" on one side and "off" on the other, that a crap dealer uses to mark off the point number on the layout.

discard rack The plastic holder into which used cards are placed in a multiple-deck blackjack game.

do bet Any bet at craps that favors the shooter over the house; the same as a *right bet*.

don't bet Any bet at craps that favors the house over the shooter; the same as a *wrong bet*.

don't come A bet at craps made after the come-out that the shooter will lose if the next roll is considered a come-out roll.

don't pass A bet at craps that the shooter will lose.

double down To make a second bet on one's hand at blackjack in return for which one agrees to accept one and only one more card.

Double Exposure 21 A version of blackjack, first introduced at Vegas World, in which both of the dealer's cards are dealt face up.

double odds The option of making a free odds wager at craps that is equal to twice the size of one's line bet.

double-progressive slots Slot machines that have two different giant progressive jackpots, each growing independently and capable of being won on alternate plays of the machine.

double-up system A betting system that involves doubling the size of one's bet after every losing wager; the same as the *Martingale system*.

down with odds If the player has a place bet and his come bet has been moved to cover the same number, he may instruct the dealer that he wants "down with odds," which means that he wants his place bet returned to him after the dealer has subtracted enough money to serve as a free odds bet for the come wager.

dozen bet A bet at roulette that one of twelve numbers in sequence will win.

draw ticket A keno ticket on which the selected numbers have been punched out so that the ticket may be used as a grid to be superimposed on players' tickets to facilitate rapid identification of winning tickets.

duplicate ticket The ticket that is given to a keno player as a receipt for his bet when he submits his original ticket to the house; the same as an *outside ticket*.

early surrender An option at blackjack that was at one time available in Atlantic City casinos whereby a player could concede the hand and forfeit only half his bet even if the dealer had a possible blackjack.

Eastern craps A style of craps, found in some foreign casinos and some illegal casinos in this country, in which come bets and place bets are not permitted; the same as *New York craps* and *5 percent craps*.

the easy way   A total of 4, 5, 8, or 10 when rolled with different numbers on the two dice.

86   For a casino to ban someone from playing at its tables; the same as *bar*.

en prison   A feature of roulette as played in Europe whereby a player whose even-money bet loses is allowed to retain the bet if it should win on the next spin.

even bet   A wager at roulette that one of the eighteen even numbers will win.

even up   Said of a wager that offers no mathematical advantage to either side.

field   Uncircled numbers marked on a keno ticket that are to be played in combination with one or more king numbers circled on the ticket.

field bet   A wager at craps that wins if the shooter rolls a total of 2, 3, 4, 9, 10, 11, or 12 on the next roll and loses if he rolls 5, 6, 7, or 8.

15 across   A set of place bets at craps covering each of the box numbers for three units except for the point number, which is not covered.

first base   The first seat at the dealer's extreme left at a blackjack table.

five-number bet   A bet at roulette that one of the numbers 0, 00, 1, 2, or 3 will win; the same as the *house special*.

5 percent craps   A style of craps, found in some foreign casinos and some illegal casinos in this country, in which come bets and place bets are not permitted; the same as *Eastern craps* and *New York craps*. (The name is a reference to the fact that in these games the only way to cover the box numbers is with buy and lay bets at a 5 percent commission.)

flat bet   1. n. The portion of a wager at craps that is paid off at even money, as opposed to the part that is paid off at true odds. 2. v. For a blackjack card counter to make the same wager each hand rather than varying the size of his bet according to the count.

floorman   A casino executive who is responsible for supervising play at two or three tables.

free odds   A wager on the point at craps that can be made by any player with a pass or come bet and that is paid by the house at true odds.

French wheel   A roulette wheel that contains no double zero.

front line   The space on a crap layout where a player places his bet if he wishes to wager that the shooter will win; the same as the *pass line*.

front money   Cash deposited by a player at the casino cage against which he draws when he gambles.

full odds   The maximum amount allowed by the house to be wagered on the free odds bet in proportion to one's line bet.

get out   To succeed in breaking even after having sustained a heavy gambling loss.

ghost   A stop on a slot machine reel that has been left blank rather than filled with a symbol.

goose   The device used for drawing the twenty selected numbers at keno.

Grand Martingale   A betting system that involves doubling one's bet plus one unit after each losing wager.

graveyard shift   The work shift in a casino that runs from 2 A.M. to 10 A.M.

greens   Casino chips valued at twenty-five dollars each.

grind   A small-money bettor.

grind down For the casino to succeed in winning all a player's money over a long period of wagers over which the house edge has an opportunity to operate.

grind joint A casino that caters primarily to small-money bettors.

grind system A gambling system similar to a reverse d'Alembert that requires the player to increase his bet by one unit after each win.

hand 1. A player's set of cards in any card game. 2. At craps, the shooter's entire series of rolls of the dice up to the time he sevens-out; the same as his *shoot*.

hard hand A blackjack hand that does not contain an ace counted as 11; the opposite of a *soft hand*.

the hard way A total of 4, 6, 8, or 10 when rolled with the same number on both dice.

hardway bet A wager at craps that the shooter will roll a particular total (either 4, 6, 8, or 10) with the same number on both dice before rolling either a 7 or that particular total with different numbers on the two dice.

hardway hop A wager at craps that the shooter will roll a particular total (either 4, 6, 8, or 10) with the same number on both dice on the very next roll; the same as a *hardway on the turn* or a *one-roll hardway*.

hardway on the turn A wager at craps that the shooter will roll a particular total (either 4, 6, 8, or 10) with the same number on both dice on the very next roll; the same as a *hardway hop* or a *one-roll hardway*.

head-up game A game between only two opponents, for example, a blackjack game with only one player seated at the table opposing the dealer.

heel a bet To offset the chips in a wager so they are half on and half off the bottom chip of the stack as a means of distinguishing the bet from other types of bets in the same space on the layout.

high hand One of the two hands into which a player in Pai Gow divides his four dominoes.

high-low A one-roll bet at craps that combines wagers on totals 2 and 12.

high-low system The most basic type of blackjack card counting system in which each card is assigned a value of either $+1$, -1, or 0; the same as the *plus-minus system*.

high roller A gambler who plays for high stakes.

hit To draw an additional card to one's hand in blackjack.

hold'em A form of poker popular in Nevada casinos.

hole card The second card of the dealer's hand, which he deals himself face down.

hop A wager at craps that a particular combination will appear on the dice on the very next roll.

horn bet A one-roll bet at craps that combines equal wagers on totals 2, 3, 11, and 12.

horn high A one-roll bet at craps that combines wagers on totals 2, 3, 11, and 12 with one of the four totals being covered for one more unit than each of the other three.

hot Said of a player who is experiencing a winning streak; also said of a table, a deck of cards, or dice that keep winning for the players.

hot and cold system A betting system that involves always wagering on the side that won the previous time in the hope of catching a long streak of winners on one side.

house edge   The mathematical advantage the casino enjoys on a wager; the same as the *P.C.*

house odds   The ratio at which the casino pays off a winning bet.

house special   A bet at roulette that one of the numbers 0, 00, 1, 2, or 3 will win; the same as the *five-number bet.*

house ticket   Any special kind of keno ticket offered by a particular casino that is not available at any other casino.

inside bet   One of the six wagers at roulette (straight-up, split, street, corner, five-number, and line bets) that are made in the central, numbered portion of the layout.

inside numbers   The box numbers 5, 6, 8, and 9 at craps.

inside ticket   The ticket on which a keno player records his bet and that he submits to the house along with his wager; the same as an *original ticket.*

insurance   A wager at blackjack in which the player bets that the dealer is holding a natural.

juice   The 5 percent commission that the house charges on buy and lay bets at craps; the same as the *vig* or *vigorish.*

junket   A trip arranged and paid for by a casino to bring a group of gamblers to play at their tables.

junket master   The organizer and supervisor of a casino junket trip.

keno board   The electronic board bearing numbers 1 to 80 on which the selected numbers are lit during each drawing for the information of keno players.

keno counter   The location where keno tickets and wagers are submitted and where winnings are collected

keno lounge   The area of a gambling casino where the game of keno is conducted.

keno runner   A casino employee who roams through various parts of the casino and hotel to collect keno wagers from players.

keno writer   The casino employee who collects players' wagers, issues them duplicate tickets, and pays off winnings at the game of keno.

king number   A single number that has been circled on a keno ticket to indicate that it is to be played in combination with other numbers marked on the ticket.

king ticket   A keno ticket that contains one or more single numbers that have been circled to indicate that they are to be played in combination with other numbers marked on the ticket.

Labouchere system   A betting system that involves adding to a written series of numbers after each loss and crossing out numbers in the series after each win; the same as the *cancellation system.*

ladder man   The casino employee who oversees a baccarat game while seated at a high chair.

lay bet   A wrong bet on a box number at craps that the house pays off at true odds after first charging a 5 percent commission on the short end of the bet.

laydown   A wager.

layout   The diagram printed on a gaming table that identifies where different bets are to be placed.

lay the odds   For a wrong bettor to make a free odds wager.

level-one system   Any card-counting strategy that uses no more than the point values $+1$, -1, and 0, as opposed to more advanced systems that may use as many as seven different point values for the various cards.

line bet A bet at roulette that one of six particular numbers will win.

live crap number One of the craps combinations, either 3 and 12 or 3 and 2, that pays off for the don't-pass bettor.

long end The side of a wager that has to pay more than it stands to collect.

loose machine A slot machine that has been set to return in the form of payoffs a high percentage of the money it takes in; the opposite of a *tight machine*.

low hand One of the two hands into which a player in Pai Gow divides his four dominoes.

make your point To succeed in repeating your point number at craps before rolling a 7.

marker The IOU form that a player must fill out when receiving credit from a casino; the same as *paper*.

Martingale system A betting system that involves doubling the size of one's bet after every losing wager; the same as the *double-up system*.

Mickey Mouse chips Special non-redeemable chips sometimes issued to players on junkets.

mini-junket A trip arranged and paid for by a casino to bring a group of gamblers to play at their tables; it is distinguished from a *junket* by the fact that the players' stay at the casino lasts only one or two days.

money wheel A carnival-type game employing a large vertical wheel marked with U.S. currency around its border; the same as a *big six wheel* or a *wheel of fortune*.

monster hand A period in which one shooter at craps keeps the dice for an exceptionally long series of rolls before sevening-out.

multiple-coin machine A slot machine on which a player may play more than one coin simultaneously.

natural A perfect hand. At blackjack, this consists of a two-card hand containing an ace and a ten-value card. At baccarat, it consists of a hand totaling 8 or 9 on the first two cards. At craps, it consists of a 7 or an 11 on the come-out roll.

negative progression Any betting system that involves increasing the size of one's bet after each losing wager.

New York craps A style of craps, found in some foreign casinos and some illegal casinos in this country, in which come bets and place bets are not permitted; the same as *Eastern craps* and *5 percent craps*.

nickel Five-dollar chip.

no action A term signifying that the casino refuses to cover a particular wager.

odd bet A wager at roulette that one of the eighteen odd numbers will win.

off To remove a wager from play at craps for one or more rolls of the dice.

one-roll bet Any wager at craps that must be decided on the next roll of the dice.

one-roll hardway A wager at craps that the shooter will roll a particular total (either 4, 6, 8, or 10) with the same number on both dice on the very next roll; the same as a *hardway hop* or a *hardway on the turn*.

original ticket The ticket on which a keno player records his bet and that he submits to the house along with his wager; the same as an *inside ticket*.

outside bet One of the even-money or 2-to-1 bets at roulette (high/low, odd/even, red/black, dozen, and column bets) that are made outside the central, numbered portion of the layout.

outside numbers The box numbers 4, 5, 9, and 10 at craps.

outside ticket The ticket that is given to a keno player as a receipt for his bet when he submits his original ticket to the house; the same as a *duplicate ticket*.

Pai Gow An Oriental game played with dominoes.

paint A picture card (jack, queen, or king) at blackjack.

paper The IOU form that a player must fill out when receiving credit from a casino; the same as a *marker*.

parlay To double one's bet after a win.

pass A win by the shooter at craps, either by rolling a natural on the come-out or by successfully repeating his point before rolling a 7.

pass line The space on a crap layout where a player places his bet if he wishes to wager that the shooter will win; the same as the *front line*.

pat hand Any hand in a card game to which one would not normally draw additional cards.

patience system A betting system that involves waiting until a certain number of decisions on a certain side have occurred before making a wager.

pawn Any of the numbers marked in the field in a king ticket.

pay line Of the several rows of symbols visible through the reel window of a slot machine, the one row that actually determines whether a player has won a payoff.

P.C. The mathematical advantage that the casino enjoys on a wager; short for percentage. The same as the *house edge*.

pit An area consisting of a series of gaming tables arranged back to back.

pit boss The casino executive who is responsible for the conduct of all games within a particular pit during a work shift.

place bet A right bet on a box number at craps that the house pays off at less than true odds.

player hand The first of the two hands dealt at baccarat.

plus-minus system The most basic type of blackjack card-counting system, in which each card is assigned a value of either $+1$, -1, or 0; the same as the *high-low system*.

point The total, either 4, 5, 6, 8, 9, or 10, rolled on the come-out at craps, which must be repeated before rolling a 7 in order for the pass line to win.

power of the pencil The authority on the part of a casino executive to issue complimentary hotel services to a player.

press To increase the size of a wager (most often doubling it) after it has won once.

price 1. The total sum wagered on a keno ticket. 2. The house percentage on a particular wager.

producer A term used by casino executives to refer to players who are consistent heavy losers at their casino.

progressive jackpot The grand prize offered on certain kinds of slot machines that keeps growing each time the machine is played until someone wins it.

progressive meter The LED number on a progressive slot machine that records the changing size of the giant progressive jackpot.

progressive slots Slot machines on which the highest jackpot is not preset but rather grows each time the machine is played until someone wins it, as opposed to *straight slots*.

prop A player employed by a cardroom who plays with his own money in those games in which he is directed to play.

proposition bet 1. The wagers located in the center of the crap layout. 2. Any longshot bet at a casino game.

push A tie between a player and the dealer in blackjack or between the player hand and the bank hand at baccarat.

quarter bet A bet at roulette that one of four particular numbers will win; the same as a *corner bet* or a *square bet*.

quarters Twenty-five-dollar chips.

rabbit ears The two transparent tubes into which the twenty selected numbers are forced during a drawing at keno.

race A term sometimes used to refer to a keno drawing. This comes from the fact that, at one time, every keno ball bore the name of a race horse as well as a number.

rail The high, padded border that encloses a crap table.

rake The commission a cardroom charges on each pot in its poker games.

rating card A special form that casino executives use to record the playing of junket participants and other high rollers.

razzle A seven-card stud version of lowball poker popular in Nevada casinos.

red bet A wager at roulette that one of the eighteen red numbers will win.

reds Casino chips valued at five dollars each.

reel One of several loops inside a slot machine that spin each time the handle is pulled, stopping eventually to determine whether the player has won a payoff.

reel strip The covering on a slot machine reel that contains the symbols that determine whether the player has won a payoff.

reel window The glass display area in front of a slot machine through which the player views the reels.

replay ticket A duplicate ticket from a previous keno game that a player submits as his original ticket for a bet on a subsequent game when he wishes to bet on the same numbers again.

RFB privileges Free room, food, and alcoholic beverages provided by a casino to a high-rolling player in return for his patronage.

rich deck The undealt portion of the deck at blackjack when it contains an overabundance of cards favorable to the players.

right bet Any bet at craps that favors the shooter over the house; the same as a *do bet*.

running count The count kept at blackjack that is adjusted as each new card is dealt out.

run the shoe For a player at baccarat to maintain control of the shoe by dealing nothing but winning bank hands until all the cards have been exhausted.

seven-out For the shooter at craps to lose by rolling a 7 before repeating his point number.

shaker The container holding three dice that is employed in the game of Sic Bo.

shift boss The casino executive who is responsible for the conduct of all games during a work shift.

shill A casino employee whose job it is to pose as a player in order to attract players to a slow table.

shoe An oblong box used to hold the cards as they are dealt in a game of blackjack or baccarat.

shoot   At craps, the shooter's entire series of rolls of the dice up to the time he sevens-out; the same as his *hand*.

shooter   The player at craps whose turn it is to roll the dice.

short end   The side of a wager that has to pay less than it stands to collect.

short odds   Payoff odds on a wager that are less than the true odds on the risk the bettor is taking.

shuffle up   For a blackjack dealer to shuffle the cards frequently, perhaps as often as every hand, in an effort to thwart card counters.

Sic Bo   An Oriental game in which players bet on what combinations they think will appear on three dice when they are shaken.

sick gambler   A compulsive gambler.

single odds   The option of making a free odds wager at craps that is equal to the size of one's line bet.

slot arcade   A gambling casino consisting entirely of slot machines.

slot floor   The area or areas of a gambling casino that contain its slot machines.

slot mix   The mixture of loose machines and tight machines, nickel, quarter, and dollar machines, and progressive and nonprogressive machines that a casino utilizes to achieve maximum profits from its slot machines.

snake eyes   The total 2 at craps.

soft hand   A blackjack hand that contains an ace counted as 11; the opposite of a *hard hand*.

split   To divide one's blackjack hand into two separate hands when one has been dealt two cards of the same value as the initial two cards.

split bet   A bet at roulette that one of two particular numbers will win.

spot   A number on a keno ticket that has been marked with an X for betting purposes.

square bet   A bet at roulette that one of four particular numbers will win; the same as a *corner bet* or a *quarter bet*.

stack   A group of twenty roulette chips. Roulette chips are only sold in stacks.

stand   To decline to draw any further cards to one's hand in blackjack.

steaming   Said of a gambler who is playing recklessly in a desperate effort to recoup his losses.

stickman   The crap dealer who pulls in the dice after each roll and pushes them to the shooter for the next roll.

stiff   A blackjack hand that might exceed 21 if one more card is drawn but that is not good enough to constitute a pat hand, i.e., a total of hard 12 through 16.

stops   The various points at which a slot machine reel may stop when the handle has been pulled.

straight slots   Slot machines on which all the payoffs are preset and unvarying, as opposed to *progressive slots*.

straight ticket   A keno ticket that contains only one wager and that involves the selection of anywhere from one to fifteen numbers; the same as a *basic ticket*.

straight-up bet   A bet at roulette that a particular number will win.

street bet   A bet at roulette that one of three particular numbers will win.

surrender   An option at blackjack available in a very few casinos whereby a player forfeited only half his bet if he was willing to concede the hand before drawing any cards.

sweat   To watch, as in "to sweat a game."

swing shift   The work shift in a casino that runs from 6 P.M. to 2 A.M.

table games   The games of blackjack, craps, roulette, and baccarat, as opposed to slot machines and keno.

take down   To retract a wager (usually at craps) before it has come to a decision; the same as *call down*.

take the odds   For a right bettor to make a free odds wager.

tap out   To lose one's entire bankroll.

third-base   The last seat at the dealer's extreme right at a blackjack table.

32 across   A set of place bets at craps covering all the box numbers with five units each on the numbers 4, 5, 9, and 10 and six units each on the numbers 6 and 8.

three-way craps   A one-roll bet at craps that combines wagers on totals 2, 3, and 12.

ticket   The piece of paper on which a keno player records his bet.

tight machine   A slot machine that has been set to return in the form of payoffs a low percentage of the money it takes in; the opposite of a *loose machine*.

toke   A gratuity.

toke hustling   A dealer's actions designed to aggressively encourage players to tip him.

tough player   A skilled gambler.

trente et quarante   A banking card game found in European casinos.

triple odds   The option of making a free odds wager at craps that is equal to three times the size of one's line bet.

true count   The running count at a blackjack game after it has been adjusted to reflect the approximate number of cards still left undealt.

true odds   The actual likelihood of an event occurring.

26/27 across   A set of place bets at craps covering the box numbers with five units each on the numbers 4, 5, 9, and 10 and six units each on the numbers 6 and 8, except for the point number, which is not covered. Depending on what number is the point, the wager will involve either twenty-six or twenty-seven units.

underground joint   A gambling casino that operates secretly in a jurisdiction where gambling is illegal.

up-and-back   A trip arranged by a casino to bring players to play at their tables for a period lasting eight to twelve hours; participants receive a discount on their expenses from the casino.

up-card   The first card of the dealer's hand, which he deals himself face up.

video keno   A kind of electronic slot machine game in which a keno card appears on a video screen, the player selects anywhere from one to ten of the numbers on the card, and the machine then randomly selects twenty numbers that determine whether the player's selections win a payoff.

video poker   A kind of electronic slot machine game in which a poker hand appears on a video screen, the player has the option of improving it by drawing more cards, and payoffs are given based on the rank of the hand.

video slots   Computerized slot machines that utilize computer graphics of slot symbols shown on a video screen in place of the standard mechanical slot machine reels.

vig/vigorish   The 5 percent commission the house charges on buy and lay bets at craps; the same as the *juice*.

wash A situation in which a win on one bet exactly cancels out a loss on another, simultaneous bet made by the same player.

way ticket A type of keno ticket on which a player makes several simultaneous bets all of the same type, for example, all eight-spot bets.

wheel The casino's term for the game of roulette (never "the wheel of fortune").

wheel chips Special casino chips used only at roulette and no other game.

wheel head The revolving, central portion of a roulette wheel that contains the numbered slots.

wheel of fortune A carnival-type game employing a large vertical wheel marked with U.S. currency around its border; the same as a *big six wheel* or a *money wheel*.

wheel roller The casino's term for the dealer who conducts a roulette game.

working Said of a wager at craps that counts for the next roll of the dice.

wrong bet Any bet at craps that favors the house over the shooter; the same as a *don't bet*.

Gambling Books Ordering Information

Ask for any of the books listed below at your bookstore. Or to order direct from the publisher, call 1-800-447-BOOK (MasterCard or Visa), or send a check or money order for the books purchased (plus $4.00 shipping and handling for the first book ordered and $1.00 for each additional book) to Carol Publishing Group, 120 Enterprise Avenue, Dept. 40525, Secaucus, NJ 07094.

Beating the Wheel: The System That's Won More Than $6 Million, From Las Vegas to Monte Carlo by Russell T. Barnhart
$12.95 paper   0-8184-0553-8   (CAN $17.95)

Beat the House: Sixteen Ways to Win at Blackjack, Craps, Roulette, Baccarat and Other Table Games by Frederick Lembeck
$12.95 paper   0-8065-1607-0   (CAN $17.95)

Blackjack Your Way to Riches by Richard Albert Canfield
$12.95 paper   0-8184-0498-1   (CAN $17.95)

The Body Language of Poker: Mike Caro's Book of Tells by Mike Caro
$18.95 paper   0-89746-100-2   (CAN $26.95)

The Cheapskate's Guide to Las Vegas: Hotels, Gambling, Food, Entertainment, and Much More by Connie Emerson
$9.95 paper   0-8065-1530-9   (CAN $13.95)

The Complete Book of Sports Betting: A New, No Nonsense Approach to Sports Betting by Jack Moore
$14.95 paper   0-8184-0579-1   (CAN $20.95)

Darwin Ortiz on Casino Gambling: The Complete Guide to Playing and Winning by Darwin Ortiz
$14.95 paper   0-8184-0525-2   (CAN $20.95)

For Winners Only: The Only Casino Gambling Guide You'll Ever Need by Peter J. Andrews
$18.95 paper   0-8065-1728-X   (CAN $26.95)

Gambling Scams: How They Work, How to Detect Them, How to Protect Yourself by Darwin Ortiz
$11.95 paper   0-8184-0529-5   (CAN $15.95)

Gambling Times Guide to Blackjack by Stanley Roberts
$12.95 paper   0-89746-015-4   (CAN $17.95)

Gambling Times Guide to Craps by N.B. Winkless
$9.95 paper   0-89746-013-8   (CAN $13.95)

How to be Treated Like a High Roller by Robert Renneisen
$8.95 paper   0-8184-0580-4   (CAN $12.95)

John Patrick's Advanced Blackjack
$19.95 paper   0-8184-0582-1   (CAN $27.95)

John Patrick's Advanced Craps
$18.95 paper   0-8184-0577-5   (CAN $26.95)

John Patrick's Blackjack
$12.95 paper   0-8184-0555-4   (CAN $17.95)

John Patrick's Craps
$14.95 paper   0-8184-0554-6   (CAN $20.95)

John Patrick's Roulette
$19.95 paper   0-8184-0587-2   (CAN $27.95)

John Patrick's Slots
$12.95 paper   0-8184-0574-0   (CAN $17.95)

Million Dollar Blackjack by Ken Uston
$16.95 paper   0-89746-068-5   (CAN $23.95)

New Poker Games by Mike Caro
$5.95 paper   0-89746-040-5   (CAN $7.95)

Playing Blackjack as a Business by Lawrence Revere
$15.95 paper   0-8184-0064-1   (CAN $21.95)

Progression Blackjack: Exposing the Cardcounting Myth by Donald Dahl
$9.95 paper   0-8065-1396-9   (CAN $13.95)

Win at Video Poker: The Guide to Beating the Poker Machines by Roger Fleming
$9.95 paper   0-8065-1605-4   (CAN $13.95)

Winning at Slot Machines by Jim Regan
$5.95 paper   0-8065-0973-2   (CAN $7.95)

Winning Blackjack in Atlantic City and Around the World by Thomas Gaffney
$7.95 paper   0-8065-1178-8   (CAN $10.95)

Winning Blackjack Without Counting Cards by David S. Popik
$9.95 paper   0-8065-0963-5   (CAN $13.95)

(Prices subject to change; books subject to availability)

"TENDER AND FUNNY . . .

See's swift prose, her dead-on dialogue with twists of knowingness depth-buried in it, energizes the adventures."

—*Los Angeles Times*

"With this compelling work . . . See evokes an L.A. rarely seen: a place where unexpected beauty blossoms in the margins."

—*Time*

"A wondrous fantasy of artistic—and human—triumph . . . In *The Handyman*, novelist Carolyn See takes a wry and playful look at artistic inspiration and the sheer nuttiness of life at the edge of the millennium."

—*The San Diego Union-Tribune*

"Misleadingly conversational in tone, borne aloft on deceptively offhand currents, *The Handyman* ascends, detail by detail, into the realm of mysterious profundity Carolyn See has made her own. Only a master novelist could have written this book; only Carolyn See could have informed the mastery with such grace."

—PETER STRAUB

"Engaging . . . The people who call on Bob for help are a wonderfully drawn, motley cast of Angelenos, including a harried mother of two children who have Attention Deficit Disorder and a gay man whose end-stage AIDS is more than his partner can handle. . . . Ms. See is never saccharine. Her quick wit, sharp tongue, and lively pace keep the book grounded and enjoyable."

—*The Wall Street Journal*

"[A] vibrant and provocative novel . . . With deft narrative pacing, See follows a scene of slapstick domestic chaos with a searing portrayal of a young man dying of AIDS. In a compulsively readable narrative, she conveys a philosophy of life for the Y2K and beyond. . . . Witty, insightful, and compassionate, this book has a beguiling message and mainstream appeal."

—*Publishers Weekly* (starred review)

Please turn the page for more reviews. . . .

ALSO BY CAROLYN SEE

Dreaming: Hard Luck and
    Good Times in America

Golden Days

Making History

Rhine Maidens

Mothers, Daughters

Blue Money

The Rest Is Done with Mirrors

The Handyman

The Handyman

A NOVEL

Carolyn See

BALLANTINE BOOKS · NEW YORK

A Ballantine Book
Published by The Ballantine Publishing Group

This is a work of fiction. All incidents and dialogue, and all names and characters, with the exception of a few well-known artists, are products of the author's imagination and are not to be construed as real. Where the real-life figures appear, the situations, incidents, and dialogues concerning those persons are entirely imaginary and are not intended to depict any actual events or to change the entirely fictional nature of the work.

Library of Congress Catalog Card Number: 99-91831

ISBN 0-345-42660-6

This edition is published by arrangement with Random House, Inc.

Manufactured in the United States of America

Cover design by Kristine V. Mills-Noble

First Trade Paperback Edition: April 2000

10 9 8 7 6 5 4 3 2 1

for Robert Laws

my bon vivant

brother

JOHN SIMON GUGGENHEIM
MEMORIAL FOUNDATION
90 PARK AVENUE
NEW YORK, NEW YORK 10016

GUGGENHEIM APPLICATION
STATEMENT OF PLAN
August 15, 2027

ROBERT HAMPTON Y LOS TESTIGOS

BY PETER LAUE

My "plan," if I should receive this grant, is to trace imagistic connections between the very earliest work of Robert Hampton (eight surviving paintings, as well as a small collection of wooden animals, all owned by the self-proclaimed "Testigos" or "Witnesses"), and a large body of his intermediate work, most of which has been kept off the market and is currently stored at his main compound between Cuernavaca and Mexico City.

In 2025 and 2026 I was able to travel to Los Angeles, Lausanne, and the south of France to track down and interview the original "Testigos." My work on them has been accepted by <u>Art of the Americas</u> and will be published in November of this year. Since this material is not yet in print, however, I will be quoting from it here fairly extensively.

I have also been fortunate enough to have received a grant from the Lannon Foundation, which allowed me to journey, in January of this year, to the Hampton Compound. During the two weeks of my stay I was allowed access to many of the stored paintings, and was also able to secure an invitation to return for a year to continue my work. A Guggenheim grant would cover my travel and living expenses during that time.

I feel confident that no other scholar has approached Hampton's work from this point of view. Most criticism has either concerned itself with his vast museum pieces (and has been, as a consequence, heavily theoretical) or has dealt only with Los Testigos and the rest of the Hampton myth in purely biographical terms. I would hope that a year of close research may combine the two approaches and yield up the first authentic, significant Hampton scholarship.

My "Statement" will be divided into three parts: (I) A few words on Robert Hampton, his career up to this point, and the criticism it has so far generated; (II) A short account of "Los Testigos," the surviving artworks in their possession, and the position the artist holds within this band of early acquaintances; (III) A very brief summation of what I was able to find during my stay at the compound.

I. THE ARTIST

By the year 2015, Robert Hampton had been acknowledged by most European critics to be perhaps the preeminent international artist of the new century. By most accounts, he had been among the first to cast off the debilitating angst of the twentieth century, and the ever more sterile conceptual art that had become the emblem of its anomie and affectlessness, so popular then, so dated now.

He is rightly said to be obsessed by light, color, and space. Along with this facile Renaissance comparison, he is often ranked with Renoir, Manet, and Monet, though scarcely ever said to be in their debt. Indeed, he has been more often mentioned in the same context as Latin literary figures from the century's turn, such as Gabriel García Márquez and Tomás Eloy Martínez.

I believe—though many of my colleagues might disagree—that the artist precedes the critic: The language with which to properly assess Robert Hampton's work does not yet exist. In my view, most contemporary critics have attempted to define his techniques, his world view, in the stunned, barbaric idiom with which the first astronauts described the moon. Second, for reasons that, frankly, still remain unclear to me, Hampton has so far been revered—venerated, even—quite as much for his life, his "myth," as for his work.

Hampton presently makes his home in the inviting countryside between Mexico City and Cuernavaca. (He also keeps a studio in a small town near the southern tip of the Baja California peninsula.) His home outside the capital is, as I have said, a spacious compound, where he lives with his wife and his three children, Valerie, Samantha, and Benjamin. His stepson, Teodoro M. L. Hampton, has long kept a guest house on the property, and together with his mother, manages the day-to-day workings of the artist's enterprise. It was Teodoro's idea to open the grounds once a month as early as 2015, so that both serious students and the general public could ponder the connections between art and life so essential to the development of this artist's vision. Hampton has been rigorously schooled, his stepson likes to say, in all the techniques of the previous century, and even studied (for a very short time) at the École des Beaux-Arts in Paris. But he turned his back on all that, and cast his lot with the new world and the new century.

The family makes no attempt to hide or close itself off: Visitors often glimpse Valerie and Samantha playing tennis; Ben frequently drops by with friends. There are always picnics and parties somewhere on the grounds. Teodoro Hampton, dazzlingly handsome and endlessly courteous, never tires of pointing his siblings out to the pilgrims, reminding them that these young adults were once the models for the "golden" children whom Hampton has painted through the years. He himself, Teodoro reminds them, appeared in Twilight, The Pool Series, Cabo, La Bufadora, and many other early works.

Often, the artist joins his stepson. Hampton moves among the crowd, shaking hands—a slight, tanned man, wiry, with close-cropped graying hair, and sometimes the whimsical conceit of a bolo tie fastened with turquoise. He resembles nothing so much as an American family man, and, of course, he is that. (His own mother resides on the property, but is seldom seen.) He states repeatedly that he owes a great deal, everything, to his wife.

People speculate ceaselessly about Señora Hampton, who has long been considered one of Mexico City's great beauties. In public, she dresses simply, her slim arms heavy with the gold jewelry her husband makes for her. She seems to many to be deceptively "ordinary" in her behavior, the very picture of open American friendliness. But in financial negotiations regarding her husband's work, Mrs. Hampton has been notoriously astute. With the help of her assistant and Hampton archivist, Barbara MacKenzie (whom Hampton met years ago at Otis Art Institute in

Los Angeles), Señora Hampton speedily amassed the artist's fortune. She was quick to realize the monetary value in his work, to see that the thirst consumers developed for it corresponded directly to its scarcity. By keeping at least half his work off the market she has made her husband a very rich man. There are even tales that she accomplished this at first against his will—that he would have been content to live quietly as an artisan fashioning tourist "rubbish" on the Baja coast. But when one is in the presence of those vast canvases, which sing with color and energy, one discards that story as apocryphal.

Hampton's early, smaller, more accessible work is still most beloved by the general public. When pilgrims visit the Hampton Compound or any of the major museums, they are most apt to leave with reproductions of some of his twenty-four interpretations of <u>The Junction Between Earth and Sky</u>, all 36″ × 44″, all filled to bursting with color and detail. In technique they have sometimes been compared to Le Douanier Rousseau, but these comparisons are specious. Rousseau's world is closed and dreamy; the light that pours from Hampton's canvases is tropical, searing, totally untamed.

Much has been written about Hampton's secular saints in <u>The Junction</u> series—the dying boy watched over by an ardent lover or devoted father; the anti-virgin, or Lilith, a woman who compels desire even as she admits to, flaunts, her age. And of course the exquisite, water-soaked families painted in hot light and cool blue gardens, who incontrovertibly live in another world, but where? These worlds confound the viewer. Part of Hampton's appeal has always been that his vision is often literally inexplicable: as I have suggested, the critical vocabulary has not yet been invented, the terms not coined, that explain and define his work.

But it is my contention that these twenty-four paintings boast an even earlier provenance: eight primitive prototypes; <u>The Child and His Guardian</u>, <u>The Child Assumpted into Heaven</u>, <u>The Guardian Alone</u>, <u>The Aging Lilith</u>, five floral still lifes (and, of course, <u>The Animals</u>). All currently owned by "Los Testigos," the Witnesses.

II. LOS TESTIGOS

In Los Angeles a zealous group of disciples—self-styled "Testigos" or Witnesses—insist they knew the artist in his youth, and they speak of him as a man of both saintly modesty and fierce passion. They turn up again and again, in interviews on public television, in Sunday supplements, even in learned journals. This group has little in common except that they all claim to have known Hampton in his youth, at the turn of the century.

Jamé Hareh-Tran runs an animal sanctuary in the barren canyons to the north of Los Angeles. She recalls Hampton as a spiritual healer and natural lover of children, a man who, merely by coming into a room, banished the sorrows of the abandoned and the lonely: "My children loved him. He was wonderful with my animals. I myself adored him beyond words." Mrs. Tran has in her possession six unique and probably genuine wooden Hamptons—two monkeys, a snake, a bird, a turkey, and an iguana rendered in his distinctive signature green, the theological color of hope. She has mounted these artifacts in temperature-controlled, museum-quality frames in the receiving room of her wildlife refuge.

Other Testigos revere him as well. Henry William Hurst owns three prototype acrylics of what he calls <u>The Child</u>

<u>Jesus at the Junction of Good and Evil</u>. He also claims to be the original "Guardian Lover" above the dying Savior with the caste mark. It's difficult to associate the graying, distinguished public-health activist with the fervent "Guardian," but Hurst's argument is unequivocally backed by these intriguing originals that unmistakably bear the magic signs of the early Hampton. Hurst's longtime companion, Alec Austen, also claims to have known the artist.

Two other prominent Californians knew Hampton at that time. David and Shelley (Ross) Baxter were both acquainted with him during a fateful summer, and—like Hurst and Austen—claim to have met each other through the good offices of the artist. "We were all in our twenties," Baxter says. "He's the one who introduced me to Shelley. He helped her that summer, when she was at loose ends."

It's difficult to think of investment banker Shelley Baxter as ever having been "at loose ends." Mrs. Baxter has served on many boards, including that of the San Diego Museum of Modern Art. (It was through her personal efforts that the museum was able to acquire the Hampton <u>Paradise Lost and Found</u> triptych, which claims its own room at that site.) Her husband, a respected urban planner, claims to have been influenced by Hampton at a critical "junction" in his own life. "When we conceive of communities, we often get caught up in our own inventiveness, in an aesthetic that puts the 'plan' before the individual. Put another way, we philosophize ourselves to death. We give people what they <u>should</u> need instead of what they love. Hampton knows—always did know—that people crave air, gardens, animals, children. My communities make room for all these elements."

The Baxter home boasts five contemporary Hamptons—

floral masterpieces in lavender, yellow, morning-glory blue, a bamboo piece in his signature green, and a slightly later hyperreal <u>Nasturtium Study</u> in dark orange. More significantly for this study, they also own four prototypes of these large works, hung in a small den and generally kept from public view.

The Baxters maintain their friendship with the Hamptons, seeing them several times a year, as does Valerie Le Clerc, reputed inspiration for the <u>Lilith</u> series. An elderly lady of great dignity and rectitude, she resides in the Hollywood Hills home she has owned for decades. (Her dearest friend for many years has been Laura Huxley, widow of the legendary Aldous Huxley, and Madame Le Clerc has said that if she herself has ever made any "contribution" to the larger world, it is because of Huxley and Hampton.) "Many of us strive and strive for nothing," she says. "That was the essential mark of the last century, and I believe it was a source of the pervasive discontent of that time. When I first met Robert, I was struck by his utter lack of striving, his absolute reluctance to claim his own greatness. To know him was to love him."

"Love" him? Can it be that Valerie Le Clerc was the original Lilith? When asked this, Madame Le Clerc laughs. "Get out your calendar," she says. "I was close to sixty in 1996." Still, an astonishing early <u>Lilith</u> hangs in her bedroom, so disturbing in its eroticism that the observer—however worldly—blushes to see it.

Perhaps the most unexpected of all "The Witnesses" is June Shaw, controversial professor of gender philosophy at the University of Lausanne. "Robert Hampton and I were lovers at the turn of the century," she claims. "Before we formed our attachment, he could have easily been dismissed as a loose construct of erroneous assumptions and badly thought-out premises. He was an idiot savant, if you will, utterly unconscious of himself and the world in which he lived. Our coupling changed all that. I brought him to an understanding of carnal knowledge. I am Lilith—as is any woman who dares to make that desperate choice." Absolutely nothing in Professor Shaw's physical appearance ties her to <u>Lilith</u>, and there is no corroborating evidence that she was ever Hampton's mistress and muse. But there can be no denying that June Shaw may have, more than any other American critic or scholar, contributed to Hampton's early artistic reputation, insisting upon his greatness and on her own contribution to it. (And it was she, in an early monograph in 2009, who coined the term "Testigos," also insisting upon the Iberianization of the word.)

Are there other Testigos? Only one woman of legendary charm—much married—who has drifted from California to the south of France for close to three decades. Some years ago, thanks to a postdoctoral grant, I was able to track down "Kate" in the town of La Ciotat on the Mediterranean coast; that preliminary interview, in fact, has led to my lifelong preoccupation with Los Testigos. Kate is an attractive, ample woman, very much a "Hampton beauty." Her diffidence, too, is Hamptonesque. "I'm not even sure he's the person you're looking for," she told me, "Or that I am. I can't believe he's '<u>the</u> Robert Hampton.' For one thing—I think we were lovers once, but I hardly remember it. And wouldn't I remember it? I can tell you one thing. The boy I remember was dear. To me that counts for more than being a great lover <u>or</u> a great artist." She laughed, and added, "Maybe that's why I've been married so often. Maybe I'm still looking for a man like Bob."

As I stated before, I was able to spend two weeks during January of this year at the Hampton Compound. Señora Hampton was enjoying a visit from her married stepdaughter, and several students from around the world were beginning a season of "color fellowships" under Hampton's supervision and the more direct tutelage of Teodoro M. L. Hampton. With the artist's permission, I was able to spend many hours in the large studios where the artist stores his completed, intermediate works. Once again, I was struck by the fusion of the ordinary and the divine—the "sacredness" of Lilith, the transcendent quality of his floral still lifes, the inexorable insistence upon the infinite within the quotidian. Even in this cursory search I was able to find dozens of paintings that hewed to the themes of the Testigo works—the dying boy with his devoted guardian; the same boy assumpted above city crowds; the pagan woman, nude, again and again, assuming the posture and demeanor of a saint. It's often been said that Hampton is a "visionary"; from the evidence of these paintings I would argue that he has perhaps always been a Christian mystic in his own world view, obsessed with the miraculous, the divine.

Independent of the Testigo themes, I also found numerous depictions of women and girls, plainly dressed, walking in air, walking on water. And I was struck in particular by another pair of "saints" who turned up repeatedly and are plainly from the same early and intermediate periods; men who resemble Saints Peter and Paul but are dressed as American peasants, dreamy men, benign of visage, invariably presented against a celestial silver background. Threads of ineffable fire spurt from their fingernails, as miracles—dare we speculate?—waiting to occur.

When I asked the artist about these representations, he said only that he was glad I had discovered them, and that, yes, they did carry great significance. To be truthful, Hampton was less than forthcoming about his work. At times, I believe, he found my questions amusing.

Soon after that first interview, we were called to dinner, a family dinner like so many others at the compound, with its commanding view of the valley descending toward Cuernavaca. Tables had been set up under awnings outside, by a brook and waterfall of the artist's own construction. Lanterns were lit in the twilight; exotic Hampton "animals," birds and reptiles elegantly lit, could be glimpsed in the surrounding trees. A few small children romped on the lawn as the adults conversed. Robert Hampton ate with a good appetite; his wife—her arm about the waist of her visiting stepdaughter—remained standing until she was sure the party was served.

I admit that at first I was too shy to join the others. I kept to myself out on the darkening lawn, envying all of them in their easy pleasure. But Robert Hampton looked up and saw me in the dark. He got up from the table, came and took me by the arm. I was a lonely scholar, an outsider, no longer. A grant, of course, would allow me to pursue all this much further.

Peter Laue

PETER LAUE
LOS ANGELES,
MEXICO CITY
AUGUST 15, 2027

The Handyman

Part One

In May of 1996 I flew to Paris from Los Angeles, to get settled in the city before I enrolled in the fall semester of the École des Beaux-Arts. I was twenty-eight years old; I had a bachelor's degree in Fine Arts from UCLA and ten thousand dollars in traveler's checks. I'd spent one summer in Paris before, when I was eighteen. I'd been out of school for five years, "finding myself"—thinking I might be an artist—but that search had turned up nothing. In Paris, at least, I had the idea that I could see what others had done, and what I might do. I was scared shitless.

My plane landed at Orly at quarter of six on a cold Tuesday morning. I had a long wait for my luggage, since I'd brought enough in theory to live for a year, and I had a hard and embarrassing discussion with a cab driver when I finally got out of the airport. I'd expected to feel great, but the jet lag—maybe—kept me from being happy as the taxi drove through suburbs and grimy fog.

I had to keep reminding myself that a lot of other artists had come to this city. All of them must have had a first day, and that day had to have been lonesome.

I kept waiting for the city to turn into something beautiful, but I had a fair wait. After about forty minutes, we came in sight of the river, and yes, everything was as great as everyone said. I gave the driver the address of the Hôtel du Danube on the rue Jacob, on the Left Bank. It was too expensive for me but I'd allowed myself a week there, since it was close to the École, the Musée d'Orsay, the Louvre, and Saint-Germain-des-Prés, the oldest church in Paris. I think I would have to say that everything in me at that time pointed in one direction, to find out what it meant to be a fine artist, to put my life on the line for art, to combine everything I'd learned and everything I felt and then distill that into paintings. It hadn't happened in LA—"the art scene" in LA was crap—but if it were going to happen anywhere, it would happen here. In two years I'd be thirty, and then the whole thing would be ridiculous.

The cab pulled up to the Hôtel du Danube at ten in the morning, and right away I saw I'd made a mistake. The lobby was dark and glossy and touristy, and a clerk my age gave me a chickenshit stare. I asked for their smallest room and I got it—a dark little cubicle toward the back with a single bed, a shorted-out television, an armoire set at an angle on the sloping floor, and wallpaper that went on all the way across the ceiling—brown cabbage roses on a tan background. The one small window looked out on a roof made of corrugated tin.

I felt lousy, but, again, I put that down to jet lag.

After I washed my hands and face I went out for a walk. I knew a run would make me feel better, but I thought I should know where I was running before I suited up and started.

I walked along the rue Jacob to the rue des Saints-Pères and turned up toward the Seine. The sun was out by now. Things looked the way I expected, but not the way I expected. The river was amazing. I could look across it to the Louvre and that was amazing too, more than I could register, more than I could take in. That so many people, so long ago, had been so dedicated to beauty! I thought of LA, weeds sprouting from the sidewalks and retaining walls bulging with dirt from the last earthquake and all the stucco bungalows on the sides of all the hills and how they faded into that beige background of dead ryegrass. I thought of Salvadorean women on Western Avenue with little kids in strollers and more kids strapped to their backs. Everything I remembered seemed monochromatic and sad.

I came back from the river, walking in the direction of the hotel. I thought I should see Saint-Germain-des-Prés, and the famous cafés on the boulevard Saint-Germain. I was getting hungry. Take it a step at a time, I thought. A thousand people, a thousand thousand people have done what you're doing. They got through it. So you can get through it.

Half the people around me were French, but most of the other half were American—hunched together on sidewalks, poring over guidebooks and maps. The French pushed past them. The shops had windows filled with high-class tourist junk—etchings cut out of books and framed, tarnished jewelry you could pick up in LA in thrift shops for ten bucks. And stuff only a moron might want— life-sized stuffed leather pigs.

Saint-Germain-des-Prés was great. Old, old, a mass going on at the far end, groups of Parisians and tourists wandering around in the dark. It calmed me down. I was facing a depressing fact, the fact that I didn't want to go into a place by myself for lunch. I had to remind myself that I was an American, well educated, able-bodied, with enough money to last a while. Picasso had done it (not that he was American). Hemingway could do it. (But thinking of myself at the Ritz Bar in a trench coat might have made me laugh, if I could laugh.)

I came out of the church into the cobblestone yard and looked over to my left, at the café where Sartre and de Beauvoir had eaten lunch every day, if you could believe the guidebooks. I walked off on a diagonal to my right, toward a café that to my knowledge had no reputation at all. I sat down, ordered a *Croque Monsieur,* a *salade des tomates,* and a glass of red wine. Not quite what I expected, because there was a red-faced Irishman stuffing down a pair of fried eggs right next to me, telling a story about the computer company he worked for and how he'd just come in from Hong Kong the night before and how he'd be damned if he'd take the company house out in the banlieues, he'd live in the city or nowhere. On my other side, an American woman in a tight suit explained to someone who looked a lot like her mom that the French were terrific pill poppers, and that she, the daughter, was terribly disappointed that her mother had let herself go, because how could she introduce her to François, when she was looking like that?

Everyone I saw had someone to talk to; everyone had a friend. Everyone had somewhere to go. Everyone had a plan.

I paid my check and walked back to the hotel.

My room faced away from the sun and smelled of mildew and smoke. I pulled off my clothes, got under the covers, and slept.

When I woke up, it was the next morning. I ordered coffee and croissants and the maid brought them up. I sat in bed and ate and began to feel terrible. I got ready for the voices that would be rolling by soon, and sure enough, here they came: my dad, the redneck Texan carpenter who'd taken off when I was fifteen. "You're gonna be a *what*? An artist? Gimme a *break,* Bob!" My mom, sitting alone in her apartment down on Virgil: "That's fine for *now,* when you're still young, but pretty soon life is going to catch up with you. You can't go on living for yourself and expect to get away with it." Living for myself. Man, she was convinced of it.

My old professors: "Hampton, pretty good. No, a B+ is a good grade, especially at UCLA. No, I'm not going to change it. No, I can't tell you what's 'wrong' with the painting! It's just not A work.

I know A work when I see it, and I don't see it here. No, I can't tell you what to do. I can tell you how to get a B, but no one can tell you how to get an A. If I could, we'd all be out on a yacht spending our millions."

Or, "You'd make a fine teacher, Hampton."

Or, "Disney needs animators. You work very rapidly and you're good with detail."

Or, "Did you ever think of special effects? You've got a real craftsman's eye. We're living in the special-effects capital of the world, remember."

But that wasn't what I wanted. I wanted to knock them out. I wanted to knock their socks off. I wanted to change their lives through my art.

Yeah, well.

I got up and took a shower and headed on out to see the Musée d'Orsay.

The day was cold and cloudy and getting inside the museum was a relief: it was warm in there, it was beautiful. The art was something. Manet's *Déjeuner sur l'herbe,* his *Olympia.* How'd he get that light? Renoir's *Dancing at the Moulin de la Galette.* How'd he get that great light?

I went through the museum, feeling worse and worse. The Renoirs—and Renoir wasn't even my favorite painter, for God's sake—made my stomach tie up. I stood for a long time in front of *Danse à la ville* and *Danse à la campagne,* and remembered what one asshole professor had said to me about what I could do to get an A. "You must be born again, Mr. Hampton! You must be born again!"

What if I couldn't be born again? The two pairs of Renoir's dancers—in the city, in the country—showed me a million things in terms of light and technique and even social commentary, but something else in them made me feel like crying like a kid. Some people, somewhere, had been as happy as that.

It didn't matter, because no one in this century painted like that anymore. I tried to remember, back in LA, Tony Berlant using nuts and bolts and metal in all his pieces, doing it for years now. Had Berlant been born again? Born again to what?

I got out of there after a couple of hours and went into a place for lunch, big chunks of veal in a red-orange sauce. I paid too much for it. I went back to the hotel, waited for an hour, went out to a café, and started talking to a good-looking American guy who worked for a French computer firm. Everyone did, he said. Work in computers.

"This is the best café in Paris, absolutely the best. Do you play squash? I make it a point to play three nights a week. Keep in shape. Have to. Going to the École? I have a friend who went there. Best education in France. Absolutely the best. Ever been married? Neither have I. That's the reason I stay over here. They can't get to me here. Not that there aren't plenty of women. *Plenty* of women! How long have you been here? *A day!* I've been here twelve years, off and on. Ex-pat for life, I imagine. Are you free for dinner? Like Greek food? I know an excellent place, right in this neighborhood. Best place in France. Here's Jean-Pierre. Jean-Pierre! Over here! Bob, here, will be going to the École. I told him it's the best . . ."

"Where are you from?" The Frenchman wore a bright red crewneck sweater and a look like he had a sewer right under his chin.

"California. Los Angeles."

"And you come *here*? That is bizarre. Everyone in France wants to go to Los Angeles. It is our Mecca. We all want to go there."

"More wine, don't you think?" The American guy seemed pretty happy about things. "Greek food tonight?"

The next morning I woke up with a hangover and a feeling of doom. This is it, man! You're here, this is it! Cut the crap, do what you're supposed to.

I crossed the river and headed toward the Louvre. I knew it

was banal or bourgeois, but all I really wanted to see was *The Raft of the Medusa*. Then I'd head out to the École, sign up early if I could, get a newspaper, look for a decent room or maybe even an apartment.

Down in the museum's basement I started to sweat. I checked my jacket and backpack and headed up into wings of art, and more art. Too much of it! Renaissance stuff and pre-Renaissance stuff, and Saint Stephens and Saint Sebastians, and miles of virgins and angels. I recognized everything I'd ever studied and saw a thousand things I'd never seen before. I thought of all the men who'd had something like the same dream I had, *to knock their socks off!* To be born again! Would I ever get hung in a museum? Forget it, I couldn't even get a single show. I didn't even know what to paint.

I heard myself panting for breath. I'd just go see *The Raft* and then head over to the École. I spent another couple of hours looking for the damn thing, if only to know for sure that other people sometimes felt like they were drowning, slipping off, losing it altogether. But *The Raft of the Medusa* was undergoing restoration "due to humidity." It stood behind a tall plywood partition. Just a few desperate arms poking up beyond the plywood. Help! We're drowning over here!

The École des Beaux-Arts had very ornate and wonderful gates. They were closed tight and chained with a padlock. I didn't know why they were closed, but it wasn't going to matter. I pushed my face against the cold metal bars and looked in at the gray, rainy courtyard. Who had I been kidding?

I went back to the hotel, dressed for a run, and headed west along the south side of the Seine, passing churches and buildings and more buildings. Not my home. Not my city. I got to the Tour Eiffel and turned to cross a bridge across the Seine. Was this the Trocadéro?—dozens of black guys my age were selling umbrellas to nobody, shivering in the cold.

I ran back to the Hôtel du Danube, and went thudding through the lobby. I sat for a long time on the edge of the bed, then showered, took a nap, got up again at six, and went to the café where I'd met the American guy.

He'd just come from his psychoanalyst. "I tell him my troubles in French, it's good for both of us. Do you want to have dinner? What about Czech food? Something Italian?"

"Do you mind if I ask . . . how old are you?"

"Forty-two, why?"

We ate Italian, "the best in France." I'd had better on the Santa Monica Promenade. We didn't get out of the restaurant until after midnight, and walked over to the Île de la Cité for ice cream. The city's lights twinkled in the freezing drizzle. We ordered double cones, pistachio and chocolate, and started back another way, and there, on a bridge that separated one part of the island from the other, I checked out maybe a couple of hundred students, most of them American. They sat right out in the rain, huddled up in duffle coats, smoking dope, having a great time. None of them looked up. They were all at least ten years younger than I was. I'd waited way too long. Who did I think I was kidding?

So that was that. I flew back to LA. I'd enroll at the Otis Art Institute in September, brush up on design for a semester or two, get work in advertising, drafting, maybe special effects. Maybe get an MFA, finally, and teach. Figure out something to do for the summer. I'd think of something. On the plane back, I asked myself how I felt. My gone Texan dad gave me the answers: like a sick flea on a pig's butt. Lower than a toad. Wronger than a three-dollar bill.

So I was back again in LA. In late sweltering May there I was again, the way I'd been so many times, at the housing center at UCLA, going over the hundreds of apartments and roommate slots that came up empty at this time of year. I'd had it with the West Side though, and was looking for something else. No more trendoids. I couldn't stand the strain.

I found something pretty quick. A chance at a house, shared with three others, over in the Silver Lake area, halfway up the Micheltorena Hill. A room of my own. Three hundred a month. My old neighborhood from when I was a kid. Picture window in the sunken living room. Ocean view from twenty miles away. Central location.

I drove east from UCLA in my old car, with a feeling of retracing my steps, zooming along Sunset all the way through Beverly

Hills and the Strip and Hollywood, and finally to the western border of the place I'd be calling home again if this house looked OK: Vermont Avenue, perpendicular to Sunset. Three blocks to the north, Mom and I had lived for a while in a fifth-floor corner apartment that overlooked The Dresden Room, formerly a pickup joint for zombies, now too hip for words. There were a couple of bookstores and a little theater in that same block, but you'd never know it from my mother's life. She went down to the street to shop for groceries in the store right below her, and then she went right back up to sit by the window. Then she moved to Virgil and did more of the same thing. I tooled through the intersection and tried not to think about it. No more wide lawns or even straight-up businesses now, just free-floating weirdness—used-car lots, mini-malls, Vietnamese manicure shops, Korean banks, Mexican restaurants, a public television station. Sunset Boulevard, still plugging along, all the way from the beach to downtown LA.

I hit "the Junction," where Santa Monica Boulevard came into Sunset at a diagonal, and hills sloped up sharply on either side of me. Sunset was at the bottom of a little valley here, and along the tops of all these hills old palm trees made a fringe like shredded lace. It wasn't the banks of the Seine, but if I had a home, this was it. Amok Books was somewhere around here, and Saint Francis of Assisi Elementary School over to my left, and in the next block, Micheltorena Elementary, where I'd gone for a while as a kid, since Mom and Dad and I had once lived on the south side of Sunset. We'd lived all over, around here.

The Junction was mostly Mexican now, but it was still my old neighborhood, seedy, rundown, right in the middle of things, ten minutes from downtown, and just a look away from the Hollywood Hills, the Hollywood Sign. You could take wild-card streets like Hyperion over to Los Feliz, which could sneak you around the Zoo and the new Forest Lawn and out to the San Fernando Valley, or you could follow Sunset for a few blocks in the other direction, make a left and end up by Silver Lake itself. People on the City Council liked to live over there.

Central location. Central to what?

I turned left, up Micheltorena, and my hands got damp on the wheel. It was steep! I knew I wasn't going up the whole way, I'd be turning left halfway up on Dahlia, but still, the people who'd laid out these streets in the first place hadn't given a shit. They just eye-balled it and went straight on up. A few blocks over on Maltman they'd shut off a whole city block years ago and let it go back to weeds because cars couldn't make it. I'd played war plenty of afternoons on that wilderness plot when I was a little kid.

This hill had seedy old apartments at the bottom and fancy estates at the top, and classy little Neutra houses all along the middle. If you could make it halfway up in this world, you knew you were OK. A little less than halfway up, as I was taking the hill in second gear and trying not to think about it too much, I made a sharp left on Dahlia and there was the house, just a double garage and a front door visible from the street. But a lot of houses were like that on this hill, I remembered that. This one had a thin little stucco lip showing on the street, and probably a big hanging jaw of rooms out back, stuck onto the dirt and hoping for the best.

I rang the bell and after a minute or two a thickset guy about my age opened the door. He wore shorts and a T-shirt, had a big crazy smile and bloodshot eyes. Pretty stoned.

"Come on in. Name's Dave. Show you around."

Very cool in here. Dark and quiet. I peered down a long hall to a patch of bright light, but Dave was moving slowly, giving me the tour. "This would be your room, first one on the left. The middle one is where Austen lives. He's studying for his first qualifyings and his language exam. He's in there now. Hardly ever comes out, except to organize student strikes. And down in the corner room, Kate. She's a hostess over at Cha Cha Cha. Good Caribbean food. Getting married pretty soon. Here's the living room."

Three steps down, and then a big white room with a couple of chairs and a couch and an old piano. And a good-sized picture window that looked across twenty-five miles of LA to a thin ribbon of ocean.

"Great view."

"Yeah, it's why I took the place. And I like the neighborhood. In transition. That means falling apart. I study over in here."

Three steps back up, Dave had staked out a corner at the dining-room table. "I'm reading all of Adorno right now, are you familiar with his work? No? Want to split a joint?"

An hour or so later, I let Dave get back to his Adorno and began to unpack. Not much to move in. There was already a bed and bureau in what would be my room. All I needed to buy was art supplies so I could work on my portfolio for Otis in September.

Back to being a student again. For what? For what.

Sometime during the hour when Dave and I had been kicking back, Austen slumped out to the kitchen for a sandwich. He'd been soft and sluggy, big and miserable looking, and he hadn't wanted to get stoned. "Got to study," he'd said. Then he'd slumped away again, looking pitiful.

Dave smiled. "Guy doesn't wash much. Stays out of everyone's way, though."

I'd felt pretty good in the little room with Dave, talking about art, about how I didn't know what my real material was supposed to be, but how if all I was really cut out for was to be some sort of graphic arts techno-freak, I'd just as soon pack it in. And I talked a little about Paris. It wasn't as awful as I'd thought it would be, to talk about it. Dave was philosophical.

"Isn't a lot of that Paris myth just a fictional construct? A way we have of placing what we think we want out of our reach? The Paris you want was over by 1925. You're not Picasso. You're— what'd you say your name was?—Bob. Some people might say *this* is the right place to be. For now, anyway."

Driving west a little later on Sunset, still in a pot-haze, I spotted a Ford dealership, and eased on in. If I was back in America I might as well buy American. I needed a van to carry my canvases, I told myself. Plus, I had some sort of idea about being mobile, picking up, getting out, going somewhere, starting over. You could live in a van if you had to. And the Paris money was burning a hole in my pocket.

After a couple of hours in the sun, getting harangued by two guys my age wearing terrible suits, I could at least be glad I wasn't selling Fords for a living. I was embarrassed at how much I liked my Aerostar; but if I were ever the kind of guy to be thrilled, I'd have been thrilled. It was tan, with tan leather seats, and two sets of other seats in the back that folded down to make a bed and clear windows along the sides so people wouldn't think I was a pervert. It was clean and smelled of *new car*!

It was great to make the down payment in traveler's checks, blow off my trade-in, great to watch the sweating salesmen look with big eyes at my bulging money holder. He was the opposite of the clerk at the Hôtel du Danube. I didn't even condescend to haggle about the price. Was this what the great American artist drove, a big tan van? Was this what the great American artist wore, khaki pants and a clean T-shirt and white high-tops? Why not?

I looked in the rearview mirror, and got a grip. Same old face. Brown eyes, curly brown hair, moderately tan skin, medium mouth. I could be a bank robber and rob a million banks, and put a million million bucks in a million numbered Swiss accounts, and no one would ever recognize me, because I was so totally and completely average. I thought of myself in an art-house photo, dressed in a black turtleneck, blowing smoke rings, looking serious, and had to laugh. *"Robert, will you change out of that ridiculous sweater at once!"*

That made me think again of my mom. I'd been staying at a motel since I'd got back, and hadn't told her I was home. I stopped at a coffee shop on Virgil, had a tuna salad sandwich, looked across the street at the apartment where she lived. Dreary, dreary. In all the years the two of us had lived together, she'd never told me I was just like my dad, but she showed it in every sigh and glance. That alone gave me a lot of sympathy for the guy. He'd taken that walk when I was fifteen, literally taken a walk, and never come back. I still kept up with my dad's side of the family. There was a lot of family over on that side, they'd never let me get lost. Over here, on this side, there was no one but my mom.

The apartment house had that old smell. The sad smell of being old. I thought of the Hôtel du Danube. That place was *really* old but it didn't smell as bad as this. I climbed up two flights, went down a dark hall, and knocked. Waited while she decided to open the door.

"Mom. I'm home. It's me. Bob. Surprise!"

"What's wrong? Why are you here?"

"I decided to come home, that's all."

She stood back from the door. "Come on in then."

The same faded furniture I remembered from forever. She hadn't ever bought anything new. She wore slacks and a blouse, and her hair hung limply around her tired face. I glanced across the room and saw what I was looking for—a padded occasional chair with an oval back. It was pulled up to a window. She'd sat in that chair staring down at different streets for years now.

"I've been having this terrible headache. It starts down underneath my left shoulder blade and comes up over my head and ends right here above my eye."

"Ma! Aren't you supposed to be asking me why I came back from Paris?"

"You want to talk about yourself and I want to talk about myself. I don't have to ask you. You'll tell me soon enough."

"Did you take any aspirin for your headache?"

"Aspirin upsets my stomach."

"What about Advil?"

"That's worse."

"What *do* you take?"

"Nothing. My system can't take drugs."

"So. What have you been doing then?"

"There comes a time in your life when you've got to slow down. The things you used to do in your life, you can't do anymore."

I tried a little joke, it was the only thing I could think of. "Ma, you never leave the apartment, so how can you slow down? Like it takes you longer to take a shower?"

"You think because you're young that life won't catch up with you. I'd like to be around when it *does* catch up with you. You think you're too smart to go through what I've been going through, but you're not. I'm all alone, Bob."

"I realize that. I *realize* it! Look, I just stopped by to say I'm back in town, and to give you my phone number."

"You won't be staying here?"

"I found a place over by Micheltorena."

"I would have thought you'd stay here."

"Ma. It's not a good idea."

I looked down at her. Who was to say that life wouldn't catch up with me in the same way that it had caught up with her? She was only eighteen years older than I was, only forty-six, and I thought of her as having been exactly like this for as long as I could remember.

"You wouldn't be so sad if you got out more. I mean it. I'm not kidding."

"I get out."

"No. No, you don't."

She looked away from me. I'd hurt her feelings.

"Look. Who am I to talk? I went to Paris and I couldn't make it, so I came home. So who am I to lecture you?"

"You have your whole life ahead of you."

"Actually, I don't. Actually, I'm getting on in years."

"You're still a young man."

"Not really, Ma. I'm almost thirty! Thirty in two more years."

"Life is an awful thing," she said. "It has so many terrible surprises. I wish there was a way to keep them from happening to you, but there isn't."

"Turn around. Let me rub your neck a little. Maybe it will help your headache. Then I have to be going."

She bent her head and I pressed my fingers into her back. You could have played the guitar on her shoulder blades.

"Not so hard!"

How long it had been, I wondered, since somebody had touched her? Really touched her?

"You ought to try and get out more."

"I'll try."

I breathed the smoggy, heavy air on Virgil like freedom itself. The inside of the van seemed the perfect shelter, everything my mother's place wasn't: clean, impersonal, and new, new, new.

I drove around a while, then found a Kinko's on Sunset. I bought some paper, drew a hammer, a screwdriver, a lightbulb, and lettered:

WHATEVER'S WRONG

I CAN FIX IT

CALL BOB!

I wrote my new phone number over and over at the bottom of the page, then ran off a hundred copies, used the paper cutter to turn the numbers into a fringe, bought a box of thumbtacks, and spent the next two hours inching the van along Sunset, Santa Monica, Vermont, and Wilshire as far down as Hancock Park, putting up my posters on phone poles and car washes and Laundromats.

The heat had broken by the time I'd finished and most of the rush hour had cleared out of the city. I drove back to Micheltorena feeling pretty good. A car and a job. Not bad for one day.

The front door was open and I walked down the long hall to the sound of friendly talk. Through the picture window the sunset across LA looked red and wild. At the far end of the city that strip of the Pacific gleamed like a neon sign.

"Bob? That you?"

"Honey, I'm home," I said.

"Come on and meet Kate. And Austen's even come out for a few minutes."

I walked up three steps to the dining room and there was Dave, eyes still bloodshot, big smile on his face. Austen sat at the table, his mournful head drooping. A smiling girl, overweight but sexy, with nice breasts and sleepy eyes, leaned against a wall.

"I've been trying to get them to tell me what they want for dinner. Not that I'd *make* it! I'm curious, is all. Maybe you can tell me. What do you want for dinner?"

"Come on in," Dave said. "Don't mind Kate. Be part of the family circle. Want part of a joint?"

I checked out the room. "Don't mind if I do," I said. "Man! What a day. Bought a van. Went to see my mom. I'm going to be a handyman this summer. They gave me a cell phone with the van. Customer incentive. I'm drowning in the mainstream."

"Honey," Dave said, "bring Bob a beer. He's had a day."

The crazy thing was, Kate did it. "Just this once," she said. "Don't get any ideas."

The handyman job got off to a shaky start. Predictably, some flaky young woman needed me to go to a Hollywood motel, pick up a package, and hand it to her later at the corner of Sunset and Vine. *Sure.* And spend the rest of my fast-fleeting youth in the slammer. Respectable jobs were even worse. Nobody had anything to work with. I spent what was left of my money making shopping runs on Home Depot, picking up a hammer and nails, a couple of screwdrivers, a miter box because my dad always swore by his, and some cans of motor oil in case someone was going to need their oil changed. Trying to be prepared.

My first real job was building a treehouse for a small boy in a deformed tree behind a crummy little house over on Berendo. I thought I did a pretty good job—extending a sturdy four-by-six platform out along the strongest branch, but the kid had expected a regular cottage and threw a screaming fit when he saw what he

got. His mom tried not to pay; I insisted on my ten-dollar-an-hour
price, and got it. Then I realized in the van driving home that I'd
forgotten to charge for the lumber.

One night that first week, I got a call from an out-of-breath
woman. "How tall are you?" she asked. "You can't be too tall.
What's your inseam?"

I couldn't remember the last time someone had asked me that.
Probably never.

"I need you *now*. It's an emergency. Be sure to shower before
you come."

"No drug stuff," I said. "I can't stand the stress." But she'd
hung up.

I drove to a beautiful art-deco apartment on Wilshire, close to
the Ambassador Hotel. A frazzled-looking concierge expected me.
"Better make it snappy. Apartment 621."

I heard the argument before I knocked on the door. A drop-dead
gorgeous babe in a lamé gown with spaghetti straps looked me over
and said, "Fine! Go on in and get dressed. We're late."

"Go ahead and try it, cunt!" Some guy was yelling from the
other room. "You haven't got the guts! You'll be the laughingstock!"

"I don't think so. I don't *think* so!" She pushed me into a bedroom where a tuxedo was laid out across the double bed, waiting.

"It's not going to fit . . ."

"It *will* fit. *Because I say so!*"

It did. I looked pretty good, I had to admit it. Even the pumps
fit. Patent leather, and they had bows.

She grabbed my arm and marched me to the den. A beaten-
down guy peered into his computer, then looked at me with a lot of
hate.

"This night's important for me," the babe said. "So Steven
picked tonight to lose his brief in the computer. I wonder if he'll
manage to find it once we're gone."

"Cunt!"

"Say, listen," I said. I didn't think it was right to speak that way to women. But she ignored both of us. "Bye, now!" she said sweetly, and started out ahead of me, wagging her lamé butt.

As we rode down the elevator I had to tell her, "I only have a van. It's new, though."

I danced the night away with a bunch of Women in Film and their escorts, took a crisp hundred for my pains, and stayed around to watch her pick up an award. I was glad I'd brought my regular clothes along with me in a paper sack. I didn't want to go up to that place again.

I loved the painting and building, but wiring confused me totally. I usually pretended I knew what I was doing, but if it could be moved, I took whatever it was out to an electrician. Generally speaking, I got paid in cash, I met new people, I didn't have to think much. But there was a certain amount of sadness to a lot of this work. Somebody else should have been doing these jobs. I noticed it my fourth day, when some hysterical mother called from King's Road above Sunset to say her daughter had locked herself in the bathroom. Could I come quick, *now*, and take the door off the hinges?

I went right over, thinking a tot might be drowning in the tub, but when I got the door off there was a girl in her teens, her face pushed into a corner by the shower curtain, crying her eyes out. She ignored me completely and asked her mom, "Where is he? Why didn't he come home?"

Her mother said, "He just stepped out of the office. The way he always does. What did you think? Did you think he'd come home for this?"

Ten dollars an hour. In cash. They generally fed me. But I didn't really luck out until the beginning of my second week, when I went to work for a regular family where there seemed to be a lot to do. The Landrys lived down in the flats of Hancock Park on a very well-kept street. The houses were almost-mansions, but not quite. The place had been built in the twenties and needed some pretty serious work. Mr. Landry was a big-time sports agent and hardly ever home. Mrs. Landry seemed nice but disorganized. A lot of the time she was chasing after her son, Tod, who looked to be about three. And there was a great-looking stepdaughter, Millicent, left over from Mr. Landry's previous marriage.

I took a couple of days to tighten up a loose Landry banister, and hang a picture of some Canadian hockey team in Landry's office, and fix all the leaky faucets, and begin a painting job in Millicent's bedroom. Then Mrs. Landry got a bright idea. She hated the white cement around their backyard swimming pool, she said it looked like a bad hotel. This was Landry's house from that same previous marriage and he wouldn't spring for Mexican tile, he said it looked faggoty. Mrs. Landry got the idea, why not paint the cement around the pool—and there was a lot of it—cerulean blue? Not that she had a clue what cerulean blue really was. But then she could buy discount terra-cotta pots over by Olympic and Twentieth, and have Ono fill them with red and pink geraniums, and then maybe I could paint the lawn furniture and the place would start looking pretty good. You could see she had time on her hands.

Two, maybe three weeks' work. Maybe a whole summer. Because in spite of Ono coming over once a week to water and trim, and a chunky little Mexican woman named Conchita who stopped by four hours every morning to clean up, the place was too big, you could see that the whole enterprise was out of hand. The kids were a handful, and the lady of the house was way too far behind.

So I said sure, I'd do the cement. I bought samples of paint from Home Depot, and something made me buy sealant, not just to keep the paint from chipping or flaking, but to see if I could create a great surface. I was thinking I'd do several coats and seal them all. Sure, this surface would never back a fresco, because you had to mix lime and cement with the paint to create a fresco surface and it took fucking forever to do it, and it couldn't ever even be a mural, because murals went on walls, and this was just a huge floor of cement that went for miles around the swimming pool and out to the ivy-covered back fence—way too much cement, because some owner, probably Landry himself, had been too cheap to put in lawn back when he should have, or the tile that would have made the yard look great. All I had to do was paint the cement, but I'd make it a background for whatever might come up. I thought I even might paint on it later. I drove out to Fontana one day and bought marble dust to put in the paint mix. I thought I might make it the greatest blue in the world. What the fuck—I didn't have anything better to do. And I'd have a brush in my hand again.

I thought you could have some dignity painting a white surface blue. Giotto did it; Botticelli did it, plenty of other guys had done it. Even the ceiling at the Sistine Chapel must have had guys like me, not doing the big biblical stuff but painting in the blue, the cosmos. The . . . stuff. Mrs. Landry said she wanted the blue to match the sky in summer. Yesterday she'd said that, then early today she'd looked down into the deep end of the pool, like she was looking for something else, the answer.

"Could you more or less make it match the water in the pool? Enhance it? Make it, I don't know, *more* like the water than the water?"

I liked her a lot, I didn't mind her talking that way. I peered into the pool with her, standing by her but looking sidelong at her fore-arms as she stood, slanting a little forward, in one of the long brown-and-gold dresses that she seemed to like wearing around the house in the mornings. I looked at her unpolished fingernails with garden dirt under them—in the week I'd been working here, she'd told me about forcing narcissus in the basement and growing flats of jalapeño peppers because the ones in the store weren't hot any-more. I think I already said she had time on her hands. She'd pulled weeds. She'd snipped little pink roses off a monster hedge of them as soon as they looked like they might even think of turn-ing brown.

I had a few samples I was playing around with. I took a brush, four inches wide, stiff bristles, cheap—I was just playing around at this point—and dipped it into the first can, laid a thin margin along the line where some of that white cement met green, stubby grass.

Too pale. Too much like today. June in California. Fog burning off. Not enough color. Going to be hot later, though. I could see taking off my shirt, lying back on white cement, just going *yah!* Scaring Mrs. Landry to death.

Eleven in the morning. Well, I'd been busy. Touched up a place in the bathroom where Tod had thrown his boat at the wall. Weirdo kid. Rousted Angela Landry's stepdaughter, Millicent, out of her fluffy little dream room—which was about as big as a basket-ball court—white carpet, white bed, white pillows, white this, white that, so that I could give the inside of her dressing-room al-cove a second coat of pale lemon yellow. It had been her idea, Mil-licent's, and I did it in just over an hour, while Millie and Mrs. Landry stayed outside, telling the gardener where to plant flats of perennials.

Millicent wore white satin nightgowns I already knew about, because just this morning I'd seen her yawn and stretch and grin at me and run her fingers through her fine blonde hair as she swung her tan legs so far over the bed that I almost—but not quite—caught a glimpse of *it,* which would have been a treat, but I didn't. "All *right!*" she'd said to her stepmom, on the edge of being really bratty, but not wanting to give up the other glamour thing she was pulling on me. "All right, I'm *coming*! Couldn't you have gotten me up a little earlier?" And then she twitched her slick little boobs right past me, as Mrs. Landry peered into the dressing-room al-cove, probably trying to find the answer to a whole other question.

I moved along, crawling backward on all fours, working on the margin between grass and cement. I laid down another blue, and knew right away it was too bright. But unless you tried out the wrong ones, you might not get to the right ones. A white satin nightgown. It made me grin. White silk blouses, white slacks, loose and soft. A stage Millicent was going through. I felt really old, like I'd been through all my own stages.

Too bright. Too raw. Well, I had time to play with this stuff.

I hardly ever saw Mr. Landry. Always on the phone. Television deals. Endorsements.

After barely a week, I knew I didn't like him. I didn't like to look at him. I tried to stay out of his way. Tried not to overlap. I felt very thin and brown when Landry was around.

Sometimes I felt as old as the hills. Man! I felt *older* than the hills. Twelve years older than Millicent, almost twice her age. And what did I have to show for it? What had I ever done? What was I going to do? And on and on. I stood up to get the kinks out of my back, and stretched. A couple more blues to try. I'd lay them out by the other side of the pool. Then I'd knock it off, quit for the day. Head down to the beach. Tomorrow I'd come back and work a full eight hours. In September I'd be back in school. I didn't give a shit because a hundred years from now, who'd *give* a shit?

I put down one four-inch-wide line of deep charcoalish blue that by some magic seemed to have some gold in it. Even though it had to dry and Mrs. Landry had to say yes to it, this might be it. I might not have to do any mixing. It looked to me like a great blue, a perfect blue that might catch some elements of water and air and sky, so that when people came out into this garden they'd see those fat nasturtium borders and white daisies, and new pots of geraniums, everything easy and open. Their eyes would follow the flowers to the deep blue of this—just cement!—and then to the reflecting sky and then down, perfectly, to this small deep pool.

You can see I was spacing.

I stood up and walked over to the edge of the pool. I took a couple of deep breaths and looked the way Mrs. Landry did, into the deep end, kind of absentminded, for the answer.

And I saw Tod curled up at the bottom, with his thumb in his mouth, taking a nap.

I dove in. It couldn't be true, anyway. It had to be a mistake. Tod looked dark, shadowy, a real dark blue. Or it could be a shadow I'd seen, or a joke, or a dog. I came up for breath. Water clogged my lashes, so I could only see light. I went down again. If I weighed more I could have gotten further down. I kicked my legs into the dark, brushed against cloth, came up, and gave it my best shot, dove down again. Maybe it was just cloth, just trash, or somebody had thrown something in. But I grabbed hold of the kid. I held him like a grocery bag, stood at the bottom of the pool, bent my knees, and jumped. We went right up, through the surface of the water into wet sunlight. I couldn't see a thing.

I got to the edge, pushed Tod over onto the cement. I sank back down, I couldn't help it, and took a big breath of water. I'm not much of a swimmer. Then I got out.

"Hey," I said. "Hey!" I called. *"Hey!"*

I couldn't remember any of their names.

I turned the kid over on his stomach, then over on his side. Then I stood up and grabbed him by his heels and shook him good. I pounded on the kid's side like he was a television that wouldn't work unless you gave it a couple of smacks.

Each thing I did brought a little more water out of the kid, until I laid him back down again. He looked dead.

"Somebody help me out here," I said, but my own voice sounded clogged, it was like talking underwater. I watched water draining off the kid onto the cement, staining it black.

"Come on," I said. "Come on."

Another part of my brain clicked in. I remembered going on a date with Tori, some girl from high school, who'd taken CPR. She said first you had to call their name: "Annie, Annie, Annie, Annie!"

I said that, because I couldn't remember the kid's name. I yanked his head back and pushed down his tongue and held his nose and blew into his mouth, but I tried to be careful, because I'd always wondered, watching people do that, couldn't you blow out their lungs? Couldn't you explode them?

I blew again. One, two, three, four, five. I pressed down on Tod's chest. "Tod," I said, and my whole body shuddered. "Tod, Tod, Tod, Tod!" I blew in again. It crossed my mind that it was like kissing a sea urchin, small, cold, soft, wet, wiggly. *"Hey!"* I yelled, "Come out here, somebody! *Millie! Angela!*" But in big houses, it was hard. You never could find anybody. You never knew if they were there or not. A person could die.

"Tod, Tod, *Tod!*" You could say I kissed him again. A junior high school kiss. Pressed his chest. Kissed him again. Dug my fingers into his hair. Pressed his chest. Breathed into him. The kid gave a lurch, and I got a mouthful of crud. I turned the kid on his side, pounded him, spit the crud out into the pool. Green and yellow vomit that floated for a while, then sank to the bottom.

"Come on, *goddamn you!*" I wiped my mouth against the back of my hand, put my mouth over the kid's mouth, remembered to plug that nose, blew harder now. I was pissed. Don't pull this with me, you little shit! I saw the kid's chest move on its own, or thought I saw it.

"Millicent! Mrs. Landry!"

They hung over you all the time when you were trying to work, but when you needed them for anything, they were out getting their nails done, or their hair washed, or trying on track shoes when they didn't even run! Useless, damn useless women. I blew into Tod some more, and pressed on his chest.

It seemed like hours to me. It seemed like the sun had already dried the back of my T-shirt, when finally I heard a high shrill scream like something you might hear at night, a coyote in the hills, and then another, younger scream, like a tea kettle. I knew they were calling 911, and Tod's mom was standing over me. I heard her crying, but I didn't feel like I could look up. I was concentrating now, concentrating like when I used to be painting, really painting, working on a picture that I thought might be good.

So I heard her crying and I could see her somehow off to my side, see her legs through the thin cotton of that brown caftan, and hear the other one screaming away in the front yard, and I heard a big car roaring up the driveway. That would be Landry, I thought, but keep away from this one, Bozo—this one's mine. He did, Landry kept away. He stood there and watched, while Tod's chest every once in a while rose by itself, and an arm or a leg jerked, and his mouth got warmer and warmer and I breathed into him. It was junior high all over again. I thought, it's almost like making out in a movie. I'm getting him warmer now. But no one made out in movies anymore. I'm so old, I thought. Older than goddamn God.

This made tears come out of my eyes. I thought, if I screw this up it will make my life worse than it is now, and I can never come back here. And I can never go anywhere. I kept blowing into the kid, one, two, three, four, five, until I heard the girl, Millicent, out in the front yard screaming like a banshee, and sirens answering back at her. Then the real guys came and pulled me off. I stood up, dizzy and crazy, and looked all around, at the thick hedge that lined one side of the pool and the ivy-covered fence at the back and Landry's plum-colored Cadillac and the big white Spanish house with the red tile roof and the blue sky where the haze had finally burned off and the white wooden Adirondack chairs that didn't seem too far away. I put one foot in front of the other and made for a chair and got there. I sat down, put my head on the warm glass of a patio tabletop.

I knew I cried, but it didn't matter, because there was nobody paying attention. I cried because I knew the kid was alive, but not that alive. He'd been down in that pool way too long. What was it with people, how could they let it happen? I couldn't seem to get over the fact of all the parents who let their kids sink and drown. And right about then I heard Landry in the distance asking, "Who's responsible for this?"

You, butt-fuck! You! I thought, but it made me feel a little better. It meant the kid had to be really alive, up and around, bright as a penny, better in no time, or the dad wouldn't take that tone. I heard the two women saying in some kind of duet, "I thought, *you!*" I even thought, Christ, maybe I was the one who was supposed to take care of him. Then the ambulance got loaded up with the bunch of them, but before that Landry crunched my shoulder with his big jock hand and said, "*Thanks,* son." Millicent knelt down in front of me with her face all tear-stained and said, "You saved my brother's life! I'll never forget you, never!" And beat as I was, I couldn't help noticing those chirpy breasts under her white silk shirt.

Then I felt like I was caught in a vise. A big armful of brown hair covered my nose and mouth and a head pushed on my neck. There was a breast across my chest and another along my back. I thought she might break my ribs.

"Please, *please!*" I said, but Mrs. Landry held on for a minute more. Then she ran off and got into the ambulance, which drove away. I was alone in the yard again. The house stood there as if nothing had happened. The three blues on the cement lay there. I thought again the third one might be the right one.

I walked across the lawn into the kitchen—small, for a house like this—cracked open the refrigerator, and pulled out a beer. I drank about half of it. I noticed my wet shoes were making tracks on the floor so, still a little woozy, I bent over and took them off, put them on the back steps to dry in the sun. I finished my beer, set the bottle on the sink, found another one. It was quiet.

I had to take a piss, and it surprised me. How could anything ordinary ever happen again? How could everything just go *on?* I walked through their formal dining room, past their living room, and found the powder room. She'd said she'd had it redone recently. She couldn't seem to decide what she wanted things to look like. And the house really belonged to Landry.

This room had bad light, the kind that drained you of color in the daylight. I looked in the mirror and my face was like a dead leaf, thin and brown and spindly. My brown hair was close-clipped and looked like Brillo. I didn't look like any de Kooning, Laddie John Dill, Tony Berlant. I wasn't any Ed Ruscha. Kicking back a century, I wasn't any Manet, Monet, Courbet. I wasn't fucking anybody. I looked like my mom, my dad.

And this was what a jerk I was: I was watching myself in the mirror, and it wasn't even my mirror, while a little kid was off maybe dying someplace.

I walked upstairs, found Millicent's room again, went to her bureau and opened the top drawer. Cosmetics, jewelry, tampons, Kleenex. I opened the next, deeper one. Aah! White satin! I slid my arms in.

"Something you looking for?"

Conchita. Concerned and still a little teary. I'd forgotten she'd still be here. But it struck me funny. I couldn't get embarrassed about it.

"Just browsing."

I grinned at her and she grinned back.

But after that there was nothing to do but go. I couldn't stay. I couldn't paint around the pool, for Christ sake. So I had to go. Was this all there was to it? What was it now, two in the afternoon?

I didn't even put my paint and brushes back in the van; it would have seemed like thinking about the wrong things. And I didn't feel like biking or running or going to the beach anymore.

Two of my roommates were home. Kate, and Austen, back from a student strike.

The thing was: in five years, three years, two years, even, Kate would be helping to manage a good restaurant, pulling money in. Maybe she'd become one of those fancy female chefs. She was going to marry her boss at Cha Cha Cha. They'd have kids. It would happen. And Austen would never finish whatever degree he was after, but all those student organizers he hung out with would finally get it that all he wanted to do was protest, and they'd put him in a position where he could really *protest*. And pretty soon he'd be giving speeches and getting on cable television, because there would always be something to protest about. And finally he'd run for mayor. But he'd have to get . . . some good shirts. He'd have to lose some weight.

But me? What was I going to do? Where would I be in five years, three years, two years? I was twenty-eight. Twenty-eight!

I leaned in Kate's door and she put a finger over her lips. "Austen's feeling pretty bummed," she whispered, "He didn't get arrested."

Through the door to his room, I could see Austen lying face down, his legs all over the place, spread out on his unmade bed.

"Tough. Tough luck."

Kate nodded. She was propped up in bed watching the cooking channel on her own TV, the volume turned down low. She wore a bra and some bikini panties under a short kimono. She had a pretty good stomach going there. It was summer, she worked the night shift, so she generally didn't get dressed until late in the afternoon. She lived in the corner room because she paid the most rent. The place was usually littered with spilled powder and opened cologne and thrown-around underwear, but I liked it. I liked her. You couldn't get too lonely with Kate around.

"A kid nearly drowned at work today. In the swimming pool. I saved him. I guess I saved him."

"You're kidding."

"No, I did. I really did."

"That's amazing, Bob. That's great."

"I guess he was down there a long time. I wish I'd seen him sooner."

"You really did it? You got him out?"

"Yeah. I did."

"Did 911 come?"

"Yeah. But he was better by then."

"They say kids can stay under a long time. If it's cold enough."

"Yeah."

I ducked down the hall and closed Austen's door.

"So, Kate? Want to do it?"

"*No!*"

"Why not?"

"Are you crazy?"

"Come on! Special occasion. You can be my hero medal. Don't I get something out of this?"

She gave a last look at the television, where some guy was getting busy with a whisk, and crunched herself up off the bed.

"Your room," she said, "but keep it quiet."

I had the only neat room in the house. The few finished pictures that I still cared about and a dozen new, stretched canvases stored along one wall in wooden racks. There was a painting in progress up on an easel, a bureau as neat as a sergeant's, a twin bed with a white cotton spread, made up and clean.

She fell back on it and looked at me. "Well, come on over then!"

It was like paddling around in a lake, it seemed there was too much of her. Her breasts went all over the place. It wasn't going to be easy. Or, maybe I was wrong. Maybe it would go OK. She grabbed on to my dick and didn't let go, so maybe it would be fine.

She kept sticking her chin up at my face. I realized she'd seen too many movies, she was arching her neck because she wanted to be kissed. (Or felt that was the way it ought to be going.) I was supposed to go all powerful on her, *surmount* her, go over that chin ridge of bone.

But there was so much of her. I really just wanted to put my head down between those big breasts and take a snooze. Her mouth seemed enormous, like the ocean. I tried for the pleasure. Because the bottom half of my body was going along OK, doing what it was supposed to do, so I wouldn't disgrace myself. I opened my eyes to get my bearings, to catch my breath.

Kate's face was broad and sweet. She had pale skin with blue shadows under her eyes. She worked too hard, she didn't get enough sleep. Her hair spread out along the pillow was that curious gray-black-brown. People never say girls have gray hair but they do—that deep charcoal gray. She opened her eyes, smiled at me, and ran one of her hands through my hair. She was so comradely, so friendly, that I almost started bawling. But her other hand slipped my dick in, and I closed my eyes.

Pretend you're drowning. Pretend you're leaving. Pretend you don't live on this earth! And then I did clamp my mouth on hers, trying to get the life back that I'd given out this morning, trying to add onto my life instead of subtracting. Every mouth is every mouth. Suppose this was the way you breathed?

I clicked into another way of thinking, let myself consider Millicent's chirpy little breasts and crackly little bush showing through white satin, Millicent's deep dresser drawer full of white satin stuff, instead of Kate's sturdy white cotton. Millicent's tear-stained face, her fervent *thank you*. I'd heard of contortionists who could go down on their own selves, think how tired your back would get! I felt myself falling where I wanted to go, to the bottom of the pool, getting out, going away, not myself anymore. I remembered getting crunched out of shape, hair in my eyes and mouth, one breast on my back and one on my chest and my vertebrae pushed all out of line by someone so—

"Yah," I said. "Thanks. How was it for you?"

She heaved herself up on one elbow, gently sliding me off her. "Well," she said kindly, "have you ever had a TV dinner?"

"Oh, please," I mumbled. But I didn't feel too bad about it.

"What's the story again? You really saved that little boy? How'd you know what to do? Did you take that course?"

"I don't know if I saved him. They drove off. But I did everything I could think of."

I told her everything, starting from the cans of blue paint.

"You weren't supposed to be watching him, were you?"

"*No!* I thought about that, but no. I don't know who was. I thought I was going to be sick once or twice. I thought he was dead." And I told her parts of it again.

"You were brave," she said. "Not many people could really do that. They'd hop over to the phone and call 911. You were brave."

"Well, it was a *kid*!" But taking everything into consideration I began to feel a little better. Because I'd been feeling like shit.

"Someone should have been watching."

"There's a lot of things in this world that ought to happen," I said, "that don't."

"You did a great thing. You did a swell thing." She locked her arms around me and covered my body with a friendly leg and I began to think we were going to do it again, and I'd give it more attention this time, when Austen knocked on the door and then opened it.

"Isn't there anything to eat in the house? I had some tuna made up but somebody took it."

Austen's face was squashed and fat. His sweatshirt had stains on it, you could see his bellybutton pushing out against the cloth. His sweatpants were filthy, he probably hadn't combed his hair in a week. Kate laughed, and I sat up in bed.

"*Christ*, Austen! No wonder they wouldn't arrest you. You look like a mattress. Think about it. You couldn't get arrested!"

"I just thought somebody might want lunch. You can't spend your whole life fucking around."

Later, while Kate opened more tuna and mayonnaise and rummaged around for bread, I got on the phone. I tried Kaiser and Hollywood Presbyterian and every other hospital I could think of, until I finally tracked down the Landry family and got Millicent to talk to me.

"He's breathing on his own," she told me. "He's got one of those little oxygen things on his nose. So that's good. He opened his eyes once or twice. He hears us, I know. He hears his mom. But they don't know. They don't know. He didn't talk very much anyway. You know, he's only just three. But he's not saying anything now."

The next morning I got up early, made my bed, microwaved some oatmeal. How could I go back there? I thought I might understand, maybe for the first time, how my dad could have left. It turned out to be a kind of antimagnetic thing. I'd rather have been any place in the world than where I was supposed to be—down on my hands and knees in the backyard of the Landry place. I put on some paint clothes, walked in my socks past Kate, still curled up in her room, and past Austen's snores to the bathroom. Dave was still asleep downstairs.

"You should have been a great artist," I told the dickhead in the mirror. "That's what you should have been." I brushed my teeth and left. It wasn't even eight when I let myself in through the gate of the house down in Hancock Park and walked out past beds of impatiens and ranunculuses and a carpet of brand X grass to the pool. Too much cement here! How could people be so dumb? Then

I forgot about it and thought about the paint. Once I looked at the colors again, I knew I was right. Even in this early morning light the third blue had depth, you could look down into it.

I began stirring up a batch. I thought I'd give the rough surface lots of coats, play around with more sealant, change it here, change it there, see if I could get a feeling of sea to sky, with clear air captured in it. One of the few good things I could do was play with paint—I had a light hand with it, the way some cooks had with pastry. I could always get air into my work by painting with the grain and then against it. I did that on wood. Cement had no grain, but I could figure out ways to make the color float. As if anybody gave a rat's ass one way or the other.

Around ten, Conchita brought me some iced coffee. I liked the buzz. The June fog burned off early and I took my shirt off. The blue was perfect. I loved it. It drove everything else out of my mind. You could say I worked my mind like a blue scrim. There was stuff behind it but I couldn't see it.

So I was almost surprised when around twelve-fifteen the big Landry Cadillac eased up the driveway and stopped by the three-car garage. I rocked back on my heels and watched as Landry opened the door and Millicent got out of the back seat. On the other side, Mrs. Landry opened the door by herself, pushed the door open with her arm and hip, and got out of the Caddie holding Tod.

Thank God.

I took a couple of steps forward and then thought better of it, as she came around the car and stood with her husband and stepdaughter. She held the kid under his rump, cradled his head in her neck. His arms fell loose. Even from here, I could see his eyes were closed. Asleep, from the car.

"I'll sit out here for a while," Mrs. Landry said. "The sun will do him good, won't it, Tod?"

Millicent went inside. Landry kept standing there, looking down at his son.

"Bob." Mrs. Landry said. "Come on over. He's fine, don't you think? A little groggy, but they said we could take him home. He looks good, don't you think? A little sleepy, but they said that's to be expected. They said they did everything they could do. The paramedics said he'd be dead if it weren't for you. So we have a lot to thank you for, don't we, Tod?"

I put down my brush, walked around the pool and put out my hand. "Mr. Landry."

Landry looked at me. "Somebody should have been watching the kid. Was it you?"

"Honey . . ."

He shut up his wife with a look. "I have to know. Was it you?"

But I knew that was wrong. "No. It wasn't me. I worked outside almost the whole time yesterday. Starting by the lawn. You can see where I worked. The first time I saw him was when I looked in the pool." I almost said *I'm not the baby-sitter,* but I didn't. I did say, "Aren't you supposed to have a fence around it?"

"It was Conchita then. She should have been watching. Then maybe this wouldn't have happened." Landry looked down at his wife. "Maybe *you* should have been watching." He headed over to the kitchen.

The kid opened his eyes and saw me. He smiled and reached out his hand.

"Yo! Tod! You had us worried yesterday." I squatted down, took the kid's fist, and had to keep from dropping it. It felt like a salamander. Still wet, clear through. No muscles in the fist. Just damp life.

"Tod? Howzit going, kid?"

Tod smiled and closed his eyes.

His mom held him hard. "They say he's operating at about

eighty percent. They say he's got to have some physical therapy. But that's easy in this city. We've got a lot of it, it's all over. Everybody does physical therapy."

"Did you sleep at all, Mrs. Landry? Don't you think you'd better go inside and try to get some sleep?"

"I'll stay here a while."

And I thought she felt the same way about going inside that house as I'd felt about coming over here this morning.

"The truth is," she said, "we all should have been watching. All of us, all the time."

I heard Conchita shout, and watched as Landry, head down, trotted out to the Caddy, backed it speeding down the driveway, grinding gears, spinning wheels.

"He's . . . having trouble with all this," Mrs. Landry said.

She closed her eyes, her arms clamped around Tod. After a minute or two, I did the only thing I could do. I went back to painting the cement around the pool.

And the crazy thing was, when I looked up once, the kid had gotten loose and crawled over again to the side of the pool. He had his head stuck way over the edge, looking at his reflection, or further, to whatever he thought was down there.

I sprinted over and grabbed the kid. *"Can't you . . ."* What could I say? "Let well enough alone?" I saw that his mom was dead asleep, her lips open, sweat on her forehead. I took the kid inside to look for Conchita. But she was in the maid's room, crying and packing.

"No, not *me*," she sobbed. *"I'm* not going to be the one. That *sinvergüenza,* that hole! I don't stay here. I leave him with his shameful life. I leave him with his pig ways. *Manso,* coward, monster! Let *him* die, instead of the rest. *He* is the one!"

I went upstairs, carrying the kid, looking for Millicent, and heard her talking on the phone. Because of the fancy private school she went to, I knew she must be an old hand at emergency rooms all over LA. Rich kids tried to destroy themselves as a hobby. It was what they used for small talk later on in college. For a minute, I thought like an old fart. I thought that when I was a kid, *if* we'd had a pool, and if *I'd* fallen into it, I would have sunk right to the bottom and died. Because even if there'd been an emergency room around, no one knew where it was, and my mom didn't have a car, and we couldn't *afford* a catastrophe. So I didn't fall into pools, or cross streets without looking. Because I knew better. That's the frame of mind I was in.

"They gave him oxygen, and they gave him some tests, and they said there might be some brain damage, but they don't know. They're going to be sending somebody out to work with him. But he's so little they can't really tell anything yet. Boy! My dad had a spaz attack. But Angela's the *one*. She cried all night."

Millicent was looking at me as she talked, frowning and waggling her manicured fingernails in some kind of hello. "You know who the *real* hero was? Bob. The guy who does a lot of painting around here? Bob is the one who saved my little brother's life. He was a hero, there's no other word for it."

Tod had fallen asleep again in my arms, so I nodded at Millicent, tried out a heroic smile, and backed out of the room. I was familiar with the upstairs. Besides painting that alcove, I'd worked up here hanging pictures, spackling, painting other stuff, firming up that banister. I moved along the polished wood floors to Tod's room, and put the kid down as carefully as I could on his "youth bed," a kind of modified crib covered with stuffed animals.

All over the room were the trophies of being a big boy—posters and pennants from it seemed like every damn professional and college team in the world. That would be Landry's doing. But what would a three-year-old care about the UCLA Bruins and the USC Trojans and the Loyola Lions and the Occidental Tigers? These felt rags were just somebody's stupid hopes pinned up on the wall. Even I could see that these hopes weren't going to be happening.

God, I thought, the kid's only goddamn *three*. Doesn't he get a *train* to play with, or some goddamn Lego blocks? But except for the stuff on his bed, toys were in short supply. Or Conchita had put them away before she hit the road.

Tod slept with his mouth open, looking halfway between a corpse and an angel. Or one of those pre-Raphaelite kids that didn't have any blood in them.

"Man," I said out loud, "this is shit. No kidding." But the whole house ignored me. I could still hear Millicent blabbing on, turning the whole mess into high school chat. And Landry was probably off at his office by now, screwing sports management out of another gazillion bucks, and the lady of the house was chilling by the pool. So the whole conspiracy seemed to be: we will take this little inconvenience and we will absorb it. We won't even see it. What's *your* problem?

I looked down at Tod again, pulled the bedspread out from under him and tucked him in underneath it, so he couldn't get loose without at least a little squirming. Then I walked past Millicent's room, where she was still talking. She waved again as I turned to go downstairs. I went back to the pool and cleaned up my paints, took another look at that mom who was still sleeping, totally zonked, and got out of there. I couldn't stay around anymore. It was just too weird.

But—talk about weird! That afternoon there I was, getting ready for a social event. One of my uncles on my father's side was having a birthday, my uncle Dan. So after a run down Effie Street and out along Hyperion, and a nap and a shower, I pulled out a clean T-shirt and khakis and ironed them while I watched part of an *Oprah* rerun. I found a box of cigars I'd bought at the drugstore a couple of days before, wrapped the thing in newspaper, painted *Happy Birthday Dan* on it, and while I waited for it to dry, went outside and hosed down my van.

Fresh, shaved, washed, I took the van onto the 405 Freeway just ahead of the afternoon rush-hour traffic, heading down past the South Bay Curve through the badlands of Gardena and Carson, where they said the rats at the Carson Mall were big as cats, *bigger* than cats, big as terriers, and down through Wilmington to Seal Beach.

My dad's family spent their summers in a trailer park close to the beach. They loved the lifestyle. There wasn't just one trailer; the family had pretty much taken the place over. Five mobile homes down there had *Hampton* wood-burned on decorative plaques tacked to their outsides. A hundred years ago most of my dad's side of the family had traveled all the way west to Texas by way of Virginia and Tennessee. Then in the thirties they made the big push to California, very proud of the fact that they were one of the oldest failed families in America. My aunt Ada and uncle Jack lived in a shiny silver Airstream from the fifties, perfectly kept up. My two bachelor uncles, Bowlie and Hack, lived in a cut-rate slot off to the back in another Airstream, badly tarnished and dented. Aunt Teresa and her lunk-husband, Otto, and their three kids had moved up to a double wide with plenty of Astroturf carpet inside and a flock of flamingos in gravel outside, beyond parody, beyond anything. I also had a couple of elderly aunts down there, Tess and Vera—still very active in some church or other—and, of course, Uncle Dan and the woman he lived with, Wendy, a nice girl who'd run away from her real husband on her wedding day and worked in the Department of Motor Vehicles.

All these were my dad's family. For a while in the fifties they'd lived in no-down-payment tract homes in Torrance and Maywood, but as Uncle Danny had told me often enough—he'd be sixty-something this birthday—the Hamptons didn't take much to hard work or settling down. One by one they'd slid off and out and back into the trailer culture. They had it pretty good. They spent winters out by Glen Ivy Hot Springs in Riverside, soaking in those springs all day, strolling back down the dirt road they've got out there to their trailer park, drinking margaritas at the bar they had at that place, lying out on air mattresses outside when it wasn't raining, looking up at the stars. Real work wasn't anywhere in it. In June they picked up and headed to Seal Beach, where they'd stay until deep fall. They worked for places like the phone company, or at temp jobs, or handyman stuff. They swam in the morning and got tanked at night, even the churchgoing aunts. My mom had always hated all of it.

But I felt, no matter what, I deserved a family. The Hamptons might not have been the ones I would have picked, but they were the ones I had. And back when I'd decided to go to college, they hadn't bugged me about it. Even when I'd decided to go with being an art major in my junior year, they hadn't yelled at me that I'd never make any money because they'd never made any money, so why should I be any different? They'd tease me every once in a while about turning out to be a nance, but their teasing didn't have any sting in it.

By the time I pulled through the park's rickety gates I could see that the barbecues around the community house were already smoking. Three picnic tables were set up under trees, and there'd be more in an hour or two as beach bums and housewives and people around the park nosed in. I knew the food; I knew the program. Life out of a bad TV commercial, or maybe my dad's family was where those bad commercials had come from. I could already see those half-gallon plastic soft-drink bottles on the tables. I knew hamburgers and hot dogs would be the order of the day, and my aunts' potato salad that was about half hard-boiled egg and choked with relish, and yes, actual dishes of green Jell-O with little marshmallows, and barbecued beans, Dan's specialty, and Wendy's onion dip. Uncle Jack always spent two days making a big pot of chili, cutting up the beef by hand. He'd entered that chili in plenty of cook-offs and never even won an honorable mention, but he loved the stuff and he never changed it. By about ten at night, strangers would drift in stoned to the eyes, and they'd finish it off for him, so it always got eaten up.

I took in the whole road-ness of the scene—Pacific Coast Highway right outside the park, and just beyond that four-lane stretch, the flat pancake of beach. Beyond the sand, the flat dim ocean with gray fog coolly coming in. And right in front of me, the rundown community house with *Happy Birthday Big Dan* on a banner slipping off to one side, and the charcoal drenched in lighter fluid. If I couldn't be where I wanted to be, I could at least sniff the fog and the smoke and let that Jell-O slide around in my mouth and hang out with my dead-ass family.

My aunts and uncles talked about the basketball play-offs, and how the Lakers hadn't been the same since Magic Johnson had played the prima donna and let the championship slip through the team's fingers because of his boring AIDS. "It's because he's so into *It's my last chance,*" Dan said. "He's in, he's out, he's in, he's out. He wants everybody else to forget the AIDS thing, but *he* can't forget the AIDS thing. Like he's the damn poster child. He ought to grow up."

Aunt Tess and Aunt Vera pursed their lips. I didn't think I could stand to hear some churchly rant against homosexuals, but it turned out to be my aunt Teresa who nursed a grudge, for another whole reason. "What I want to know is, what happened to all the women—men too, maybe—that the man slept with? How many people did he infect? Did he pay them off or what?" Teresa, God, I could remember, used to be beautiful. Now her face looked like a gravel bed, splotchy and sad. I wondered what my dad looked like now, if he was still around.

I looked over at the guys at the table: Otto, Teresa's lunk-husband, stared across PCH at the ocean; Dan looked at his unopened presents in a sort of noncommittal way; but here were Uncle Bowlie and Uncle Hack, lighting kitchen matches one after another, giving me big silly grins. What was *that* about?

It didn't feel right, so I slid off the picnic bench and went to look for somebody to play a little volleyball with before dinner got started.

It wasn't until much later, after a long game, and a bunch of hot dogs and some of Jack's bad chili and a couple of joints kept half-heartedly out of sight of the aunts—not until we polished off the cake with sixty-three candles on it, and took care of the melting ice cream on paper plates; not until someone turned on the lights outside the community house and everything started gleaming in a foggy yellowish haze, and a bunch of other people had dropped by to wish Dan a happy birthday and stayed to eat and drink, and that bad chili was finally getting eaten up, and some music or other was blaring away, that I saw Bowlie and Hack looking sideways at me again, smiling flirtatiously.

I thought, I've got to stop smoking this stuff because it makes me paranoid as hell. I smiled nervously at my bachelor uncles and thought about getting up and getting out of there, but I was too stoned. Instead, I focused my eyes on the table where party wreckage made some interesting designs, the paper circles and crumpled napkins and the arms and hands of all these Hampton guys as they held, or didn't hold, their beers . . .

Uncle Bowlie passed me a note. *Want to burn up a building tonight? Fifty bucks for you?*

So it turned out that it wasn't Tess or Vera or Teresa or Wendy who had the righteous tantrum, but me, Bob, standing out by my uncles' ratty old trailer trying to make sense of it all but yelling, yelling like a fool, saying, "Why didn't you *tell* me?" and Bowlie suggesting, reasonably enough, "Well, kid, we *are* telling you. That's what we're doing."

I was pretty stoned and way out of control. "How long has this been going *on*?"

Bowlie said, "Long as I can remember. Live in a house, burn it down, collect the insurance. No problem. We had to branch out though. No more houses." He gave me a game little smile.

"There's no harm to it," Hack said. "Nobody gets hurt."

"Does everybody *know*?"

"Well," Bowlie said, "sure. Everybody's got to make a living. Don't go all prissy-ass on us."

I turned and trotted back through the park, past the party that was still going on, and got into my van and gunned the motor. I drove back up the 405 and turned right at the 10 to head back home, but I couldn't do it. Instead, I turned off on Wilshire and saw that I was going to be driving back into Hancock Park. And there I was on Sycamore, cursing myself for a fool, knowing that a strange guy in a van after the sun went down was bound to be picked up here by the cops. Then I'd be a criminal like the rest of my family.

It wasn't even midnight yet. Quite a few lights in the neighborhood were still on. I parked on the street across from the Landry house. The moonlight was bright. I looked at the bland white façade, the smooth lawn, the brick path up to the front door, the arbor that supported the wisteria Mrs. Landry liked and that I'd already tried to anchor to the second story. I stood against my van and waited, watching for movements on the second floor. The light was on in Tod's room, and in Millicent's. There went Mrs. Landry, carrying the kid. I went on waiting, maybe a half hour, maybe more. Lights along the street began to go out. People watching *Nightline* or *Charlie Rose* decided to call it a day. Tod's light went out. And a hall light, dim and further on in the house somewhere, out. Finally, Millicent's. The master bedroom faced the pool, but they had to be asleep too. I knew their bedroom, quiet and big.

My neck was getting stiff, and I was starting to shiver. But I couldn't seem to get back into the car. I'm going to, I said to myself. I'm *going* to.

Then, like a pretty picture in a frame, maybe a Fragonard, there was Millicent, her blonde hair curling all around her face and catching the moonlight, her skin showing up dark against that white satin nightgown she was wearing. She leaned her elbows against the sill and checked out the moon and the neighborhood.

Of course she spotted me.

She waved a big wave and gestured at me to come on over. I walked across the lawn, feeling stupid, and she whispered down to me, looking positively thrilled, "Come on up!"

"How?"

"The arbor!"

I knew how shaky the damn thing was, but I certainly wasn't going to be able to walk away now. I shinnied up the strongest pole and felt the whole structure creak. I thought of the Hancock Park security cops, thought of Landry, the irate householder, waving a gun. Then I pulled my body to the top of the arbor and more or less danced across it over to the window where she was waiting to pull me in. I was covered with twigs and leaves and blossoms, and I shook myself like a wet dog as I stepped inside. Not very romantic.

"I'm an orphan," I whispered. "I don't have a family anymore."

Even then I wasn't sure what was going to be up. Was she going to tell me about her troubles at school? Or dish about her stepmom? Or get sad about her little brother? Or just listen to my own sad story? Because I was getting ready to tell it.

But it didn't look like it was going to be any of that. She pointed to the door to the hallway, and twitched her fingers to show it was locked. She tiptoed over to her bed—white and puffy and covered with pillows and flounces—turned the sheet down on both sides, then jumped on in, her hands clasped around her knees. I thought of Mr. Landry, mega-agent, and my own hands got damp.

"Hey!" I whispered, "Get out of that *bed*! I'm gonna get my ass whipped by your dad!" Of course, *I* was the one who'd danced across the trellis in the goddamned middle of the night, and come in the window, and hung out like a vagrant in front of the house, just waiting for the security cops of Hancock Park to cruise by and pick me up. But I was trying to stay on the high road.

Millicent patted the sheet beside her and gave me a terrific grin. The moonlight brushed over her like an egg-yolk glaze; the light caught her teeth, she was her own light show. Amazing! Amazing that I should be here with this beautiful girl.

"Come on over!"

"This is a bad idea," I whispered, kicking off my shoes and sliding onto the fresh-smelling sheets. "This is a *terrible* idea. I've got to be getting out of here right away." But just thinking of that arbor made my heart sink. I knew I'd plunge through going back down. I could see it in my mind's eye—the cops zooming up, Landry storming out, poor Bob Hampton sitting in the middle of the lawn covered with flowers and splintered wood. They'd put me in jail. They'd shoot me full of holes.

Meanwhile, my right hand had begun to run, all by itself, along the silvery curves of her slick little body. She was muscular and twangy, of course she *would* be, she was Landry's daughter. Even her breasts had a springy give to them.

"How old are you anyway?"

"Eighteen?"

"I don't think so!"

"I'm going to be a senior next year. Then I'm going to USC." She'd wiggled over next to me, she was practically under me now.

"Don't you, don't you, have a boyfriend?" I said this into her neck, my nose cushioned by banks of her blonde hair, my lower lip brushing her fragile collarbone.

"Not really. Don't talk."

"Wait, though. Wait a minute." I reached in my back pocket, pulled out my wallet, found a condom, a couple of them. "I hope," I whispered, feeling like somebody's grandfather, "that you always remember to ask for these. It's very important."

My legs were pulling themselves out of my khakis and briefs, my arms getting rid of my T-shirt, my body sliding down against the sheets. She turned on her side and grinned at me.

"Isn't this *cool*?" she said, and I said, "Sshh."

It was like being caught in a brisk wind, like being out on a long sail in a choppy sea. I'd reach for her, she'd reach for me, I'd pin down her arm, she'd pin down mine, I'd reach for her breast, she'd turn onto her stomach. I began to think she really hadn't done this all that much. She wound up on her back, finally, and I jumped on top of her and held her shoulders in one place with my upper arms. Then it was done and I came to myself in a sweat, sick about how much noise we might have made.

It didn't seem to bother her at all. She snuggled down in her pillows, ready to jabber.

"You know, he looks like he's going to be OK. He's kind of strange, but he was always kind of strange. Like he never did get out in the sun enough? He has this transparent look? Daddy always wanted a son, that's all he could ever talk to me about, that I was fine for a daughter, but a man needed a son—write a poem, plant a tree, have a son, *you* know. That's some Spanish proverb, boy did I hear *that* when I was growing up! So now he's got this new wife, she's not so bad. To tell the truth, she's pretty nice, and she puts up with him pretty well, but now he's got this new, actual son, and from the minute he saw Tod, you could see my dad was disappointed in the whole thing. It was a son, but not the son he wanted.

You could just know, looking at Tod, he was *never* going to play catch with anyone, and now he *sure* won't, but he never would have anyway. My dad, he's a nice dad, and I love him, but he's *limited*, he's got these serious limitations, so I try to just love him the way he is, and I appreciate that he wants me living with him because my mother gives me a pain actually, she's the type who has fat taken from her butt and gets it pushed into the backs of her hands so she'll look like a teenager? But she's not a teenager, *I'm* the teenager, and she's got this underwear that she orders out of really good catalogues, because even *she* knows she's too old to try it on in stores. She *won't* grow up, she just can't, and my dad, even though he's kind of a geezer, at least he's a pretty OK man, so I'm glad I'm living here, and Angela's OK, she's quite nice, and I love Tod, he's a little sweetie, he's just the sweetest thing . . ."

I stretched out flat on my back and looked at the ceiling while she went on. I knew I ought to be thinking about noise and I did, for a minute, but then I thought, she's on the phone all the time anyway. If they hear anything they'll just think she's on the phone, because isn't she always on the phone?

I knew I ought to be thinking about getting out, but I was just so comfortable.

"Seeing Tod like that made me wonder about his soul. You know, when he was almost drowned, and you were working on him? And they say the soul goes out of its body? Where would a little soul like that go, if he's only three? Actually, he just turned three. Don't you think he'd be watching you and thinking he'd have to come back because you were working so hard? And he decided to come back because it would hurt people too much if he didn't come back?"

I felt myself drifting off. I'd have to leave soon but my whole body felt like it was melting right down into the sheets. I sniffed a little. Smelled sex and bubble bath and clean sheets and detergent.

"But what does that say about little kids in Peru who've got that nutrition disease where their hair turns red and they just die like flies? They have souls too, they must have, they've got to. But nobody worries about where *their* souls go! Do you think that's a *Christian* thing, that you've got to have an identity before you can even have a soul?"

She shook me awake. "Did you know they're sending Mormon missionaries down to South America, and they think that those original tribes they've got *rowed* across the Atlantic from Israel a long time ago?"

She shook me awake again. "Don't you think you'd better get out of here? You're going to get into trouble!"

In the morning sun she looked perfectly bright and fresh. Her nightgown didn't even have a wrinkle.

"Oh, God." I pulled on my clothes and looked out the front window. "Oh, *God*."

"Just go on down the hall. They're all still asleep. But you'd better get *on* it."

I crossed to the door, opened it up, closed it, and began walking down the hall. Of course Mrs. Landry saw me as she came out of Tod's room. She must have been in there most of the night.

"You're here early. I'm glad. I've got something else for you to fix." She beckoned me into Tod's room where the poor little kid lay tucked into his youth bed, surrounded by those stuffed animals of every size and shape.

"His lamp broke last night. It isn't the bulb, it's something else. The wiring. He loves this lamp."

The base of the lamp was Grumpy the Dwarf. I took the lamp and wrapped the wire around it.

"You probably want to fix it downstairs. So Tod can sleep."

"Sure."

I worked an hour on the damn lamp, then I said I had to go out on an errand. I took the lamp to a repairman who fixed it in five minutes. I stopped off at McDonald's for some coffee and an Egg McMuffin, then headed on back to the Landry house, where I dropped off the lamp and laid down another coat of blue along one side of the pool.

Around noon, I drove home to get some more sleep, but the messages were piling up. It seemed like everyone in LA needed something fixed.

The Walker family lived above Los Feliz, in the hills, in another of those massive, white stucco Spanish jobs. I pulled up in front and checked the address, but I recognized the place before I found the number. The lawn needed mowing. Windows along the front of the house hung open any old way. The gate to the back slumped. I sat in the van a minute or two, feeling stretched all over from my night with Millicent. Then I heard a piercing scream—from the Walker house, of course. I took a deep breath, opened my door, and got out of the van.

"I'm Bob Hampton. Handyman?" I smiled at the woman who began tearing at my T-shirt and gulping like a fish before she choked out, "In there, in *there!*" Then she gave it up and began to scream. Again.

The living room was huge and ugly, full of kelly green furniture against ivory wall-to-wall carpet. But she was waving me into the dining room, where a couple of middle-sized kids pushed at each other. A big refectory table had old food and dishes all over it and up against a wall a very big reticulated python writhed around in a glass cage.

"I *told* you," Mrs. Walker raved, and lunged at the boy, "I *told* you, Hugh, never, never . . ." She began to scream again. "Aaaaaaaah!"

Hugh caught his mother's drift, dodged her sweeping hand, and his sister took it—right on the chin.

"Samaaaantha! Get out of the waaay!"

But the little girl, chubby and about ten, with a lot of macramé on her dress, decided to stand her ground and scream back at her mother.

"What's up?" I said. "What's going on? Is there something I can do?" I noticed that while the two females were howling, Hugh had withdrawn a little, folding his arms, trying not to snicker. "Can I do something?"

"The rabbit got loose," Hugh said. "The snake needs his lunch. Uncle Sam is hungry."

"I *told* you, Hugh! I *told* you! Never, never try to *feed* him!"

Hugh smirked and Samantha looked confused. Mrs. Walker stopped to take a breath and then let loose again. Samantha and her brother listened to their mother's screaming along with some appreciation. It really was kind of an art form.

"Ma'am? Ma'am? Could you"—I had to raise my voice—"could you tell me where the rabbit is? Do you want me to try to find the rabbit?"

Mrs. Walker whacked Hugh, got him straight this time. The kid staggered and felt the side of his face where his mom had clipped him. He looked over at me with a lot of outrage, and then he began to roar.

"You *criminal!*" He yelled at his mom. "This is *child* abuse! I'm calling the cops! Right *now!*"

"Just *try* it! Eeeeeeee!"

In the middle of all the noise, Samantha looked at me and gave me a shit-eating grin. Then she pointed to the corner of the room where a mangy rabbit sat, looking pretty sick.

"It jumped out of the sack. I told Hugh he shouldn't be doing it, but he did it anyway, and the rabbit got out."

"God, it's just a poor little rabbit. A live one!"

"They have to be alive or the snake won't eat them. Snakes don't like dead things."

Mrs. Walker and her son went on screaming. Hugh, by this time, had got into a pretty loud groove.

"So what is it I'm supposed to do? Give the rabbit to the snake?"

"Yes. *She's* afraid the snake will get out. It's happened a couple of times before."

Mrs. Walker grabbed Hugh by the arm and the two slammed together up against the table. "Insolent, impudent, I'll show you! I'll *show* you!" Hugh didn't seem to be hurt, but he yelled over to me. "Look what she's doing! Be my witness! Call the cops! Call the *cops*!"

I walked over to the rabbit and picked him up behind the ears. "I'm sorry, buddy," I said, and carried him over to the cage. I slid open the top with my left hand and tried to drop the rabbit off my right, but the rabbit loved life more than I gave him credit for. He turned just enough to hold onto my forearm with his back paws. I tried to shake him off, but he wouldn't budge.

Then the snake bit me on the wrist. It hurt like hell.

"*Shit!*"

Hugh and Mrs. Walker stopped screaming and started to laugh. The snake went after the rabbit, who came running right up my arm. The snake went after it, up my arm, and across my chest.

Mrs. Walker began to scream again. "He's getting out. I *toooold* you! He's getting *ooout*!"

I grabbed the rabbit with my right hand just as it made a last-ditch attempt to escape down my left arm, and threw it into the cage. The snake had to stop and think about this. He was still wound pretty tight at the tail around my right arm. He reared back from my chest and gave me a long look. Then he decided, fuck it, it was just a hobby, went slipping back down into the cage, and gave the rabbit an evil eye. The rabbit settled down to wait for the worst. I slid the glass back and clicked the cage shut. I was dripping blood all over the place.

"Be sure he doesn't get out," Mrs. Walker said. "We want to be sure he doesn't get out. He's done it before and we had to call the Fire Department."

A half hour later, after they'd bandaged my hand and given me a couple of cold beers, I stood in the laundry room while Mrs. Walker talked.

"I got a little behind. Michael says there's no excuse, that I don't work outside the home, so it ought to be easy. But I'd like to see him try it! Blanca quit, Rosario quit, and Candelario quit. There's only me. There's only *me*!" She began tuning up to cry again. "It's those damn kids! They don't give me any help. They don't give me any respect! I can't do it. I *won't* do it! They can do anything they want to me! But they can't make me *do* it!"

The room we were standing in had about two feet of dirty clothes on the floor, wall to wall. I bent down, picked up an armload, opened up the washer, jammed the clothes in. Not exactly handyman work, but what the hell. "Detergent?" I asked. "Do you have some around?"

"I don't *know*!"

I found some on a shelf, and started the washer. "Ten dollars an hour," I said. "And I got here at two."

I went into the kitchen, which was a shambles.

"Dishwasher?"

I saw it as I was talking and began loading up. There was so much junk and crap and dirty dishes and old food on the sink and on the center counter island that I didn't have to move to load. I just reached and reached and reached, filled the machine, found the other detergent, started it up.

I began at one end of the kitchen, clearing the way, putting dead food down the garbage disposal. I ran hot water in a bowl, poured in some Clorox, found a sponge, and began wiping my way inch by inch down the long counters. Hugh and Samantha came in and watched.

"Make yourselves useful, will you, guys? Bring in the dishes from the dining room. Stay away from that snake, now!"

They looked at me like they'd been debrained. Then they turned around to get some dishes.

"Put them on one of the counters. Any counter. That's cool." I got maybe eight more inches closer to the sink, driving the mess in front of me. "So, Mrs. Walker? Things got a little out of hand here?"

She nodded her head, but she wasn't going to say anything more.

"Can you put that load of wash we just did into the dryer?"

Her eyes filled with tears. She shook her head. "No. I won't."

"No problem. Forget it. I'll do it."

I put the clothes in the dryer, and tossed another load of dirty stuff in the wash.

"What's your first name, Mrs. Walker?"

"Jamey."

"So, *Jamey*, what's the problem?" I didn't look at her, I kept my attention down on the sink. I asked her again, "What's the problem? How long has it been like this?"

"Ever since, ever since . . . I can't be the only one," she said.

"Can't be the only one *what*?"

"There isn't any . . ."

"Yeah?"

"There isn't a . . ."

I came upon a dish of what looked like Stouffer's spinach souf-flé, something my mother used to fix for herself, but it was actually a dish of mold. I put it down the disposal. I couldn't hear her over the grinding noise.

"What?"

"Reason to live."

She was maybe forty, her wild eyes were a very bright blue. Her skin looked tight and tan; she'd probably had a lift. I don't think I'd ever seen a sadder face in my life.

"Jamey. Don't feel bad." I put my arm around her and patted her shoulder. Hugh and Samantha stared at us, goggle-eyed.

"You kids. Keep those dishes coming. Jamey? Are you divorced or something?"

"Business trip. Michael's coming back tomorrow. That's why I called you. But that's . . ." She took a long, shaky breath. "That's not—it. I've got . . . there's no reason for me to . . ."

"Don't think about it now. Why don't you look in the fridge and hand me any bad food you see, OK? You kids! Go upstairs and see if there're any more dirty dishes up there. Just do it. When's Mr. Walker coming back?"

"I *said*. Tomorrow. Around noon, I think."

I worked five hours steady. I set Samantha to folding laundry, and sent Hugh—who gave me a certain amount of lip—out to mow the front lawn. At about five, I could look around the kitchen and decide that it was clean enough. My hands were Clorox-soaked and wrinkled. I felt as tired and crabby as any housewife. Mrs. Walker hadn't been good for much. She sat at a table and watched me the whole time, sniffling a little, and rubbing at her eyes.

"If Rosario and Candelario hadn't quit, this wouldn't have hap-pened," she told me at one point.

"Yeah, but if you're going to go around yelling like that . . ."

"You don't know a thing about it!"

"I do, though. I do."

By eight that night, the place looked OK. I took my money in cash.

"Tomorrow morning you want to go out and get your hair done or something, then you'll be up to speed," I told Jamey. "And kids, make your beds before you leave for school. That way it'll look good for your dad."

"Ah, who cares," Hugh said, but Samantha said, "Bob? Are you ever coming back?"

"Ask your mom," I said. Mrs. Walker looked skeptical. It seemed as if she might be homesick for the dirty clothes and old food.

They walked me to the van, but on the way, brushing by a wall of ivy, Hugh heard a scuffling noise. "Look! Mom! There's a possum in the ivy! Quick! Let's see if we can get him out!"

"Bob!" Mrs. Walker screamed, and dug her fingers into her hair, "Bob! *Looook!* There's a possum in the ivy!"

But I wouldn't look. There was no way they could make me look. I hopped in the van, made a daring U-turn, and skidded down Vermont, past Los Feliz, and back again into the land of the marginally sane.

Within the week, Dave and Austen and I were looking for another roommate. Kate finally moved in with the owner of the restaurant where she hostessed. Her corner room was left clean and empty, a lot better than the room I had. I considered making a run for it, but my own room was already filling up with house paints and art paints, and the closet worked as a storeroom; it wasn't worth the trouble.

Austen's middle room smelled like a dog had died in it. And anytime of the day or night when I walked by Austen's door, I could hear him groan, groan in the most terrible way.

"What the *hell* is he doing in there?" I asked Dave one afternoon, but Dave had his reference books around him and a chess game going with himself and a Walkman at the ready in case he needed some music, and a stack of ham sandwiches and a pitcher of lemonade and a bag of chips, and a hand of solitaire laid out. He only smiled. He got a kick out of Austen.

"He's using the summer to study for his German exam but he can't stand to give up his groundbreaking work on Australian aboriginal syntax, and he can't keep two foreign languages in his head at once. That's what he told me, anyway. Plus, he keeps organizing Hispanic students on campus and they don't respect him because he's not Hispanic. So he groans."

Dave gave me another big smile. "That's why I keep my amateur status. Take only extension classes, or ones down at City College. A life of learning without the agony. As if there were any jobs, anyway! For a linguist? A philosopher? I don't think so, laddie."

I hesitated. It wasn't for me to ask. It wasn't any of my business. But I asked him anyway.

"You make a living now, don't you?"

"Layout. Take-out layout."

"I'm sorry?"

"Those ads you see in the paper for ten million television sets at Adray's, or fifty million CD players at Circuit City? I do those ads. The regular advertising guys hate to do them. I've got a network of places that know my name. I could work forty hours a *day* if I wanted to."

"But . . ."

"But what?"

"Do you . . ."

"Do I hope to make something of myself someday, young man?"

"I guess."

"Yeah, I do."

"I guess I meant—what do you want to do later?"

Dave reached over to a pitcher and poured himself some lemonade. "If something doesn't happen by the time I'm thirty, I guess I'll have to do something. But I think I have that much time to figure things out."

"Things?"

"I want to figure . . . what's the right stuff to be doing. Which is why I majored in philosophy. But it's not the theory I care about. When I read *La Nausée,* I get distracted. Like, why does Sartre hate the bourgeoisie so much? What's wrong with Sunday lunch in a restaurant after church? When I was in Paris, I noticed he got himself a big bourgeois tombstone right next to Simone de Beauvoir, you know what I'm saying? He didn't have any qualms about that."

"When I was in Paris . . ."

"Not the place for me. But, hey, what *is* the place? Isn't that one of the things a man should figure out first? And then, who is the woman? The right one, I mean. And what's the right work? And will all that make you happy? Or should we even want to be happy? And how much do we serve the community, or should we even bother? If we can manage to be totally self-sufficient, maybe that's a service in itself. Like, I have everything I need in this room except for a place to sleep, and that's right downstairs."

"No girl, though."

"If I wait long enough, the right girl will come. Or I'll have to go out and find her. She could be right around the corner."

"No friends?"

"I sat here and thought about a friend. And you came in. And there's always Austen."

I had to laugh. "Do you talk to him like this? No wonder he groans!"

"No. I don't talk to him like this. The guy's barely holding on."

"What are you going to do about the room?"

"I had the guys over at the housing office put up a notice for a female. We need one to civilize the atmosphere. What I'm doing is conducting an exercise in human behavior here. What's the best way to live? I've already figured—you need a house with a female in it."

After what I'd already seen this summer, I had to wonder about that. LA had plenty of houses with women in them. It was the men who seemed like they'd all stepped out for a smoke. And could anybody anywhere pass Mrs. Walker off as a civilizing influence? I sat down at the table, looked around, got up, went to the kitchen, came back with a glass. "Can I have some of that lemonade?"

"Sure."

"I used to think that life without art was useless. That life without art was the way my family lived."

"Yeah?"

There was no point in telling him how bad I was feeling. "Otis wants a portfolio. A minimum of twelve pieces, including four to six drawings from life—a self-portrait and some still-life drawings. And pieces that show my 'color sensibility.' I guess I have the whole summer to think about it. But I . . ."

"You know what I've been thinking? Plato envisioned a city, but he didn't care about building it. I've thought it might be interesting—fun—to be a city planner, but any city planner you meet is a bureaucrat in a gabardine suit. All he can think of is how to build a promenade so pedestrians can buy coffee. I'd like to hit that place in the middle where you've got the material *and* the idea, and they come down together. Like finishing up your bacon and your pancakes at the same time."

"Yeah, but what if the people you're working for don't like bacon or pancakes?"

There didn't seem to be much more to say. But it was OK just sitting with Dave, looking out the window. Four-thirty in the afternoon. Watching the eucalyptus leaves in the sun. Maybe I'd work a little on a self-portrait later. The last thing on earth I felt like drawing or painting was myself.

Then the house shook. I think we both figured it was an earthquake. Some other kind of explosion? For some reason I noticed a line of bright-colored crockery on the sideboard, pottery mugs that had jumped a good quarter of an inch. Bright yellow. Deep pure green. Turquoise. And the greatest red, looking like it came straight from the clay it was made from.

We heard footsteps in the kitchen. "Hello? *Hello!*"

"Out here," Dave called.

"The least you could have done is answered when I said hello."

"Didn't we answer?"

"Not until I forced the issue."

She stood about five-four and weighed maybe a hundred and ten. Her brown hair was pulled back across her great big head with plastic barrettes, and her forehead was shiny with sweat. Her eyes were small and a slab of bright red lipstick waggled around on the bottom half of her face as she talked. She was wearing a brown suit that could break your heart if you thought about it, a definitive shit brown that carried a green sheen like ham that's spent a month in the sun. Brown lace-up oxfords. Where did she even find shoes like that?

"Are you looking at my breasts?"

"*No!*" I said.

"I am *not* a sexual being to you!"

Dave seemed to remember his position as rent-taker and philosopher in this house and tried to get the upper hand. He did it the wrong way, though.

"What the fuck are you talking about?"

"Don't you use profanity with me! I'll be writing to the housing office as soon as I get settled in."

She looked like a certifiable nutcase. She couldn't stand still. Her arms jerked around all over the place, her eyes rolled in her head, and her big red mouth gaped. She had good teeth though. The suit was the problem. She might have looked OK without the suit.

"Just go on doing what you're doing! You're *asking* for it!"

"The housing office sent you?" I was trying to keep up the conversation.

"What do *you* think, moron!"

"But . . ."

"Is someone going to help me with my cartons? Show me my quarters?"

Dave tried to assert himself again. I could have told him it was a losing proposition. "Don't you want to take a look at the room first?"

"A *room*? *One room*?" She started waving a three-by-five card. "I was told this was a three-bedroom home with another room in the basement and a double garage and a view of Catalina if the weather is good, a kitchen, dining room, and sunken living area. I demand full access to every room in the house, and fair rotation on the parking spaces!"

"I don't think you want to stay here." Poor Dave, again.

"If you *try* to tell me that this room is already taken—"

"OK. *OK!* I'll show it to you. Bob, you want to come with us?"

"My parents know where I am, you know. So does the housing office. Don't think the two of you can try anything."

But Dave was already up and out, cutting through the living room and up into the hall to Kate's old corner room. I followed along after both of them.

"This is it."

It really was a great room, with sunlight and eucalyptus and scotch broom and morning glory just outside the windows. A double bed, bureau, good mirror. Kate had left it looking good.

"There's a bullet hole in the wall!"

I wished I could draw with the speed of light, and capture the look on Dave's face.

"Right here!" She scraped at the stucco with a stubby fingernail. There was a bullet hole all right.

"I demand a different room."

"This is the best one in the house. Bob should have taken it, but he didn't want to move his paints."

She turned around to me, pushing out a bony hip in my direction, and spread her big lipstick mouth over that great set of choppers. "Oh, do you paint? How inspiring!" Her poor suit was so stiff it didn't bend along with her.

"Would you like to see my room? You're welcome to it."

We walked down the hall, the three of us. It was like escorting a short circuit.

"This is a *dungeon*," she said, and gave me a sour look. Then she said she had to see Austen's room. After a low warning knock, Dave opened it.

"Go away," Austen moaned. "Leave me alone."

After the door was closed, the girl sniffed. "That's *disgusting!*"

Dave made his way back to all his junk in the dining room. "So, do you want the room or not?"

"What about the downstairs?"

"The downstairs is mine. You can write a letter of protest to the president of the United States if you feel like it, but that's going to stay my room."

"I suppose you have a separate shelf for me in the refrigerator? And in the kitchen cupboards? I'm on a very strict diet."

We helped her move her boxes into her room. When we got finished with that, she gave us a weeny little grin and said, "I'd like to be alone for a while. Then I'll come out and visit, and we'll get acquainted."

I guess we just stared at her.

"Well? Didn't you notice I haven't even told you my name?"

"What is it?" I asked. She was like a scorpion, ugly but pretty; mean, but wonderful to watch.

"I didn't tell you for a reason."

"Yeah?"

"It *was* June Shapiro. It's June Shaw now. I didn't want to be a victim of anti-Semitism."

Dave slammed away to his part of the house, he would have punched her out if he could have, but I stayed around.

"You go to UCLA, then?"

"Of course."

"What's your major?"

"Philosophy. I'm a senior."

"Great."

"I transferred from Arizona State. I had to get away from my father. He abused me as a child. Often."

"That's tough."

The next morning, I looked around the kitchen for my loaf of bread, and put water on to boil for coffee. A dozen eggs were hard-boiling already, and about six raw onions had been chopped up and piled on the sink. My butter was missing. I saw where it was, melting in a saucepan. Three quarters of a pound of it!

"Hey!" I said.

No one answered.

"Hey! *Who took my butter?*"

A thudding sound came from somewhere.

A long time ago somebody had built a partition down the middle of the kitchen. It had a little alcove to fit a refrigerator in, but it was too small, so our refrigerator sat outside. The partition couldn't be torn down because there was an old-fashioned back porch on the other side of it, with a washtub from the Stone Age. Austen sometimes took his instant oatmeal into the little refrigerator alcove to eat, sitting on the floor with his legs crossed. He liked it in there.

The alcove shuddered. Sort of a repeat of the earthquake from yesterday. I went around to the back porch. June Shaw stood by the washtub, which she'd filled up with steamy water that reeked of ammonia. She wore a black bikini and hiking boots. She'd hooked her fingers over three or four wooden coat hangers and was pounding them as hard as she could against the sides of the tub.

Washing out coat hangers. Why not?

"Don't you want to keep it down, June? It's not even seven-thirty. People are trying to sleep."

Austen stormed out of his room, took a look at both of us, and stormed back to bed. June set her chin and went on banging.

I watched her for a minute. "If you're counting on waking up Dave, you're going to have to do more than that. He sleeps downstairs, remember, and he sleeps pretty sound. Maybe you could shoot a cannon off outside his window."

She tossed her hair and doubled up on the pounding.

"What are you trying to do, anyway? Why don't you let them soak? How does a hanger get dirty in the first place?"

"I'm watching you watch my breasts. Men love breasts that move."

She had me. I turned my back to her and went to the kitchen, where my toast was burning and what used to be my butter was bubbling like mad and turning dark brown.

"Fuck it," I said. "Oh, fuck it." I headed to my room to get dressed and go out to Denny's for breakfast. Before I left, I heard her screaming. "What happened to my *ghee*! You turned the fire up under it. How *could* you?"

I had a day's work in front of me, sanding down the walls of a new restaurant, then painting on primer. I didn't need this shit.

That night when I came home the smell of curry was all through the house, and I knew where my butter had gone. I was dead beat. I grabbed my towel and headed to the bathroom for a shower. My hair was full of plaster dust, my nails were split, and my disposition was shot. I decided not to go back the next day. They'd already paid me in cash, eighty dollars for my eight hours, but the work was worth at least a couple of hundred. It was close to seven o'clock, and I was too damn tired to even think of doing anything but crashing. I splashed water in my face and took a look at myself in the mirror, my bloodshot eyes, the plaster dust in my nose that looked like coke. Life was too short to live like this.

When I turned around to get in the shower I spotted something on the tub. It looked like a little red mouse.

I picked it up by its string and dropped it into the toilet and thought of Botticelli's *Venus* and Manet's *Olympia*. Either the great artists had it wrong or I was meeting the wrong kind of woman. Then I thought of Millicent Landry dressed in white satin and those athletic little breasts like baseballs with erasers on them and heard myself grunt. I'd take a shower and forget the whole damn thing.

Feeling clean at least, I wandered on out to find Dave, who looked unusually content. "Try some egg curry. June made it. Not bad at all. With Indian dried fish and homemade onion chutney. She says you can have some if you want."

"Where is she?"

"Some yoga class. She really is pretty good at that stuff. She was practicing down on the patio outside my room this morning. Had some Indian ragas turned up pretty loud. I was going to tell her to turn them down, but when I got to the window I saw she was topless. So I let her go ahead."

"Did she see you watching?"

"Nah. I was a regular Peeping Tom."

"Don't count on it."

My stomach growled. Against my better judgment, I went prowling in the kitchen, found some steamed rice and scary yellow curry. Spooned in some chutney. Cracked open a beer.

"Tod? Do you want some grapes? Do you want some grapes? They're right here, son. They're already washed. Do you want some? Take a bite. Do you want one? Just answer me, yes or no. Tod? Tod? Do you want some grapes?"

"I don't think he wants any."

"How do you know? Did you take some kind of class in mind reading?"

"I think . . ."

"There's no way you could know what he wants or doesn't want."

"That's not true."

"Tod? Talk to me, son. See these grapes? See? I'm eating one right now. Mmm! Good! No seeds either. Nice and cold. Don't you want one just like me? Answer me, yes or no. Answer me, Tod."

"He's not *going* to answer you, can't you see that?"

"Shut up! Shut up."

"I'm only saying . . . he won't answer you. Or he already would have."

"Do you want to fight? Is that what you want? Do you want a fight from me?"

"I was just saying . . ."

"Do you think he can hear us? He can hear us, can't he? Because he moves his eyes to look at us. He can talk too. Does he talk when I'm not home?"

"I . . ."

"What does he say, then? What does he say?"

"He's barely three! Even before, he didn't make much sense."

"You didn't listen to him! You didn't pay attention! People ask me, no, I mean it, they're always asking me, how come you always spend time at the office? Isn't that *rough,* hanging out with your clients? But at least with athletes, you're with people who understand the concept of discipline. Who have a purpose. People who know what their job is."

"You're saying I don't do my job?"

"I don't have to say it. Nobody has to *say* it."

"It was an accident."

"When I'm gone, does he talk?"

"He hardly talked before. He was slow in talking. You know that."

"Now he'll never talk."

"It's only been three weeks! We don't know what's going to happen."

"What do you want, Angela? Do you want me to pretend that what happened *didn't* happen? It happened."

"I know that. I know it."

"All I ever wanted in my life was a son. I thought I'd never have one. When Linda divorced me, I thought I'd never have a son. Then I had one."

"*We* had one. *I* was the one who *had* the son."

"I had a son for a little less than three years."

"You still have him!"

"I wanted a son, to teach him what I know. Every man should be able to have at least that out of life."

"You still *have* him. We still have him."

"Why do you lie? I never pegged you for a liar. Live and learn. Angela? I'm talking to you!"

"You're talking to hear yourself!"

"I come home for lunch, and I ask my son a simple question, and . . ."

"Please!"

"A simple question! And he looks at me. He looks at me, Angela! And I don't know what to think. All I know is I get a call at the office one morning, and I drive home, and there's some guy working on my own son. I want to know where you *were*, Angela . . ."

"Please."

"You had to be some place. Talking on the phone? Taking a shower? Ordering groceries from Gelson's? Hassling Millicent? Doing your goddamn nails?"

"I don't know where I was. I've told you a hundred times. I don't remember where I was."

"I know where you weren't. That's the important thing. I know where you weren't. Don't you? Don't you? Don't you? Angela? And now you're crying again?"

"I was in the house. He got out some way, I don't know how. And he fell in the pool."

"That's right."

"I was in the house. I don't remember what I was doing."

"Angela?"

"You talk as if I wanted it to happen. Why would I want that? He's my son too, he's my child. I don't know what to do, anything more than what we've been doing. But I have to tell you one thing. One thing! If you keep doing this, you're going to lose both of us."

"*You?* You're not going anywhere, because where would you go? What would you do?"

"I'm asking you, please."

"I just want to know . . ."

"*That's enough.*"

"Angela?"

"*Please.*"

"I guess . . . I suppose I'd better be getting back to work."

"Fine. That's fine."

"Are you going to be needing anything? Should I pick up anything at the store on my way back?"

"No."

"Will you call me if you think of anything?"

"Yes."

"If Tod . . . if he says anything, will you call me?"

"Yes."

"I guess I'm going now. I'll be back around seven."

"Fine."

"I can be home earlier."

She didn't answer him. His steps clicked away on cement and she called after him softly, "What about the fence? You were the one who didn't want there to be a fence."

I waited until the Cadillac rolled out the drive, then I came out the back door from the kitchen. I was pretty sure Angela knew I'd been there. She sat at the patio table, shaded by the umbrella, holding Tod on her lap. One of his hands was tangled up in her hair. He was sweating.

"Is there something I can do?" I hated to see her look so sad.

"He doesn't know what he's saying."

"You tell me if there's anything I can do."

"I know what you can do. There's a bottle of wine in the refrigerator. And some fruit juice. Why not bring out a couple of glasses?" She leaned back and got the cricks out of her neck. Tod tightened his grip on her hair. Mary Cassatt, I thought. Too bad I can't paint like that.

When I came back with glasses and the bottles, Tod reached out to me. "Who," he said.

I took the kid. "That could mean *you*," I said.

"It could," she said, and smiled.

When Millicent came home a half hour later, she brought out another glass, and the three of us played around with Tod until some late afternoon fog chilled down the yard.

A day or two later, I was back in their laundry room wedged behind the dryer. Something about the wiring wasn't right. Man, my weak point. The washing machine was working OK, shaking this whole part of the house, smelling up the room with bleach, but the wiring behind the appliances was iffy and the dryer had quit. It was a real quiet morning, right around eleven o'clock. I'd been here since eight, working hard.

You have skin like peaches.

I focused on the pipes and wires just beside me, and I actually saw the place where the dryer had burned out. For once, it looked easy to fix. I wiggled out and sat up, brushing possible dust out of my hair, and trying not to sneeze.

"I need some duct tape."

"It's out in the garage, on the shelves to the right. Can I put this load in the dryer?"

"Yeah, but wait before you turn it on. I *think* I can get the wiring right by now." In four weeks, she'd figured out that half the time I didn't have a fucking clue what I was doing, and I didn't mind her knowing. How could I mind? Every day after I woke up and had my breakfast and took my run, I got in the car and came over here, and saved almost everybody else for the afternoon. If I ever thought about it, I dreaded that there wouldn't be any more work for me here, but every day another damn thing would be busted. A house like this was like a big machine, always breaking down.

"After that, I've got a Chinese scroll upstairs in the hall. The wind blew too hard last night and tore it about a third of the way through. And two of the drawers in Mr. Landry's bureau won't shut."

I gave the dryer my best shot, then stood by Angela as she hit the switches. It began to whirl and heat up, and I slid back behind the machine to watch for sparks or smoke. It looked like I'd actually fixed it.

"Did you say something before?"

"You've got dust in your hair."

The scroll had a pretty bad tear. We both carried it down the stairs and unrolled it on the dining-room table. I told her that I'd take it to a real restorer, but she said that they'd bought it for less than twenty dollars, so it wasn't worth it. I fished around in the "everything drawer" in the kitchen, found some wide Scotch tape, cut off four inches, taped it to the back of the scroll.

"Good as new. Maybe better."

But I hit a snag with Landry's stuck drawers. For a while I made them worse than they were, so that I couldn't pull them out at all and I couldn't push them back in. About that time, Tod woke up from his morning nap. He tiptoed up behind me, as I was stretched out along the floor, trying to look up and underneath to see how the drawer runners actually looked. The kid stuck both his hands in my hair. It seemed like that was his new thing to do. I yelled, with lots of false surprise. "Oh my *gosh*! What *is* that?"

Tod laughed like a maniac and ran from the bureau out into the middle of the bedroom to hide behind the bed.

He did it again.

And then he did it again.

"Tod, that's enough, honey. Let Bob do his work."

"I *want* to play," I said, and this time I caught the kid as he sneaked up behind me. "This beats working any day." I realized it was true. This wasn't how grown-up men were supposed to spend their time, but God, this was nice. Angela was wearing one of her long dresses and her hair was loose; she curled up on a chair in the corner of the bedroom and caught Tod every time he ran in her direction. For some reason I thought of Paris and that guy who worked in computers. He had the wrong idea. He was working too hard.

"You know," she said, "we could get out of here. We could—I don't know—we could take Tod to the zoo. It's Saturday. I'd buy your lunch. And," she added in a rush, "I'd pay you for your time, because you'd be baby-sitting."

"Sure thing," I said, and caught Tod as he threw himself down on my chest again and grabbed my hair. "I can't fix these drawers anyway."

Griffith Park was only fifteen minutes away from Hancock Park, but it seemed like a parallel universe, a different world. I had memories about that place that went as far back as when my mom and dad were still together. On Sundays, in the far past, I'd get scrubbed up and dressed in a short-sleeved shirt and baggy slacks and they'd take me out to see the bears (on the left side in the old zoo, as you climbed up the steep entrance slope) and the monkeys and elephants, and then cut out early to hit the pony rides. (I still had pictures of myself somewhere, looking nervous and a little bit geeky, holding on for dear life as my pony walked around the ring.) And then the train museum, where you could climb up and down on trains for a half hour or so, and then the merry-go-round, jammed right up against two green hills, just a great place.

But that was then. As we drove on into the park and I got ready to get lost—because didn't everybody get lost when they drove into Griffith Park?—it seemed like we'd turned off Los Feliz Boulevard straight into Mexico. The lawns, which I'd always remembered as more or less deserted, were packed with big family picnics, moms and dads and grannies and a million little kids. All the public barbecues were in use and a layer of smoke made a low roof over the whole scene.

"Let's get out of the car," Angela said. "Let's look around."

I had a moment's worry about gangs—Landry wouldn't be crazy about it if one of us came home with a gunshot wound, unless, of course, it was me—but I parked the van and we got out, and all of a sudden I felt a serious jolt of happiness. Life, outdoors, in LA. Families, kicking back. The smell of good food. Music coming in fragments from all over the huge ratty lawn. What could be better? I looked over at Angela and Tod. They both had the same smiles.

We ended up eating tacos from a vendor. Tod found a couple of little kids who were rolling a big ball back and forth in the shade under a tree. I wished I'd remembered to bring a blanket to sit on, but Angela had changed into Levi's, so we sat on the lawn and watched the kids roll the ball, catch it, laugh, look at us to make sure we were watching, laugh, send it out again, wait for it to be caught, catch it again, laugh again, look at us again, and so on. Maybe twenty feet away, on a big patchwork of blankets, some moms and aunts and grannies sat and smiled—at the kids, and at us.

Guys too. I saw two or three of the toughest-looking hombres in the world lying there, playing with their kids. And a fat guy in an undershirt lay on his back with his mouth open, snatching forty winks, with a fat little kid snuggled up under his arm, snoozing in exactly the same way. If I'd been drawing, it would have been great to do all of this, a park series, except no one would want it, or believe it.

But if I decided to use acrylic, I could do something really beautiful in an old-fashioned way, with the lawn's faded green, and the patchwork of old bedspreads, and that fat guy with his look-alike kid, and especially Tod with his big ball and his never-ending laughs.

I actually grunted out loud. Because no matter how good my draftsmanship and speed and technical skill, my taste was all in my mouth, as one of my professors had so kindly told me once. I didn't have a clue. Little kids on the grass! I'd end up painting on velvet if I didn't watch out.

But Angela heard me and misunderstood. "It's amazing, isn't it? And we luck into it like this." She sighed. "I want to thank you for coming with us. I wouldn't have had the nerve to come alone. Look at Tod. Look at him!"

Roll the ball, wait for it to be caught, catch it, laugh, look around to see who's watching, laugh like crazy, roll it out again. Sometimes it pays to be a little kid.

Because then he gets to sleep for a half hour, scooped up against his mom, while I forage across the lawn for soft drinks, and come back with three wet bottles of Peñafiel and three big straws.

The sitting ladies smiled at me as I came back.

"*Su hijo?*"

"Oh . . . *sí*," I said. "He's mine," and ducked my head nervously.

"*Qué bonito!*"

"*Gracias,*" I said.

Later on, we drove up to the zoo itself. It was too late to go through the whole thing, but Angela thought she remembered a Children's Zoo that would be OK for Tod. It was hot, July hot, but not impossible. We walked up the slow incline, each holding on to one of Tod's hands.

"I used to come here," I said, "when my mom and dad were still together."

"My parents and I used to come here too." She didn't look very happy, so I said, "So, no bears? They used to be my favorite. And didn't they used to have just two broken-down seals?"

"Yes."

The Children's Zoo loomed up on our right, and we pushed through the turnstile. A bunch of baby goats, their heads on a level with Tod's, came up looking for food. I put some quarters in a machine, came out with kibble, and crouched down by the kid. "See? Put some in your hand, Tod. They'll come right up and eat." I stood back up and watched as the animals pushed and jockeyed for position as if they'd never seen food before. Tod shrieked with happiness and held his ground.

"You can't tell me he's not better," I said, but as I turned to look at Angela I saw she might be crying.

"So!" I said. "Were you any fun before all this stuff happened?"

"*Was* I? Before I got married, you mean? The life of the party. Dances and parties, my middle name!"

"I wish I'd known someone like you. All I ever wanted to do was be an artist, and I was a real pain about it, with my boring secret life, my *artiste* life."

"I never had any ambition. I just want, like what we have today. Like . . . that time in the day when nothing's happening. As if it were three in the afternoon, on a weekday. Or four. And everything's in order. You don't have to start dinner for a couple of hours. And you're out in the backyard. Or on the porch. And the kids are fooling around. Or one of your friends comes over. Just hanging out. On a lawn. Because, in my life, even though it's so ordinary, I can't seem to get to it."

"Here's how rare it is, Mrs. Landry. I never saw any of that except at your house, and I'm twenty-eight."

"*Where's Tod?*"

He was gone. We looked around the dusty enclosure. The goats, full of food, were dozing, sitting under a pepper tree. The chickens had taken shelter in a little open coop. A few bedraggled sheep looked at us without much interest. A baby llama chewed on some hay. At the far corner, a few humans clustered together and pointed at something.

I hotfooted it over there, feeling sick.

There was a pond, full of muddy water. Two calves knelt to drink, very picturesque. In the pond, Tod stood up to his waist, laughing, batting at the calves' faces with both his hands.

"Does anybody own this kid?" an old man in a baseball hat asked the crowd. He held on to a little girl with both hands. She looked as though she'd give a million bucks to hop in the water with Tod.

"Oh. Oh, God." Angela was standing next to me by now, both hands over her mouth.

I jumped in, scooped up the kid, sloshed out.

"Was it fun, buddy? Did you think it was time to cool off?"

I tried to keep smiling at the disapproving adults and envious kids, tried to stay mellow as a keeper in a uniform came over. "Is there anything wrong here?"

"Not a thing, took a dip to cool off, is all. Come on, Angela! We don't want to be late getting home!"

Walking back down the asphalt slope to the parking area, I took it upon myself to say, "Try and be cool. We don't want to upset him, he doesn't know what he did. You're going to be wetter than *he* is, if you don't stop crying!" And to the kid, I said, "So, *Tod!* Went for another swim, did you? What *is* it with you, boy? Was it the water you went for, or the cows?"

Tod held on to me with one hand and gestured expansively at the parking lot, the park, the whole world. "Saw a cow!" he said happily. "Saw a cow."

Two in the afternoon. Maybe three. Everything OK. Couldn't be better.

It inspired me to drive over to Atwater Village, after I'd dropped them off, to an art store with great prices. I stocked up on my favorite acrylics—Prussian Blue, Payne's Gray, Dioxazine Purple, Cadmium Red Extra Deep, and Phthalocyanine Green—too dark for me, maybe, but pure and translucent. He saw a cow, did he? Cadmium Yellow. Cad Yellow. Thal Green.

The bungalow sat back from the crumpled sidewalk on Manzanita, a few blocks down from the hill, baking in the sun. It had been painted white once, but that had to have been a long time ago. Another one of these sorry places I'd grown up with. I'd walked home from school along here. If Micheltorena was on the hill, Manzanita was in its valley, a shallow, disreputable street just north of Sunset where engineers must have been so at a loss about how to level the damn land that they gave the whole thing up and ended it in a staircase; you had to climb up on foot from here to the boulevard to do your shopping. Not that any of these people cared. Immigrants, senior citizens, bummed-out guys whose only social life had to be with their parole officers. Who around here had gotten it together enough to call a handyman?

White paint, on old, old wood bleached by the sun, splintered off by weather, and the brown wood underneath bleached to silver. That combination of white and silver looked good if you didn't think of the poverty that went with it. A slanting roof with asphalt tile, a front porch that went the width of the house, those pudgy columns of beach rock and concrete that builders used to like in California at the beginning of the century—and big, stringy hydrangeas on either side of uneven steps going up. Unmowed lawn, of course.

Ask for Hank, the phone message had said. The door opened and a tired-looking guy looked out. He was still probably in his twenties, wearing a black T-shirt, with an orchid tattooed on his arm. His hair was dyed matte black, but he looked strange—he looked like a hick. A bad smell came out around him.

"Hank?"

"Bob?"

"I'm the guy you called."

"Sure. Don't you remember me? Come in."

The shades were drawn in here. The windows were closed and the smell was worse.

"You do remember me? At that restaurant a couple of weeks ago? You had the machine and you were sandblasting the walls? That *under new management* deal? And out in the side yard, where some people were filling out applications, we got to talking when you were taking a break?"

"I guess I don't . . ."

"You said it was a good thing every day wasn't like this one, and I said, oh, you're not a painter then? Then you said *this isn't painting,* and you said you were a handyman. I said what do you do mostly, because, see, I already had a reason. And you said I do anything, anywhere, any time. So I asked you for your number, just in case. I didn't get that job, by the way."

The kid was a nervous wreck. What was going on here?

"What can I do for you?"

"I've got a friend here who's sick."

I got the picture right away, but I thought I might have it wrong. Weren't people with AIDS supposed to have it together by now, with Project Angel Food coming over every day with hot meals, and people dropping by to walk your dogs? Bringing you your AIDS cocktails?

Or so I'd heard.

"We rented this place about two months ago. We're here from Ohio. Southeast Ohio. It seemed like a good time to come. It's a good place to be out of."

Hank stood chatting with me in the hot dark room as if we'd known each other for years.

"Can I open a window?" I was afraid I might gag.

"Only out here, I think. The light hurts his eyes."

I pushed open the front door and lifted up a couple of windows. I remembered the furniture in here—I actually could identify some of it—as hotel issue from when I was a kid, moving from one fur-nished apartment to another with my folks. Painted stuff, stiff and off-balance, flaking. *Man!* That smell.

"We had a lot of fun for exactly one month before Ben got sick. I got my hair dyed and my ear pierced. We went to the beach. We'd never seen the ocean. It's different out here from Ohio. We went to readings up at A Different Light. It was like heaven, you can't imagine. To meet people like your own self. You know what we've got in Althea? The Tri-State Headquarters of the Klan. The Ku *Klux* Klan. Not a good place to be. Ben grew up in Carbonear, about thirty miles away. Do you know where we met? At a *church picnic* in Carbonear. They have a lot of survivalists out there, guys who hunt with crossbows, and both of us had been thinking for quite a while we were setting up to be targets. If there's anything they hate worse than an unfortunate nigger back there, it's a . . ."

"Hank? Is there something I can help you with here?"

Hank put down his invisible cocktail glass. Started to come to the point. "I think I bit off more than I could chew. I didn't know how sick Ben was, or even that he *was* sick. That's how dumb we were in Althea. He's just a kid. I shouldn't have taken him away from home. I brought him into a clinic one day a couple of weeks ago, but we can't *begin* to afford those drugs, and he doesn't have pneumonia, so they wouldn't admit him into a hospital. They treated him like he had AIDS, you know? Which he does, of course. They say he needs home care, but I don't know anything *about* it. Neither one of us has insurance. I worked with my brother-in-law back home. We had a delivery business. I don't know anything about taking care of people.

"Where is he?"

"Back here."

In what would ordinarily be the dining room, a thin little form stretched out on a twin-bed mattress. They'd covered up one window with foil to block out the light, but there was still enough light for me to catch the shine of urine and puke on the wood floor. Hank went on talking.

"I had to call somebody. Nurses are too expensive. I didn't know what to do." And, in a lower voice, "If I didn't call someone, I was afraid I might leave. Just walk out the door. I didn't know this would happen."

The kid turned his face toward us. It looked like the face had three eyes, and when I came closer, I saw that in a way it did. The kid was wearing a caste mark. His face was wet with sweat.

"How long has he been like this?"

"A couple of weeks, like I said. Maybe a little more. The hospital won't take him unless he has pneumonia, and he doesn't. He has a gastric upset. That's what they said."

"Do you have a washing machine here in the house?"

"No. The landlady's going to have a fit when she sees what he's done to her sheets. She only gave us two sets. We don't have much money, you know. I don't know what I can pay you."

"How are you, buddy?" I leaned over the kid so he could see me.

"I've been better." His voice was thin and shaky. He looked about thirteen.

"It's true you don't like the light?"

"Hurts my eyes."

I dodged out to the kitchen, rummaged around mostly empty cupboards and drawers, found a dish towel, doused it with cold tap water. "Put this across your eyes. I'll work around you."

I checked out Hank, in his jeans, black T-shirt, bad jewelry.

"You say you don't have any money?"

"If you're worried . . ."

"You must have enough to shop. I mean, while I strip the bed and get the laundry together, you walk up to the Junction and buy some food. Just go up the stairs at the end of the street. Jell-O, ginger ale. Chicken soup. Things for when you're sick. Have you called up Angel Food?"

"What's that?"

I rubbed my forehead. I didn't really know where to begin.

Hank got defensive. "We don't have a phone. We don't know anything about this place! We came into LA on a Greyhound off Highway 70 and took another bus out here from downtown. We got off at the wrong stop, we found out later. We got off at East Hollywood when what we wanted was West Hollywood."

Ben gagged, moved his head off the bed, aiming for a pot on the floor beside him. Hit it, almost. The kid had nothing to throw up, but that didn't stop him.

"OK. Get going then. You do know where the grocery store is? Right there at the Junction? Walk two blocks, climb those stairs, turn left. It's across from the elementary school. Ginger ale and Clorox. Chicken noodle soup. I'll be working right here."

Once I was alone with the kid, I took a quick turn through the house. In the one bedroom, Hank's room, there was a bed, a few magazines on the floor, and a couple of posters on the wall, some guy on a motorcycle, another naked guy with a big dick. The high life! The kitchen was filled with empty cans and roaches and dirty dishes.

But the dining room was the big problem. And the bath. The kid had aimed for the toilet a few hundred times, but missed.

"Just lie there!" I called to him, not that he was going anywhere. "Don't move. I'll take care of everything."

I found a rag and some Comet in the bathroom, and splashed chemicals around on the basin, the toilet, the tub, the floor. I picked up dirty towels with the tips of my fingers and threw them into a pile in a corner of the dining room. But it was hopeless in here. Beyond thinking about.

I had a brainstorm. I went outside to the backyard, found a garden hose, poked it through the bathroom window, hosed down the entire cubicle, walls and all, for about ten minutes, as though I was washing a car. I'd give it time to dry and go in and scrub more later. If you broke the whole house down into six units—living room, Hank's room, bath, kitchen, Ben's room, *Ben*—one unit was slightly under control.

Five to go.

I headed around the side of the house to the kitchen, and opened all the windows. I smashed a few roaches and looked in the refrigerator. It was almost empty. So, you could say the kitchen wasn't as bad as the Walkers'! You just had to break it down into components.

I spotted a sad trickle of shit across the kitchen floor, grabbed the mop, found some 409 and some other junk. I cleaned it. I slammed some dishes through scalding water. I opened up the back door. Went outside, breathed fresh air.

I was there, outside, as Hank came in with a couple of sacks of groceries.

"I'll put those away," I told him. "You need to go back to the store. I think you need some of those—what do you call those things? Depends. And more Clorox. A couple more bottles."

Then I worked on the living room, putting off Ben until last. Nothing too bad out here. Nothing much to do. But bleak, *Jesus*! I mopped the hardwood floor and pushed the rickety tables and chairs into some kind of phoney order. But they needed a couple of extra chairs for the front porch, so the kid could get outside if he ever felt better.

"Are you having a nice time?"

"Huh?"

"Are you having a nice time?"

I went to the dining-room door and looked over at the kid. His head was thrown back, his eyes were hidden under the towel. The smell in here was, if anything, worse then ever.

"Are *you*?"

"Splendid," the kid said. "Splendid in every way. You troops have outdone yourselves."

His lips were horribly chapped and cracked. And where were his clothes?"

"Where are your clothes, uh, Ben?"

"When I get them too dirty, Hank throws them out. They really do get dirty. But I'm running out. Of my clothes. I never thought this would happen. My head feels like it's coming right off my body."

"How old are you, Ben?"

"Everyone asks me that."

"Well? How old are you?"

"How old are *you*?"

"Twenty-eight."

"I'm seventeen." The cracked lips smiled. "Just a child. A mere child. A youth."

"Stay there."

As if he were going anywhere.

I didn't know who else to call. I trotted out front, got my cell phone out of the van, and called up the Landry house. Millicent answered.

"I need some help, Millie. Some twin-bed sheets, two or three sets, and some double ones too. A pair of your dad's pajamas, two if you can get them, and about six old towels. Do you think you might have an extra rubber sheet around, left over from when Tod was a baby? As soon as you can do it. I'm over here on Manzanita north of Sunset by the Junction, about ten minutes away from you. By the staircase, do you know where that is? Can you do it right away? Tell your stepmom it's an emergency."

I waited on the porch until she drove up in that high school deb car of hers, a new Audi.

She was curious as hell. "Anything I can do?"

"No. I'll call you later. Thanks!"

I put clean towels in the bathroom and threw some more Comet around. Then I waited for Hank, who seemed to be taking a damn long time with those adult diapers. I walked around outside the bungalow, just breathing fresh air.

Hank came back with two boxes of Depends. "He's been lying there five days," he said hastily. "I have to tell you, maybe it's been more than a week."

I ignored him and walked back into the dining room. I took hold of Ben's forearm and gave him a little shake. "OK, kid, I'm going to change the sheets now. We're going to clean you up."

I pulled back the blanket and the top sheet. *Oh, God. Oh, Christ.* I stopped breathing and reached forward, grabbing Ben around the waist. "Can you stand up? Can you walk?" I marched the kid through the kitchen and called over my shoulder to Hank, "Come on! Come on out in the yard with us. Turn on the hose out back. Not too hard. Just steady."

In the backyard, I peeled off Ben's pajamas. They stuck to him in places, and when they came off, they left raw skin. I dropped them in a pile and stood bracing the naked kid. He shivered bluish-white in the hot sun, and kept his eyes closed. A tall rickety wood fence kept the neighbors from looking, as if they cared.

"Come on, Hank! Just turn the hose on both of us. Rinse us off. We'll give him a real shower later." Finally, I had to reach out and grab the hose from him. I turned it on myself first, straight down on the top of my head. The cool water felt great, and began to dent the smell.

"See what I'm doing, Ben? Take a look. Just rinsing off. It feels really good. Cover your eyes if the light hurts. Here goes." The water drifted down the kid's head in little rivers, and Ben tilted his face to it. He smiled, but his knees began to buckle. Hank rushed forward and grabbed him from the other side. I kept hold of the hose. I tried to think of it as an anatomy lesson, a memory from some long-gone UCLA art class. I pooled water in the hollows of the kid's collarbones and ran it down his chest and over his arms and lifted his arms to get under them. Brownish, reddish water pooled for a minute on the dry grass around him before it disappeared into the earth. I rinsed the kid's front; his little dick, his thin little thighs, his little kid feet. But when I took the hose around to the kid's back, I had to gag again. There was a pad of caked shit the size of a saucer in the center of his crack and up into the small of his back. And at the center of each cheek and at the point where his shoulder blades hit the sheets, there were four open sores. I kept pouring water gently, gently, over the sores, and over the pad of shit that shrank down and melted and finally disappeared.

I wanted to say something to that dyed and tattooed idiot Hank, but the guy had called someone, finally, and he hadn't run away. It would have been easy to do but he hadn't done it.

"Here's the deal," I said to both of them. "I'm getting a blanket and putting it down in the middle of the backyard. Ben's going to lie on his stomach and get some sun. I'm putting the mattress out in the sun and bringing out the old sheets. Hank, you're running the hose on them. Then I'll take them to the Laundromat."

They did what I said.

The dining room, once the sheets had been stripped, the bucket cleaned, the windows opened, the floor swabbed with Clorox, didn't smell so bad. I bundled together all the sheets and towels, put them in the van, got to the Laundromat run by two Hispanics by the Junction. I shoved the loads in, got them washed and dried, and came home to find the two guys, one dressed, one naked, quiet and peaceful out on the back porch. Hank was sitting and Ben lying on his side, his head on Hank's thigh. Ben's hair was fluttering in the breeze, and Hank, looking dead beat, caught strands of it in his fingers. A long way from Althea.

"How're you feeling?" I put my hand on Ben's shoulder.

"Better. Splendid in every way," the kid said, and smiled a dreamy smile.

"Great. 'Cause now we're taking a real shower. Getting you really clean."

It turned out to be fun, in a crazy way. The three of us got soaking wet, half in, half out of the shower, trying to keep track of a cake of soap and a bottle of shampoo. Hank was probably relieved not to be preached at. Ben, with his dreamy smile, kept sticking his head straight into the warmish spray. Maybe he was so sick he didn't know any better. Maybe deranged. Or maybe both of them were just damn glad not to be alone. Who knew?

After the shower, I said Ben had to have another sunbath. Then—what about the sores? I didn't have fucking clue one. Minute by minute seemed to be the way to take it. I poured some ginger ale for the kid to sip and found bottles of beer in the fridge for Hank and me. The three of us sat on the back porch and drank. Then we got Ben dressed in a Landry pajama top that hung on him like socks on a rooster. The kid stood and let himself be dressed with his eyes closed, looking happy.

"Do you want to go back to bed now?"

"For a while."

We took him back, made up the bed, put him down on his stomach, spread a sheet lightly over him, and then went back outside with another couple of beers.

"You've got to do some stuff," I said.

"I know. But what? We don't know anyone. I'm afraid to leave him alone."

"I'll make some calls. Get you some help. How much money do you have?"

Hank reached into his pocket.

"*No!* I mean for doctors or food. Or calling home."

"Oh. Enough, I guess. For a couple more months."

"What do you want to do? What are you *going* to do?"

"I don't know."

I went out to the van again for my phone and called AIDS Project LA and Project Angel Food—the only two places I knew about. I drove back to the store and got another six pack, a couple of hamburgers, a half gallon of milk. Then Hank and I sat down on the back porch.

I told him about my calls. "They'll send someone by tomorrow, if they can. I'm going now. I'll drop by tomorrow afternoon. Listen. Hank?"

"Yeah?"

"Those diapers. You've got to put them on him. Don't let it get like it was. But you're the one to do it. Not me. And be sure he keeps drinking some ginger ale. He's probably dehydrated. If he gets worse, call 911. *Make* them do something."

"All right. All right."

"OK, then, I'm going to see you both tomorrow, in the afternoon."

I tiptoed through the house, past the kid who was sleeping now, drawing long shivery breaths.

"Does he like to look at anything special? I could paint him something, maybe. A picture." The little room looked like a sorry jail.

"I owe you money."

"Not for today."

"I don't like to see you leave."

"You know my number. I'll be back, tomorrow, after my other work."

I drove off thinking I was OK, until my whole body seized up in a sob. I held on to the steering wheel and cried. When I got home I went straight to the shower and used up all the hot water. Then I got paranoid about possible holes in my skin and poured peroxide over my hands. I finally got a grip, more or less, and went out to the dining room where Dave sat, predictably, with a beer and a joint and an open book.

"I saw, ah . . . I saw an AIDS case today. A bad one."

Dave shook his head. Looked out the window. What was there to say?

I picked up a deck of cards, peeled out a game of solitaire.

Austen slouched into the kitchen, opened up some cereal, and looked into the room where we were. His eyes were bloodshot, his expression all spacey.

"Don't you guys ever work?"

"Lay off, Austen," Dave said. "Bob's been out all day with an AIDS guy."

But Austen couldn't come around. "Sor-eee!" he said, "How was I to know?"

I looked up from my cards. "You don't," I said, echoing the

thought pattern that had zoomed in and around my head for the last eight or ten hours, "have fucking clue one. About any of it. About anything. Not fucking clue one. OK?"

"Sor-*eee*," Austen repeated, into the silence. "Well, I'll go back to studying, then."

"Do that," I said, and put my hands over my eyes. "He had sores. Where he'd been lying there. No one to help him."

"Sorry," Austen said again, as he went back to his room. "Sorry."

"You baaastaaard! I'll kill you, Hugh! Eeeee!"

Ten in the morning, in the Los Feliz hills. Against my better judgment, I'd answered another call from the Walkers. What *was* it with these people? I eyeballed the lawn and saw it had to be mowed again, probably hadn't been cut since the last time I'd been here.

The double-garage door was open and Samantha stood there, holding her arms straight out. She looked like she'd been crucified by invisible forces, and of course she was screaming to beat the band. Hugh stood close but not too close to her, grinning sheepishly. He gave me a feeble wave.

"What now?" I asked.

Hugh shrugged. "I don't know."

"He killed my guinea pig! He *killed* her! Oh, Guinea, Guinea, *Guinea!*"

I looked down at a cage on the garage floor. The guinea pig was dead all right. It had been eating a piece of navy-blue flannel, and lay on its side with a mouth full of flannel and a puffed-up stomach. It looked smug and self-satisfied, and dead as a box of marbles.

"Who gave him the cloth?"

"He did! He did! *Heeee* did!" Samantha came at Hugh, her fists going like crazy machines. He backed off, snickering, dodging her blows.

"My God. You kids. Well, before we do anything else we better have a funeral. Where's your mother?"

The kids exchanged a glance.

"Upstairs. She said we were driving her nuts." Samantha sounded like she thought the charge was unjust.

"I can't imagine why," I said. "Is that your ambition? To drive your mother into the nuthouse, and you only have this summer to do it?"

Now they both shrugged, and looked around.

"Let's go. Somebody find a shovel. We'll go out back."

"We're too old for funerals," Samantha told me. "You bury him. We'll wait here." She seemed pretty queenly about it.

"Too old for funerals but not too old to sound like an air-raid siren?"

"*Yeah*," Hugh added, and Samantha lunged at him again.

"How's the snake?" I asked, as I poked around the garage for a shovel, and they both answered together, "Oh, fine."

"I've got an aquarium now," Hugh said. "Lots of stuff. Some very good fish."

"Mom got this *turkey*," Samantha whispered. "She's weird."

The funeral turned out to be pretty good. We put the guinea pig in a shoe box and lit some sparklers they'd bought for the Fourth of July. Mrs. Walker came out to watch, clutching her head. "I've got a terrible migraine," she moaned. "I can't take this much longer. These kids are driving me mad. I can't be expected to do all this alone."

Hugh and Samantha looked at her with concern, but neither of them seemed particularly inclined to change their ways.

"Where's Mr. Walker?"

"Playing golf in Hawaii. With clients. I didn't want to go. I *hate* those stupid businessmen in their stupid madras shorts. Besides, what would I do with Hugh and Samantha? I can't take *them* anyplace!"

"Ah, Ma," Hugh said.

"They both have ADD, did I tell you that? Both of them. Attention Deficit Disorder. Can you imagine? They can't pay attention."

I didn't know what to say to that. "What do you want me to do around here?"

"The turkey needs a pen. He makes a terrible mess. I don't know what I was thinking. I wanted a peacock, but the man told me they make too much noise."

"Did you ever think of a dog? No offense. But a dog, like other people have?"

Mrs. Walker waved over at Hugh and Samantha. "They're allergic. To *everything*. House dust, pollen, tree bark, tobacco. Especially dog hair. We can't have anything with fur."

I thought of the crud I'd seen in the Walker house, the dust to end all dust, but I didn't say anything.

"I've done everything I can," Mrs. Walker said. "No one can say I haven't done everything I *can*."

Mrs. Walker was dressed today in beige linen slacks, a silk blouse, and white sandals with high heels. She looked great. For what? I got the momentary sinking feeling it might be for me. The four of us stood out back in the summer morning by the guinea pig's grave. The backyard was run down, but not out of control the way it had been two weeks ago. I flashed on Rudyard Kipling, *The Jungle Book,* and my brain took a hike. She could be a memsahib out in India somewhere. We could have been burying a mongoose, not a guinea pig. And time would be stretching out in front of all of us with nothing to do ever except wait until midnight when, if we were lucky, one of us might get to see the elephants dance. Why not? That's probably what some family was actually doing over in India right now.

"OK," I said. "Where do you want this pen? Hugh, why don't you come with me to the lumberyard? Mrs. Walker, are you going to be getting any more . . . fowl, or will this be for just one turkey?"

We decided on a place near the back of the yard, near a wall of dying, decrepit ivy.

"I just want my children to have everything a normal American family has," Mrs. Walker said. She did look especially cool in all her silk this morning, but wacky. "Pets and books and music and lessons. But because of their ADD all of it rolls right off them."

Hugh and I worked for most of the morning on the turkey pen. When it was finished, it looked solid and good. We'd both taken off our shirts and Hugh's back showed some sunburn. He seemed like an OK kid.

"Now that it's done, we've got one other thing to do," I said. I liked the look of the pen, I felt kind of dumb that I liked it, but I did. It felt good to know I could put something like that together.

Hugh shot me a grin. "I know. Catch the turkey."

For the next hour, the four of us chased the turkey around the yard. Mrs. Walker changed out of her silk into brief shorts and a halter top. Looking pretty good.

The turkey didn't want to get caught, but it finally got tired of the screams and the chasing and allowed me to fall on it. I grabbed its feet, turned it upside down, and heaved it into the pen. Samantha and her mother decided to get affectionate.

"Oh, *look* at it! A turkey in a *pen*. Turkey. Turk*eee*!"

I rolled my eyes. You couldn't hate these people. I almost liked them. And that right there was about as stupid as putting a turkey into a pen.

I went in the kitchen for a glass of water and was standing by the sink holding the icy glass against my forehead when Hugh came tearing past with Samantha right in front of him, running hard. "You *bitch*," he screamed at his sister. "I'll kill you. I'll *do* it this time!"

Hugh caught hold of her T-shirt, yanked her around to face him, pulled back his right arm, and clipped her square on the jaw. He knocked her out cold. Mrs. Walker came in from out back, took it all in.

"What *now*?" she shrieked. "What have you *done*?"

"She turned up the heater on my fish! They're dead, all of them. She *boiled* them to death."

Mrs. Walker didn't take it too well. "No!" she wailed. "*Noooo!* I can't stand any more of this."

Samantha opened her eyes and looked at her brother. She must have figured she was safe on the floor. "*You* were the one who put the flannel in the cage. You killed him."

Hugh was going to kick her, but I pulled him back.

"Hey! Cut it out. We'll clean the aquarium and go get some more fish. Do you have one of those nets around?"

Poor old Hugh seemed fully crushed. He watched as I skimmed what seemed like a thousand poached bodies off the top of the water, and scraped tears off his cheeks. I tried to get his mind off it.

"Do you know the phone number of the place where you got all this stuff? Why don't you call them and see if there's anything we can do, or if we have to change all the water or what? Maybe we can go on over and stock up again right away. Go ahead, do it, Hugh."

The temperature of the water was already going down and the filter seemed to be working OK. I put my face close up to the glass and began going over every inch of the aquarium, trying to find any more dead bodies. Just a couple left, down at the bottom.

When Hugh came back, he looked a little better. "They say . . . it will probably be OK. And we can go over there right now."

The two of us drove to a fish store on Melrose. The quiet in the van was a relief, and Hugh seemed glad to be going out again on a guy's errand with a guy.

"So, Hugh. I don't want to butt in, but what *is* it with you guys?"

"What do you mean?"

"Jeez, Hugh! You're always trying to massacre your sister, that's what I mean. Or she's always trying to massacre you. Can't you, uh, go to camp or something? Now that it's summer?"

"Got to stay home with Mom."

"Maybe she'd like some peace for a change."

"Can't do it."

"But . . . what's the deal here? I don't know how to tell you, but most of the world doesn't carry on the way you guys do."

Hugh shrugged his shoulders. "So?"

"No, I mean it. It's not good for you. I mean, think of the fish. This morning they were happy fish. Now they're in fish heaven. Think of the guinea pig . . ."

"I hate that stupid pig!"

"So, Hugh. What grade are you in?"

"Seventh. Eighth next year."

"What school?"

"Thomas Starr King."

"I went there when I was your age."

Hugh shrugged again.

"Couldn't you go over and see some friends? Spend some time away from the women?"

"I told you. We've got to stay home with Mom."

"Who says?"

Hugh shrugged.

"What?" I asked. "What?"

"If we went away, she'd be alone."

"So? A lot of women stay in a house by themselves. Or maybe she could go out—do whatever they do. Play bridge or something. Get her hair done. Have lunch with a friend."

"She hates that stuff. Besides, she doesn't have a taco."

"I'm sorry?"

"A taco. On her combination plate. That's what Dad says."

"And that's why he's never around?"

Hugh looked worried. "He's around."

"What about this taco?"

"Like floors missing in her elevator shaft? That kind of stuff."

"Your mom seems OK to me. A little high-strung, maybe. At least she hasn't murdered any animals today."

We were on Melrose now, and I kept an eye out, looking for a parking place.

"She doesn't come from out here."

"What?"

"She doesn't *come* from out here."

"You could have people over. Your own friends."

"To my house? Yeah, right."

The fish store was air-conditioned and cool. My mind kept wandering. Like, here were these watery worlds rising up on every side of me, closed universes where fish didn't yell at each other and no fish was alone and no fish had to choose a meaningful career. Nobody bothered them, and they didn't bother anybody.

The clerk found a computerized list of all the fish in the Walker inventory and boxed up an army of specimens, all in white cartons, like a big Chinese dinner. He was in a pretty good mood. The store was making solid money off this. "Say. Want an iguana? I'll throw in an iguana for another twenty bucks. Just came in this morning. Full grown. Shouldn't really be here. Got to get him off my hands. They're easy to take care of. Put him in an aquarium with some gravel on the bottom. Feed him flies. Maybe hamburger. Nice bright green. No allergy problems."

I wondered how many kids had been taken by Westside parents to allergists for those tests, and now they could never own a puppy again. Which probably accounted for the thousands of homeless pets all over the city. Which accounted for all the Westside animal rights activists.

"Can I?"

"Can you what?"

"Have the iguana?"

"Why not? Pick up another aquarium for it. Your mom probably won't mind. It's all going on her card."

We didn't talk much on the way back. I could feel the presence of the iguana on the seat behind me. He wasn't in a good mood.

Of course, when we got back to the house and unloaded the fish, and I told Samantha to keep her hands off the aquarium thermostat from now on, and then let her open some of the cartons to let the fish fall in, she was the one who opened the one with the iguana in it.

"It got *awaay!*"

The iguana zoomed out the back door and scrambled out across the lawn—avoiding the ivy, thank God. It ran up the trunk of a large sycamore tree, where it settled down, and got into the groove of pretending to be a set of green leaves.

"OK," I said, "all right." I was getting tired of this. "Someone get me the ladder."

From then on, I decided to consider the afternoon as a study of color and almost-still life, something I'd be putting in my portfolio for Otis; the silver brown of the tree trunk, the midsummer green of the leaves—Thal Green?—the entirely different green of the iguana, who seemed to have quite the personality, now that I was getting to know him.

Even though it was July, a trick in the Los Feliz hills seemed to make the sun go down early, and the colors got a lot deeper as the direct light disappeared. It was beautiful up in the tree. It looked to me a lot like the insides of those aquariums—leaves brushing against each other, the tickle of the iguana's claws against tree bark that I could barely hear. The yelling down on the grass faded away. If they were going to keep on making that racket, they'd have to do it in their own world. I was out of it now.

"You going to make it easy for me? Or are you going to make it hard?"

The iguana ignored me. He was snippy beyond words.

I settled in.

Mrs. Walker and the kids got bored and went inside.

The afternoon darkened down.

The iguana kept an eye on me. Then it seemed like it didn't keep an eye on me. That it might be thinking of something else.

About a half an hour after that, I snapped out an arm and grabbed the thing behind his head.

"Two can play," I told him. "Two can play your game."

The iguana had a fit but I held on like death as I skinned down the ladder, trotted across the lawn, and banged on the back door with my free hand.

"Open up! Samantha! Hugh! Be ready to give him something to eat."

In the kitchen, once they got the iguana put away, they treated me like a hero. It was out of the question for me to go home, Mrs. Walker said. I had to let them take me to dinner. Why not? I didn't have anyplace else to go. I stood in the kitchen under bright lights drinking a gin-and-tonic Samantha had made for me, and listened to them discuss the pros and cons of where to eat: Chan Dara? No, it was bound to be too crowded by this time of night, and besides, Hugh was sick of Thai food. Anywhere Italian? No! Too hot for it. Spicy food is good for you in hot weather, Hugh said, but the women overruled him. Italian food isn't *spicy*, Hugh, it's just rich! Well, well . . . what about Mexican food down at Barragans on Sunset? But Mrs. Walker thought the neighborhood was too iffy after dark. What about that Caribbean place, Cha Cha Cha?

"I'm getting faint," I said, but drunk was more like it—the gin hit my empty stomach pretty hard. "Is there a Tony Roma's around here? Don't ribs sound good?"

The restaurant glowed like a darkroom. We turned out to have a great time, gnawing on corncobs and spareribs and acting dumb. Hugh and Samantha built stockpiles of ribs by their plates and before dinner was done they began lobbing them sneakily at each other. Their mother told them to cut it out, but then stockpiled a few of her own. I thought it might be a good idea to do the same.

After the waitress had brought us second rounds of g-and-ts, I watched Hugh as he aimed for his little sister, and just as Hugh threw, I threw at Hugh, catching the kid above the ear, right by his hairline.

"*Yow!*" Hugh yelled so loud that the noise in the restaurant stopped for a minute and people at other tables began to look around in the dark to see who had caused the commotion.

The four of us stared down at our plates.

"*You* did it," Hugh whispered to me.

I did my best to look pained. "You did it, Hugh. I saw you. Picking on your sister like that. It's a disgrace. Mrs. Walker, I don't see how you put up with these little bandits."

She leaned back and gazed at them fondly, a shiny layer of grease at the corners of her lips. "They're completely out of control," she said. "The bane of my existence." Then, to the waitress, "We'll be taking these bones home. I'm making soup stock."

Back at the house I came in for one last drink, and the bones from the doggy bag began to fly. It went on for almost an hour. Finally, the Walker family ganged up on me and pelted me with bones which I grabbed and put away in my own stockpile until they all ran out. I got to my feet and threw up my hands. "I surrender!"

"What are you going to do with those bones?" Samantha asked suspiciously.

"Bury them?" I suggested.

"Out by the guinea pig?" Hugh blurted out, and then fell over, crippled with laughing. He thought he was the funniest thing in the world.

Even Samantha laughed.

"What we could do is make a ring of bones around the grave, like Stonehenge. I could come by tomorrow afternoon. We could do it together."

"Now it's time for bed," Mrs. Walker said. "Go on. You know it is."

Samantha hugged her mom and then hugged me. "Tonight was *fun*," she said. "You're coming back tomorrow then?" Her broad face was blissed out. She was a sweet little kid.

"Sure. After work. We'll stick in those bones. Maybe I'll paint some of them."

Hugh waved and disappeared upstairs. Right on the edge of being a cool dude. Samantha went after him.

"You know," Mrs. Walker said, "I just remembered. I never did put feed in for the turkey. He has water in his pen but no feed. Would you go out with me to put some in? I get a little nervous in the dark."

She didn't look nervous. She didn't look nervous at all. All the laughing, and certainly the gin, had loosened up the muscles in her neck and along her jaw. Her hair was a thick natural blonde with some silver in it, and it gleamed in the yellow light.

"Can we have another drink?"

She nodded again, and mixed us a couple of strong ones. We sipped on them as we wandered through the garage, found a plastic bucket, loaded up on feed, and went on out across the lawn.

It was dry as Africa. I kept thinking of the iguana in the tree, and that luminous, concentrated green. How many iguanas had escaped from how many cages in this city? How many reptiles were out there tonight in magnolias and sycamores and jacarandas? What if this were a jungle pretending to be a city? I'd had a lot to drink.

Something rustled out in the ivy. "You ought to let me cut some of this back," I muttered, and I was surprised at how throaty my voice sounded. I groped for the pen's fence, found it, and pitched in the bucket of feed. The turkey was asleep for the night, but he gave a reflexive gobble.

Mrs. Walker took my hand and pulled me behind the pen, right up against the ivy. I couldn't say I was surprised; I'd been considering the possibility all night. Would I draw the line at a woman who could be almost forty? Hell, no! Why should I draw the line? She was squirmy and pretty and jittery and vague and drunk. Her lips went all over my face like she was a pony looking for a sugar cube, and I just stood there, letting her do it. She shucked off my shirt and took off her blouse and then her skirt. Her arms went all over me like a spider monkey. She had a surprising amount of energy. I got out of my jeans and next thing I knew I was flat on my back in the dry grass. I put up one of my hands to touch her breasts, but she pushed it away. "Stay still!" she told me, and I did, still as the iguana had been in the tree, keeping from coming by imagining Hugh or Samantha snooping out across the lawn. I concentrated on the dusty smell of the ivy and the lawn and the jungle smell of Mrs. Walker, and the breathing sounds of the snoozing turkey and the husky breath of Mrs. Walker, and the amazing circular feeling of being screwed right into the baked dirt of the Los Feliz hills.

When she finished—which I had to notice, because her whole body went rigid as a crossbow, I allowed myself to come and cursed myself for not having brought a condom with me. But who could have known I'd get lucky *here*? She slid right off me and sat in the grass.

"I miss it so much."

"Is he gone a lot? I guess he is, huh?"

"Not him! Yes, he's gone a lot, but I miss . . . staying up late, until . . ."

"I have to go home now," I whispered. "I can't play anymore."

"Oh, you!" She rapped at my chest with her fingernails. "This isn't even what I was talking about. This was nice, but I mean those *real* nights. Now that I'm married, I'll never have those real nights again."

"What about your husband?"

"He's all right. He's a schmuck, actually. I can't stand him."

"No, I mean . . ."

"Robert, I couldn't pick him out of a lineup. He's a bleb."

"Isn't there something you could do?"

"There's nothing else I want to do. So there's no point leaving him. Or kicking him out." The change in her voice told me she'd given it some thought. "Besides, what would I do then? I don't want to work, it's a waste of time. I like staying home with the kids."

The kids. I suddenly saw myself, buck naked, flat on the grass between a wall of ivy and a turkey pen with their mom. The thought, which should have shrunk me down to nothing, worked the other way. I reached for her, but she pinned me back to the grass.

"Wait! Stay still. Let me get on."

"You're all romance," I said.

She didn't bother to answer.

I concentrated again on breathing, making it last, inhaling dust and the smell of sweat. I was still pretty drunk and that made me think I could see things the way the iguana saw them. It seemed very important—to be able to live in a separate world, up in a Thal-Green tree, perfectly quiet in a world of leaves and breeze and elegance of air.

"The one place I always wanted to go was Calcutta. Doesn't that seem splendid in every way?"

Ben was better now, but you could see he was still weak. He got up sometimes to sunbathe in the backyard, but he didn't like to go out in public. He stayed in the dining room on his bed and watched people move around him, and he was hardly ever alone; Hank stayed with him.

"Why Calcutta? You talk about it all the time." I'd done a little straightening up around the house and was spelling Hank so he could go for a walk. I had a surprise in mind for later, and I asked the kid again, "Why Calcutta?" But Ben had dozed off.

In the three weeks I'd known these guys, I'd changed my mind about Hank. The guy had a lot of courage. Courage to come out to LA to live the life he'd always wanted, but more courage to have stayed in that Ohio town for the whole first part of his life, living with his Christian parents, impersonating a tough guy when he drove trucks for his brother-in-law, fending off country girls who— over the years—had thought he was "cute."

And I couldn't even measure Ben's courage.

Every afternoon, I tried to come by. Every afternoon when Hank got back from his walk, we'd pull a couple of beers out of the refrigerator. The two of us would sit on the front porch, just a couple of guys in Levi's and T-shirts, chugging our brewskies and watching the life of this little street, Chicana girls pushing babies in strollers, old, forgotten white ladies who hadn't moved out after their husbands died, and a lot of young guys washing their cars. Hank would tell me what it was like talking to strangers on the phone about their setup. He told stories of missed appointments and lost papers and counselors at AIDS Project Los Angeles, who started out sounding like they could do something but got less and less enthusiastic when they heard the whole story—that he and Ben were from out of state, that they didn't have insurance, that neither of them had job benefits, or family, or money, or even a car.

Then he'd change the subject, and it turned out he was homesick. He talked about what it was like back home—the American plainness of it—miles of woods and grassland and scrubby hills that never got anywhere and that hadn't changed since the whites took the land from the Indians. The one-street town of Althea, all built of red brick. The truck-driving school they had there, where guys who couldn't read or write learned to drive semis as big as a football field, and what *bad* drivers those guys were! The strip joints outside of town, where you watched girls you'd gone to high school with take off their clothes.

The churches. Hank had been raised a Methodist, and he would say, even now, that he believed in God. The best thing about the church had been piling into buses and going out in youth groups and young adult groups to meet youths and young adults in other towns, which is how he'd met Ben. Carbonear was famous for its all-day picnics. Every town back there had those all-day picnics, because none of them had movie theaters; you had to drive ninety miles to Columbus to see a flick, so it was better to pile into a church bus on a Saturday morning in the spring and head out to Carbonear or somewhere else and sit down on a curb in the sun and watch hours of barbershop quartets and banjo players and funny-looking girls in homemade costumes doing clog dancing. Later, they'd all go over to some church basement, or out to a meadow full of ticks, and eat chicken and potato salad and apple pie and Cool Whip and then go home. Singing sometimes, as the bus drove dark roads in the night.

A couple of days ago, Hank had said, "I thought, if I even thought about it at all, that my whole life was going to be that way, a big lie, a tragedy. But one Saturday I took my eyes off the banjo players and there was this beautiful boy, just a kid, sitting on the curb a few feet away from me, leaning back against a streetlight in the sun. He said, 'I'd rather be in Calcutta, wouldn't you? Or out with General MacArthur's troops in Corregidor?' And I thought, my God, maybe there *is* a God. He said, 'Would you like to go down and take a walk by the river?' Just like that. We both got up and left the street and the people and walked a couple of blocks over to the river that goes through that town. We slid down the mud banks until we got to the water and walked for about a mile up to where it looked like the Indians might still be living. Then we had sex. I was a virgin up until then. But Ben wasn't."

I listened, and thought about my poor mom. Or my dad. Or myself, is more like it. Or poor everyone. Waiting around in life watching the equivalent of bad clog dancing, and maybe there would never be the person who would catch your eye and say *I'd rather be in Calcutta,* or whatever words it took to wake you from your sleep.

"I'd been saving all the money I ever made because I still lived at home. God knows I never went out on dates or bought clothes, or even took a drink. The fourth week we were together, I asked Ben if he wanted to go out west. We thought of San Francisco, but Ben said he wanted heat and squalor. Something as far away from Carbonear as possible. We got it! We got the squalor part right. We got the heat too."

Today I'd brought my paints, and one of my new stretched canvases. I'd had the thought to paint Ben, in "Calcutta." The drawing itself was pretty much in place. I worried now about the feelings, and the color. The trick would be to get the pure blond Ohio part of the kid, together with the India of his dreams. And give Ben something good to look at from his bed.

I set up my easel and chair in the dining room and began to lay on paint. I laid out pale Ben, just as he was, flat and thin on his single bed. I painted in his caste mark. Amethyst. I got the perfect color of his almost-white hair against the faded turquoise sheets the Landrys must have had for a long time before Millicent nabbed them.

All around the bed, I'd sketched in my idea of India. Luscious curling vines with monkeys in them, and more monkeys eating mangoes. In the foreground, I painted in blocks of children, naked and ghostlike, beautiful beggars, standing next to each other in crowded streets. But I gave them all handfuls of gold coins. I put coins in all across the bottom of the canvas, and didn't hold back on the glitter. Above Ben, I'd drawn in some kind of god. I knew zip about Indian religion but I painted a handsome prince and made him look a lot like Hank, with black hair and a tattoo. The prince would be dressed in purple silk, every finger of his hands covered with jeweled rings. And he'd send out rays of golden light. The light and coins would circle around the sleeping boy in a shining haze.

Ben had drifted off to sleep again and I thought some more

about the picture. After a while, I mixed up two or three shades of deep lilac. I painted over the caste mark in the picture, changing the amethyst spot into a perfect vanda orchid. (They always said I was a good craftsman.) Then, using the same brushes, I painted an orchid over the caste mark on Ben's own forehead.

I worked very fast on the Indian jungle and the naked children, and as the sun began to go down, I cleaned up my paints and folded my easel, and propped the painting against a far wall. An Angel Food volunteer came by—a stout little woman with cartons of pureed vegetables and carrot juice. I took her into Ben's room to check out the work.

"Amazing!" she whispered. "You've made them both into saints from heaven."

When Hank came back, winded and sweaty from his walk, he covered his mouth with his hand. "You saw what made me fall in love with him. You have a gift, you know that?"

We lit a bedside lamp and waited for Ben to wake up. When he did, we propped up the painting at the bottom of the bed so he could see it. "I love it," he said. "It's so beautiful. It's the most beautiful thing I've ever seen."

"Now, look at this," I said. I found a hand mirror and held it so that he could see the orchid on his own forehead.

"Oh, I love it. Oh, it's splendid in every way."

"Bob, we need you!"

"Yeah, who is it?" The sun was barely up but already my room was stifling. The air was so thick you could gag on it.

"It's his birthday, and he's going to be home for once." She giggled, and I recognized the lunacy. Mrs. Walker.

"How's the menagerie?" I asked groggily.

"Oh, Bob. The menagerie's OK. You were a big help last time."

"How do I answer that one?"

"Oh, Bob! What I mean is, Michael actually said a few nice things when he came home last time. He said he almost thought I might be getting my act together. I guess . . . we might be really trying again."

I pulled myself up to a sitting position, and kicked off the sheet. A stone July scorcher coming up. "That's nice," I said.

"So it's Michael's birthday a week from today on the twenty-

sixth, and I thought I'd give him a party. Seven hundred of his closest friends."

I had to laugh in spite of myself. "You want me to come over and
scrape the slime off the floor? You want me to paint the snake?"

She sounded almost prim in the way she chose to ignore me.
Like I was a bad little kid who'd forgotten my manners.

"We'll have to have it outside, of course. A garden party. I'm
renting a tent and a dance floor. And I'm calling the caterers today.
But we need some *decor*. And we'll need extra people for passing
hors d'oeuvres. The caterers want twenty-eight dollars an hour for
each extra person they bring. Don't you live with some people?
Couldn't they help out? And didn't you say you were a regular
artist? Didn't I hear you say that? Couldn't you whip me up some
decorations?"

"Ten dollars an hour. For my friends, too. How are Hugh and
Samantha?"

"They like the idea of a party. Can you come over this morning?
We've only got a week. Did I tell you that?"

"Have you sent out invitations?"

"Telegrams. Three hundred of them. Hugh's doing it today.
With the Rolodex."

"How's the laundry situation? How about your dishes?"

"Oh, *Bob!*"

I hung up, got up, went down the hall. Dave was already awake.
He hunched over the funnies and brushed powdered sugar off his
chin. A package of doughnuts lay open and I grabbed one.

"Want to pass some hors d'oeuvres next weekend? Wear a snap-
on bow tie? Ten bucks an hour."

"Sure!"

Even in the awful sun, a party seemed like a good idea, until I
drove up and saw the Walker house again, which still looked deso-
late and peculiar on this street with all its manicured respectability.

I went around to the back. At least nobody was screaming, but they might have been past the point of screaming. The three of them, Mrs. Walker, Hugh, and Samantha, stood outside in the sun, looking at the yard. Lawn needed mowing, of course. But the whole place looked raggedy-assed. All in all, beyond help.

Samantha ran over and hugged me. Hugh gave me one of his careful waves and a self-conscious smile.

"We're giving a party!" Samantha said.

"Cool! So what are you going to do out here?"

Mrs. Walker took a couple of deep breaths. She wore Levi's shorts and a flimsy white blouse, and she'd been lying out in the sun a lot. She looked good. "Fix it!" she said brightly. "You can do that, Bob!"

I don't know why, something about these people cheered me up. *"No problema,"* I said.

I drove down Sunset and over to St. Francis of Assisi Catholic Church, found the pastor, and asked if he had some parishioners of good character to do seven days of intensive gardening. Ten dollars an hour. After only fifteen minutes, I drove back with Lorenzo and Martin, shy young guys who carried their own machetes. I dropped them off in the backyard and they began on the ivy and the lawn, turning on water wherever they could find it. The rental people were there on a planning visit, and I got a map of where the tent and the dance floor were going to be. Hugh and Samantha stayed in the kitchen, still burning up the phone lines to Western Union, sending out invitations. Their mom stood by the sink, looking distracted.

"Mrs. Walker? Could you go for a jungle motif?"

The next four days I spent hours constructing larger-than-life plywood cutouts of climbing monkeys and bright birds to hang from trees, and representations of their snake and the iguana and that damn turkey. I wore out nine blades on my coping saw. Work with what you have! Lorenzo and Martin and I made daily afternoon runs to Armstrong's and bought every plant we could find that had orange or yellow or blue in it, and, as the sun went down, the men planted them. I found some Japanese lanterns over on Sawtelle and spent an afternoon wiring them. RSVPs began coming in. Samantha kept careful records.

I got the kids to help me as painting apprentices, showed them how to lay first and second coats of paint on my plywood, and then set them up to do some detail work after I'd painted in the big stuff, so that before their eyes plain wood began to turn into jungle mania. They loved it.

By the next Sunday morning, when the party people brought in the tent and set it up, the place looked great. I couldn't stop admiring my snake, seven feet tall with a piercing stare, turned up against the sycamore, and my green iguana, which ran to four feet and reclined in a hedge, illuminated by a couple of those battery-driven ground lamps. If parties succeeded on looks, this one was aced.

Austen and June Shaw said no to the hors d'oeuvres job, of course, but by seven Dave and Kate and some of her friends turned up, in black pants and starched white shirts. Looking good. A DJ had set up at the far end of the yard, over by the turkey. Dave checked out the newly painted pen, the stupid-looking turkey, and said to me out of the corner of his mouth, "Is this where you . . . ?"

I nodded. The music started, low and sweet. Lanterns came on. Out front, Lorenzo and Martin, spruced up, were acting as valets.

"Ah, the good life," Dave remarked, and I could only agree. What wasn't to like?

The party began. The back lawn filled up. Dave and I hopped to it, carrying out trays from the kitchen full of endive with blue cheese, and crisps dabbed with sun-dried tomatoes, and jicama with crab salad. White linen seemed to be the order of the day, and, in the middle of it all, the birthday boy came out, a fortyish guy with a puffy face. Just about as blebby as Jamey had said. Happy birthday, Michael! He stood by the snake, under flattering light, being jovial, shaking hands, taking credit for all my work.

I switched to trays of champagne and white wine. Some of the people here were my age or younger, but most were in their thirties, pushing forty. Mr. Walker sold ads for a television sports channel so most of these people were either in sports or television or advertising. Real cool or trying for it, young women in short skirts and strapless tops, basketball players looking like linen giraffes. Plain old salesmen in blue blazers, praying for Scotch. Everybody hoping this was going to be an A party, waiting for it to become one. Bob Marley came from the DJ, and a few awkward couples moved out onto the floor.

An hour later, it *looked* like an A party, as if I'd ever seen one. I noticed Dave, always the philosopher, standing at ease with an empty tray, talking earnestly to some guy. Saw Mrs. Walker, tautfaced and nuts, nudging an old fart with a purple face. Saw Hugh and Samantha, dressed up and on what passed for their best behavior, sipping what looked to be white wine out of juice glasses. People kept pouring in through the side entrance to the yard. It was dark now, and the lanterns were shining. There was about an hour more to go until dinner was served. I went back in the kitchen for another tray of wine.

And came out and did my job, just doing it, asking, "Wine? Wine? Wine?" And they all wanted it and drank it down and I took another tray of empties to the kitchen where the caterers were getting tense, and came out again, loving those lanterns, which I'd actually wired right, and my terrific plywood animals, thinking, yeah, it *is* a jungle at this place, it was cool to make it a jungle, saying, "Wine? Wine?" And the person I said it to next was Mr. Landry, who gave me a crazy look, picked up a glass, and drank all of it down.

"Wine?" I said to Angela Landry, who had been crying. Her eyes were bloodshot and swollen.

"Yes, please," she said.

Then, down in the dark, I saw another person, felt another kind of energy. I heard the kind of scream I was used to in this place, but this scream was serious. "Bob!" It came out, "Bah!"

Tod hung on to my knees for dear life.

Hugh took the tray away from me and Samantha was right there, leaning down. "Did they bring you to a grown-up party, little chiclet? What a drag that is! Come on, let's go inside. We'll play upstairs. This is so boring down here!"

Tod transferred his grip to Samantha, and she hefted him up like a sack of grain. Hugh followed along and I thought I'd better go too, through the crowded noisy kitchen, as Tod leaned over Samantha's shoulder and yelled right at me, "Bah! Bah!"

Upstairs, we pulled out Hugh's old action figures, and got Tod to laugh after a while, and then he got really giddy. He ran all around Hugh's room four or five times, touching the walls, whooping and yelling, and then he took off his shirt, holding up his arms like a champ, turning around and around, taking bows.

Samantha saw it first.

"Look at this," she said, outraged. "Just look at it."

Across Tod's thin shoulders there was a thick, red palm print. Tod looked around, stopped whirling, his point made.

"That *asshole*," Samantha said. "And I thought we were bad over here."

But the next morning when I called over there, Angela said that I must be mistaken. Then she said it was a wonderful party, and even remembered to ask if I'd done the decorations. "I think it's important for you to go on with your art," she said. "You have a lot of talent." The blue around the pool looked fabulous. And no, she didn't need anything done around the house just now because I'd done such a good job earlier in the summer.

"That's just wonderful," I said. "That's really swell."

Part Two

The job was beginning to get me down. For a week I'd been walking in mud, swimming in Redi-Crete, losing money, losing my temper. I'd spent two days with a dickhead Hollywood bachelor putting
bookshelves in an apartment that already had built-in bookshelves.
I bought raw wood, layered it with thinned whitewash so the grain
would show, and put up the shelves. The bachelor, working out
intermittently in the second bedroom—his "weights room"—
decided at the end of two days that the work wasn't good enough
and I wasn't going to get paid. I lost it and began yanking boards
out of the wall, leaving some pretty good holes.

"Stop that!" the bachelor yelled at me. "You're defacing my
property!"

"It's only your property if you pay for it," I said. "I'll sue you for
fraud, you've been wasting my *time*!"

As I drove away, it occurred to me that the guy had been home for both those days and the phone hadn't rung once. He was just one more bummed-out orphan of the storm, desperate for company. But that left me with a van full of whitewashed bookshelves I didn't have any use for. I dropped off a few at Ben and Hank's, along with some cement blocks, and stowed the rest in the garage.

My next job was for a woman I couldn't seem to like, a fretful wife in her thirties who walked around her own house with a clipboard in her hand, getting organized for God knows what. She wanted all of her rooms painted white, *off* white, and we spent a morning at the paint store working on colors. I bought gallons of the stuff, custom blended, with my own money. After I'd finished the living room, she said it looked too sterile; I'd have to take the rest of the paint back and start over.

"I can't take it back. It's custom-blended." The inside of my chest felt like a brick. These women! They pretended to be dumb, they ignored the world. And thought they could get away with it. "I paid for this with my own money, remember."

I ended up taking the rest of the paint in trade, along with the brushes, stacking cans in the Micheltorena garage.

One morning I drove up Beachwood, way up in the Hollywood Hills, and parked just under the Hollywood Sign. I could feel myself getting ready to lose my temper. No lawns here, and very few homes that you could even see from the road. Just walls of trumpet vine and rockrose and ivy—not dusty and overgrown like the Walkers' but neatly clipped, and deep, watered green. The morning seemed fresh and clean and unlived-in, and made me feel out of place. Who'd need my services up here? I got out of the van and looked around.

Beachwood Drive, a slice out of a mountain, with another great view—Los Angeles by the mile. To my left, the glass towers of downtown. To my right, twenty miles away, that same pale ribbon of Pacific blue we saw from our house. No one around. The sound of a mockingbird working himself up, trying one trill after another.

I felt a sharp stab of resentment, no, make that rage. Never in my life would I be able to live like this. It wasn't just the money, although these Hollywood Hills were paved with gold. It was the ease, the confidence, the organization that I'd never be able to figure out. The best thing I could hope for in my little life would be a house in the Valley, and the last thing in the world I ever wanted in my life was a house in the Valley.

I looked at the number on my card, and the number on a redwood wall. They matched, all right. I pulled an elaborate bell-ringing thing, and a door in the wall opened.

"Bob? Come in. Did you have trouble finding the place?"

I had to adjust my attention, bend my head down. The woman talking to me stood about five feet, what my dad used to call a little-bitty thing. She looked pretty old, in her fifties somewhere, very tanned, with messy bright platinum hair, deep-set eyes. Her voice was low, husky, and she had an accent.

"Mrs. Le Clerc?"

"Come in."

She turned and walked through a narrow tiled courtyard. I ducked my head and followed her. Hanging planters of fuchsia poked at me from above and shallow pots of purple and gold pansies around my ankles made the going rough. What does she need me for? I thought. This place is *fixed* already. We got to the house and went into the kitchen. A wall of glass opened it up to that great city view.

"I was just having my coffee. Please join me."

Espresso. And orange juice straight from the squeezer. Fresh French rolls.

"What can I do for you, Mrs. Le Clerc?"

"My husband died two weeks ago. I need to go through his things. My friends have endured enough with this. And I don't want to do it alone."

"I'm sorry."

"It was a surprise, although nothing like that is ever really unexpected. He was reading, and then he wasn't. He looked up from his book and then he wasn't there anymore."

I drank some coffee. Didn't know what to say.

"That was about ten at night. I stayed in the room with him until the next morning. I pulled a chair up to his and took his hand. Even when he was still warm, he wasn't there. I'm afraid I don't believe in an afterlife, and I find that I ask myself a banal question. If there's no afterlife, where did he go? Where will I go? Or you?"

"How long had you been married?"

"Twenty-four years. Not that long. We weren't young when we met."

"Can your children help?"

"We never had children. It was our choice."

"What did your husband do?"

"He was a professor of philosophy. We built this house in 1972. Buying the land took almost all we had. We put up first one room, then another. We had friends who stayed with us and worked. Shall I show you the house?"

"Please."

It was a beautiful place, peaceful and cool. It had a Mexican feel to it. There were high white stucco walls and big sheets of plate glass open to the view in each room. She had dusky Saltillo tiles across every floor, and Mexican or Central American hangings in dark corners. Japanese and Chinese low tables. There seemed to be not one library, but three of them, small and dim and clean. Downstairs, they'd put in a big enclosed garden with dark wood furniture and low, vivid flowers. The colors were so clear and deep they seemed to color the air itself. I'd heard of that actually—an interior-decorating trick.

And off this garden, cut right into the slope of the hill, there was a downstairs room, their master bedroom, the walls so clean in their whiteness they seemed to have blue in them, glacier blue. A big bed, covered in sky blue. As peaceful as a church. A great place to be dead in.

"We'll be working here. I have the boxes ready. Some of my friends advise waiting to throw things away, some of them say not to wait. I don't think his shoes or shirts can save me."

All I could do was shrug. I felt like a moron. I couldn't resist glancing at my watch. Only twenty to eleven. It was so quiet in here!

"Golf shoes. He loved golf. A place he could get away from me, and from his mind. These were hiking shoes—oh, these are old. He came from Europe when he was young, just after the war. Twenty-five years later I came here from Guatemala, because of the civil unrest. My parents were German planters. I was supposed to marry into that society, but I couldn't bear the thought. And then, of course, it became impossible. We came to California in 1971 and I took a summer-school course in philosophy. Wally taught a very popular undergraduate course in Existentialism. He said that suffering was a choice we made, that we could all choose not to suffer. I thought he was mistaken, but I admired his courage. These are his teaching shoes. I think he shopped once a year, laid out his clothes every morning, put everything on without thinking."

She dropped four identical pairs of shoes into a large box, flung in tennis shoes and one pair of evening pumps, and started on another box. "He was loved by his students and hated by his colleagues. He was authentic, do you know what I mean? He'd been through the war and seen evil, and he spent his life finding weapons against it. His colleagues pursued their careers. And, of course, they disapproved of me. I was a blonde shell, a *bomb*shell. And now I have to say good-bye to his teaching suits, which he owned and used since I first met him."

"Shall I take these upstairs?"

"Not yet."

She rolled up clothes and placed them carefully in a carton.

"But later, he tended to mistake stasis for peace. He cherished quiet, lack of movement. He pared down all his motions. He was a great believer in economy."

As she bent over, I could see the back of her neck. Her hair was up. I could see tendons flex with her movements. She was so tan!

"Look at these shirts. One of our very few quarrels. He felt I should iron them. I became very haughty. A woman of good quality is not going to iron shirts like a peasant girl! But he felt that he should be cared for, physically cared for, by a person who loved him deeply. I couldn't do it. God didn't put me on earth to be a servant, I told him many times. It was one thing for us to work together on this house, quite another for me to serve him personally."

"What are your plans? Will you be staying here?" I hated the thought that this woman might end up sitting on an oval-back chair like somebody else I knew, looking out a window all alone.

"I don't know. I've spent time on this place, making it beautiful. And where would I go? When I go back to Guatemala, I have almost nothing to say to the women I grew up with. Since I have no children, in their eyes I'm worthless. They may be right, I don't know. But I do know that I've filled these boxes. Will you take them away for me? And will you come again? Can you come tomorrow, before I lose my courage, doing this?"

"Of course," I said, and began carrying up cartons, loading them in the van.

When I'd finished, I looked around for her to say good-bye and found her in the kitchen, staring out over the city. She gave me too much money, two twenties. "And these are for you, if you want them." She handed me another bundle, and I ducked my head so I wouldn't have to look at her as I said good-bye.

When I got in the van, I opened the package and found five V-necked men's cashmeres, fresh from the dry cleaners, thick and expensive. Green, coral, cream, gray, tan. A small fortune in cashmere.

So I should have felt good as I went back down the hill toward Franklin. But I didn't.

I headed for home, but stopped first on Western Avenue at the Salvation Army. I drove around the back and handed off the cartons to a man who casually slung the clothes into a huge Dumpster. All of Mrs. De Clerc's folding and rolling for nothing.

Don't you at least want to keep the suits together? I almost asked. But it wasn't my business.

"So, Mr. Le Clerc," I said, as I walked around the van, pulled myself up and climbed in. "Rest in peace, OK?"

I came by Mrs. Le Clerc's at 9:30 the next morning, and made sure not to eat breakfast before I got there. I told myself it was because of June Shaw poking around in the kitchen in spandex biking shorts chopping dates and raisins for a foul-looking granola. That was true, of course. Mornings in our house were light years away from Valerie Le Clerc's perfect espresso. But there was another aspect to it.

I'd mentioned it to Dave the night before, as we'd shot baskets down at the foot of the hill by Micheltorena Elementary.

"There's a side effect to this job." It was easier to talk if I kept messing with the ball—bounce, bounce, *shoot*, recover. "I hadn't thought of it or I'd have got into it sooner."

"Yeah?" Dave liked to say he practiced silent basketball, ball as Tai Chi. He stood in the dark playground, solid and centered, just in front of the basket, willing the ball to come to him. When it came close, he snaked out an arm, recovered, threw, scored more often than not. I ran around all over the place.

"I've been getting a lot of play. For a change. Comparatively speaking. I told you before, I think. Kind of unexpected."

Dave decided to sing. "The man comes to our house every single day, Papa comes home and the man goes away. Papa does the work and Mama gets the pay. And the man comes to *our* house every single day!" He snagged the ball, sank a basket.

"Where'd you hear that?"

"My dad used to sing it to my mom."

"If people . . . knew . . . the whole world would be out working as a handyman." I missed a shot. "I do wonder about these women, though. Don't they have anything to do? I mean, all the way around. They're sitting in houses with nothing better to do."

"That's what women do, lad. If they don't work. They sit in the house and then they buy groceries. Do men have it any better? Make stuff, sell stuff, make stuff, sell stuff. Go to war when they can't take it anymore."

He was getting off the point, as far as I was concerned. "Some of these women, they scare me."

"My dad used to say . . . If you want booty, you can't be particular." Dave snagged the ball. Mystical energy.

"If it's falling in my lap, how can I say no?"

"Yeah, but where do you draw the line?"

"June Shaw?"

We both laughed.

Parts of this conversation kept running through my mind as I pulled up in front of the Le Clerc house. I did the best I could not to notice them. I tried to focus instead on the clean smell of the damp earth in the first garden, and the smell of rosemary, and the just-watered pansies and camellias. And the smell of that great coffee. All I wanted was breakfast! I knocked on the kitchen door and she slid it open for me.

Instead of making orange juice, she'd sectioned oranges in two crystal bowls.

"What's that other great flavor in this?"

"Amaretto. To go with the almond croissants."

I ate like a king while Mrs. Le Clerc took an occasional orange section for herself and gave me a few paragraphs about her family home in Guatemala—a hacienda at the base of a beautiful mountain, where coffee plants disappeared in cloudy mists at the peak. Wide verandas, where the ladies of the house gathered in the heat of the afternoon to gossip and play canasta. The strangeness of the beginning war years when soldiers, not even out of their teens, threatened all but the very richest families. Fortunately, they were among the very richest. Long afternoons and evenings, when she and other well-brought-up girls of the area drove to the country club, sunning themselves by the pool, drinking rum-and-Cokes (with their mothers' grudging permission). They heard gunfire from time to time, but told themselves that it had to be a defective car backfiring, or maybe the *paludismo* trucks that plied the back roads squirting pesticide into stagnant ponds to exterminate malarial mosquitoes—maybe the tubes were stopped up and that's what made the popping sound. Until the smell of cordite drifted into the grounds of the club itself, and the mothers made anxious calls to the police for an escort home. Except they couldn't be sure they could trust the police.

And the final fateful morning she told me about, when she and her mother and her aunt drove fearfully to the airport, carrying only what they could take in big straw handbags, so that watching eyes in the jungle along the road wouldn't know they were leaving, but accept the flimsy idea that most likely they were driving to the airport to meet a few more visiting relations from Germany or France.

And the men in the family stayed stoically in the hacienda with the few servants and field hands whom they thought they could trust, and eventually every last one of them died in flurries of gun-fire on steaming afternoons, humid moonlit nights.

"God," I said. "That must have been awful."

Mrs. Le Clerc shot me a disapproving glance, as if to say, I give you some of my very best material, and that's all you can come up with? She cleared away the dishes. "I think today will be harder for me. We're going to sort through papers."

I'd been right the day before. There *were* three libraries in this house. She showed them off to me. Her own—Valerie's—was given over entirely to works by women. She stood me in the doorway and rattled off names—Vita Sackville-West, Anaïs Nin, Djuna Barnes. She had three paintings in here, which I frowned at, trying to get the point. A small reproduction of Our Lady of Lourdes, a nicely rendered Kwan Yin, and another smoky-looking Asian goddess with a hundred arms, an eye in the palm of each hand. It was dark in here, with a smell of dried flowers.

"When we built this house, I insisted on a place for myself. I still thought I might create something of my own."

"There's a saint, I can't remember which one, who hid bread under her cloak, and when her jealous husband ripped back the cloak the bread turned to roses."

"I'm afraid I don't follow you."

"I thought," I said lamely, "something like that might look nice in here."

The next library, no more than an alcove, held the stuff most people had. Even my mother, even my Seal Beach uncles had some of these books. Just not so many and not so organized. There was a small fireplace right in the middle of the wall, with two chairs pulled up beside it.

"My husband, when he felt sad, would come home and say, 'Can we have drinks in the snuggery?' "

"The snuggery?"

"Yes. This room."

His own study was a different story. Papers and more papers. Books mashed any old way into shelves that sagged under the weight, and more papers pushed in on top. No computer. Two filing cabinets so full that some of the drawers couldn't close.

Mrs. Le Clerc closed her eyes as though she had a headache. "I'm afraid you have to do it."

"I wouldn't know where to start."

"He retired years ago, but he never threw anything away. He liked to have a cluttered desk. To be a work in progress. He entertained his students in here until the day he died. Still working on their dissertations. Some of them going bald!"

I steered clear of the desk and headed for a file, opening the top drawer. Breathed in the smell of old paper.

Philosophy 101. Plato. Socrates. An exam in five parts. Pick three. Be specific. Cite all sources.

Jesus.

There must be a hundred copies of this one exam.

"Should I keep samples, one of each, of the things I find? These exams?"

She'd pulled a chair up to a window and sat forward with her hands in her lap, looking out, striking a posture that gave me the willies.

"There are no more students, are there? No classes *or* exams."

Philosophy 383. Sartre and Camus. Choose three of five questions. Cite all sources. Plagiarism will not be tolerated.

Another fistful of papers. I pitched them all out.

"What are these?"

"Offprints. When someone got published in the old days, the periodical would send the writer offprints of his article, and the writer would hand them out to his friends and enemies to show that his career was going well. Wally rarely published, but his colleagues did."

I began a stack of my own. I'd take them home to Dave and June and Austen, let them dig around.

Silverfish. Dust. Paper clips and staplers and erasers and ball-points old as the hills. I got one file drawer finished.

And more of the same. Correspondence in colored cellophane folders.

"Throw them out," Valerie said. "It's over now."

He had envelopes dating back to the fifties and forties and books with pages torn, and advertisements for products that didn't even exist anymore. And of course, classroom texts, heavily under-lined by the professor himself.

"Throw them out. I know what he cared for and what he hated. I don't need the books to remind me."

I was hot. The room filled with dust, and Mrs. Le Clerc didn't seem to feel like talking. I'd filled eight big Hefty bags when I heard the chime of the front door and Valerie excused herself.

In a few minutes, two young guys and a nervous woman appeared in the room with a dolly and an armload of flattened cardboard.

"Take all the books. As quickly as you can."

The woman, a pretty creature with wavy hair, said, "The uni-versity is very grateful."

I couldn't believe what I was watching. The guys hauled down books by the armload and the lady pushed out cardboard to make boxes. They loaded up a dolly, wheeled it out. The dolly came back, and left, came back, and left. Within half an hour, all the book-shelves in the room were empty.

They left. I thought I'd better speed up, and filled another seven bags. She wanted her husband gone, I'd get rid of him for her. By something like three in the afternoon, everything but the desk had been cleared out. The desk itself still had stacks all over it—those offprints, that looked pretty pitiful now, a stack of snapshots, and a collection of the weird stuff that ends up in any office—a carved box, a pewter mouse, a plastic dog with jaws that snapped, a portable shrine of the Infant of Prague. I was sweating, covered with dust, and starved. Ready to eat a horse and chase the driver.

Valerie brought in sandwiches, ham on pumpernickel with hot mustard, Perrier, and a decanter of brandy.

I sat at the office desk and wolfed down the sandwiches. I thought I knew by now why she wanted everything out. The outlines of the room were coming clear; I could see she wanted it for something else. I saw that she was watching me eat. She only had a little brandy.

"This may be the best meal I ever ate."

"You worked very hard. I'm grateful. I couldn't have done it myself. He didn't like people going through his things."

Was she afraid she'd find a secret? Another life that didn't belong to her? Something as separate from her as her afternoons at the country club were from him?

"You look tired. Should we stop for today, and you come back tomorrow? Would that be possible? Could you come around four? Do you like to paint, *house* paint? Would you like to paint this room? Not tomorrow, but later? Tomorrow, would you like to go on the roof and sweep leaves, clean out the gutters? Is four too late for you?"

I leaned up against the desk with my legs sprawled out. The brandy had gone straight to my head. All I could do was nod yes, sure I'd come back.

By the time I got down to the bottom of the hill, I'd come back to myself enough to try and get a grip. I'd forgotten to ask her for today's money, every bone in my body ached, and any thoughts of a magic afternoon seemed insanely out of the question. I thought I must have been nuts to even think of it.

In your dreams, Bob, in your dreams.

But what kind of weird dreams were they in the first place? When I thought about that, I knew I was in trouble.

I slept late the next morning and creaked when I got out of bed. I spent a lot of time in the shower, letting the water smooth out the knots in my neck. In the kitchen, I found the offprints I'd brought home scattered across the counter and floor. I went out for breakfast, did some errands, came home, felt the need for another shower, saw that the time was coming up on three.

I got in the van, stopped by a liquor store, looked for something she might like, and bought a bottle of Fernet Branca. I realized I'd cleared a grand total of about twenty bucks from two days' work—and three good meals—but I wouldn't get rich if I went on this way. (But maybe I'd learned I'd never teach for a living, or go back to a real university, ever, and maybe that was worth something.)

As I knocked on the kitchen door, I registered a scrabbling in my chest like the beginning of an acid trip, and a tightening in my groin. *You idiot,* I said to myself, and then she was there.

Old! Why couldn't I keep *that* in my mind? Why wouldn't I remember? Her tan skin had been lightly oiled, and her platinum hair was pinned loosely up off her neck again. She wore a house coat of some dark orange gauzy stuff. She smelled like spices. The whole house smelled like spices. She took the bottle from me, smiled, put it on the table. Was I fucking *nuts*?

She led me to the back garden at the bottom of the house, the one outside the master bedroom, and began asking my advice. She'd always loved trees and flowers by the house, and then a shallow patio, and then a vegetable and herb garden beyond that. But one of her friends had suggested building a deck out from the kitchen just above. That would be good for morning sun, but a deck would cast most of this downstairs area in shade, and would that be a good thing or a bad thing?

She stood under an acacia tree and sunlight dappled through it, tracing patterns on her skin and hair. There was a fig tree, and a pomegranate, and the postage-stamp flagstone patio with two chaise longues padded in deep blue canvas pushed together. Low redwood tables stood on either side with carafes of red wine and ceramic platters of figs and apricots. That spicy smell again.

"You wouldn't want to lose this." I was having trouble with my voice. "Everyone has a deck. What do you want a deck for? Nobody has this."

"I get so tired of thinking what to do. Maybe the best thing is to do nothing."

She drooped a little. Then she was lying down, the dark orange dress against dark blue. What else could I do but lie down beside her? It was so great out here, so comfortable. She poured us both some wine.

"My whole life I wanted to be an artist," I told her, and then I spaced, looking past her at green pomegranate leaves, dusty fig leaves, the blazing orange and yellow of nasturtium borders. "No one in my family had ever done anything like that before. They thought I was crazy. We're the kind of people who live in trailers. My uncles live in an old Airstream. I was an art major at UCLA. Then I worked in advertising for a few years and made a good living, and did some painting, but I still wanted to be an artist. A real one. *In my dreams,* right?"

I told her about going to Paris, about the cold and the rain and how I couldn't figure out the École des Beaux-Arts, how I didn't have the nerve. She listened, and drank, and opened up a fig, licking into it with her narrow tongue.

"I'm beginning at Otis Art Institute in the fall, you know the place? But I look at what's out there, I'm talking about *art* now, the art scene, and I can't imagine being a part of it. I don't like what they're doing. And I certainly don't know what *I'm* doing."

"I wonder if it's not life we're supposed to pay attention to. Life tells us. What we're supposed to do."

I turned to look at her. Her eyes were closed, her face tilted up a little to catch the sun as it filtered through leaves. Sun made her face glisten and I noticed that while her skin stretched taut against her jawline and cheekbones, she had those give-away tiny lines above her upper lip. The sunlight caught those lines. Coruscation, was that what they called it? Those tiny lights that the sun made on the sea?

"Your skin has coruscation from the sun. The sun keeps catching it, lighting it up."

I propped myself on an elbow and kissed her lips. Her tongue was like the rest of her, thin and dusky and aromatic. *Whoa!* What was *this*! I took off like a rodeo horse. I tried to cover her body with my own, lie down on top of her while I took off her clothes and my clothes at the same time. What the *hell* was I doing? It seemed very important to pin down her legs with my own, pin down those tan feet with my shoes, even though common sense told me I was going nowhere with this, especially with my briefs and khakis and all her orange gauzy stuff. I pulled my head back to get a look at her and she tilted her head a little to the side, her lips parted in a smile, her eyes closed. I bent my face down into the crease of her neck and breathed in as hard as I could. *Whoa!* I drew the smell into my lungs, held it, let it out. She shivered.

I got out of my clothes like a madman while she lay there, eyes closed, waiting. I began to bunch up pieces of her orange gauze and saw that she sunbathed naked. Her nipples were dark brown against her tan, flat breasts. Her body was tan, lean muscle. The hair she had down there was anchovy brown.

And that's where I went, trying to get to the source of that dusky, spicy smell. I felt her fingers tracing patterns on my neck, and thinking about it later I could say time stopped. It was a question of staying there until I found it, the source of it, *it*. I wiped my wet face with the back of my hand, and I smelled it on my hand, again.

"What is it?"

She opened her eyes, smoothed her hair, looked at me.

"*What is it!*"

"When you left yesterday afternoon, I soaked for two hours in a bath with Shalimar. But that was too sweet. After I'd dried, I cut lemons in half and rubbed them all over my body. I picked a sprig of rosemary and slept with it . . . *there*." She pointed a careless finger. "And a few other things this morning."

I scrambled around for a condom and came into her like a regular lover, and her lean legs wrapped around my neck. She was as limber as a chimp. I grabbed her dusty left foot and held it to my nose, inhaled lemon and spice and heavy perfume, and came.

"Whoa!" I said, "How could he have died when he had *this*?"

I felt terrible for saying it. Just terrible.

"When I saw you, I knew I had to have you. I knew it before I saw you. To keep from . . . Something that would . . ."

"Don't even tell me. I can't believe this is happening."

I came into the house quietly, after two in the morning. Austen's light was on, and I thought Dave might still be up, but I ducked right into my own room and turned on the overhead light. I held my forearm to my nose, inhaled. She was right, plain perfume would have sickened both of us, after all we'd done. But just remembering what we'd done jerked my sore dick up against my pants. It had been through the mill.

I got out of my clothes and laid out my paints in a hurry, pulled out a canvas, grabbed a #2 pencil.

Just to get the outline. A saint picture, a picture of Saint Valerie, but instead of roses, rosemary. Instead of Old Testament linen in those traditional folds, just sharp, oiled, tanned skin, with pubic hair like anchovies. A cloak of dark orange. And at her feet, glowing lemons and nasturtium. More rosemary for the halo, scratchy, dusty green all around her body. Her face, tilted to one side, expecting pleasure, happy about it. The lines above her lip, they had to be there. Tomorrow, before I mixed more paints for the hard work of it, I'd get some real rosemary, grind it in.

Ben was sick again. Hank had called Ben's new "Buddy for Life" the night before, and he'd come over and driven Ben and Hank to the emergency room, but it turned out to be the same old story. He wasn't *that* sick, and they couldn't get him in. Just the flu, they said, or an upset stomach. The Buddy—Buddy for Two Weeks, Hank called him, because that was how long he'd been assigned to them—was a nice guy, a heterosexual in his forties. He'd been in a fight with his ex-wife, who'd kept calling him on his cell phone, in the car and in the hospital waiting room. The phone kept ringing and the guy kept yelling into the phone, so after he'd driven them back home, Hank decided he couldn't come over anymore. "I told him *adiós*," Hank said. "We've got enough trouble here without going through somebody else's divorce." So then Hank called me.

It was a midafternoon in the second week in August, and hotter than hell. The heat bleached the color out of everything in sight, squeezed every drop of sweat out of every person it touched, evaporated the water and left the grease. How was it, I wondered, that the people in the paintings by old masters always looked so *bathed,* even if they'd lived in Florence in the summer? I'd answered Hank's call and come straight on over this morning, but it wasn't my idea of a good time. Not that I didn't want to help, but it was so fucking depressing.

In the five or six weeks since I'd met them, Hank had gotten a little more of their act together. He'd dealt with APLA and found that Buddy for Life. People kept wanting to walk their pets, except they didn't have any. Volunteers had brought over more linens, and plenty of rubber gloves and rubber sheets. The lady from Angel Food stopped by three times a week. Besides coming by in the afternoons, I had stayed with Ben a few evenings so that Hank could get out a little. He did go out. He was determined to "enjoy" himself. He'd had dinner at Millie's on Sunset and gone out to Dragstrip 66 on Riverside Drive. He'd been doing some body building; he'd dyed his hair a heavier black and cut it in a cooler do. But under his hip hair his face still looked like it belonged to a kid from Ohio. "I dreamed about this life for as long as I knew about it," he told me, "but I don't fit into it. No one wants me around. Except for Ben, of course."

Ben had been throwing up every twenty minutes since about six o'clock the night before. The linen situation was under control; Ben almost always had rubberized squares under his behind now like the ones they used for babies. Every time he threw up, he had some diarrhea, not much. After he was over being sick, Hank put on gloves, rinsed out the square, put it in a plastic laundry hamper. The poor kid had nothing left in his system, nothing but bile. After it came up, Hank would give him a little cup of 7-Up, which Ben drank right down, and said, "Oh, that was wonderful!" He'd lie back under a sheet and doze for exactly fifteen minutes—you could time it. Then he'd sit up on the edge of the bed, swallowing hard, and start coughing, and swallowing harder, while Hank, and now me, would start saying, "Is there anything we can get you? Do you want anything?" Until the five minutes had gone by, and the kid picked up a yellow plastic bucket and puked in it.

Then, after he was done, Ben drank more 7-Up and lifted his skinny butt so that Hank could put down a new rubberized pad. I took the bucket out back, sloshed it with a hose, left a skim of fresh water across the bottom, came back in, sat down by Hank. It was just the three of us, and the situation.

"The guy from Shanti, he calls a couple of times a day," Hank said. "He's like a stereotype. He's taken the Course in Miracles. He says he doesn't get up in the morning, not even to go to the bathroom, until he's read his lesson. And the people from Angel Food are Course in Miracles people. They tell me to expect a miracle. I can expect one as much as I want, but that doesn't mean it's coming any time soon."

It had to be over a hundred degrees in this room. I'd bought them a couple of fans from Home Depot, which moved the air around but didn't cool it off. Nothing could cool it off in here.

"I can stay a little while longer," I told Hank. "Do you want to go for another walk? Get some fresh air?"

"I could walk for fifty miles and it wouldn't change anything. You know what's weird about the Shanti people? The Angel Food people? They don't know what to do any more than we do. They're just as scared as we are." Hank closed his eyes. "I don't think I can stand this. I don't think I can go on with it."

I got up, went for a tour of the little house. There was my painting right by Ben's bed, and another painting I'd done of Hank alone where the biker poster had been. There were a few dirty dishes on the kitchen sink—I rinsed them out. I turned on a sprinkler in the front yard.

I got an idea for another painting—the Junction, just the way it was, poor and crowded, full of gang kids and immigrant families. Santa Monica pitching into Sunset, and Benjamin, sick and sweet, wonderful and splendid in every way, being assumpted into heaven. Everyone in the street looking up with polite interest.

"I've got a deck of cards in the van. Want to play some cards? Gin rummy?" I wanted to go home, but I knew I couldn't.

"Why not?"

We played through the afternoon, or at least until around seven, when Hank noticed that Ben had gone thirty-five minutes without throwing up. This was good news, he told me, and whispered that maybe they both might get to sleep through the night if Ben kept tapering off. I thought it over, thought it over some more. I couldn't get a handle on it. I couldn't figure it out. The kid was seventeen. He was going to die, going to die right here, in this time frame, in this city, in this house, probably. There was nothing I could do about it.

By 8:30 I couldn't stand it over there a minute longer. I couldn't think of a good reason to leave so I just left. Hank stood at the front door and watched me go. I could feel him looking at me, but I didn't look back.

Driving home, I began to freak all over again. I hadn't worn gloves all the time I'd been handling Ben's vomit. I knew I didn't have any cuts on my hand, but there was the beginning of a canker sore somewhere inside my mouth. (I remembered one of my granddad's raddled old girlfriends coming up to me once at a picnic: "Did you ever have a sore right *here*?" And then having to listen to some terrible story about venereal disease back in World War II.) Suppose I'd stuck my fingers in my mouth this afternoon? Bitten my fingernails? It could happen.

"Suppose you're fucking nuts," I said out loud. "That could happen too."

Still, I felt queasy as I pulled into the garage. My stomach heaved. "Probably just a virus. The kid probably just had a virus, and maybe I caught it," I muttered. Then I thought, damn *right* he has a virus, and maybe I caught it! But as I stepped down from the van, something else caught my attention: big, loud man's sobs. Coming from the kitchen.

Austen had installed himself in his favorite place, the empty refrigerator alcove. He sat on his broad butt with his knees up to his shoulders and sobbed into the hem of his sweatshirt. The whole front of his shirt was soaked with tears and snot. June Shaw knelt down by him trying to pat his shoulder. Instead of being grateful for the attention, he tossed his head away from her and kept on roaring. Even Dave had come out to the kitchen to see what was up with the guy.

"What happened?" I asked. I had to raise my voice above the noise.

"He got some kind of letter," Dave said, "from the university. He's out."

"I'm not well," Austen sobbed. "Call a doctor. I'm dying. I'm going to die."

"Well, *shit*," I said. I went to the fridge, found a beer on my shelf, opened it up. "What a fucking crock."

That caught June's attention. "Toad!" she said. "Scum!" She scrambled to her feet and shoved me hard in the chest. "Oaf!"

I clenched my fist and raised it, remembered she was a woman, and stopped.

"He got dropped from graduate school! That's the end of his career! It wouldn't matter to someone like you. You couldn't understand it!"

"What are you picking on me for? I didn't do anything. How'd he get kicked out?"

By this time Austen had managed to curl his big sleepy body into a fetal ball. He mashed his face against the far wall of the alcove and turned his back to us. The partition shuddered with his sobs. He made a hell of a racket.

"He missed the German deadline because of his work on the hunger strike. We'll have them up on charges for this!"

"But didn't he miss his deadline? Isn't that what the letter said? So, he knew what he was doing, didn't he?"

"Moron!" June really did seem upset.

"I just want to ask both of you something." And only my day with Hank and Ben would have allowed me to ask it. "The whole world knows there aren't any jobs out there for what you people are trying to do. So what are the both of you even doing in school? Why don't you get real jobs, so you don't have to pull this stupid shit any more?"

She shoved me again, hard. For a second time! This time I shoved her back. She went flying across the linoleum, landing with a thud against the stove.

"OK, *buster*," she shouted at me, "get ready for the lawsuit of your life!"

But I felt something in my body, beginning somewhere in my solar plexus and flooding up behind my ears. I watched myself, about one-tenth of me still calm and interested while the other nine-tenths began to go berserk.

"Give it a rest, you . . . baboon! Get out of this room before I break your scrawny arms. Out. Out!" I surprised myself. It wasn't like me.

She worked her lipsticky mouth but she didn't move. Maybe she couldn't.

"You aren't worth my time," I told her. "You!" I said to the beige lump in the alcove. "Get up, you worthless heap!" I watched as my own running shoe shot out and began prodding Austen's soft back. "Get up. Get up! Be a man. *Fake* it, for Christ's sake!"

"I'm not well," Austen said. "I've been through a lot. People have died in my family."

I kept pushing at him. "Do you know anything about it? You don't know anything about anything."

"Don't take that from him!" June Shaw screamed, but I showed her my clenched fist again, and she took a step back.

"Get up! Act like a man."

"Maybe he'd like to go to his room," Dave suggested, but I grabbed the back of Austen's shirt and tugged. "You think life is awful? *I'll* show you awful."

"Don't! You'll tear my clothes." But one way or another, Austen got up.

"Wipe the crap off your face. I'm taking you for a ride."

Austen sat beside me in the van while we made the short run down to Manzanita. His big body still quivered and sighed every once in a while, but you could see he was getting curious too. We parked and I went around to the passenger side to open the door. "Get out, asshole. We're paying a visit."

Hank opened the door right away. "How'd you know? He's gotten worse again."

I could feel my temper draining away. "I've got a friend here, Alec Austen. He wants to help out. He's going to sit with you for a while. I'm going out for some burgers for all of us. And some more beer."

Hank spoke right to Austen, telling his same old story. It didn't seem to matter that he was talking to a stranger. "I can't do it anymore. I know I have to, but I'm afraid I can't. I'm afraid of what I'll do."

Austen let himself be led into the next room. I watched his face change as he saw Ben.

"Back in a while," I told them. They didn't answer.

Through the evening, Austen helped with the bucket and rubberized pads. In between, the three of us sat out in the living room, talking, keeping our voices down.

"Where's his medication?" Austen asked at one point. "Even a Thorozine suppository for the nausea would have to help. And all the other drugs. Why doesn't he have them? Aren't there clubs where you can buy them wholesale?"

Hank explained again that they'd just come out from Ohio, that they didn't have much money. That they couldn't go to their families. That some organizations were helping, but they couldn't afford protease inhibitors. Or much of anything. I watched that familiar expression of sullen outrage come over Austen's face.

It was so late by now, and I was so tired. I sat nodding in my chair, getting up with the other two every twenty minutes, until, about one, the intervals began stretching out again. The kid appeared to settle down. It looked like he might be tuning up for a real sleep.

"I guess we'd better be going," I said.

"I'm staying here," Austen whispered to Hank. "Is that all right?"

I drove home, aching for sleep.

So, by the end of August, Austen had another cause. He lurked in the hall outside his bedroom when he was home, and all of us took to using the back door to avoid his little sermons. "Did you know that thalidomide can stop mouth ulcers from AIDS in only four days? Not only that, but it significantly reduces the amount of the virus, the viral *load,* in everyone who takes it? People have to organize to outsmart the drug companies. All *they* want to do is get rich off this epidemic. Why would you want to eliminate your own best market? Does Philip Morris try to get people to stop smoking?"

Austen gave us all reproachful stares, as though we'd been out spreading AIDS. But June Shaw practiced militant abstinence, and Dave's Tai Chi method hadn't worked with sex, so far.

"You're the Typhoid Mary, Bob," Dave told me, trying to joke about it. "You're the one who turned him on to this. And you're the king of unsafe sex around here."

I had more than one shiver of doom thinking about just that. I always had plenty of condoms but never quite enough. I even thought, sometimes, of going down to be tested. But I didn't go. Common sense told me I was OK, but late at night, lying awake, common sense didn't always work. And there was Austen the hall sentry now, telling everyone who came through the front door to repent, abstain, refrain.

So, none of us came through the front door if we could help it.

It was late, late August, the worst time of the year in LA. Dog days. August 18th was my absolute last chance to enroll in Otis for the fall semester, their last semester in their "picturesque" downtown location. I had to get my portfolio downtown quick if I wanted either a scholarship or financial aid. I loaded up some stuff and rolled on down in my van to Wilshire Boulevard by MacArthur Park. The admissions people liked my work, although I'd never managed to do the self-portrait. I got in, with a partial scholarship and a substantial student loan. Instead of illustration or surface design—which would at least guarantee me a future career with some commercial outfit—I chose a couple of classes in fine art, kind of a last wave at what I knew now I could never be. Classes were due to start September 3rd.

The end of summer. I came home from a day replacing doorknobs and water faucets in a bad motel on Western Avenue, stinking of sweat and roach powder. I couldn't get over the idea that some people deliberately chose to live in ugliness, as if there weren't enough of it around already. I'd seen unflushed toilets, even with water in the pipes, because people were too—what? depressed? demoralized? trashy?—to move their arms up to a flushing position. I'd seen bathtubs filled with magazines, because people hadn't planned on taking a bath any time soon. And roaches. My God.

I ducked into the shower and heard screams from the kitchen, female screams, almost as bad as Mrs. Walker's when the snake got out. I knew I should go over and see the Walkers, she'd called and left a couple of messages, but I couldn't. They wanted too much from me, these women. They thought I was there to fix stuff for them and have sex. I was function and form to them, not content. "They don't care about the *real* Bob," I said out loud as I showered. I meant it to be a joke on myself, but my voice came out serious and bitter. The screams were still going on as I got dried.

In the kitchen, June Shaw held the telephone to her head and shrieked into it. She wore a white lace bra and panties, a cardigan sweater and tennis shoes.

"I've always paid back every loan I've got from you *with interest!* Ten percent interest! I will *not* type my life away like you did. I *will* have a career, whether you help me or *not!*"

I slid past her to the dining room, where Dave had opened his shoe box and was rolling a joint. He had a ball of hash about the size of a thumb in front of him, with a nice pile of shavings. Dave sprinkled them in with the mounded weed, then licked and twisted the paper.

"Want some?"

"Yeah." I reached in my wallet and pulled out some twenties.

"Not necessary."

"Take it. For next time."

Dave folded the money into his pocket. "Hot as hell."

"*Tell* me. I must have had five thousand cockroaches on me today."

"Hard day at the office, dear?"

"Ah, man . . ." I sat down and shook my head. I felt like shit.

Dave gestured toward the kitchen with his head. "She's having a guy over for dinner tonight. Wants to put food on this table. Wants me to move my stuff."

Of all the women in the world, we had to be living with this one.

"OK," I said. "Let's do it now. It'll only be worse later." The hash gave me that itchy feeling in my chest, and I took another deep drag on the joint. I heaved myself up and grabbed a pile of books. Dave took another one, and we stowed them under the sideboard. Two more moves and the table was clear, except for the shoe box and the hash, which we took with us to the sunken living room.

"She's not going to like this," Dave said. "She was looking forward to another fight."

"Her mother's getting it now."

"Yeah. Would you say it was *hot* around here?"

I went back down the hall to my room to take off my shirt and hang it up. The door to Austen's room was open. "Did you know there's a church in Pasadena that does more proportionately for AIDS victims in this city than Shanti and APLA put together?"

"No," I said. "How's Ben? I'm not going over this afternoon."

"The same."

Dave waited for me out on the living room couch, and we spent the next couple of hours getting seriously stoned.

June's date stood her up. By that time it seemed like too much trouble to move everything back in the dining room. By eight o'clock the sun had gone down, and by nine it got dark. One more day gone.

No one bothered to turn on the lights. Dave and I sprawled on the couch. June and Austen were in here some place.

"I have to decide what I want to do after I graduate," June said. Her voice was surprisingly low. "I want to do women's studies, but there's no point to it. Men hate women. I have to be well known in my field, whatever field it is, and the deck is too stacked against women."

"At least you're still in school." But Austen didn't sound too messed up about it.

"I want a life. A life. Just a life." Dave talking.

"You have a life," I said. It seemed like it took an hour to say it.

"I don't think so. I don't think we do. Do you know where we are? Halfway up a hill. People don't even know where we are. We're like the clear skin between zits. They can't even see us. They can't even find us. They don't know we're here."

"You have to do stuff. *Deeds,*" Austen said. "You have to have a reason."

"My mother hates me." June reached out in the dark, took a joint from my fingers.

"Christ's sake, June. She doesn't *hate* you. Isn't that kind of *old*? That whole idea?"

"She does, though. Never liked me at all."

Dave coughed. "None of us are married. We don't have children. None of our parents have ever even seen this house. In the simplest philosophical terms, we aren't here."

"We're here." Austen's sweaty face was round as a pie plate. It moved as he spoke. "We're here. But there's so much to do. I can see that. I'm afraid we can't do it."

Moonlight shone through the picture window. My eyes saw them all in outline: Dave, on my right, slumped on the couch in perfect relaxation, and then the square of moonlit glass and the piano that nobody played, and then Austen, crouched on a thrift-shop hassock, tormenting himself as usual, poor guy. Down on the floor, all white skin and right angles, was the electric June. Where were our families? Our parents, our children? We're all we've got right now, I thought. This is what we've got. The room, which never seemed too grounded to begin with, slipped its moorings and sailed with us across the sky. You can't worry too much about a speck of cosmic dust, I thought, sailing away. It isn't worth the effort.

"The thing is to be famous. Make them *know* we're here." June's voice had an interesting tremor to it tonight, like a scratchy violin. Probably from yelling so hard.

"Your voice," I said, "sounds like a violin."

"Man," Dave said. "These artists."

"I'll never be. An artist. You know what I need? A cold beer for my hashed-out throat."

I woke up the next morning, and knew before I opened my eyes that I wasn't alone. Information came in; a head resting by my head. A bed that wasn't mine. When I did open my eyes, there was the sun and that damn eucalyptus. Not my tree, though. This was the corner room. Kate's room. June's room.

I moved, very slightly. Her arm came further over across my ribs. I wasn't going to be able to sneak out of this.

Quietly, I moved my head back to see her more clearly. As long as I'd done this fool thing I might as well pay attention.

Her skin was perfectly pale and very clear. How would you paint it, that skin? Her lips without the lipstick had a nice old-rose tint. I could see her hand on my chest. She had long fingers, close-clipped nails. She was very clean. Thin arms. She breathed quietly. She smelled good.

She opened her eyes and blushed.

I kept quiet, waiting for the cyclone.

She got up, carefully keeping her back to me, went to the closet, put on a robe, and went out to the bathroom. I could have jumped up then, sprinted down the hall. I could pretend it never happened. I stared at her few outfits in the open closet. That shiny brown suit. Those matching brown oxfords.

She came back in quietly, closed the closet door and the door to the hall. She'd combed her hair and splashed water on her face.

She sat down on the bed, looked at me, glanced away.

"Listen," she said.

I listened.

"I'm sorry." Her voice still had that scratchy violin texture. It made me take hold of her hand.

"No. Don't. We can't do this again."

I widened my eyes. *Why*, I telegraphed. *What on earth do you mean?* I didn't dare open my mouth.

"There's a disparity, an intellectual disparity. It's not your fault."

I turned my head away from her.

"There's no room for a person like you in my life. We have to go on living as though this never happened."

Acting completely on their own, my hands opened her robe. Her breasts stared watchfully out into the distance. Her body had a separate personality. A nice one.

"*Don't!* We have to pretend we were never together."

I let the robe fall back in place. Remembered the bed had another whole side to it and rolled on out. I found my shorts and got them on some way. I pulled on my T-shirt. Then I stopped for a minute. Put a hand on her cheek. She blushed again, hung her head.

I got out of there quick. Headed for the kitchen. Poured some coffee.

Dave was already up, and looked at me with something like awe. "God's gift to women," he suggested. "Would that be it?"

All I could do was shake my head. Words failed me.

CHAPTER

16

A few days after my night with June Shaw, I stood in the driveway of the house while a nice woman in her thirties wrapped me up in crepe-paper ribbons. I wore a shirt and shorts and tennis shoes, which left my arms and legs free to be wrapped. The woman had lettered a sign that she fastened around my neck:

ONE FULL DAY OF SERVICE
ONCE A WEEK FOR
SIX GLORIOUS WEEKS

She fooled around with extra crepe-paper strips, tying a big floppy bow around my neck.

June came out the door, dressed today in barf-green socks, green shorts and shirt, and a Donald Duck baseball hat pushed back on her head. She took in the two of us and sneered. "Some-body's present? Aren't you *farfetched*!"

"Yeah?" I said. "Look who's talking!"

"Who is that person?" my wrapper asked.

"She lives here."

"A roommate?"

"Up to a point."

"Well, you *will* be a present. A nice gift. Remember, we want you to go the full eight hours, ten to six, or maybe eleven to seven. It's the time as much as the work. We all chipped in for this. Shel-ley might want to send you home but you just stay, keep her com-pany. We're all so worried about her. She doesn't know what hit her. Once a week for six weeks. See if you can cheer her up."

"I may have to speed up the process. I'm going back to school in a week or so. What happened again? She broke up with her husband?"

"He did that thing where he didn't come home from work one night. He only talks to her now through a lawyer. She had no idea it was coming."

"How do you know her? Did you go to school together?"

"The park. We all take our kids there. We've known her from her first one. That's three years ago. She doesn't show up anymore."

I was wrapped up like a mummy by now. The only thing left was to hoist myself into the van. The woman getting me as a gift lived right here on the hill, only two blocks away. I wished that I could get a look at myself dressed as a present, but that wasn't going to happen. I took a check for today's work in advance, grabbed a he-lium balloon she handed me, zipped along Dahlia and turned right on Micheltorena toward Sunset, heading down for less than a block.

Again, the unmowed lawn tipped me off. That, and a few dozen shitty plastic toys on the porch. The house looked like it might be ready to burst into tears. I got out, walked up the path, and knocked on the door.

The woman who answered was taller than I was but looked at least ten years younger. She looked like a great big child.

"Shelley?"

"What is it?"

"I'm a gift."

"I don't want one." Her face was swollen and pink.

"Your friends—all of them from the park—got together to give me to you as a gift. What does it say?" I fumbled with my sign, turning it so I could read it. " 'One full day of service once a week for six glorious weeks.' I'm a handyman. So put me to work."

It was a crappy little house, and it was a fucking mess, just for a change. The windows were closed and the summer air had cooked up that familiar smell of rotten food and very old diapers. Christ, I thought. I'm a handyman, not a housemaid. I watched my step as I followed her out to the kitchen table, where she must have been sitting. I passed a kid sleeping on the couch, one crying over in the corner, and, here on the table, a third one, sweaty and white and half asleep, strapped into a baby seat.

"What do you want to do?" She didn't seem the least bit surprised or pleased.

"Could you give me a hand getting unwrapped?"

She only looked at me as I started pulling off my strips of crepe paper.

"Should we start with some laundry? Do you have a machine here?"

She nodded. She seemed unconscious, totally dazed. I looked around the kitchen. It was something like the Walker house the first time I'd seen it, every inch of surface covered with dirty dishes and dirty clothes and kids' crap of every kind, but this place was small and cramped and old and dark. I found a machine on the back porch, checked to be sure there was detergent, and put in the first load, bending down and picking up stuff right next to my feet, right where I stood. *Pòco a pòco.* Another world going down the drain. How many people around the city were in a fix like this? How long had she been like this?

"Do you mind if I open a couple of windows?" The smell of the place was close to making me gag. I went back into the kitchen—there wasn't any dishwasher—ran water in the sink, and began washing dishes. She sat at the table, not even looking at me, and two of the kids still went on crying. How could things get so bad? How could anybody let things get like this?

I filled the drainer with a first batch of clean dishes, went to the back door, opened it, and checked out the yard: just a sad trash heap of weeds and broken toys. But the fresh air was good, and that gave me an idea. I found an empty trash can, put it on the porch, and made a run through the house picking up bags of used Pampers off the floor, throwing them in the trash. Then I opened up all the windows, every window in the damn house.

Two hours later I was still at it. Loads of laundry, batches of dishes. I hit the bedrooms and peeled off dirty sheets. One kid who'd been crying quieted down and napped on the floor. The woman—Shelley—had some papers, along with the baby, on the kitchen table. She stared at them and ignored me. Around one in the afternoon, I said, "Would you like me to go out and get us some hamburgers?"

She barely nodded her head. I got a little irritated. I'd been working my ass off! Still, I got in the van, peeled out, hit a McDonald's and the mom-and-pop down at the Junction, came back with three burgers, six cartons of milk, some bread and peanut butter. And a huge box of Pampers.

Back at the house with Shelley and the baby, I pulled some more curtains back, cleared a patch among the papers, and noticed that they were bills. And that she was crying again. God! These leaky women!

"Have some lunch and you'll feel better." I handed her a burger and went out to the kitchen for some clean glasses. She chewed down the burger and drank all her milk. The whole time, tears dribbled down her cheeks.

"What are you doing there?" I said, conversationally. I certainly wasn't going to ask her how she'd gotten into a situation like this.

But it was the wrong question. She began to cry out loud.

"I can't do it. I don't know how."

She was covering a checkbook with her hand. I could see the number, 101. A new account.

"They say they'll cut off the phone if I don't pay the bill."

"Did your husband leave you without any money? Is that it?"

"No. I get two thousand a month until the divorce. And he's paid that twice, direct to the bank. But I've never written a check. He said I'd never be able to figure this out, and I can't."

"What do you mean, you can't?" And I thought that June Shaw would have taken this woman out and shot her for gross incompetence.

Like a bad kid, she moved her hand away from the checkbook a half-inch at a time. "I can't figure it out," she whispered. "He said I couldn't do anything and I can't. I don't know how to do it." Next to where it said PAY TO THE ORDER OF, she had written *two hundred and two dollars*.

"I've never written a check in my life. I married Sydney the day I got out of high school and he said he'd take care of everything. He did! He took care of things. But why did he *do* it? Why did he even marry me if he was going to do this? How could he be so mean?"

"Wait, wait. We can fix this." I found some paper towels to clean up the remains of the burgers, checked to see that the rug rats were still dozing, gathered the bills up into one stack. There weren't that many. I opened the checkbook, told her to mark 101 *void* and said, "It's easy. And don't worry if we make a mistake. We can fix it." An hour later, the paid bills were in a stack.

"Stamps?"

Her lips started quivering again and I said, "No! Stop! I can't take the waterworks!"

"Waterworks?"

"No more *crying*! Please. Now, I need your help sorting some of the clean clothes. Do you remember which stuff belongs to which kid?"

She did, sort of.

And another two hours saw the last of the dishes done, the beds aired and changed. The kids were all awake by now, looking dazed, like they'd been through a bomb blast. Shelley, raw-boned and fully miserable, had gone back to the table, watching me work.

"This won't do any good," she told me. "You have to know that. You can fix this up all you like, but it doesn't change anything. I figured that out. You clean something up, it just gets dirty."

"Where's your family? Where's your mom and dad?"

"They said I was big and stupid and I thought, all right, you want me to be nothing, I'll *be* nothing. But I *can* do this, I can get married and you'll never see me again. And so I did. I'll never ask them for anything."

"You don't see them?"

"No, because then they'd see they were right, that I'm stupider than they even thought, so, *no.*"

"They don't know your husband left?"

"They don't even know where I live. And that's it. That's all I'm going to say about it."

"OK," I said. "Here's what we're going to do next. We're putting these kids in the tub, all of them, and soaking some of the dirt off. What are their names?"

"Jennifer, Sophie, and Spencer. They're three, two and almost one. And don't ask me why so many. I don't *know* why so many!"

I put them in the tub with a squirt of detergent, sat Shelley down on the toilet to watch them, put in one last load of filthy wash, then came back.

"Did he leave you a car?"

More crying. God, she was tiresome.

"He left a car, but I don't drive. He said I was too dumb to drive."

"Do you have any plans about what you're going to do?"

"No. *No.* Kill myself, probably."

I'd found some clean shirts and shorts and pulled the kids out of the tub one by one. Dried them off, dressed them.

"Here's the deal, Shelley. You're going to take a shower. I'll watch the kids while you do it. Be sure to wash your hair. You'll feel better."

Out in the living room, I tried talking to the little rats, who were about as outgoing as their mom. But when she came out, drying her hair on a towel, at least she looked a little better.

"I'm going to go out and do some shopping for you," I said. "If you sit out on the porch, you'd get some fresh air, you'd feel better. The kids, too."

I jammed the van down to a Von's and stocked up on more milk, Pampers, baby food, canned soup, cereal, hot dogs, orange juice, vitamin pills, ice cream, cookies. When I came back, they were still lined up on the porch steps.

It was close to seven by now, but I didn't feel like I could go home. It was as though they'd melt, completely unravel, if I turned my back on them.

"So, Shelley? I know you have these good girlfriends, because they gave me to you as a present. Can you call one of them?"

"I really don't know them all that well."

"OK. OK. This is what we're going to do. We're going to open up some soup. We're going to have some dinner. Then I'm going to clean up. Then I want you to watch television until ten tonight and then try to get some sleep. I'm not supposed to come by until next week, but I'll be by tomorrow. Try not to let the stuff pile up. Put the dirty clothes in the washer right away. Rinse the dishes right away." I looked around the grim little living room. "What's your favorite color?"

"Yellow. And blue, I guess."

"You like flowers?"

"Sure."

"I'll bring you a present tomorrow. Try to keep everything a little bit picked up. I know it doesn't mean anything in the long run, but give it a shot."

Before I got to bed at one in the morning, I'd turned out one very nifty canvas of yellow daisies and one of bright blue lobelia. Between the grocery money and the art supplies, my day put me in the red about ten bucks. Well, fuck it!

The next day I was over there by seven, running an old manual lawn mower through the dead grass of the front lawn. After I whacked a couple of nails in the living-room walls and stuck up the pictures, I looked over at the big horsey girl and saw the beginnings of a chapped-lip smile.

"Looks good," I said. "Now. I'm supposed to be back in six days, but I'll probably stop by in a day or two. I want you to have some lists made up for me. What needs to be done around here, and what you'll be needing to buy, and . . . what you think you might be doing with your life. Don't even think about arguing with me, Shell! I'm going to be over here, and I'm going to be needing those lists."

I checked the kids; they looked OK. I looked at the drab house, the bright pictures. "OK, Shell? Are you listening to me?"

I drove the couple of blocks back home. It was no more than

10:30 in the morning. Just twenty-four hours since I'd been wrapped up like a present.

I stumbled into the house, called one of the women who'd hired me, and told her they'd have to take turns checking up on Mrs. Ross. I left a note for Dave asking him how he felt about doing some house painting. Then I hit the bed and tried to get some sleep, but I couldn't. The world was too damn sad.

The third morning I drove over to Shelley's house with a long narrow painting of an iguana for Baby Spencer. I liked how it looked; green and gold with Thal-Green scales on its belly and bright red claws that looked like polished nails. I brought two more flower paintings for Jennifer and Sophie's room, sweet peas, pink and blue. Very girly, but what the hell, they were girls. I hung around there for a couple of hours and talked to Shell.

That night I brought Dave by and we both rolled around on the floor for a while, playing with the kids. It was great but weird to see how just that little bit of attention could change them. And dropping by kept Shelley from sliding back into her coma.

She'd been good about her lists. I'd brought her different colored pens. In green ink, she wrote down groceries, in blue, what the kids might need, in purple, what the house needed.

The fourth day she was ready for me—beds made, kitchen cleaned up, the kids in pretty good shape and ready to go. We were going to pick up some clothes at Target. I'd already gotten her to throw out any stuff that was too grungy, or that wouldn't fit anybody anymore.

I'd been pestering the toddlers and their mom about their favorite colors and what they wanted to do. I was beginning to get the idea that maybe you couldn't change the world but you could paint sadness over, brighten the whole thing up. And maybe the bright stuff would bleed down into the interior and start changing it. It couldn't hurt! And here Shelley was, the big horsey girl, on the fourth day, her hair washed, in a clean sundress, pale but determined, ready to start.

"I couldn't do any of this if you weren't here," she told me, as we piled into the van and she buckled Spencer into his car seat.

"You used to before."

"Not really. Syd works in the clothing business downtown and he never let us go out by ourselves. He'd bring stuff home, all the stuff he couldn't sell, or what his friends couldn't sell. That's why we all look so lame. Then he'd tell us we *looked* lame and he didn't want to be seen with us! So he didn't take us with him to very many places. This is harder than writing checks, almost. I don't . . . I haven't been in . . . like even a mall, since high school. I don't know what sizes the kids are. I don't know, oh, where to buy a bedspread."

Christ! I wanted to say. Why'd you stay with that crazy creep! Why'd you hook up with him in the first place? But I'd said something like that yesterday and she'd almost defended him, saying that she was the one who got pregnant and she was opposed to abortion and she was the one who, after the first two girls, had thought that maybe a son might put Sydney in a good mood. She was the one who let the house go, and herself, so that Sydney could hardly bring himself to look at her. "I think," she'd said, "he didn't know what he was getting into any more than I did. He thought he was getting just a teenaged girl, and I was. But that's a stupid person to marry."

Sydney had even hit her a few times, but she defended him. "I would have hit *myself*, if I could have figured out how to do it." I could see her point, but I'd reminded her that Sydney-the-Creep had kept her away from her old friends, and wouldn't take her out, and just plain treated her so mean for so long that finally she ended up agreeing with that creep on his creepy assessment of her.

"Yes, but he—"

"We're not going to talk about The Creep anymore! We're going to talk about you and the kids. If you had seven pieces of clothing for each one of you, which ones would they be, and what color would they be? Make a list of them, right now."

She had. The lists were ready right now.

She sat in the passenger seat beside me, breathing deeply as I headed down Micheltorena and took a right on Sunset. Baby Spencer had already fallen asleep and the two girls, dressed up and on their best behavior, looked out the windows in the back. This was a big deal for them. Man! This job was a heartbreaker. The best thing was not to think about it. Not to give it a thought.

Target shared a parking lot with a Stroud's and a few other places. We took our time in Target, finding a nice girl to help us. I told the clerk that the kids had grown so fast nobody knew what size anybody was anymore. The girl helped them and our big shopping cart filled up with shorts and bright-colored tennis shoes and underwear.

Then I said to Shelley, with a sappy grin, "Now, *honey*, we've got to find something for you!"

She looked like she might tear up again, so I nudged her and said, "Color! Remember your favorite color. And let's go find some stuff."

We bought her three big T-shirts in white and yellow and navy blue, with shorts to match. And tennis socks with gold lace on the cuffs, and white tennies.

It was still early, no more than eleven. Out in the killer sun, I noticed a Fantastic Sam's and herded them all in for haircuts. The guy, a sweating Middle Easterner, made all kinds of faces at their raggedy-ass cuts but shampooed and clipped and snipped, and in less than an hour they all looked pretty good.

Then I grabbed Shelley's house list, checked out the kids, who seemed in a daze of happiness, figured they were up for one more errand, stashed what we'd already bought in the van, and rolled everybody into Stroud's.

"Two bedspreads, three pillows, something for the crib, and we'll get the rest later. Pick your favorite color now!"

The girls had no trouble picking lavender cotton for their twin beds and Shelley went straight to a swirling floral print that had a lot of light gold in it. "Because when I said yellow, I really meant gold." With no hesitation at all, she bundled pillows into their basket, and when we got to the cash register she had her checkbook ready, with her Social Security card as identification.

"Don't you have a driver's license?"

"I don't drive," she reminded me. Incredibly, Shelley started laughing, and looked over her shoulder at me.

"Before this month is over, Shell, you will."

I had a bright idea in my mind. I bought them all more burgers at McDonald's, then headed south on Vermont to LA City College, paid to park, and hustled them all out onto the lawn in front of the Administration Building for a picnic. "Because I just wanted you to see how close this place is to your house, Shell, and how easy it would be to take some courses."

She looked trembly. "The one thing Sydney promised is that I'd never have to work. He said if I stayed home with the kids, I'd never have to work. So I don't have to go to school, do I?"

"Staying home all day with three kids is a regular barrel of laughs. I couldn't help noticing how much you've been enjoying it."

Sitting on the grass with the sun shining down on her freshly cut hair, she looked absolutely young. Of course, she wasn't much older than any of the students out here with us on the lawn.

"I know I have to earn a living some day."

"Nah. That's not what I'm talking about. I don't want you to learn how to mess with somebody else's medical records or work on the computer for some asshole. Remember, Shell, what I've been saying to you? *What's your favorite color?*"

"I don't know. I don't."

"That's why you take college classes—to find out what you like."

"I'm too stupid."

I didn't even try and argue with her. "What's your favorite subject? There has to be something."

She looked at me, drawing a blank. The kids, who might have been carriers for sleeping sickness, had crashed by now, all three of them, their cheeks against the grass.

"You don't want them to grow up hearing you say that, that you're stupid?"

"No!"

"Well, so? I'm going into the Ad Building to pick up a fall catalog and schedule of classes. When I come back, I want you to have a list for me. OK? OK?"

When I came back, she did. French. History. Music.

It was a start.

By the time we got home it was after three in the afternoon. Shelley and I worked together putting things away, and put on the bedspreads. She actually laughed a couple of times. I couldn't help it, I was impressed. The hellhole with four suffering souls in it I'd come into just a few days ago had changed into a plain, semi-cheerful cottage with a nice mom and three cute kids. They still seemed sandblasted by life, but they weren't going to kill themselves anytime soon.

"You know," I said, as we drank lemonade and rested, "I have two thoughts. Dave's going to help me for a few days doing some painting in here, OK? And—what about a class in estate planning?"

"What's that?" At least she didn't look like a whipped dog, admitting there was yet another thing she didn't know.

"You know those ads on television, where they say if you'd started saving a hundred a month when you were twenty-one you'd have a billion bucks to retire on when you're sixty-five? Well, you're only twenty-two. And you can certainly spare a hundred a month, maybe more. You just have to learn how to invest."

"I can't do that!"

"Neither can I. But if you took a class in it you could teach me. You could give me tips."

"That would chap his ass!"

"Excuse me?"

"It would chap Sydney's ass if I got rich!"

"Then I think you've got to do it."

"I can't go to school. It's a nice dream, but I can't drive and there's nobody to stay with the kids."

"That's your car in the driveway?"

"Sydney's other car."

I jumped up, grabbed the phone, dialed my own number. "Dave? I'm at Shelley's. Can you come over for an hour and watch her kids? I'm going to give her a driving lesson."

In five minutes Dave was there. I had to tease her and threaten her but pretty soon I maneuvered Shelley out to the car, where she sat in the driver's seat, telling me she couldn't do it. But then she changed her mind. Jerking Sydney's Acura into reverse, she made a wide, crazy circle out into the street, crunched into first, and careened down onto Sunset. I sat in the passenger seat and prayed. But she did remarkably well, so well that I got her to stop by a nursery to pick up a couple of pony packs of marigolds. "Since I didn't know until today gold was one of your *real* favorite colors."

Her smile was unexpected, and still incredibly new. She smiled as she drove us back, remembered to signal on Sunset when she turned left, and she didn't spook going up the hill. She even hit the driveway pretty well, before she stopped the car with a tremendous jolt. Dave and the kids waited on the porch and waved. I was proud of her, blown away by this whole Pygmalion trip.

"I did take Driver's Ed, you know," she said. "I got a B in it."

She looked new and fresh. I took the credit, wished there was someone I could tell about it.

That same week, I showed up at Valerie Le Clerc's dressed to drive her on what she said were "important errands," in pressed khakis, blue shirt, nice tie, white linen sports jacket. I got a kick out of her asking me for this. I'd taken the van to be washed and stowed my handyman junk in the hall outside my room, which made June Shaw sick. "What a dilettante!" she'd said, as she surveyed my hammer, screwdrivers, miter box, boom box, and then, checking out my dressed-up self, "Going to the *doctor*?" which she evidently thought of as the last word in cutting insults.

I hopped up into my clean-and-neat vehicle, headed on out. It was one in the afternoon, a scorcher of a day, but Valerie seemed fresh as dew waiting for me in a pale gray pantsuit with a long lavender scarf. She wore wraparound aviator glasses and looked too cool for words. I liked her a lot.

"Where to, Madame?"

But, man, she wasn't young. Her neck showed it. The backs of her hands showed it. Cruising down Beachwood, I argued with myself. Who *cares*? Who's the person in charge who tells us who we should want and who we shouldn't? I consciously thought *rosemary* to stop my mind. It worked. My dick jumped. Valerie put a hand on my thigh.

"I thought we could have a day off," she said. "I thought I'd take you to lunch."

Under her direction, I drove west on Sunset through bleached-out Hollywood, with its whitish asphalt pavement and scorched buildings. And further west through the Strip, where it was still sweltering but at least business was booming, with guys dressed like I was today and chic young girls sitting out in sidewalk cafés where the temperature had to be 110. No Mexicans here, except rich ones and busboys; a different world from Silver Lake, the Junction, the Micheltorena Hill. Every sign here was in English.

We zoomed on all the way to the coast, then south to Ocean Park. I concentrated on driving, past crowds of pedestrians who didn't seem to be doing jack shit on a weekday, nothing, nothing at all.

"Turn here," Valerie said.

I did, and parked. We walked back up to Main. She stayed ahead of me and I watched her, a little squirt of a thing, elegant as hell.

"Here," she said. "I thought this might be fun."

Lula, a Mexican restaurant, with windows open to the sidewalk, painted in lemon, whole walls of lemon and bright green and tingling blue, but what made my stomach turn, made me know one more time I was a failure, were three or four giant paintings by Carlos Almaraz, some of his great freeway stuff. I had to remind myself Almaraz was dead by now, and it was pointless to envy a dead person. But here were more paintings, pieces by Frank Romero, huge graceful cars in motion.

Romero was only twenty years older than I was, maybe twenty-two years older. He had a big house and a bundle of money and a great rep.

I had nothing.

By now we were seated out in the courtyard, next to a wall of huge skeletons by Eloy Torrez, skeletons dancing, partying down.

"Don't look *that* way, look *this* way," Valerie said, so I sat next to her and looked out across a lemon-yellow courtyard banked by purple bougainvillea. The colors made me nuts. Here were a lot of upper-middle-class . . . *butt-fucks,* eating lunch surrounded by color, taking color as their own, their right, chomping down tacos, soaking this up as if they deserved it.

A couple of margaritas calmed me down.

"I love to come here," Valerie said. "This is how the world should be. Good food, drinks, windows open to the street. People having a good time. Not thinking! I even like the skeletons. They say Mexicans are in love with death. Why not? Better than fearing it, certainly."

"Yes, I will," I said. To my third margarita.

"The music, too," she said. "I love the music." She reached over, patted my upper arm. "I only came here once with my husband. He thought it was tasteless. But I came here with other people. Friends."

Was there something I should be asking her?

"Don't have a fourth one," she said. "I need you this afternoon." A better part of my mind began to register: yellow walls, that bright bougainvillea coming out of planters at the top. And the courtyard open to the sky.

We drove up the coast to Santa Monica. Again, she asked me to park and I did, out by the palisades. I saw the blue ocean and felt the sea breeze. Old men in white trousers walked through a green but mangy park along the top of the cliffs. Valerie jumped down from the van and I followed her across the street to another building painted in an alarming shade of yellow. The Hotel Oceana.

We went up the steps into a crashingly terrible lobby painted like one of the worst, last Picassos. Valerie leaned into a counter, checking in. "Le Clerc. Suite 314?" I thought, this is it, I'm a gigolo for sure.

The elevator opened on the third, top floor. We looked down into another courtyard, this one with a pool. Again, color smashed at us—mustard yellow? No, they'd oranged it down, but it was bright, way too bright. I followed Valerie to the room, where two yellow adirondack chairs flanked the doorway. She opened the door. I followed her in, and had to laugh.

More yellow! Just fucking bright yellow. And the bedroom was done in ink-blue wallpaper with two big white beds. And the bathroom was painted a clammy persimmon. Someone had gone nuts in this place. Or had a lot of fun.

She'd been here before, this morning. The second white bed had a white nightgown, white pajamas, a basket of fruit, some chilled champagne, some fresh herbs. For a second I thought *this is going to be too weird*! But I shuffled a little drunkenly up to her and planted a big kiss on the back of her neck. The years peeled back, or, more to the point, they didn't matter. I yanked off her cool linen and there she was in a lot of steel-gray satin and we thrashed around the bed, loud and athletic.

The first time was over and it was only three in the afternoon.

I wanted to do it again. Immediately. But she felt like a shower, just a shower, so I took one with her.

She cracked open the champagne and I sprawled out across the bed, drinking, feeling fine. I could do this forever. Make a living at it.

She closed the wooden slats on the windows. The second time

we did it in real deep gloom. I felt myself losing myself, I gave my-self up to it, didn't think about it.

At six, she ordered up caviar from room service.

I stretched out on the bed and listened to her set up a little pic-nic in the living room.

Caviar. There were people in the world who did nothing else but this. Eat caviar. Drink champagne. She'd cracked the wooden slats again so that one wall of the suite opened up to outside light, and I saw that the yellow walls colored the air in here, made every-thing golden.

A couple of hours later, while the sun was still up, she opened the door and went boldly out to put her arms on the railings that marked off this curving third floor. I followed her in my paja-mas. Three floors below us, the pool was empty, inviting and—to my eyes, anyway—sinister. You could cool off there, or die. The yellow building pressed around me, each story marked off by banks of purple petunia, blue lobelia. Down by the pool, someone had set up a buffet. Businesswomen in party dresses, the long flowered print skirts of Southern California, drank white wine and laughed.

At the other end, a grandma was having trouble with three lit-tle kids. "Careful! Be careful! Janet! Antoinette! Michael! You'll fall—"

Janet and Antoinette teetered safely along the side over to the lobby and the drinking businesswomen. Michael headed straight to the pool and plunged right in the deep end.

My whole body lurched. I climbed onto the railing, but Michael bounced right up to the surface and hauled himself out. His mother appeared and yanked him into the room. Hell was going to be raised. I felt queasy. I went back inside.

I told Valerie about it, about Tod, about Landry, about Milli-cent. About Angela.

We sat on the couch, holding hands. It was dark now.

"Valerie, this has been wonderful, you've been really wonderful . . ."

"I know we have to stop. You have to find your own life. But I wanted to give us this afternoon."

"What . . . will you do now?"

"Find out ways to be happy." She patted my arm. "*More* ways to be happy."

I didn't know what to say.

"I need to be of use," she said. "I suppose I'm sorry now I never had children. Wally and I thought mostly of ourselves."

"Wait a minute. Children? Are you telling me you like kids?"

"Yes, of course. How could I not?"

"I know a woman and some children who need you. I mean, they *need* you! But kids are messy. They're hard work. Can you deal with that?"

"Robert! What else am I supposed to do? Go on fucking and hosing until the grave?"

"Fucking and hosing? Did *you* say that?" I reached across the couch and grabbed her. For the last time.

"But remember," she said later in the dark, "I want you to remember about color. I never had enough of it, but you can have as much of it as you want. That's why I brought you to this silly, wonderful place. And don't mistake peace for happiness, as I did, for so long. Don't stay indoors, because time is so short, there's so much to see. And . . ."

"Don't worry. I'll remember all of it." A wave of what you'd have to call tenderness washed through me. I wanted to hold her and hold her, and not think about anything.

And I did.

On my last day—actually my eighth—as a present for Shelley, I got there early and brought Dave along to help. We were going to paint the girls' room and wanted to get done by noon. We moved beds around and laid drop cloths and I mixed up a pale yellow that—along with my flower pictures and those lavender spreads— made the space look like the inside of a really good Easter egg.

As we were cleaning up I got one of my ideas and checked with Shelley, who was out back watering the new flowers and playing with the kids. Would she like just one yellow wall in the living room, to pick up some sunlight in the morning? And maybe some whitewashed bookshelves, since I had those boards in my garage. Sure, she said, and Dave and I got busy with drop cloths all over again. We were finished by one in the afternoon. She gave us lunch. Dave could have gone home, but there didn't seem to be any point to that. We were all having a pretty good time.

"Would you guys like to stay for dinner? What if I made a couple of salads and some lemonade?"

She was looking great today, sleek as a seal, flushed and clean and happy. "Why don't I call that Valerie Le Clerc and see if she'd like to come over? I'd like the kids to know her better if she's really going to be taking care of them."

Yeah, sure, we said we'd like to stay. It wasn't as if we had anything better to do.

"But this doesn't mean I'm really going to do it, go back to school. I'm not promising anything!" For a big girl, she was acting downright kittenish.

Dave spent most of the afternoon putting up a swing for the girls in the backyard; I drove out for a few more pony packs of flowers. Valerie came over about five with a couple of bottles of wine and an apple tart. When Jennifer and Sophie saw her come in, they went straight for her legs and held on.

I kept thinking that this was my last day. I'd be coming back by, of course—Shelley and I were friends by now—but this was my last assignment in a professional capacity this summer. I took a lot of pride in what I'd done here. Shelley had her learner's permit to drive, her finances were in order, she was beginning classes on Monday at LACC, if she didn't change her mind, and the house looked great, considering. But mainly, Shelley herself was my big source of pride. All she'd needed was some friends. And a car. And a nice place to live. And a project. I had to think about it from an educated point of view. Could you really override a whole shitty life in just eight days? Maybe that was oversimplifying it. But what if it wasn't?

The afternoon turned into evening. It was hot, but not too hot, and we all took turns with the kids. We thought about eating outside but opened every window and the back door, and set a table in the living room instead. Things were looking good! I'd painted this table and these chairs a pale green last week; Valerie didn't have to worry, I was going ape-crazy with color here. I'd slapped a brush on everything that gave the least hint of being sad and gloomy. I'd surrounded this girl Shelley with the colors of what—bravery? I'd made it so she'd . . . have to be happy.

Because the thing about Shelley was that she didn't seem to have any yearnings to be someplace else. She didn't seem to be feeling all that bad about her husband; she took every little improvement or triumph as if it were winning the World Series or the Pulitzer Prize. I felt strange taking money for having fun hanging out with her. But when I remembered my first couple of days over here, I thought, yes, I deserved all the money, and probably a bonus.

Dave turned on a sprinkler, an old-fashioned one, in the backyard, and brought the girls in the house to get their hands washed. I set the table—was I going to turn out to be an interior decorator after all this?—playing around with yellow napkins against the green wood. Valerie went out back to get some mint to put in a vase—for the fragrance, she said. Then she and Shelley brought out bowls of tuna salad and spinach with olive oil and hard-boiled eggs. I put on a CD of Elvis Costello from my collection, another thing I'd added around here to cheer things up. Baby Spencer, who'd just started to walk, staggered from room to room playing peekaboo with anyone who'd go for it. I took a deep, appreciative breath. The place even smelled good, mint and fresh paint and food and flowers, a lot different from the stink I'd found when I'd come in eight days ago. We wandered around, getting set up at the table, and finally we were all sitting down except for Valerie—looking very nice tonight—who made one last run to the kitchen to bring out a plate of fresh fruit.

Then the front door opened and Sydney Ross walked in. It had to be him. He was a wiry man, you could see he worked out. He wore a shiny sports jacket, and looked straight at the floor. "We've got to get something straight!" he raved. "I left because I *had* to!

Life had become intolerable for me. My parents say I was irresponsible. Have you been talking to them? I forbid you to do it! *You* were the one who was irresponsible! I will *not* be railroaded into coming back. They can't make me do it. You can't make me do it. I'm still a young man. *No* one should be forced to live the way I was living."

"Sydney," Shelley breathed, and he looked up and took us all in. I could see that, for half a second, he thought he'd blundered into the wrong house.

"Sydney," she said again, and looked sick. "Would you like some dinner?"

"No. No thank you!" Still, he stood in the doorway, looking around. Valerie poured lemonade. You could hear ice cubes clinking in glasses. Elvis kept on singing. The kids looked at him. Sydney Ross narrowed his eyes. "What have you done to this place? Who are these people?"

"I'm the handyman," I said, in the loudest voice I could manage, "and this is Shelley's new baby-sitter."

"I'm just a friend," Dave said, waving affably. He was already sitting down, helping himself to the tuna.

Sydney got a look on his face and Shelley lowered her eyes. "I don't know about this. I don't know about this at all. I turn my back on you, and you fill the place with strangers!"

I kept on standing, kept my eyes on Shelley. She looked at me and took a deep breath. "They're not all strangers. What about the children? Don't you remember *them*?" She took a deep breath again, leaned back in her chair, and tried out a shaky grin. "Don't you? Sydney?"

"Well, goddamnit!"

He turned and slammed the door. And was out of there. We sat for a moment in stunned silence. Then Shelley squared her shoulders, gave a brave little smile, and said, "Well, what are you waiting for? Eat up!" After a little wave of nervous laughter, the rest of us began eating. The salads were great. Valerie's tart was terrific. And Shelley looked content.

After dinner, the women stuck the kids in the tub for their bath. Dave and I cleaned up in the kitchen. Valerie read the kids a story and said she'd be back on Monday for Shelley's first day at school. By then it was close to ten o'clock and she left.

Still, I hated to leave. My last day as a professional handyman, unless I got work on the weekend. The three of us watched a rerun of *Law and Order,* and after that I pulled myself to my feet. "Come on, Dave. We've got to give Shell a chance to get to sleep." But he didn't move. I sat back down again and we stayed on the couch as the eleven o'clock news came on, and went off.

"I guess I'm going to stay here for a while," Dave said.

Shelley grinned. A real grin this time.

"Oh," I said. "*Oh.* Well, OK. See you later."

Then I thought of wretched Sydney. "Well, *goddamnit,* Shelley," I said, "who *is* this man! Don't you think I deserve an explanation?"

But my handyman career wasn't over yet. Mrs. Landry called me Saturday morning to do some work. The arbor in their front yard had pulled away again from the front of the house. Ono thought it must have been because of a bumper crop of wisteria. I had a sneaking idea that I knew better. I'd heard the damn thing creaking and crunching as I'd done that Cyrano-Romeo thing at the beginning of the summer. Thank God, Millicent wasn't anywhere around this morning as Mrs. Landry walked me through it: "Ono didn't want to clip the vine until the last of the major growth was over, and I agree with him. But yesterday, you can see right here, he spent the whole day with it, and when he got finished, well, you can see, the arbor just pulled away from the wall, here, here, and over here."

We stood out in the front yard. Of all the neighborhoods I'd worked in this summer, I thought, Hancock Park didn't have it. The money was here, but the imagination was somewhere else, above Los Feliz where the Walkers lived, or up in the Hollywood Hills where every steep slope hid either a shack or a palace, or even where we lived, where houses always gave you a surprise. Here, it was two stories and a lawn, two stories and a lawn, two stories and a lawn.

I was jealous, I knew that's what it was. I was poor, they were rich, something like that. No. I was furious that Angela Landry would sell out herself and her kid for two stories and a lawn.

"I don't know how you're going to fix it. The arbor is wood, the wall is stucco—I don't know."

"Is it OK if I sink a couple of four-by-fours, probably three of them, one on either side, one in the middle, up against the wall, paint them white to match the walls, then lay a one-by-four on top of them, flush with the wall, just under the lattice? I'd stay away from the roots of the vine, of course. But I'd sink the four-by-fours in cement. I'll take all day today to put in the first set, the vertical ones, then I'll come back tomorrow morning and finish the job in a couple of hours. Eighty to a hundred bucks, and money for materials."

I'm not very tall, but she looked up at me. It was hot this morning and she had little beginnings of sweat under her eyes and along her cheekbones. She looked tired. But who wouldn't in this weather? I hadn't seen her since the Walker party.

Then she'd called, with that talk about the arbor.

"What do you think, then?"

"I'm sorry?"

"I said, what if I give you a blank check for the lumberyard and you start right away? I'd like it to be done before Ono comes back on Monday. He says the whole arbor ought to go; it doesn't go with the rest of the landscaping."

"*He* doesn't live here, does he?"

"I don't want to argue with him. It's better to just get it done."

She was wearing one of her long dresses, but it was so hot—and the humidity was so bad—that around her collarbones the cloth stuck to her skin.

"Can I give you the check? Bob? And you'll have it done by tomorrow noon?"

"Sure. How's Millicent? How's . . . Tod?"

"Fine."

"OK. So, give me the check. I'll start right now."

It was so hot. Hard to get anything done.

But I took some measurements and drove to the lumberyard and got the wood and a few bags of Redi-Crete and started work. In design terms, Ono was right, I could see that. The arbor cut the white front of the house in half. The wood looked dilapidated against the stucco. It had been somebody's bad idea to plant wisteria here, but it wasn't my problem. All I had to do was fix it.

I took off my shirt, found a shovel and gloves, and started digging three holes against the front of the house. The holes had to be fairly deep—about two feet. I tied a bandanna around my forehead to keep the sweat out of my eyes and every push of the shovel made me feel a little better.

Around 11:30, Mrs. Landry and Tod backed out of the driveway to do some errands. It was the first time I'd seen him since the party, but Tod remembered me. He leaned out the window and waved. "Hi, *Bah*! Bah!"

I went over and grabbed his fist in my hand.

"Bah! Wanna play?"

"Later. When we come back," his mom said, and I went on with what I was doing.

An hour or so later, another voice said, "Bob?" I turned around to see Millicent and a couple of her friends in white shorts and shirts, all part of one smothered giggle. I knew the friends must know about me, and even though I felt like a fraud, I let them take it all in, some California version of whatever that guy's name was,

Lady Chatterley's lover. The only reason I didn't hold my stomach in was that all the work I'd done this summer had trimmed every ounce of fat away. The cool handyman, for sure.

"How are you, girls?" I said, and wiped sweat off my forehead with the back of my hand.

"Oh . . . fine," Millicent said. She didn't even introduce her friends. "We're going upstairs now. Maybe we could go to a movie tonight?" She was talking to me. More giggling, from the girls.

"Well, OK," I said. "But I've got to get my work done now."

Every man should be a handyman. I'd never had a summer like this in my life.

I'd placed the vertical four-by-fours in their holes, poured the Redi-Crete by late afternoon, but the sun wouldn't be going down until eight or later, so I gave them a first coat of white paint. When Mrs. Landry came back, I said, "Millicent asked me out to the movies, is that OK with you?"

"I guess so. I guess it's all right. Be home by twelve, though. She wouldn't like me to say that, but be home by twelve."

When Tod came out in the front yard, I showed him what I'd done, then threw him up in the air a few dozen times. Millicent came out with those two nameless girls in tow, and said could we go see *Lone Star* at the Beverly Center? I'd be by at 7:15, I said, and packed up my van and left.

Back at the house, I played it for all it was worth.

"I need the bathroom, June. I've got a date. With a blonde. A young one! Of the opposite sex. You ought to try it some time."

"You plank," she said. "Go away."

"Even cretins get to have fun. How's *your* love life? Going out with that guy in the wheelchair who invented black holes?"

"Toad!"

I peered into the smelly gloom of Austen's room.

"I'm going out, Austen. On a date with a beautiful blonde."

"Grow up, Hampton."

Dave leaned back in his chair and gave me the answer I needed.

"How do you do it? It's been so long since I've had actual sex I don't even remember it. I might still be a virgin, I'll have to check the files. Although that might be changing soon."

"We're only going to a movie." But I didn't believe it and neither did Dave.

"Isn't she just a kid?"

"Yeah, yeah."

A nice kid. She was waiting outside when I came, and I was glad about that. A nice chat with Mr. Landry was not what I'd been looking forward to. She wore a white sundress with little straps. Her hair looked healthy and shiny, and she kept tossing it as we drove west to the Beverly Center, where the whole world seemed to be out, enjoying the last few nights of the summer, drinking cappuccinos, licking frozen yogurt.

"My last year was my hard year, because that was my junior year when you have to put in your first applications to college, and keep your grades up too, but I did it, and I applied to Harvard and Yale and Wesleyan and Brown, and Stanford, and, of course, Berkeley, but I really don't want to go there. We took one of those college trips back in April, Daddy and Angela and me. There was a terrible thunderstorm at Harvard. Angela liked Yale, but I really hated it. I won't get in there anyway, but I probably *will* get into Wesleyan, and probably into Brown. And this next year, this senior year, I'm only going to be taking drama and journalism, because I got everything else out of the way."

She paused for a breath and looked up at me. We strolled the third floor of the Center, waiting for the movie, checking everybody out.

"Daddy says kinesiology is nice. All of his best clients are always getting injured. But, naturally, he'd want me to do something he can relate to. Sports medicine. Or broadcasting. Or PR. Daddy really wants me to go to UCLA, but no way."

"Want to get away from home?"

"Not really. I *love* Tod! And Angela is nice."

During the movie, she put her hand on my knee. I kept my distance. We were in the real world now, the date world, and anything I tried would go down in real-world history. But it was nice, taking in a movie in high summer with a beautiful young blonde.

Afterward, she wanted ice cream. We sat at a little table with iron chairs. I watched her demolish mounds of it, bit by bit with her curling pink tongue, and then bat her lashes at me.

"You're bad!" I had to say. "You know it, too!"

"I'm playacting," she answered. "That's all."

At home, the first-floor lights were on. "Walk me to the door, give me a kiss good night, then go on up," she whispered. "I left the window open."

"Are you sure?"

"Sure!"

Why not? It was only playacting. We walked up the path to the front door, playacting. Millicent turned to me and said, "I really had a good time, Bob!" I said, "Me too, Millicent! I hope we can go out again sometime."

She said, "We'll see. I'm pretty busy getting ready for senior year. But you can call me."

I bent to give her a good-night kiss, and her tongue darted into my mouth like a minnow. My dick jolted against her and widened her eyes. "Night, now!"

I walked to the van, parked it a block away, walked back, remembered that first night, took a look at the house, realizing again that this was the last night of the summer, then shinnied up the arbor and into Millicent's room. She was waiting for me in one of her satin nightgowns. Playacting, but what a play!

I peeled off my clothes, grabbed my condoms, and leaped into her bed. Her skin felt like it did the first time, toned and buff and young. I began kissing her like crazy, really loving the look of her square white teeth in the moonlight, and the smooth blonde of her hair, and the dark of my arms against her white slippery satin. I was going too fast, but I had all night to make up for it.

"Millicent? Millicent? Have you seen . . . ?" The door opened. Mrs. Landry turned on the light, turned it right back off. "Oh. I'm sorry!" Closed the door. Her footsteps receded down the hall.

"It's OK. She won't tell. She's all right. Come on. It doesn't matter. She's OK."

Oh! I'm sorry.

I took a deep breath, let it out. Rolled over on my back. Looked at the ceiling.

"I'm going home now, Millie."

"You don't have to. Really."

"Yes, I do."

Sunday afternoon I stopped by Mrs. Walker's to say good-bye. Since the night of the big party, I hadn't been over once, but I couldn't go back to the Landrys' today, and I couldn't think of anywhere else to go on this last day before school started.

Starting back at school meant I could simplify my life. I'd be a student again. A student for as long as I could swing it. Then I'd find a . . . girl. Then I'd get a job. Work for the studios. Go back to advertising if I had to. Get a condo. (Just the word, *condo*, depressed me.) A condo. A girl. A job. I'd fake my way into the adult community. I'd live by the beach, maybe.

Something.

But first I had to simplify my life, because this summer had gotten out of control.

Before I went over, I stopped by the drugstore down at the Junction. The guy behind the counter saw me coming, and watched as

I unhooked a package of Trojans along with some LifeSavers, and put them on the counter.

"Why not buy them by the gross? You'd save a lot of time and money."

I pulled down two more rolls of LifeSavers.

"Suit yourself," the guy said.

I drove right past the Walker house, almost got lost way up in the hills, had to turn around and come back down. Then I almost drove past it all over again. The front yard fooled me. In the month or so since I'd been here, someone had been working on the lawn. It was deep, trimmed, velvety blue-green. Someone had been pouring on water with a heavy hand. The hedges around the front door looked so alive they seemed right on the edge of strolling over and saying hi. For the hell of it, I didn't go in the front way but went around out back. It was a warm day and there was a good chance of the family being out there.

I could see the turkey shed, and recognize my own painted animals still up in the trees. But the same vivid blue-green prevailed. She must have found a great gardener.

Mrs. Walker lay out in the sun on a chaise in a bikini, the backs of her hands spread out flat so that the sun could tan them to match the tint of her arms. God, how many times had I seen that in high school? Around the borders of the yard, three or four Asian guys in short-sleeved shirts puttered and clipped and trimmed.

I walked on over to her and she opened her eyes. Her fingernails and toenails were carefully done. She looked good. Better than I'd ever seen her.

"Oh!" she said. "Hi! Long time no see."

"I came over to say good-bye. I'm going back to school tomorrow. I won't be a handyman anymore."

She hitched her body up to a sitting position. "I got separated. Did you know that?"

"What happened?"

"It was right after the party. I threw him *out*, that's what happened. Michael hated the house and he didn't care about the kids, and he didn't like me. I couldn't stand him! He was a waste of my time."

She caught the eye of an Asian who was looking at her, and shook her head. *No, don't come over.*

"Did you know I have a sister? I don't think you ever met her. She lives in Calabasas, out in the West Valley, and you know how close we are here to the freeway. You can drive out to where she lives in twenty minutes. They put a new Gelson's in out there. Actually, it's a whole big building owned by Gelson's. It's a great place to shop when I'm visiting my sister. You know I'm not much the housewife."

"You're not so bad." I wondered where this was going.

"I like the kids and the animals, but I hate all the other parts. So, next to the Gelson's they have one of those Vietnamese nail places where everybody knows each other and you can get a manicure and a pedicure for twenty-five dollars and that includes the tip."

What did I care? But I had nothing better to do than listen to this.

"Besides women manicurists, they had guys. They had guys as well as women." She was looking at me intently. By now I'd sat down on the chaise next to her, my elbows on my knees.

"For ten dollars extra those guys would massage your legs for fifteen minutes, and everyone was buying that. Because none of us ever got that at home. They didn't look at the clock either. They're real human, Bob. They're very kind. They didn't count the minutes. Can you imagine? They all knew each other, and they talked in Vietnamese, all part of the same big family. There's a little girl who belongs to the owner, about the same age as Samantha. I knew you weren't coming over anymore."

"So?"

She gestured toward the guy trimming the hedge. "So, I met Tran. He speaks English and he's really nice. And his family loves my sister and me."

"He's a manicurist!"

"More of a pedicurist, actually. He's in great demand, but that's not the point. At some point I had to look at what was going on. There could be a cartoon—*What the heck is going on!* Mike had his girlfriends, that was OK. But who's going to come after a woman like me? In this city, I'm old. Well, *you* know. What was I supposed to do? Make do with a handyman and an iguana? I'm only thirty-nine. I've got to pay some kind of attention to my life."

"A handyman and an iguana! Who did you care about more?"

"You reminded me, you know. You reminded me life can be nice. But Tran needs me. It's different. It really is."

"What about the kids?" I was amazed at how pompous I sounded.

"I told you, they're a whole family out there. It's perfect for Hugh and Samantha. About a hundred cousins and uncles and aunts. I'm only beginning to figure them out. They're not failures, Bobby! They've got this great way of living. They all stay in a big house in Calabasas with a flat roof, and after dinner they go up there and sometimes they sing or somebody plays an instrument, and they drink iced coffee. They sit cross-legged and rub each other's shoulders. The women are so ladylike, but they seem very strong! They handle all the money. Sometimes we go downstairs to sleep but sometimes we all stay up there on the roof under the stars. And when they come over here—well, you can see what they do. They're very successful, Bob. They have a lot of money. They own a whole chain of nail stores. I think they're more successful than Michael. And the kids love them."

"But . . ."

"OK, *you tell me.* Tell me what I was supposed to do. Go on!"

"I . . ."

"Get a face-lift? Find some lawyer who's already dumped his own wife? Hope to God he can stand my kids? No thank you!"

"As long as you've thought this through."

"I have."

"Well. OK." I got to my feet. "I hope these guys are good with animals!"

Her face, which had been anxious, cleared. "Guess what Tran's bringing over as soon as he can find me a good one. A Vietnamese pig! They're very well behaved. And they love children."

I stopped at the first pay phone I could find on Vermont. "Hello, Ma? I want you to know I've been thinking about you a lot. I don't know what I can do for you. I really don't. But I'll try and come up with something. I'll do the best I can."

€arly the next morning, I set up the ironing board and pressed my clothes. I stood in the middle of my room and checked it out again; made bed, half-empty bureau, clean little closet, canvases stacked against one wall, table next to the window with paints. A pretty thin life, but neat as hell.

I went on down the hall to the living room. No one home today. Dave was over at Shelley's. Austen was with Ben and Hank. June was at UCLA. The whole place looked pretty poor. I went over to the picture window and took a look out. It wasn't one of those days where you could see the ocean. Far from it. I looked down at the patio filled with weeds. Seventy years ago, when somebody first built this house, the city must have been a paradise, everything must have been new. This must have been a great place.

All I really wanted to do was to drive over to the Landry house, go on out to the backyard without checking in with anyone, start pruning and clipping and painting, feel the warmth of the sun on my back, and wait for Millicent or Angela or Tod to come on out. *Oh! I'm sorry.*

Of course, I could go and see how crazy Jamey and Hugh and Samantha were doing with that whole Vietnamese pedicuring army. The thought of it made me laugh.

My laugh sounded out in the empty house. Like I was a ghost. It was time to go.

I drove left on Sunset, dropped down to Wilshire, headed downtown. It was the last semester for Otis at this "dangerous" location, although I had trouble seeing what their real hang-up was. It was just LA. The school was close to an old municipal park, where the grass was worn right down to the dirt. I was early for class and walked around. Peddlers sold toys made from beer cans, planes and helicopters of snipped-up aluminum. I walked by the side of what used to be a pure, clean lake and what had more or less turned into a bog of garbage, old tires, paper, stuff that looked like seaweed, gallons and gallons of crap, except that the sun still lit up the surface of the water. The whole damn city was turning to shit. But what was I worried about? Who was I to complain? I'd had my chance at Paris and hadn't been able to cut it.

Two classes, one in life drawing, again. One in fundamentals of design, again. What was I even doing here? In the break between classes I stood out in the courtyard, scoping people out. Along with all the *other* people scoping people out. A mile from here, Frank Romero lived, painting those goofy cars, or elephants and stars, making thousands and thousands of dollars. Just up the street on Carondelet, Tony Hernandez, the photographer, lived with his novelist wife. Both of them were part of a legend of love here in LA. I was as far away from those guys as I'd ever been. Maybe more.

"Hey, Ace? Got a match?"

A husky guy with glasses looked past me, not at me at all, as he asked the question.

"Sorry. Don't smoke."

"No problem."

A young girl came up to me next, pale and freckled, with red hair parted in the middle and held on each side by green barrettes.

"Have you, did you come here before?"

"Excuse me?"

"I mean, is this your first year?"

"Yeah. What about you?"

"I graduated from Santa Clarita last June. I just moved into the city last week. It's big!"

Santa Clarita had to be a high school up north some place. The kid couldn't have been more than eighteen.

"You're living down here? This isn't a good place for a girl by herself. What do your parents say about it?"

"They want me home with them, but I told them an artist needs to be free."

She was so short I could see the part in her scalp, white and clean and perfectly drawn. I saw that she was shivering, and just when I was going to ask her if she was OK she took a breath and said, "My name's Barbara. What's yours?" I realized she was scared to death. Of me, of Otis, of everything.

"Bob. But you can call me Ace. That's what the guy over there called me a minute ago."

"I guess . . . class is about to start again." She'd spent all her social money on me and was heading straight into bankruptcy.

The afternoon class stretched from two to six, with a half-hour break. It was stuff I already knew, of course, but it was an easy way to spend time, with sun streaming in, and students alternately concentrating on their own work or moving around, looking at what other people were doing. Across the room, Barbara seemed to have made friends with the husky guy who'd called me Ace. I went over and took a look at her work. Very clean and neat.

Soon enough it was six o'clock. The end of my first day. I made a point of saying good-bye to Barbara and not telling her to be careful going home. It was broad daylight, and it was none of my business.

I decided to go for a walk before I went home myself, and headed up a side street, past house after house, little California bungalows painted Mexican colors now, vermilion, turquoise, lemon yellow, teal blue. All the windows and doors had been shut up with elaborate wrought-iron bars, and the little yards were either crammed with potted plants and honeysuckle and bougainvillea or left to go straight to hell, with dried-out ryegrass growing right up through creaky wooden porches.

What if you just looked at *this*, instead of going to Paris? What if you took this material, the way Carlos Almaraz took it before he died, took it upon yourself to see the magic in these little houses, with the freeway hanging in the sky like a big crescent moon? But how could you paint these big stout grannies that came huffing by without looking like some social-realist nut? And what about these gang kids, doing stuff like shopping for their folks now in the late afternoon, before they went out and killed people later? I thought again of Frank Romero and Tony Hernandez up in these scrubby hills, basically the same hills I was living in now, and how easily they'd found their material. Suppose I looked back to where I really came from? Uncle Bowlie and Uncle Hack with pink cheeks, striking match after match, or my mother in her dark apartment with ivy on that crappy wallpaper, wringing her hands and using up Kleenex. It was my stuff all right, but it was too damn depressing. *Hampton's Mother*. Christ.

I hit Wilshire again and headed back toward Otis. Down here, the buildings used to be fancy and fine. Now the upper stories held

God knows what and the lower ones had furniture stores with couches on the sidewalk. Here, on a corner, a woman stood with a galvanized tub and a dipper, ladling out soup to old Mexican guys who'd brought their own bowls and jars. It had to be menudo; I could see floating bits of tripe in there. She must cook this stuff at home, haul the whole thing down to the sidewalk, sell it off, and go home again. The men hardly talked to her. They paid her in small change, took their bowls, and ate standing up.

I walked on to La Fonda, the old Mexican nightclub across the street from Otis, doing a matinee show, probably for seniors. Over the years, it had become some kind of cultural monument. I heard the mariachi out here on the street, and stopped for a minute or two to listen to the music—pure happiness in the face of a reality that frankly didn't seem to me to be all that great. The afternoon sun tinted the windows of downtown LA a mile away a garish bosom pink. Amazing, what color did.

I turned at the corner and walked up the side street looking for my van. A new Range Rover rolled past with a squeal of brakes and tires. I automatically flinched. The Rover skidded just past me, the passenger door opened, and a girl flew out, head up, feet down, walking in air. The Rover roared on and the girl crumpled, covered with blood, right at my feet. It was Barbara, the girl from class.

Her face and eyes were sheeted with blood, I doubted if she could see. Her blouse was torn and her skirt was stained with blood. A few people on the street turned away. The matinee from La Fonda must have let out; those senior citizens, old women in little hats, began to cluster on the corner. Did I hear the Rover, coming around the block again?

"Hold on to me." I picked the girl up—she was so little—and trotted with her across the street to the door of La Fonda, where the hostess gave me a stricken look.

"She's been hurt. She needs help. She fell out of a car."

"She *fell*?"

"She got pushed. We need to get her off the street." I set her down on her feet. Her skinny little legs trembled and then her knees locked.

The woman nodded her head, took the girl by the hand, and pushed her through the crowd back into the dark club. I followed them. "I'll just be here at the bar," I said. I ordered a margarita and waited. After a while the hostess shepherded the girl back out, cleaned up and shivering.

"Who'd do this? It's disgusting."

I couldn't think of an answer and the hostess didn't really want one.

"Will you see that she gets home?"

"Sure."

The girl began to cry. Tears ran down her face and her shoulders shook. Behind her, a new crop of families in their party best filed in for the early dinner show.

"Do you want to sit here for a while, Barbara? Can you hear me? Do you want a drink?" But she was probably too young to drink.

"Can I have a glass of milk?" A nasty cut along her hairline still seeped blood; I could see that even in the dark bar. Her eyes were beginning to swell shut, her upper lip had been split.

"It's my fault," she said, "my fault. I'm so *stupid.*"

"Who was that guy? The one who called me Ace?"

"Paul. You saw him today. In class."

"The big guy?"

"Yes." She picked up her glass of milk and drank, but her mouth was in such bad shape she couldn't wipe her lip. I took a napkin from the bar and carefully dabbed at it.

"He asked me if I'd like to go out for dinner and I said yes. I went home and changed and he came to pick me up. I climbed into the car, and—you know that thing in cars where the person driving can make the buttons go down?"

"Sure."

"He . . . he pushed *that*, so I couldn't get out, and then he began to hit me. Just like that."

"He didn't try . . ."

"No! Nothing like that. All he wanted to do was hit me. He was driving with his left hand and punching me with his right hand as hard as he could. He didn't say anything or *anything*! I'd try to pull up that little lock button and he'd push it down. But I undid my seat belt and I managed to open the door and then I guess I jumped out. Or maybe he pushed me." She began crying again. "But I want to know *why*? Why did he ask me out to dinner? And why did he get so mad?"

I had to walk her home. I mentioned my car but she said no thank you so quickly that I realized she was almost as afraid of me as she was of the guy who'd beat her up.

It was getting dark by now, and the cars and trucks that passed us had their headlights on. Every time a car passed she tried to hide herself behind me. I felt like hiding too. I didn't feel like I had the courage or the strength to take on an oversized homicidal maniac. And as soon as it was really dark the gangs would come out.

"Are you sure this is the best place for you to live? It's a pretty bad neighborhood. I told you this morning."

She was crying again. I could hear it in her voice even though I couldn't see her. "I have to walk to school. I don't own a car. And I can't afford bus fare. My parents said they'd give me one year of school, and that's all."

"But what are you going to do tonight? Somebody's got to take care of you!"

"I can take care of myself."

We got to a ratty three-story apartment building that looked a lot like the place where my mother lived. LA was full of these broken-down places. The path up to the main door was lined with rickety palm trees and dying cypress. A platoon of rapists could be hiding behind all that plant life, waiting for Barbara to come home alone. I could see she'd just now thought of it.

"Would you mind walking me up to my apartment? I could show it to you."

No security, no nothing.

She lived on the second floor, in one room that faced the street.

"See? I really liked it, for two reasons. One reason is the balcony"—a little fistful of wrought iron that any human would be a fool to step out on—"and the other is this. A Murphy bed."

She went to a side wall, opened a cupboard, and pulled down a bed that fell with an iron *clunk* to the floor.

"How old are you, Barbara?"

"Seventeen."

"Where do your parents live?"

"Santa Clarita. Didn't I tell you?"

"And they let you stay alone in a place like this?"

"It's a nice place!"

She sat down on the edge of the bed. I thought about it, and took the floor. There was only one chair, and it had some dishes on it. The only table I could see in the gathering dark was an upended milk crate. I glimpsed some art supplies over in a corner, and what looked like a stack of paperback books. No curtains. No shades.

"Should we turn on some lights?"

"It's too bright when I do. There's just that overhead thing."

"How long have you been here?"

"Since day before yesterday."

"And your parents just left you here?" I couldn't get over it. She was such a kid.

"They want me not to like it, so that I'll go back home. But I'm going to be an artist!"

"*Why?*"

"I—you should know why." She sat stiffly on the edge of the bed and looked right at me. "Because I want to see things other people can't see. Live in a world that's different from the one I grew up in."

"Shouldn't you go to a regular four-year school like UCLA? Live in a dorm? Make some regular friends?"

"And after four years, get married and have some kids and live like everyone else in the world? That's what I *don't* want to do."

She was too dumb even to know that women never made it in the art world. Especially out here. She sat there like an obstinate child, testing her split lip with her little finger.

"Can I go out and get you some aspirin? Do you have enough to eat? Anything for dinner tonight? Anything for breakfast?"

"I don't need anything. I'm fine. But don't leave yet."

Then I saw that she was shaking. The whole bed was shaking. I could see a piece of blanket hanging down, shaking.

"Could you stay here tonight?"

"*Me?*"

"Yes. You can lie right beside me. I don't think I can stay here alone. I was so scared last night and that was before anything even happened."

I shook my head.

"Please. Come and lie down with me."

I was the handyman, I was the fix-it man, I was the one who knew how to do it. But after this summer, I was tapped out. And I knew this wasn't something I could fix. "I'm sorry," I said. "I can't. I can't help you. I can come back tomorrow with some groceries, and I can give you rides to places, and I can put in a deadbolt for you, but, Barbara . . ."

She didn't say anything.

"I can't give you the real stuff, I can't take care of you—because I'm all out." I almost said, I'm too fucked up, but it would have sounded too dramatic.

"I'll come by tomorrow to see how you are. Or I'll send some-one. Something. You can put the chair under the door for now. You'll be OK. But I've got to leave now. I'm sorry." *I'm sorry.*

Which didn't leave me any better off when I got outside again. "You asshole," I whispered. "You stupid fuck."

And then I couldn't go home. It was like I didn't have one. *Duh!* I nearly said it out loud. *Tell* me about it, fuck face. I ran down the short list of places I might go—so short, now that I couldn't go to the Landrys'—and there was nowhere. I couldn't think of one place.

I started to walk up Carondelet because I couldn't just stand there on the sidewalk. I passed more houses, more barred win-dows, more families framed in yellow light.

Everyone has someone. Except me.

And Barbara, of course.

You could almost laugh.

If you could laugh.

I crossed Sunset, looking around at crowds of dangerous-looking gang bangers. Go ahead. Do it! You'd be doing me a favor.

But the guys who caught my eye looked away. Even they had to draw the line somewhere.

Above Sunset, I spotted the apartment house where Anthony Hernandez lived. I'd met Hernandez once at an opening. A big good-natured Latino guy. Making a living from his excellent art.

I walked up dozens of cement steps to the old-fashioned fa-çade, peered around the sides of the building until I found the name, pressed the doorbell. What the *hell* did I think I was doing?

Hernandez opened his door, looking puzzled. Behind him, lounging in a comfortable chair, was a beautiful woman in a black sweater and pants, holding a glass of red wine. Everyone had someone.

"You don't know me. We only met once. I'm Bob Hampton."

"I've seen you around. Come on in. Want some wine?"

"Thanks." He stood inside the door. It was a small room a lot like Barbara's. It dated straight back to the twenties.

Hernandez came back with wine. "Sit down, why don't you?"

"Bob Hampton," I said to the woman.

"I'm Judith."

Hernandez leaned back against the wall. "What can I do for you?"

"I started at Otis this morning—I already got a degree from UCLA. I went over to Paris earlier this year." I couldn't go on. I felt like a damn fool.

"What's the problem?"

I took a breath and found myself telling them. I was stalled, I didn't know what to paint, it seemed like I was trapped between the two worlds, absolutely unstuck from what people might think of as normal life, but completely locked out of that other, better world, you know, that one . . . The life of art. "Like what you have," I finished limply. What in the hell was I doing?

Hernandez and his wife looked at each other, didn't say anything.

"And I'm a . . . I'm a . . . I'm alone."

"What do you want, Bob?" The woman, asking.

"How? How did you do it? How did you manage it?"

"Tony always said he'd never get married, never have children. I'd done the other thing. Got married when I was sixteen and had a son right away. By the time I was thirty-five and came out here to LA, I was alone again. One night I went to an art opening where there was a band. This darling man came over and asked me to dance."

"I never dance," Hernandez said. "I thought I'd dance that night though."

"As soon as we started to dance, Tony began telling me he planned on devoting his life to his art, and that he absolutely never wanted children or a bourgeois life. That was his whole position."

"And she looked at me and said, 'I already *had* mine. What would I want more children for? I want to spend the rest of my life writing novels.'" Hernandez laughed. "That put a cramp in my style. But the more I danced with her, the more I thought this could be the woman I'd been looking for."

I looked at Judith. "What did you think?"

"He was a beautiful man. I was willing to go along with it."

I looked around the room. "But you both have talent," I said, cravenly. "That's a gift."

Hernandez went into the kitchen, came back with the wine. "We put in the time. You put in enough time, you get something back."

"Yes, but how do you . . ."

"What Tony is saying, you don't have to think *how*. You just have to do it."

"Yes, but . . ."

"Didn't you hear what I said? I went over and asked her to dance. I don't dance! But I danced when I had to. I danced for what I needed. So I got it."

The novelist looked a little troubled. "It's not necessarily easy," she said.

But her husband shook his head, shrugged away her objections, and spoke right to me. "Sure it is. It's easy as sin."

In the Landrys' backyard, on layered, blue, sealed cement, at the beginning of dawn, I began to paint a world seen through water. The world in a wave, a swirl, a pond, a pool. I could see shapes, I saw how they lost their edges but took on something else, a shimmer and light, a transparency. People as fish. Trees as seaweed. The world floated, the way Tod must have seen it. It looked *so good!* You could swim to it. Dive down. Let yourself glide up, held by water.

I knew what Tod had seen. Of course I knew! I was an artist. I'd hauled all my house paint, all my acrylics, over here in the dark and stacked them on the lawn behind me. I'd finish the picture I'd begun three months ago. The blue background was waiting. The scope, the space, was immense, with the pool at its center.

I began laying in the house, its inside, using wide, airy strokes, white stucco on the blue cement. I painted Tod's youth bed, the first thing I remembered, such a silly thing, but nice to have short bars around you, good to keep you from swimming too far. I painted other stuff, too, halls and stairs. I put this house in the back corner of the cement by the ivy, and went on from there. The house was open like the house at the bottom of an aquarium; you could swim in and out, go through walls, doors, windows. I put in gleaming shapes that hovered and darted and changed their minds. I painted a Conchitafish in a black dress with white organdy fins, eyes so big they held all of Mexico in them, all the earth floors, all the children and parents left behind, all the tears, all the endless sorrow of women, but still I had to make it so her rump looked funny, so solid. That fish hung attentive by the door and I realized the house was small. Just like the ones at the bottom of an aquarium, and there must be a bigger aquarium and another after that, and then lakes and then the ocean and the sky.

I stopped and thought about it, rocked back on my heels and looked straight up to the ink blue of the perfect, very early morning September sky. The moon, full and silver, still stayed high up, pale and clear. I thought it was time to paint in the moon, but it wasn't going to cooperate. Don't look to *me* for help, it said. Don't look up, look *down* for the answer, into the pool.

I painted in the pool, right by the pool. Oh! It was beautiful! I absolutely got it. The most beautiful thing I'd ever seen or thought about or imagined. It had to have a bottom, and I swirled in some Alhambra tiles, some Prado tiles, but remembered they had no edges, only light and shimmer. Then I waited, figuring out the rest of the picture, and I swirled the pool over with translucent blue green, swimming-pool green. But didn't it need lights? I dotted the sides of the pool with little brown paper sacks, each with candles in them. Earth, air, fire, water. I flicked in some sand beneath the candles.

I hit a narrow space here, four by twenty feet, and I didn't want to be an asshole but I had to tell the truth. I gave the whole space to Landry, horizontally floating, filling in everything, and made him look like a sculpin, but he'd *always* looked like a sculpin, that was the beauty of it—so ugly some people wouldn't even eat a sculpin if it was the last fish in the sea, but, *hey!* Was that the sculpin's fault? So I gave the sculpin's thin lips and flat face and pale eyes a look of injured indignation—Landry getting out of his Cadillac—that even Tod might see and figure out: I am the sculpin of all I survey, so shape up, ship out, do *something!* But he was so big, so full of himself, so caught in the margins of four by twenty feet that he couldn't turn around, turn the corner, he couldn't even get into the world he owned. He could only sit there and glower, poor guy, poor fish.

The sun cut the sky. A thin, thin slice, what was it, 5:30 in the morning by now? The moon had slid away. I stood up, arched my back, licked my dry lips. I moved my paints across to the big patch of cement on the side of the pool by the house; twenty by twenty-five feet, cluttered with lawn chairs, a table, an umbrella. I dragged all the furniture up onto the lawn. Reorganized my acrylics. Then I stood looking at my surface and you could say I prayed. How would Tod see Tod's World? From underwater. And everything would be true.

I started at the left, as you might see it looking down from Tod's window, with the billowy Millicent, all smiles and white satin, with willowy pink arms, pale, wet yellow hair, and bright open eyes, and teeth like mythic pearls. I made her a mermaid, had to, of course, and spent as much time as I could in this fast-moving dawn. I had plenty of cans of spray paint, silver and gold; I made her scales silver and blurred her sweet edges with lines of gold. She was full of energy and ready to move. And then, I had to do it, even though I'd covered her breasts with a lot of blonde curls, I dabbed a dab of pure silk pink right where those other lips would be, right there across her mermaid scales, and gave them a lopsided smile. *Babe!*

Over on the right, because life is grim, I splashed and sprayed a whole school of Landry acquaintances that I myself had never met, long and brown like smelt, poking in their sharp noses and bland eyes. Concerned without being concerned, curious about Tod, just nosing around. "Is there anything we can do? Be sure to tell us if there's anything we can do." *No*, there's nothing you can do! We could flick this water with our fingers and you'd all scoot away, but you'd be back.

I was painting. If I didn't watch out, I'd be bawling. No, I already was. I was laying my life on the line. What if I made a damn fool of myself?

I knew I already had.

But I knew I'd already found out something I could use later. Be sensible! Remember that I worked best on these big surfaces, that I'd always been able to work fast, and that all the information about suffering for your art was wrong. There was enough suffering out there, you were supposed to get rid of it. Because if we swim in suffering, there must be a way to break through the surface. Like a porpoise. Like a trout.

I sprayed a few careless bubbles up from the bottom and painted a watery surface, leaving plenty of room for brilliant air. I stood way back with spray cans in both hands, spraying lightly, laying down a light grid of gold and silver, creating air.

So what if I was grounded in tradition? There was a reason for tradition. And a reason women came up from the sea. I thought of Venus, and said forget it. I thought of the Virgin, no dice. I thought of another mermaid, no, no. So I did Tod first, a shadow just beneath the surface, carefree, a sea otter, floating on his back, playing, swimming backward. *Everything I see looks great to me!*

Was I going to have time for this?

Sure.

Of course.

Absolutely.

I inhaled all the air I could into my chest, and painted her in. Just the way she was. Walking on water. Wearing that brown and gold dress, her brown hair a little tangled, her face attentive but carefree. She was doing what she used to do, and must still do sometimes, looking into the water for an answer. There was her child, her sea otter. She knew him, but he was separate now. She gazed at him with endless love. Love and loss were the same thing and she knew it.

I sprayed bright gold around her edges. A halo. Why not? If anyone deserved it, she did.

And only now did it look like I might choke, or have my usual doubts. Because, get serious, had it ever worked out that when I said what I wanted, I got it? My father, lost and gone, told me, *forget it*. Quit while you're ahead. My mother, watching TV all alone, looked sad and said, *forget it*. Even sweet Kate, lolling in bed before she left to get married, heaved herself up on one elbow and whispered, kindly, forget it. Come on back to someone like me. Isn't it easier, just to have fun? And that twinkling mermaid I'd already painted in laughed unbelievingly. You have *got* to be kidding! Where is your *brain*, Bob?

I prayed. I really did this time. God, the Father, Son, Holy Ghost, this all goes out to you. This all goes up to you. This all goes up. Ask and you shall receive. Isn't that what you said? Ask. Ask. Ask. I'm asking.

For the first time in hours I had trouble with proportion, with perspective, with knowing where to start. Then I looked at her again, saw how her back was turned a little, and I painted in myself, right there, kneeling on the waves, just the way I was. I knelt behind her, to the side of her—I knew how I looked well enough, from long lonely nights looking in the bathroom mirror—I leaned my head in at her waist. Remembered not to stint on my own crinkly hair. Let my arms wrap loosely around her thighs. And in the picture, closed my eyes.

Because only I can love you. Because I know what it is to lose heart and still have to go on. I know what it is to be alive but glassed in, stuck in the aquarium. To be looked at but never seen. Sure, maybe later you'll meet someone, but what are you, thirty-five? You haven't met him yet, have you? Unless you look down, unless you feel this light touch on your legs. Could it be that you're not seeing either? That you think you're looking for the answers but you're not looking hard enough?

Because I haven't been looking very hard, not hard enough.

I didn't want to cheat, but I gave myself some great-looking eyelashes and realizing, thank God, that I hadn't dealt enough with her left arm, I let it hang down, relaxed, across my neck. Not a commitment, but a touch that might go either way.

Could *I* really stand it? Everything that this meant? Was I really in it for the long haul?

Sure. Because what else was there? Because you can't get a camel through a needle, or whatever that was. Because my life could be almost half over and I'd never loved anybody.

Or painted anything, until today.

And the small sour part of my mind that never really shut up suggested, at least after this you know you can paint murals on restaurant walls and make a decent living. Or banks. No nine-to-five advertising, ever, after this. No more classes, either.

But the rest of me was sanctified. I knew I'd done it.

I stood up and back for the last time—on this project—shielded my eyes with my palm and took a look.

Pretty good. The sun caught the gold paint and made the whole thing shine. But there was something else shining in there. I could see it. I knew it.

Now, I prayed again, *Do your stuff!*

I turned to the house. The sun was picking up, gathering strength, burning into my shoulders. Brushfire weather. Paint-drying weather. The sun made the house some fairy-tale fortress where the princess lived, and the dragon, and yeah, the queen, and a wounded prince. Come out, I said, and take a look at what I've done. I can't stay here too much longer or I'll pass out.

A door did open. Millicent, looking fresh as a soft-drink ad, her slim body sliding around under one of those nightgowns, took a look at me and then at my painting and then at me again. She opened her mouth and took a breath. I cut her off with a finger to my lips. She took my cue and kept quiet, but came closer. I watched her toes sink into the damp grass. She smiled at her dad, and her own outrageous mermaid self, then stared, perplexed, at her stepmom and Tod. And me. She turned to look at me and took a breath again.

But I shook my head. For once, I was going to have it my own way. *It's not for you. Don't you see who it's for?* Even as I did it, I said a regretful good-bye to her and all the girls like her, all the other girls and women who were still young and pretty and silly, all the girls I'd never have now. And good-bye to Kate and June and Jamey and Valerie, and all the accidental girls and women I'd ever had—quite a few of them. Because I wasn't going to be one of those Picasso guys. This was going to be *it,* as far as I could see. You could spend the first half of your life one way, and the second half another.

I ducked my head at Millicent, and pointed her back to the house. She took a last look at the family in the heart of my painting. It's your funeral, she shrugged silently, then gave me a sweet, affectionate, blinding grin. At least something's happening! Somebody had to do something, and you're the one who did it.

Yes, I am the one.

Then my heart began to pound as if it really were a madman in the cage of my ribs. Because the door opened again and she stood there, wearing the same brown and gold dress she'd been wearing the day when . . . Tod's life had changed, and my own life began.

Suddenly, I felt I might really faint, pass out, disgrace myself; my knees might buckle. I hadn't eaten in about twenty hours. Empty, empty. I had nothing left, well, hell, I never *did* have anything but this. Myself. I concentrated on standing up. Holding my ground.

She had Tod with her. He'd just woken up and stood rubbing his eyes.

She looked too, of course. She checked it out the way Millicent had, but quicker, more thoroughly. It burned her. I could see that.

Now it came down to it. I'd done all I could do. Played my last card.

She whispered, "Are you sure?"

She walked over to me. I could see the translucence of her skin, the few lines that hadn't been there three months ago. I could see her as a child, a girl, a woman, old woman. I loved everything I saw.

This time, her arms went around me gently, and the minute they did, I felt OK. The kid came over and leaned in beside us and that completed it. Her hair smelled of this morning's shower and her shampoo. "Are you sure?" She was saying it again.

"Yes, I'm sure." Then, it dawned on me where she was, holding on to me, and I laughed out loud. *"Yeah!"* She put her backyard whammy on me, the way she had that first day, cracking my neck with her muscular little arm. I had to pull back, just to see her face, and laugh.

Then Landry was out there. Without thinking about it, I did a melodramatic movie thing. I pushed her behind me and put out my right hand. "They belong with me," I told him. "After what happened, they belong with me."

Landry thought about it. He was probably fed up with the bunch of us. "I thought this was going on. I knew it! What do you expect me to do, *fight* you for them? They're both damaged goods, as far as I'm concerned." He curled his lip and shook his head, and went back into the house. Angela watched him go. I couldn't see what she thought.

We crossed the border the next afternoon and drove through Tijuana, across stone bridges to the sea, past the bullring with its flags blowing in the breeze. We headed south on the toll road. The ocean burned with blue.

We'd spent our first night in San Diego, in a big hotel room with two double beds looking out over Mission Bay. Ordered up hamburgers and big glasses of milk, the two of us watching television until Tod dropped off to sleep, then building a nest for him out of pillows on the far bed. We watched more TV, cautiously, like old married people, until the eleven o'clock news was done. We'd showered separately and she came to bed wearing one of my shirts. I'd had a speech ready about waiting until we could find the kid a separate room. I'd remembered the night with Millicent, how Angela had caught me red-handed. I thought that maybe the only thing in the world I really knew how to do besides painting, I wouldn't be able to do.

But I remembered again how she'd held me the day I saved Tod. I trusted her to do that again. I gave myself over to her, and she did. I lost track of all of it, I got lost in it. She's crazy about me, was the last thought I had.

Now it was afternoon again, past Tijuana, and we were into our second day together. The van hummed along the mostly deserted road, and the world sorted itself out into vivid color: white sand, black road, blue sky, blue sea. So beautiful!

We drove straight through Ensenada and turned right south of town, heading out to Estero Beach.

I'd never been there and it turned out neither had she. It was an old-time white guys' resort, with rows of stone-floored bungalows along a broad lagoon, and around the waters' bend, shiny little trailers that could have belonged to the Hampton clan, with retired Americans and barbecues and pet parrots and flags. We walked past all this after we checked in. The sun was setting. Then we walked back home, along the edge of the lagoon. Halfway back, I hunkered down next to Tod and said, "We've got to get something straight, buddy. I don't want you ever going in the water unless you've got your mother or me with you. We'll go with you whenever you want, but don't go in the water alone. OK?"

And Tod said OK.

We walked back over spiky grass, past vinca and birds-of-paradise into our cool room. Again, the world divided itself into big bright pictures, coruscating silver lagoon, silver-gold sand, sunset-pink sky. Angela walked up to the main building and came back holding a pitcher of margaritas, slushy with ice.

Our second night.

I wondered what she had planned for us, what *I* had planned, if there was a plan. But then I gave all that up, letting myself drown again. She was strong, and she was mad for me. I couldn't get over it. She whispered in my ear, "You do have skin like peaches."

Late that night, I saw her get up and move out to the stone terrace. I followed her and we sat together, watching the moonlight on the lagoon.

"Angela . . ."

"Shhh."

"What are we going to do?"

"I've been thinking. For quite a while, actually. We keep on heading down the peninsula, down the rest of Baja. There's a little town just north of Cabo where they have a lot of American artists. You can work there. Start selling it."

I had a question to ask. "How long since, how long have you known . . . you liked me?"

"Since the first minute I saw you. Your hair! Your wonderful arms. The way you can't fix anything but you fixed everything. The way you are with Tod. The way you smell. Your wonderful skin. I thought I'd be too old for you, but I'm not. I'm not."

She reached across to me, grabbed my shoulders, pulled me down hard. We ended up stretched out on cool stone.

"Listen," she said, when we'd finished, and she sat on the terrace with her ankles crossed and told me a story about the life we'd have at the tip of Baja, living in a big house by the sea. I'd do pictures like the one I'd painted for her by the pool, and tourists would buy them for lots of money. I'd get a bald spot and a deep tan and wear turquoise jewelry. She'd wake up early every morning and go to the market for fresh vegetables and learn Spanish and drink hot chocolate with the Mexican wives and have some more kids. Tod would go to school and learn two languages instead of one. He'd skin-dive and maybe marry the mayor's daughter when the time came. Once a year, we'd all row out into the Sea of Cortés when the whales swam in to mate. We'd live together fifty years, and get brown and wrinkled, and Americans and Europeans would make special trips in four-wheel-drive vehicles to buy the original works of Robert Hampton.

I got up then and went over to the cooler where we'd stowed the second half of the pitcher of margaritas. The whole world seemed to crackle and glisten. I thought back to gray, cold days.

"You know, when I used to think about my future, I always figured it would be Paris."

"Oh, we can do that, if that's what you'd like, for a few months a year. As soon as you've got your reputation. London, too."

"I can paint you, to start with." My life shifted and creaked open again, like a rusty trunk with a hidden compartment, a

220 - Carolyn See

second, secret cache of treasure. There was a whole world in there, another whole world.

"I can paint you to start with," I said again, taking it easy, or trying to. "I can paint you a thousand ways. I can start with that."

John Simon Guggenheim
Memorial Foundation
90 Park Avenue
New York, New York 10016

To Whom It May Concern:

May I request that the following note be added to my previous application of August 15 of this year.

Re: Robert Hampton

In searching out Los Testigos in Los Angeles, I would have been remiss had I not tried to discover the Painting by the Pool, the allegorical, hastily painted work said to have been created by the artist to win the heart of his wife, who was married to another at the time. The home is still owned by Augustus Landry, first husband of Angela Hampton and father of Millicent and Teodoro. Mr. Landry answered his own door, waved me on without a word out to the back, where the painting is said to have surrounded the swimming pool.

Nothing was there. I turned to ask Mr. Landry for an explanation, but he had gone inside, nor did he choose to answer my repeated knocking.

YOURS SINCERELY,

PETER LAUE

Acknowledgments

I wish to thank the Getty Research Institute for a generous grant that included both the time to write this book and the institutional reassurance that great art may make its home in the west. I'm particularly indebted to Michael Roth and Sabine Schlosser for their kindness and to Charles Salas for his intellectual teasing and challenges.

For their insights into the mind of the aspiring fine artist, I'm grateful to Rae Lewis, Jo Anne Lopez, and dear Charles Buckley. My thanks and respect to Judith Freeman and Anthony Hernandez.

Special thanks to Ann Godoff, Lee Boudreaux, Jean-Isabel McNutt, and Robbin Schiff at Random House, Anne Sibbald at Janklow Nesbit, and Linda Kamberg de Martinez.

My deepest appreciation goes to my family, Lisa See and Dick Kendall, Alexander and Christopher Kendall, Clara Sturak and Chris Chandler. And of course to John Espey, my sweet love.

The Handyman

CAROLYN SEE

A Reader's Guide

A Conversation with Carolyn See

Q: The opening of this novel is quite notable. What inspired you to open with the text of a grant application?

A: Personal experience—I almost came to the end of my life writing a Guggenheim grant. They are not easy to write. Then one year I was a judge and got to read hundreds of these applications. There was blood on the paper; these people were so desperate. Peter Laue, the scholar writing this application, is just dying of loneliness. He almost loses it in the last two paragraphs when he talks about going down to visit and being unable to go over and join the others. He does manage to pull himself back together at the very end and assert that this grant would allow him to pursue all this much further. I am very proud of the tone of this application.

Q: Did it pose a challenge to you as a writer to open with the end of the story and then make the body of the novel compelling and interesting to your readers? Did you plan to structure the story this way from the outset?

A: Well, originally the grant was at the end of the story. I dropped it off at Random House and my former editor, a dear and generous person, said, "I will buy this if you put the grant application up front and shift from the third to the first person." And I did it—after going home and kicking some furniture. I still have trouble with the grant being up front. I think it confuses some readers who don't know what to make of it. But it also gains readers who find the application intriguing. And, in my editor's words, it gives readers a reason to care about this failure who is going around screwing girls.

The grant was easy to move; I just shifted it from the back to the front. Changing from third to first person was more difficult, but my editor was right. I thought I had cleaned up the prose and made it as guy-like and colloquial as I could. But when I had to change "he thinks" to "I think," it helped me to refine my prose in an interesting way. It kept me out of trouble because I kept worrying I had no business being in this guy's mind—I didn't know what he was thinking. It was easier to put words in his mouth because I have heard men speak, but I don't know how their minds work.

Q: **Your portrait of the artist as a young and older man does not conform to stereotypical notions of the great artist as a selfish, self-destructive individual. Why is this so?**

A: Wanda Landowska made an enormous impression upon me when I was a child. She was this wonderful musician who had a couple take care of her. She was so out of this world that it took two able-bodied people to help her navigate it. When you think of Picasso—what a wide swath he cut—you think of this self-absorbed stereotype. Yet there were good times to be had around him. Much of this negative kind of stuff originates with the people surrounding artists—friends, lovers—who like to bitch and moan. Yet nobody makes them stick around, and obviously they have rich lives while they are in this artistic orbit.

And many artists are goodhearted. Living the life of a writer in California, I have never met a mean one. I'm currently reading a wonderful biography of Mary McCarthy; she lived in this world in which she and the artists around her were as mean as snakes. But you can approach life and art and be kindhearted. Alison Lurie, Diane Johnson, Alice Adams—they're generous, good women who are also artists. Working in PEN, you see artists who are working hard for a community and doing good and decent work. It's a canard that in order to be an artist you must be selfish and self-destructive. We have all met miserable people who stay up and drink and treat people badly and try to pass themselves off as artists. "I'm an aspiring artist, thus I behave like this." But these are most often people who are not attending to or doing their work, so are they really artists?

Q: **Some harsh words are said in this novel about the state of art in the late twentieth century. Does this viewpoint reflect**

your own? Are you hoping for an artist like Bob who can transcend the irony and cynicism of our time?

A: Yes. This century has come to be known as the age of angst and depression and anxiety. As an English professor who has taught courses on how this movement started in poetry and fiction, I have dealt endlessly with these themes of anomie and depression. Writers like Ernest Hemingway and T. S. Eliot were writing out of their own personal experiences and within the context of World War I, which was a terrible thing. Works like *The Wasteland* and *A Farewell to Arms* tapped into something the public responded to. Yet there is also evidence that once T. S. Eliot married a nice woman, he cheered up and created works of a very different and more optimistic tone. These works don't make it into the anthologies—they are seen as kind of embarrassing. In the case of Hemingway, who was, of course, a wonderfully talented writer, he was dealing with mental illness all along, and this colored his work in a very particular way. After seventy-five years of the Age of Anxiety, as we enter a new century I hope we can find a new way of looking at the world.

Q: *The Handyman* **might be called a valentine to struggling artists everywhere. What do you think of this interpretation?**

A: That's a darling interpretation, and it's true. It's a valentine to artists who have lost their way. It's also a valentine to young guys. Since women have begun writing on a regular basis, a great deal of work has been produced that is very tough on men. Men have been demonized in life and art. Yet there are so many nice guys out there who are confused but who are trying do the right thing. The question is: What is the right thing?

Q: **Why do you think it's so difficult for people to find their true calling? What is it about Bob that allows him to find his way and help so many others to do so?**

A: Margaret Mead once said that in America everything looks easy because this is the land of abundance, but emotionally it's very distracting because there are so many choices. The son of a barber in a small Spanish town will probably grow up to be a barber and not be too upset about it—it's his destiny. Picasso's father was an academic artist. So Picasso grew up in the art world and was expected to be an artist, though probably not the artist he became. In this country, ostensibly, you can be whatever you want and that can be paralyzing, like when you have too many errands to do on a Saturday afternoon and don't know where to start so you don't do anything. In America, at least if you're white, you're supposed to be able to become whatever you want to be. What you want to be is a big question, and this seems to me to be a real cause for anxiety.

When Bob thinks of art, he has daydreams of Paris in the 1920s, but that world doesn't exist anymore. He has to get past his dream of art to find out what is really out there that he has to work with. And he does that by returning home and entering the world.

Q: **Do you think art can be taught in a classroom?**

A: A little bit. Skiers need coaches and so do artists. As a professor of English and writing, I teach my students to pay attention to character and plot. What is your plot? Do you believe it? Will your readers?

Years ago, a friend and I were asked to write the last episode of *Barnaby Jones*, a detective series in which the central character caught the criminal red-handed in a grassy knoll at the end of every episode. (When we wrote that Barnaby runs over to the criminal, we got laughed at because by that time he was an old geezer who couldn't run.) And there had to be a murder by the bottom of page eight with four suspects. We thought we might want to do more television writing, and we needed the money, so we didn't want to screw this up. But we really struggled with the question: Why would anybody want to kill anybody? We finally came up with the idea of an unfaithful husband, which seemed to offer real motive. Here was a reason for murder that made some sense to us, at least. You have to believe your plot.

Teaching students to pay attention to motivation, elements of time and space, and point of view are important. Just as skiers are coached to keep the skis parallel unless they want to stop, writers need to be coached. I think coaching rather than teaching is a more apt metaphor here.

Q: Since the story is told from Bob's point of view, we get his honestly brutal perspective on the people he encounters that summer. How would the other characters describe Bob during that summer?

A: They would hardly think of him at all. There's an evolution over the course of the story as they come to realize that they really like him. But he is not a fabulous artist; he's just a handyman at this point in time. He's crushed when he realizes that Mrs. Walker has taken up with her manicurist and she asks if he expected her to make do with a handyman and an iguana. In retrospect, as with Kate, who is tracked down in the south of France, Mrs. Walker remembers him as a dear, sweet boy. At the time, she did not give him too much thought, and nobody probably did. That often happens in life: Looking back, you realize that someone was such a wonderful and important person in your life, but in the moment you did not. He is after all a handyman—not a person you devote too much time to thinking about.

Q: How would Bob articulate their effect on him in 2027?

A: He wouldn't articulate it. When the scholar, Peter Laue, goes down and asks him questions about them, Bob is amused, but he won't say anything. An art historian who reviewed *The Handyman* called Bob a "dumb" artist—he does it but can't articulate it. He knows what he is doing, but he does by doing and not talking about it.

He is terribly grateful. You can see this because he's kept so many of them in his life and he keeps painting them. I am most proud of him for continuing to paint his trailer park relatives, of whom he is the most ashamed. But he has forgiven them and accepted them. He comes to recognize that their lives are just as mysterious and important as anybody else's and just as worthy of being painted.

Q: What makes Bob so appealing to the women in this novel?

A: I think because he is available to them. He is ready to not just build a turkey pen but to spend an entire afternoon trying to catch the turkey. He is willing to sit down and talk, and he listens. As a previously divorced mother, I can tell you there is a very interesting line between those men who merely react to your children as annoyances and those who are willing to engage them and join in their games. And it's not just the women. His roommate, Dave, the philosopher, is desperately lonely. He is looking for a friend and Bob is there.

Q: Reflecting on his new job as a handyman, Bob says, "There was a certain amount of sadness to a lot of this work. Somebody else should have been doing these jobs." Could you talk about the meaning of this passage?

A: That's where I'm a feminist author. We live in a patriarchy, but many of the patriarchs seem to have ducked out for a smoke. The most lonely thing in the world is to be in a room and a relationship with someone who is just not there—and it works both ways. Angela's husband is there, but he's not. He firmly believes that he's doing his job as a husband and father by returning from his absences to ask who is responsible for this mess. His daughter says that he is a nice dad but limited, and she's right. We're such a career-oriented society, and people—men and women alike—are so bent on following and advancing their careers. I do think, in a semi-metaphorical way, people should stay at home. They should pay attention to their primary, not their secondary, lives. Getting tenure or selling the most computer software is not the most important thing.

Q: **Ultimately, this novel offers a very hopeful message on the transcendent power of love and art. Some reviewers have commented that this is a bold move on your part in a literary landscape littered with irony and detachment. Do you agree with this assessment?**

A: Yes, I do. I think one of my favorite reviews refers to me as the "ever-adventurous" Carolyn See. I love that. What a nice idea. After devouring all 869 pages of a wonderful new biography of Mary McCarthy, it became clear to me that in the mid-twentieth-century New York art world, it was all about being mean. *How mean can you be?* Lillian Hellman, Dorothy Parker, Dashiell Hammett—they were like a Mason jar full of scorpions. Like the man with limburger cheese on his mustache who thinks the whole world stinks, they thought they were the center of the universe and that was how artists should behave. How tiring.

I want to ask: What if people, artists, tried to be decent and generous? Let's try this other way and see what happens. After enduring a stormy childhood and failed marriages, I finally noticed that the less awful you are, the nicer your life can be. I would like to try to point to something new for the next century.

Q: **In this novel, you reclaim Los Angeles as a utopia of sorts, though the current popular perception of Los Angeles is far more dystopian. Do you agree with this assessment?**

A: I remember a conversation I had at a party in New York a few years ago. In an exchange with an inane young man, the American version of the upper-class twit, complete with a receding chin, I mentioned that I was from California. He replied, "Oh well, I think New York is the brains of the country and Los Angeles is the genitals." As you can imagine, I was insulted and irritated and later thought of the many things I should have said in reply. Then I thought to myself, "Would I rather be stuck with the headache or the orgasm?"

Q: **There is a very large cast of characters in this novel, yet**

each is rendered vivid and distinct. How do you manage to juggle all of these voices?

A: Thank you for saying this. I am very complimented. I spent a lot of time and energy to accomplish just this. I did a huge amount of eavesdropping to get the cadences of these characters right and make them distinct. Also a lot of careful remembering, as I based some of these characters on people I've known in the past.

Q: June Shaw is a remarkable character. If she had relented, could she and Bob have had something?

A: June Shaw looks and acts like a friend from hell. Bob is rendered speechless and frantic when he wakes up and realizes that they've had sex. If June had said, "So, do we see each other tomorrow?" he would have fled the country or at least moved out. Bob does see through her mask of fiendish energy to the dear woman within. Maybe nobody else will ever see through her prickly facade to the soul. Perhaps this is why she so cherishes him.

I love June's character because she's one of those women born to make trouble. She's able to become a feminist and channel her energy. Before, women like her were forced to stay at home and make trouble there. She's so bats and tweaked, you just don't know what she's going to say next. She can't keep her clothes on. They keep flying off her because she has so much energy to burn. She's enormously smart, but also berserk, and she is going to stay that way. She is an amalgam of several women I've known who have astounded me and for whom I have great affection.

Q: This novel traces the development of an artist. Does it mirror your own process of becoming a writer in any way?

A: Well, I wish I were as kind as Bob, but I'm not. It's true that finding your own material is crucial, and I'm very lucky to have found mine. Bob's material is all around, but he doesn't know it at first. I think every artist needs to find his or her own stuff. Mary McCarthy had a grinding sense of injustice and anger toward her aunt and uncle that kept her in a tizzy throughout her life, and this was the source material of her art. Larry McMurtry is from Archer City, Texas, a little town in the middle of nowhere. He looked around and decided Archer City, Texas, was his source. Out of this came *The Last Picture Show* and *Lonesome Dove*—nobody else could have written these novels. I love it when you see an artist and his or her material in a happy marriage.

Q: How would you recommend aspiring writers learn and hone their craft? Is there a blueprint?

A: My dad had two kinds of chili he made: eighteen-hour chili, which was incredible and incredibly time-consuming, and quick chili, which took twenty minutes and was pretty good! Here is my quick-chili recipe for writing: one thousand words a day, five days a week, for the rest of your life; no more than two hours of revisions a day. Also, one charming note a week (on paper, not e-mail) to a writer, editor, or other person in the literary world whose work you admire. No asking for favors; just tell them you enjoy and respect their work. This is part of the process of constructing a literary life. And, most important, once every couple of weeks do something outrageous that a person "like you" would never do. It's important to have both an inner and an outer life—the writing and notes take care of the inner life, and the crazy thing expands you and makes a bigger person.

Q: What do you think of the phenomenon of the reading group, which seems to have assumed a new prominence in recent years?

A: It's terrific, a wonderful thing. It provides people with a chance to come together and socialize around the essentially lonely experience of reading. It's wonderful to be able to talk to others about what you have read. I think it also, in some small way, refutes the naysayers who argue that Americans don't read, that our educational system is going down the drain, that the whole country in general is going to hell in a handbasket. It's just so civilized to come together and think not just about the mundane matters of everyday life.

Q: **Do you belong to a reading group?**

A: Unfortunately, no! Since I have to read one book a week for my job as reviewer for the *Washington Post*, I just don't have the time. I did recently get lost in a wonderful unassigned book, which meant that for ten days papers did not get corrected, bills did not get paid, and I almost missed a deadline for a book review.

Q: **What would you recommend to reading groups as future selections?**

A: Frances Kiernan's terrific biography of Mary McCarthy [*Seeing Mary Plain*]. Also, a new novel, *The Dangerous Husband* by Jane Shapiro, made me laugh out loud.

Q: **What is next for you? Are you working on a new project?**

A: I just signed a two-book contract. One is a nonfiction book on how to make a literary life—the eighteen-hour chili version. The other is a novel about the globalization of the world, examining the drama around organ donorship and global adoption. It will be filled with thoughtful, intelligent, entirely decent people who get a shot at realizing their wildest dreams.

Reading Group Questions and Topics for Discussion

1. Do you think Peter Laue is going to get his grant? Why or why not?

2. As a handyman, Bob also a successful therapist. Do you agree with this assessment? Discuss the significance of the title of this novel.

3. Have you had a Bob in your life? If not, would you like to meet someone like him?

4. What do you think would have happened to the characters in this novel if Bob had not entered their lives?

5. Who do you think is the inspiration for the Lilith paintings?

6. Did you figure out the identity of Señora Hampton before the end of the novel? Do you think she was the right woman for him?

7. Why do you think Kate does not realize that her Bob became Robert Hampton?

8. Unlike the very dysfunctional families we meet throughout the course of this novel, Angela and Bob seem to have created a family that really works. Why do you think this is so?

9. Which character would you be most interested in meeting and why? Would you be interested in spending time at the Hampton compound?

10. Beginning with Bob's mother, so many of the characters in this novel seem paralyzed by their loneliness. Discuss why it can be so difficult to connect with other people.

11. As Bob compares his own far-from-privileged upbringing with the affluence of the tumultuous Landry household, he reflects, "Rich kids tried to destroy themselves as a hobby. . . . We couldn't *afford* a catastrophe." What does he mean?

12. Why do you think the housewives in this novel feel so helpless and hopeless? Why do they have so much trouble with their primary job of creating and sustaining a home?

13. This novel explores the landscape of failed marriages. How do you think people end up so trapped and unhappy? What brought these people together? What tore them apart?

14. "This wasn't how grown-up men were supposed to spend their time, but God, this was nice," thought Bob as he was playing with Tod. Why does he think this? Discuss societal expectations regarding men and work and family.

15. Hank and Ben's dreams of Hollywood fall very short. What is it about Los Angeles that drew them to it? What is the source of its pull on the popular imagination?

16. What does Bob learn while he is cleaning out Professor Le Clerc's office and, essentially, throwing out his life's work?

17. How does Bob's understanding of his art change over the course of this novel? Do you think he would have been successful if he had stayed in Paris?

18. Many reviewers refer to this novel as a fairy tale. Do you agree?

19. Describe this novel in a sentence or two. Have your group share their summaries and discuss the range of opinions and impressions.

20. How was your reading group formed? Why do you think it has stayed together? Do you agree with Carolyn See's reflections on the phenomenon of the reading group?

21. Why did your group select this novel? Have you or will you read other works by Carolyn See?

22. How does this novel compare with other works your group has read?

23. What will you be reading next? Why?

© Marilyn Sanders

ABOUT THE AUTHOR

CAROLYN SEE is the author of nine books. She is the Friday-morning book reviewer for *The Washington Post*, and she has been on the boards of the National Book Critics Circle and PEN/West International. She has won both Guggenheim and Getty fellowships and currently teaches English at UCLA. She lives in Pacific Palisades, California

Excerpts from reviews of Carolyn See's
The Handyman

"Carolyn See's tender and funny new novel begins with an extended serio-parodic Guggenheim application. . . . I am ready to award the fellowship, even if the artist doesn't exist except in See's mind."

—*Los Angeles Times*

"See manages to find redemptive grace at a time when the more predictable literary route seems to be the prophesying of gloom and doom. . . . Through her eyes, the vast Southern California landscape, with all its flaws and contradictions, is transformed into a place of hope, and yes, of beauty."

—*The San Diego Union Tribune*

"This shamelessly uplifting novel also gets it balance of light and shade just right."

—*New York Daily News*

"What does Bob get for all his good works? A lot of love, and love-making, among other things. By the time this charming fable about the intertwining of caring and creativity ends, he's discovered that he is an artist after all, in every sense of the word."

—*Hartford Courant*

"See's writing is, as befits the subject, masterly, almost painterly, and colors the whole work."

—*New York*

"*The Handyman* is a deceptively sweet tale, gently urging the reader along to its surprising conclusion and leaving us to wax nostalgic for the present, and to wonder what fresh greatness may be lurking nearby, obscured by the scrim of late-20th-century cynicism."

—*LA Weekly*

"Wonderful . . . delightful . . . Hampton is a very sympathetic and appealing narrator, and a most unlikely godmother."

—*Providence Sunday Journal*

"[T]he novel quickly takes on the brightness of a sun-dazzled swimming pool and makes a case for shadowless living—a state its hero achieves through an unlikely combination of application and hedonism."

—*The New Yorker*